THE MASSACRE OF ST BARTHOLOMEW
AND THE
EUROPEAN CONFLICT
1559-1572

The Coligny brothers

THE MASSACRE OF
ST BARTHOLOMEW
AND THE
EUROPEAN CONFLICT
1559 – 1572

N. M. SUTHERLAND, M.A., Ph.D.

Lecturer in History, Bedford College, London

BOOKS

10 East 53d St., New York 10022
(a division of Harper & Row Publishers, Inc.)

Published in the USA 1973 by
HARPER AND ROW PUBLISHERS, INC.
Barnes and Noble Import Division

ISBN 06–496620–8

Printed in Great Britain

IN MEMORY
OF
PROFESSOR
ALFRED COBBAN

Contents

Preface

THE SPELLING and punctuation of manuscripts and printed sources have been retained, though abbreviations have, in some cases, been extended. Abbreviations and short titles used in the footnotes are explained in the bibliography in cases in which they are not already obvious. For the spelling of English words, and of place names, the *OED* and *Times Gazetteer* have normally been followed. All dates are rendered in the new style, unless otherwise indicated.

I am deeply indebted and profoundly grateful to Peter Hasler, who has generously devoted a great deal of time to this book. At the revision stage his constructive criticism led to substantial improvements, and his editorial expertise has been without price; so has his constant encouragement. Any residual follies are entirely my own.

I am also grateful to my colleague Dr Caroline M. Barron, who suggested the title.

N.M.S.

List of Plates

I

The Basic Conflicts
1559-1563

THE ATTEMPTED assassination of the huguenot leader Gaspard de Coligny seigneur de Châtillon, admiral of France, which occurred on the morning of Friday 22 August 1572, was followed, two days later, by the massacre of St Bartholomew in which he and many of his confederates died. Massacres were commonplace in the civil war period and few have attracted more than passing attention, the nameless dead being soon forgotten. It was primarily the death of Coligny which distinguished this one; indeed, the massacre was the direct result of the failure of the preceding attempt upon his life, in the particular circumstances of the moment, namely the presence in turbulent, catholic Paris, of the nobility of both confessional factions, together with large numbers of their followers, to celebrate the marriage of the king's sister Marguerite to the protestant Henri de Bourbon, King of Navarre, first prince of the blood. This marriage had symbolised, and was intended to seal a policy of peace and reconciliation after the end of the third civil war in August 1570; instead, it became a political embarrassment on account of the massacre, which marked the opening of the fourth civil war.

That the massacre proceeded from the failure of the assault upon Coligny is no new idea; yet attention has never been clearly shifted from the nineteenth-century obsession with premeditation, organisation, and individual culpability, to the significant point of Coligny's death. The crucial questions do not relate to the violence in Paris – always an explosive city – but to why the admiral had to die. What were the tensions which led to the assault, and what was unique about the occasion?

The answers to these questions are as complex and varied as the civil wars themselves and the international situation, and it is only by examining the event in this dual, long-term context that it can possibly be understood. This again is not a new idea; it was stated long ago by the German historian Baumgarten[1] – doubtless among many others – but it has not been influential, and could hardly be effective until the civil wars received more careful study.

The massacre of St Bartholomew was essentially two things: a domestic episode and turning point in the French civil wars, necessarily reflecting a number of their outstanding characteristics, and an international or European incident. In both the domestic and the foreign sphere, Coligny was, in August 1572, the key figure. The two aspects were of course inseparable since the French civil wars were always of general European significance. But, while bearing this in mind, it is necessary to make the distinction in order to discuss the various elements of conflict, and to show that the massacre was neither a premeditated crime, in the traditional sense, nor an isolated outrage, but a consequence of the long-term pattern and logic of events, and of immediate pressures at home and abroad.

The long-term pattern arose from the complex interplay of personal, domestic and foreign conflicts, while the immediate pressures were primarily external. In every respect the massacre was a landmark. In the domestic sphere it marks the end of the uneasy two years' peace since August 1570 and the beginning of the fourth civil war, conducted by new leaders, in which the protestants, soon to become a highly organised confederation, began to oppose the crown itself which had first failed to protect them, and which they now blamed for the massacre. In the foreign sphere, Coligny's death had at least two immensely important results: it frustrated, in 1572, the success of the revolt of the Netherlands, and disrupted what Spain saw as an Anglo-French agreement against her or, at the least, a political com-

---

[1] Hermann Baumgarten, *Vor der Bartholomäusnacht* (Strasbourg, 1882), see Butterfield, *Man on his Past*, 193.

bination of mixed protestant forces of which, while principally occupied with the Mediterranean and the Atlantic, Philip II was always excessively afraid.

In both spheres the central theme and common element was Spain; the Spanish and catholic pressure on the internal affairs of France and the individuals concerned in them. This, in turn, affected foreign relations and the basic Franco-Spanish rivalry, which was itself one aspect of the wider European struggle against the domination of Spain – greatly complicated by the additional struggle for the survival of protestantism, which extended, in different forms, at least from the election of the emperor Charles V in 1519, to the treaty of Westphalia in 1648.

The Spanish and catholic pressure which, in the 1570s, actually came more strongly from the less vulnerable papacy than from Madrid, was the principal external force in shaping this period of French history, and is the link between the internal and personal, and the external elements governing the death of Coligny and the massacre. But in order for this force to have been so consistently, successfully and disruptively active, certain predisposing conditions were essential within the state and society of France itself, and these are naturally the same closely interrelated conditions which gave rise to the civil wars. It is therefore necessary to consider these conditions, and how this pressure was exerted from the beginning of the civil war period in 1559.

On the national level, the civil wars arose from what the French called a *concurrence*, in which five basic problems exacerbated each other, simultaneously reaching the intensity of a crisis. The fundamental problem was the collapse, and consequent weakness of the crown following the death of Henry II. This immediately gave rise to an internecine rivalry among the high nobility in the personal, political and religious fields, all relentlessly exploited by Spain. Thirdly, the nobles' struggle for the control of the council arose from the weakness of the crown and was a concomitant of their rivalry. This struggle continued throughout the period 1559–72, and was one of the principal spheres in which Spanish and catholic pressure was constantly exercised. Initially these interdependent circumstances disastrously

coincided with a national bankruptcy and the most critical stage
of the Calvinist expansion in France, hence also with a religious
crisis. As they developed, these things became so entangled that
it will not always be possible to isolate them in discussion.

The weakness of the crown was a coincidental, dynastic
calamity arising from the premature death on 10 July 1559 of
Henry II as the result of a jousting accident, and from the youth,
sickness and ineptitude of his heirs. The jousting was part of the
celebrations of the treaty of Cateau-Cambrésis by which the
rival monarchs of France and Spain had, for the most part, restored their respective conquests of the Italian wars and shelved
their enmities, solemnising their new *entente* in the marriage of
Henry's daughter Elizabeth to the King of Spain himself. Thus
the collapse of the French monarchy overtook the country with
the same traumatic impact as the king's own death, distorting
an incipient partnership into a constant threat of Spanish domination. This gratuitous Spanish advantage had even been virtually
formalised by the dying king himself, who wrote to Philip by
the hand of the dauphin, directly commending his young heir
into Philip's paternal – or fraternal – hands.[1] Henry, who was
never very statesmanlike, may well have intended no more than
the maintenance of the treaty, which was indeed essential for the
survival of France. In effect, however, he had actually authorised
that Spanish catholic pressure on France which was about to
play so large a part in the origins and recurrence of the civil wars,
and which quickly developed from plaintive admonition into
that concrete interference in her internal affairs which, in different
forms, was to last until the end of the whole European struggle
against the domination of Spain. It is possible that both pressure
and interference might have stemmed in any case from Henry's
death, but this injudicious letter is nevertheless important, since
Philip was careful to keep Henry's dying request in lively re-
membrance, and naturally enough exploited what he could

[1] *Archivo documental Español, Francia*, i, 24–5, 12 July 1559, Philip II to the
bishop of Aquila, Alvaro de la Quadra, ambassador in England. This letter is
quoted by L. Romier in 'La Mort de Henri II', *Revue du XVIe siècle*, i (1913),
148. The whole article is interesting on the crisis caused by Henry's death.

thenceforth legitimately claim to be his protective role.[1] Further-more, this tended to shield and justify members of the French catholic faction who, already protected by the respectable cloak of religion, looked to Spain for support, thereby deepening an already serious internal cleavage, and increasing the external problem of the power of Spain. Fernando Alvarez de Toledo y Pimentel, third duke of Alva, later governor of the Netherlands, who was in France on account of the peace treaty, at the time of Henry's death, quickly formulated a menacing policy, stipulating to Philip II that Spain must keep the French from obtaining any foothold in England, and favour and foment the French catholics so that, at the same time as serving God, Philip could play a large part in France and the French government. He should also work upon queen Elizabeth, who was most suspicious of the French, bring her to tolerate the catholics and, with a large force, to establish such government as seemed suitable which, Alva main-tained, would not be difficult. Ten years later, when faced with the responsibility, he changed his mind about the ease with which England could be conquered. Philip himself commanded Alva and Ruy Gómez de Silva, the prince of Eboli, who was also in France, to be very attentive to the house of Guise considering that affairs (los negocios) were now in their hands.[2]

This catastrophic weakness of the crown, resulting from the death of Henry II, which so reduced France and exalted Spain, was inevitably associated, from the beginning, with the Calvinist crisis, since the agreement of the two monarchs, contained in the terms of the treaty,[3] to address themselves to the problem of

[1] See, for example, B.N., Mss. fr. 6618, ff. 28–34 verso [1562] Spanish memoir. The document is dated 1561, which is either old style, or an error. It mentions Philip's 'si cher gaige de la couronne de France' and, specifically, Henry's deathbed request.

[2] *Archivo documental Español, Francia,* i, 20–4, 11 July 1559, Alva and Ruy Gómez to Philip II; 30, 15 July 1559, Philip II to Alva. Philip was in Ghent at the time.

[3] Léonard, *Recueil des traitéz de Paix . . .* ii, 535–57, April 1559; de Ruble, *Le Traité de Cateau-Cambrésis*; see also, Archives d'État de Genève, Registres du Conseil, 55, f. 132 verso, 23 October 1559.

religion which threatened France at home and Spain in her ad-
joining Netherlands, had turned religion into the touchstone of
Franco-Spanish relations and so, by extension, into a principal
factor in European politics. Thus one may reasonably date from
this time the great politico-religious struggle of the sixteenth
century, which could hardly have taken its historic form without
the partial collapse of France as a major power, following upon
the separation of Spain from the Germanic empire, and the
simultaneous withdrawal of England from the allegiance of Rome.

Henry may well, and perhaps rightly, have seen the strongly
evangelical Calvinist movement as politically dangerous, at least
from the moment he realised that it had begun to affect the
nobility, upon whose loyalty the crown depended and who, in
time of peace, were notoriously dangerous. But his ferocious
determination to combat this problem at home[1] was probably
enhanced by the alarming example and dynastic provocation of
the Calvinist revolution of 1559 in Scotland, whose young queen,
Mary Stuart, niece of his own overbearing favourites the Guises,
had been reared in France and married to the dauphin Francis in
1558. By June 1559 Henry had therefore determined to make war
in Scotland,[2] not only in defence of religion and the Scottish
dynasty, but also in pursuit of Mary's claim to the throne of
England, a dual objective which could equally be presented as a
catholic duty, albeit one which would certainly have over-
strained even an inquisitorial union with Spain. It was doubtless
on this account that Alva stressed the need to prevent the French
from obtaining any foothold in England.

Philip's concern with the problem of religion was more general
and less obviously aggressive, for not only had he inherited the
catholic mantle of his father, Charles V, but also his preoccupation
with Islam, less as an anachronistic crusading ideal, than as a
serious political and military reality. Philip derived power from

[1] *Archives historiques de la Gironde*, i (1859), 14, 7 December 1556, Henry II
to the *parlement* of Bordeaux.

[2] *CSP Rome, 1558–71*, pp. 11–13, 29 June 1559, Henry II to pope Paul IV.
John Knox returned to Scotland in May 1559 and the regent was deposed in
October.

the inquisition, and wealth from the Spanish church, and protestantism of one kind or another was gaining the allegiance of
those most liable to be his political enemies. In particular queen
Elizabeth, by declining his hand, had rocked the old Burgundian
alliance, and the act of supremacy in England coincided, in the
month of April, with the treaty of Cateau-Cambrésis. This, and
his marriage to Elisabeth de Valois had turned Philip towards
France, where Henry was proposing to exterminate the heretics,
when everything was altered by his sudden death. The religious
situation in France became of increasingly vital concern to Philip
because the growth of Calvinism, thenceforth within the context
of a prolonged struggle for power, represented a *political* danger
to the Netherlands which he may not have proclaimed in public,
but did not seek to conceal in private.

Within France herself, this problem of religion was paradoxically both a complicating and a simplifying factor. It was
complicating because – something new and unmanageable – it
affected all society, which was consequently sucked into the vortex
of high politics as persecution became an instrument of policy,
thereby inevitably provoking resistance. But it was deceptively
simplifying in that it obscured, behind two confessional factions,
a variety of incompatible interests. The true situation, therefore,
was generally more complex than it appeared, since the real
conflicts of the period were never embraced by that of catholic
versus protestant. This artificial alignment both enabled the
French to fight each other, and precluded the resolution of their
deeper problems, hence the sterile violence and frustrating pro-
traction of the conflict.

This division of France behind religious banners, which played
so dangerously into the hands of Spain, would not have been
possible without the second fundamental condition, the old rivalry
of the nobility and their new struggle for power upon the death
of Henry II. There were separate personal, political and religious
elements involved in this struggle, although it rapidly becomes
difficult to distinguish one from the other. Before the death of
Henry II rivalry was largely military on the one hand, and for
influence over the king and council on the other. In this respect

the most notorious contention had been between the two celebrated Guise brothers, François duc de Guise and Charles cardinal
of Lorraine, and the constable Anne duc de Montmorency. The
third in power, if the first in rank as princes of the blood, were the
Bourbon brothers, Antoine de Bourbon King of Navarre, and
Louis, prince de Condé, who lived somewhat withdrawn from
the court, never having been favoured by the king.[1] In the later
years of Henry's reign there was also a personal and military
rivalry between the one-time friends and companions in arms,
Guise and the admiral, Coligny. Coligny was captured in 1557
at the dramatic siege of St Quentin in Picardy while Guise was
in Italy. Swiftly recalled in the ensuing crisis, Guise no less
dramatically recaptured Calais from the English in January 1558
in Coligny's *gouvernement* of Picardy. Their rivalry also became
more marked and acute from about this time because first his
brother, François d'Andelot, and then Coligny himself became
protestant, although his own conversion was not really clear
before the events of 1560 began to produce an alignment of
parties. By 1559 the Bourbons were also believed to be protestant,
sufficiently at least for Calvin himself and the nascent churches
to hope for their protection and leadership. By the time of Henry's
death, therefore, a pattern of conflict already existed, although its
form and development were altered by his decease.

The political rivalry between the Guises and Montmorency
was largely transferred from the constable to the Bourbons, on
account of their rank and the prescriptive rights of princes under
a regency, or in comparable circumstances. This was an unequal
struggle which, in terms of ability, the more talented Guises were
sure to win, but its conditions were complicated by Navarre's
personal importance as a prince, and Condé's more apparent
protestantism. Guise relations with Montmorency had been too
acrimonious to change overnight. Montmorency was an old man,
and therefore disposed himself to wait upon events and retire
for a while to his safely removed, but not too distant *château* of

---

[1] The Bourbon family had been eclipsed since the defection to Charles V in
1523 of the constable of Bourbon and the confiscation of his property.

Chantilly. By the spring of 1561 his unwavering catholicism finally reconciled him to the Guises, or perhaps more accurately brought him down on the catholic side,[1] since his genuine loyalty was never withdrawn from the crown.[2] This religious element, which attenuated the once critically dangerous rivalry between Guise and Montmorency, similarly intensified that between the constable's Calvinist nephew Coligny, and the Guises, rendering it indissoluble. Coligny, however, was neither prince, courtier nor diplomat so that the power aspect of the struggle continued to exist rather more between Guise and Condé who, on account of his rank, gradually became titular head of the protestant party. But Coligny remained the more effective, and certainly the military leader, and the enmity between him and Guise is as fundamental to a study of the massacre as it is central to the story of the civil wars. Beginning in the personal and military spheres, it became sharply defined by religious divergence, first publicly evident from their ominous confrontation in the *assemblée des notables* held at Fontainebleau in August 1560,[3] and further embittered by the first civil war. This culminated in an implacable vendetta between the admiral and the house of Guise, after the assassination of the duke in February 1563, for which his family – and in particular Lorraine – sought to blame the admiral.

[1] It is sometimes alleged that Montmorency may have joined the Guises partly because he, marshal Saint-André and the Guises were called upon by the estates of Paris and the Ile-de-France in March 1561 to account for their acquisition of wealth and their administration of affairs since Henry's reign. It appears, however, that Saint-André was required to account for and restore his 'dons excessifz' received from Henry, and 'tous ceulx qui ont eu le maniment des affaires' were to render account and restore what had been misappropriated. This might not specifically include Montmorency, though he could have felt threatened, since he had been greatly favoured by Henry, particularly in the payment of his ransom after his capture at St Quentin, and which annoyed the Guises. B.N., Mss. Cinq Cents Colbert, 27, f. 249 verso, 15 March 1561, unsigned fragment on the estates, in two contemporary hands.

[2] Montmorency returned to his central and moderate role after the first civil war, in which the catholic faction was disrupted.

[3] Lalourcé et Duval, *Recueil des pièces originales*, i, 66 seq. *Récit de ce qui s'est passé à l'assemblée de Fontainebleau, au mois d'août 1560*; Pasquier, *Lettres historiques*, 45–7.

The rivalry between the nobles centred on the control of the council through which the authority of the crown was largely exercised when, for any reason, the king was ineffective. After the establishment of the regency of Catherine de Medici in conjunction with Navarre on 6 December 1560 for her ten-year-old son Charles IX,[1] all three interests, crown, catholics and protestants, struggled to dominate the council; the crown above all to safeguard peace, law and order, through the agency of all moderate and reasonable men, and the factions to wield power and patronage, and to impose persecution or secure toleration respectively. This three-tiered struggle, personal, political and religious, may be directly traced through the religious deliberations,[2] and the contradictory terms and confusing outcome of the series of so-called religious edicts issued between January 1561 and January 1562, shortly before the outbreak of civil war.[3] Indeed, the clearly moderating influence of Catherine de Medici and the chancellor, Michel de l'Hospital, in the interests of peace, may be traced from as far back as the edict of Amboise of March 1560, before the emergence of the Bourbon-Coligny leadership of a protestant party.

These conditions of multiple conflict therefore allowed ample scope for the Spanish pressure which began, like the weakness of the crown, with Henry's death, and did so much to foster and rekindle civil war, which became an increasingly important factor in Spanish foreign policy. These are the origins of Philip's fears of a protestant-political and, later, Anglo-French combination, against him. The result was to make available the support and

---

[1] Dupuy, *Traité de la Majorité de nos Rois*, 347–54; B.N., Mss. Dupuy, 128, f. 9 verso, 7 December 1560; Mss. fr. 3159, f. 8, 30 March 1560/1, *extraict des registres du parlement*; Mss. n.a.f., 3102, f. 17, 6 December 1560, Charles IX to Limoges.

[2] On 11 June 1561 the seigneur d'Esternay presented a protestant petition. This was discussed at length by the court and council in the *parlement*, deliberations described by Pasquier as 'les pourparlers de Paris'. Condé, *Mémoires*, ii, 370–2, petition of 11 June 1561; Pasquier, *Lettres historiques*, 64–5; *CSPF.*, *1561–2*, p. 178, 13 July 1561, Throckmorton to Elizabeth; de Ruble, *Antoine de Bourbon*, iii, 101–3; Delaborde, *Coligny*, i, 511–12.

[3] The texts of these edicts are printed in Fontanon, *Édits et ordonnances*, iv.

power of Spain to the extreme catholic faction, led by the Guises who had largely controlled the government from the death of Henry II to that of Francis II in December 1560. Having lost control under the regency of Catherine, in March or April 1561 they formed a politico-religious cabal, known as the Triumvirate.[1] Philip was rather more than supported in this by the pope, who had not, like him, any urgent political motives, but who, to a large extent, could only function through the co-operation and power of Spain. Thus, in mid-October 1561, just when Lorraine had ensured the failure of the *colloque* of Poissy in France, at which some religious reconciliation was debated and could well have been agreed,[2] the pope sent a legate, the count Brocado, to Spain. Brocado's instructions, dated 18 October 1561, contain an outstandingly important statement of papal policy in which Pius IV declared that if the monarchs of France and England would not obey and conform, then he intended to proceed with their deposition, in favour of Philip, upon whom those crowns would be conferred.[3] It will be seen with what perseverance and skill the cardinal of Lorraine laboured, thenceforth until 1572, to execute this papal policy, together with its concomitants as more fully expressed in the so-called 'treaty' of the Triumvirate. It is in this light that his activity should be considered, both in order to

[1] See appendix; Michaud et Poujoulat, *Collection des mémoires, série i*, vol. vi, *Mémoires-journaux du duc de Guise*, 464–5. The authenticity of this document, representing the so-called 'treaty', or *conspiration* of the Triumvirate, is questioned. It bears the date – added – 1561, when the cabal was certainly formed, but contains material which must be dated later. Its interpretation poses complex and difficult problems which, together with a quantity of further documentation, cannot be entered into here. I hope to do this in a future work on the origins of the civil wars. Guise, Montmorency and marshal Saint-André were the original three of the Triumvirate, although the group always included others, notably Lorraine.

[2] *CSPF., 1561–2*, p. 342, 30 September 1561, articles agreed upon by deputies on both sides in the matter of the sacrament of the Eucharist. In fact there are two skilful forms of words here, embodying both the catholic and Calvinist conceptions.

[3] Pius proposed to 'venire alli atti della privatione delli regni di Francia et d'Inghilterra . . .' Šusta, *Die Römische Curie*, i, 280, 18 October–December 1561, instructions for the conte Brocado.

understand what he was genuinely trying to do, and also the vexed nature of his antipathetic relations with Catherine. This will reveal the error of asserting that she ever maintained the Guise faction in order to 'balance' the protestants. Philip, for his part, was no less concerned, towards the end of 1561, about the state of religion in France, which seemed to threaten the Netherlands, partly because he feared – in spite of its risibility – that the King of Navarre who, if not precisely a protestant, was a most unreliable catholic, might resort to arms in the power of France, for the recovery of Spanish Navarre or the extraction of some other kingdom by way of compensation.[1]

For these reasons, and pressed by the pope, Philip made a careful exploration of the possibility of pre-emptive 'religious' war and, in November 1561, sent his secretary Courteville to the Netherlands, conferring on his way through France with the Spanish ambassador Thomas Perrenot de Chantonnay, brother of cardinal Granvelle.[2] In December Courteville prepared a long report[3] in which he considered, primarily, the state of the Netherlands, and what measures to adopt, and whether there were any among the French catholics 'sur qui l'on pourroit faire fondement . . .' Philip had openly declared to Ausances, a French envoy in Spain upon the business of Navarre, that if the queen mother declined his assistance 'pour redresser les abus de France par force', then he would bestow such assistance upon whomsoever else might request it, which sounds very much like compliance with Pius IV's proposals. Chantonnay conveyed this exact statement to Catherine, and Francisco de Vargas, Philip's ambassador in Rome, also conveyed it to the pope. While Catherine understandably complained, the pope expressed his strong approval, further declaring that he would proceed with the council (of Trent) and 'damn' the French heretics, and for this it was neces-

[1] Navarre also possessed property in the Netherlands.

[2] Courteville arrived at Poissy on 24 November 1561, to see Chantonnay.

[3] Granvelle, *Papiers d'État*, vi, 432–43, December 1561, rapport secret de Courteville '. . . sa Majesté avoit declairé ouvertement que orres la royne mère n'acceptast l'assistance de sa Majesté pour redresser les abus de France par force, sa Majesté la donneroit à qui la demanderoit'.

sary *to use force* (y venir a las manos), *there being no other remedy for the harm that other places and christendom might sustain.*[1]

But the duchess of Parma, governess of the Netherlands, and Chantonnay in France, who were concerned with actualities, stopped considerably short of advising Philip to go to war, whether against England in pursuit of Mary Stuart's claim to the throne – with a suitable Hapsburg marriage, which meant, at least on this occasion, the archduke Charles of Austria – or against France, in defence of the Netherlands. Chantonnay, however, whose reply was phrased with cautious imprecision, appears to have been in favour of a civil war, promoted by the Guises, and as soon as possible, because if the matter – presumably the spread of Calvinism – were not remedied the following summer, 1562, namely the next campaigning season, it would be too late. This is exactly what they attempted, though their precise relationship to Spain and the papacy does not emerge.

There was, therefore, from the start an element of discrepancy between papal and Spanish policy, not in fundamental, long-term purpose, but in priorities and tactics. Philip, with his great, imperial burden, had compelling reasons for proceeding cautiously, while the papacy and the French extremists had not. Furthermore, since the pope was impatiently concerned with a grand design, which depended upon Spain for its practical interpretation, there existed two distinct, yet thoroughly intermingled planes of policy. In practice it was inevitable that the grand design must be continuously affected by the shifting domestic conflicts of the countries concerned, and the ineluctable evolution of their historic relationships. At times, therefore, the conception was clearly apparent, and at others submerged in the confusion of events.

Thus, without quite undertaking the perilous war required by the pope, but for which civil war was at first a promising substitute, Philip did support the extreme French catholics in their efforts to thwart any degree of moderation or religious toleration,

[1] Granvelle, *Papiers d'État*, vi, 398–400, 7 November 1561, Vargas to Philip II.

to seduce from Catherine the allegiance of Navarre, and to dominate the council and crown. It is true that Philip would have 'supported' the crown itself, that he was authorised to advise and felt
entitled to bully, had it represented the most extreme catholic
element in France, and been prepared, as they said, to 'passer
oultre'; namely to employ force against the protestants, since
pastoral admonition and judicial condemnation had long since
proved ineffective.[1]

But the primary interest of the crown which, as sovereign of
the Netherlands, Philip himself had good reason to know, lay
in the imposition of authority, and Catherine would neither be
stampeded into adopting extreme measures which must result in
war and deliver her into the hands of French military leaders,[2]
nor into accepting 'help' that was tantamount to domination.
She was in fact far more afraid of Spanish power, whether
exerted directly, or through the agency of French extremists at
court, than she was of a pragmatic and humane degree of toleration, at least pending a general council.[3] This led her to oppose
the Triumvirate and catholic pressure in 1561, as indeed she
resisted the Guises all her life, and to admit into the council
moderates, and a number of protestants including Condé and
Coligny, whose exclusion would not, in any case, have been
acceptable to her co-regent, Navarre.[4] Though certain to be

[1] Philip first offered 'help' at the time of the conspiracy of Amboise, 1560.
B.N., Mss. Clairambault, 354, f. 3, 26 March 1560, d'Andelot to Montmorency;
Mss. fr. 3951, ff. 26–42, 1 October 1561, *mémoire de Limoges*; Granvelle, *Papiers
d'État*, vi, 434, December 1561, *rapport secret de Courteville*.

[2] Catherine explicitly referred to what she believed to be the Guise calcula-
tion that if war were to come she would fall into their hands again. This was
true, and also proves the antagonism between them during François' reign. La
Ferrière, *Lettres*, i, 582, [29 or 30] March 1561, Catherine to the queen of Spain.

[3] Even after the failure of the *colloque* of Poissy, September–October 1561,
efforts were still being made to reach a compromise solution to religious
differences. *Archivo documental Español, Francia*, iii, 208–10, 23 December 1561,
Chantonnay to Philip II.

[4] Condé was restored to the council on 13 March 1561. Condé, *Mémoires*,
ii, 383; Aumale, *Histoire des princes de Condé*, i, 100, says he was admitted on
15 March. Chantonnay reported on 5 December 1560, the day Francis II died,
that he feared Catherine wanted Coligny in the council. In fact he returned

maliciously interpreted, in spite of her efforts to explain, this was neither apostasy, nor even uncertainty of purpose, but a measure of the insuperable difficulty of combining political independence with the essential and inevitable catholicity of the crown – regarded as a fundamental law.

Philip strenuously opposed the presence in the council of such influential moderates and protestants, among whom Coligny and the chancellor de l'Hospital were instrumental in organising the assembly of Saint-Germain which met on 3 January 1562 and produced the first celebrated edict of limited toleration.[1] This, therefore, was the period, from the autumn of 1561, when Philip exerted the maximum pressure and influence he could to alarm Catherine,[2] both as to the state of France and his own intentions – which were indeed alarming[3] – to support the catholic faction, and to promote extreme religious measures. If his agents, the ambassador Chantonnay, the nuncio Santa Croce, the cardinal legate of Ferrara and cardinal de Tournon, narrowly failed to avert the passage of the edict of January, they finally succeeded in forcing the departure from council and court of Coligny in February 1562, and his brother the protestant cardinal Châtillon in March.[4]

---

about the same time as Condé. *Archivo documental Español, Francia*, i, 498, 5 December 1560, Chantonnay to Philip II; *CSPF.*, *1561–2*, p. 45, 31 March 1561, Throckmorton to Elizabeth.

[1] Fontanon, *Édits et ordonnances*, iv, 267–9, 17 January 1562.

[2] Catherine complained of being lectured by Chantonnay and the nuncio, and Limoges reported that Chantonnay was required to 'presser, prier, crier et importuner'. La Ferrière, *Lettres*, i, 584–7, 3 March 1561, Catherine to Limoges; B.N., Mss. fr. 6618, f. 8, 29 August 1561, de Laubespine to (his brother) Limoges; Mss. fr. 3951, ff. 26–42, 1 October 1561, *mémoire de Limoges*.

[3] The documentation on this subject is considerable; but see, for example, B.N., Mss. fr. 6618, ff. 28–34 verso [1562], as well as Courteville's report.

[4] Coligny and d'Andelot had left the council by 22 February 1562, the day the court dispersed, which rendered plausible Catherine's claim that she had dismissed no one. Sainte-Croix, *Lettres*, 39, 22 February 1562; *Archivo documental Español, Francia*, iii, 382, 28 February 1562, Chantonnay to Philip II. Cardinal Châtillon left between 3 & 9 March. Este, *Négociations*, 101–2, 3 March 1562,

Catherine, ordering all *gouverneurs* to their provinces, and bishops to their dioceses, denied having dismissed anyone, and she cannot willingly have let the Châtillons go precisely at this moment when she needed them most. This was just as Navarre, finally yielding to the Spanish and catholic pressure, opted for the Triumvirate,[1] a disastrous defection from their regency partnership without which the crown had little hope of independence. Indeed the Triumvirate went so far as to seize possession of the king and Catherine at Fontainebleau on 27 March. This acquisition by the Triumvirate of the lieutenant-general of the kingdom,[2] enabled them to make war upon his vice-regal authority. Without him, a resort to arms would not only have been *lèse-majesté*, but difficult to execute, at least in theory, in view of his position as supreme commander.

By this crisis of 1562, the basic pattern of French politics and Franco-Spanish relations, which persisted for the next ten years until the massacre, had been established. While remaining essentially catholic, the principal concern of the crown was necessarily with independence, the imposition of authority and the maintenance of peace, law and order, without which government could not function and the monarchy might perish, but for which, in the circumstances, some religious concessions were inescapable. As the catholics were implacably opposed to any concessions, this tended to force the crown into a measure of political reliance upon protestant councillors and servants, who for the most part were relatively moderate. The protestants had not, at this time, demanded more than limited toleration, and they, in turn, needed

---

Ferrara to Borromeo; *CSPF., 1561–2*, pp. 524–8, 16 February 1562, Throckmorton to Elizabeth; 545–9, 6 March 1562, Throckmorton to Elizabeth; 552, 9 March 1562, Throckmorton to Cecil. Throckmorton is penetrating on this complex crisis.

[1] I have analysed elsewhere the struggle for the allegiance of Navarre. On 28 February 1562 Navarre sent for Guise to come to Paris, and later declared that he would live in close friendship with him. Pasquier, *Lettres historiques*, 95; Sainte-Croix, *Lettres*, 46–9, 13 March 1562; Delaborde, *Coligny*, ii, 23–4.

[2] Navarre became lieutenant-general as part of the regency arrangement on 8 April 1561.

the support of the crown to obtain it. This maintenance of peace, therefore, was in their interests or, if there had to be war, then it was preferable that it should be channelled abroad, which in practice was likely to mean the Netherlands. Thus, the later military problem of 1570–2 was already implicit in the civil war situation. The catholics, on the other hand, were always aggressively inclined, partly because they largely controlled the military forces of the crown, so that hostilities would render their services essential and – another aspect of the same thing – in time of war the crown must appear to be merged with the catholic faction – which was thereby correspondingly strengthened and ostensibly associated with the international interests of Spain.

Within France, at least on the national level, the conflict was to a great extent personalised by the faction leaders, and centred in the struggles between Guises and Bourbons, and Guises and Coligny, quarrels whose form appears to have been partially dictated by the terms of the Triumvirate which stated the intention, under the auspices of Spain, not only to exterminate the protestants, but also specifically to *eliminate* the house of Bourbon. This was expanded, in or before 1565, by the catholics, Spain and the papacy, to embrace all the principal protestant leaders. The dramatic policies of extermination and elimination were, however, clearly foreshadowed by the catholics, France and Spain in 1560 before the formation of the Triumvirate, when the Guises were still in power under Francis II.[1] It was his sudden death on 5 December which frustrated their undertakings. These were already far advanced, since they had allegedly prepared four armies under the duc d'Aumale – brother of Guise – and the marshals Saint-André, Brissac and de Thermes to attempt the policy of extermination in the provinces.[2] On the personal level, elimination was first unambiguously attempted when, at Orléans

[1] See, for example, B.N., Mss. fr. 15874, ff. 106–7, 31 August 1560, Limoges to Lorraine; Henry & Loriquet, *Correspondance de la Bourdaisière*, 27–34, 30 September 1560, La Bourdaisière (French ambassador in Rome) to Charles IX.

[2] Regnier de La Planche, *Histoire de l'Estat de France sous le règne de François II*, 404; see also 364 seq.

on 31 October 1560, the Guises arrested and, without trial appropriate to his rank, condemned the prince de Condé.[1] The exact charge against him is not clear. The territories of Navarre, who was detained, were occupied by Spain, Philip II having already sent a special envoy, the grandee Don Antonio de Toledo, who can have left no doubt as to the extreme nature of his policy.[2] Civil war, which Philip in any case regarded as inevitable,[3] would, at that date, serve his interests as well as those of the catholics, by insulating the Netherlands although, via the huguenots, it quickly led to closer French relations with protestant, maritime England.[4] Such an outrage, perpetrated against princes, could not honourably be forgiven; trouble was therefore bound to ensue. According to Sir Nicholas Throckmorton, the English ambassador, Condé's life was again threatened at the time of the abortive, Guisard 'Nemours conspiracy' to abduct Henri duc d'Orléans, heir to the throne, in 1561.[5] So began the Guisard persecution of this ill-starred prince, which lasted for the rest of his life.

Coligny, who alone survived until the massacre in 1572, was the last of these Spanish and catholic enemies. All the rest had perished, whether in battle or ambiguous circumstances still re-

[1] Simon Renard, seigneur de Viremont (Imperial ambassador in France during the reign of Henry II, when the emperor Charles V was the King of Spain), later alleged that Condé was to have been beheaded, Navarre imprisoned, the constable executed, and Coligny and Châtillon burnt for heresy. 6 October 1564, Simon Renard to the duchess of Parma in *BSHPF*, xxxvi (1887), 640. Nothing is too astounding to be credible in this affair, but it is doubtful if such decisions had really been made. B.N., Mss. Italien, 1721, ff. 187–90, 10 November 1560; Condé, *Mémoires*, ii, 373–88.

[2] Granvelle, *Papiers d'État*, vi, 137–43, 2 September 1560, instructions for Don Antonio de Toledo.

[3] B.N., Mss. fr. 15875, f. 400 verso, 19 December 1561, Limoges to Charles IX.

[4] In the first place the treaty of Hampton Court, September 1562, between the huguenots and queen Elizabeth. They also, of course, had foreign connections in Germany and with the Swiss. PRO/SP 70/41.

[5] *CSPF.*, *1561–2*, p. 416, 26 November 1561, Throckmorton to Elizabeth; Valois, 'Projet d'enlèvement d'un enfant de France en 1561', *Bibliothèque de l'École des Chartes*, lxxv (1914). Jacques de Savoie, duc de Nemours was held to be the most perfect courtier of his day.

quiring explanation. There is excellent evidence that the specific Triumvirate elimination policy, as well as the extreme attitudes of Spain and the papacy were known at an early stage to both the crown and the protestant leaders,[1] whose consequent need to defend their lives and property goes far to account for their obdurate refusal, in the spring and early summer of 1562, to disarm before the catholics,[2] who speciously claimed to be serving the lieutenant-general whose right to maintain forces was incontestable.

This particular deadlock over the laying down of arms was the immediate cause of the outbreak of civil war in June 1562, which could, at least in a sense, be described as a Spanish and catholic achievement, although its inconclusive outcome was not without advantages to Philip, strongly as he opposed the peace in March 1563. Had the catholics been too successful, they would have needed him less, whereas the perpetuation of strife kept the French out of Scotland and England. On the other hand, neither the civil war nor the peace achieved anything to arrest the advance of Calvinism or to protect the Netherlands, which were Philip's initial and mounting anxieties.[3]

[1] The documentation on this is too vast to enter into here. But it is interesting to note that the 'treaty' of the Triumvirate also features among Condé's papers: Condé, *Mémoires*, iii, 209–13, and he is said to have published it in April 1562.

[2] B.N., Mss. fr. 20461, ff. 217–verso, 27 March 1561/2, Coligny to Catherine, autograph, original. Many documents relating to this protracted and complex crisis may be found in Condé, *Mémoires*, iii.

[3] B.N., Mss. fr. 6618, ff. 28–34 verso [1562], Spanish memoir, apparently addressed to someone in the Netherlands. The description *double de la déclaration du Roi d'Espagne touchant les troubles de France*, has been added.

II

The Broadening of the Conflict
1563-1565

IF LITTLE had been resolved by the first short civil war, which ended in March 1563, it had broken the deadlock between Guise and Condé, and altered internal circumstances. It is therefore necessary to consider these changes, and the further developments, between then and 1570, of the basic conditions out of which the civil wars had arisen, and which constituted the long-term pattern of events behind the massacre. It becomes increasingly difficult to isolate the Spanish and catholic pressure, the evolving religious crisis, the weakness of the crown and the quarrels of the nobility between themselves and for control of the council, which must be traced in order to see how the massacre reflected certain fundamental characteristics of the civil wars. The religious issues, for example, became virtually inseparable from the others. If the catholics had won the battle of Dreux, 19 December 1562, the only pitched battle of the war, they had not won the war itself, which was interrupted rather than concluded. Thus the war, and the peace and edict of Amboise, had finally established, if the edict of January had not, that protestantism had come to stay. The real issue therefore was the nature and degree of toleration to be permitted. With certain specified safeguards, the edict of January 1562 had permitted the exercise of the cult outside the towns, but not the construction of churches, or *temples* as they were called. The less liberal edict[1] of Amboise authorised the cult in one town per *bailliage* or *sénéchaussée*, and in places where it was held up to 7 March 1563, together with

---

[1] The 'edict' refers to the religious clauses of the peace treaty, hence the commonly used expression 'edicts of pacification'. Fontanon, *Édits et ordonnances*, iv, 272-4, 19 March 1563.

certain privileges for the higher nobility in their own houses. The nature and degree of toleration to be permitted as the chancellor, de L'Hospital, had already correctly and courageously declared in January 1562, was not a confessional but an administrative problem or, if the more extreme catholics had their way, a military one. 'Je ne veulx mettre en disputte les controverses de la religion . . . mais seulement ce qui appartient à la pollice pour contenir le peuple en repoz et tranquillité'. Those who advised the king to suppress the protestants, advised war, since, he said, the question was not 'de constituenda Religione, sed de constituenda Republica'.[1] The more violently the catholics resisted the recognition of limited toleration, the more significant the protestants inevitably became in the political sphere, which was bound, sooner or later, to mean abroad as well as at home, as both parties had foreign affiliations.

Thus the second stage of the civil wars is marked by a vitally important new factor, namely a steadily increasing internationalisation of the conflict. In practice this meant, in the first place, an increased involvement with the Netherlands and, consequently, also with Spain, the pope, and catholic princes on the one hand, and England and Germany on the other. What could once at least have been represented as a religious struggle pursued in the political sphere, became more and more a political struggle partly pursued in the name of religion. The point is worth making because the massacre – primarily of protestants by catholics – was a matter of war and politics, not religion – except, perhaps for the Paris mob – and no contemporary pretended otherwise. But while, on the protestant side, the religious content of the struggle declined – and this was further emphasised by their

---

[1] Dufey, de L'Hospital, *Œuvres*, i, 435–53, 26 August 1561, harangue to the commission of the estates at Pontoise. This is obviously a corrupt text, wrongly entitled, possibly a conflation of two speeches, large parts of which could only have been delivered to the assembly of Saint-Germain in January 1562 and not in August 1561. See also Condé, *Mémoires*, ii, 606–12. Chantonnay observed, with what sounds like grudging praise, that the chancellor was 'humanista y gran retórico'. *Archivo documental Español, Francia*, iii, 237, 5 January 1562, Chantonnay to Philip II. He is interesting on the shifting relationships of the nobles at court before the expulsion of the Châtillons and the defection of Navarre.

relative detachment from Geneva after Calvin's death in January 1564 – with the publication of the decrees of Trent and the election, in 1566, of the zealously devout pope Pius V, the specifically 'catholic' pressure on France and the protestant world not only continued, but was notably increased, and more from Rome than Madrid.

The fact that religion had become a predominantly administrative problem created immense new difficulties for a weak, impoverished monarchy, faced with widespread catholic opposition, including that of the *parlements* which should, above all, have supported the catholic crown and defended the law. The simplest possible solution was therefore desirable, whereas the establishment of a *lieu du culte* in each *bailliage* or *sénéchaussée* presented endless difficulties and was easily sabotaged. This increasingly manifest inability to implement the successive 'edicts of pacification' was perhaps *the* fundamental, domestic reason for the continuation of civil strife.[1] Without it the turbulent, aggressive nobility would have been deprived of a platform.

The implementation of the religious clauses of the peace of Amboise, the first of the edicts of pacification, therefore became merged with the struggle for the authority of the crown and its independence of Spain and the factions, which Catherine energetically resumed the moment peace freed her from the Triumvirate. It is interesting to note, as evidence of Catherine's indomitably independent attitude, that her policy at the time of the peace negotiations was different from that of both Guise and Coligny, each of whom opposed the agreement, if for totally different reasons. Nothing shows more clearly the basic continuity of Catherine's policy than her conduct at the end of each war, which was not, as historians so often maintain, a policy of 'bascule', but a steady one of reconciliation and containment, for which peace was an essential prerequisite.[2] This accounts for her

[1] This point is illustrated by the story of the edict of Nantes which I have traced elsewhere: 'The Edict of Nantes and the Protestant State', *Annali della Fondazione italiana per la storia amministrativa*, i (2) (1965), 199–236.

[2] See, for example, B.N., Mss. Italien, 1724, ff. 67–9, 31 May 1563; f. 83, 27 June 1563.

Charles, cardinal of Lorraine

Philip II, King of Spain

Catherine de Medici

Jean de Morvillier

constant, almost superhuman efforts to maintain or restore peace – which no one has ever denied – and, most particularly, to avoid war with Spain, the factor behind all others which permeated and explains her political career. Future events were to prove how intensely right she had been, since the nightmare of the 1550s, a Spanish garrison in Paris, materialised shortly after her death and, in 1597, before the civil wars were over, France was very nearly defeated by Spain. But what Philip II wanted, until much later, was war *in* France, not war *with* France,[1] and it seems that Catherine did not fully realise, at least in this period before the diminution of the Turkish threat, the intensity of Philip's own fear of war.[2] This fear, as early as 1559 (and patently evident in 1572), was one reason why he had been reluctant to withdraw the detested Spanish troops from the Netherlands, a major grievance against Spain.[3] On the other hand, he was under constant pressure from the papacy to intervene in France since the pope could fulminate, and to some extent finance, but not otherwise pursue his militant catholic purpose, without Philip.[4]

The first civil war, in which Catherine had been forced to accept Spanish military assistance, had done nothing to lessen her fear of Spanish domination, though she may well have calculated that it was preferable to request a moderate degree of help upon her own terms, than to risk Philip's unsolicited intervention which might have been on a very large scale.[5] At that time the

[1] This point of view was explicitly stated, for example, by St Sulpice, ambassador in Spain following Limoges, from April 1562. Cabié, *Ambassade en Espagne de St Sulpice*, 93–6, 12 November 1562, St Sulpice to Catherine.

[2] A memoir on Spanish finances, prepared by Philip himself, is quite enough to account for this. Granvelle, *Papiers d'État*, vi, 156–65, [7 September 1560]. Philip suffered a severe naval defeat at the hands of the Turks near Gelbes. B.N., Mss. fr. 15874, f. 36, 2 June 1560, Limoges to Guise and Lorraine.

[3] Granvelle, *Papiers d'État*, v, 672–5, 27 December [1559], Philip II to Arras (Granvelle, bishop of Arras).

[4] At the outbreak of the second civil war the pope is reported to have offered to send 3,000 or possibly 6,000 foot to France, but upon the most demanding conditions. Hirschauer, *La Politique de St Pie V*, 98–100, 101–3, two letters of 16 October 1567 to the nuncio, Michel della Torre.

[5] B.N., Mss. fr. 6604, ff. 48–9, 8 May 1562, Charles IX to Limoges. Charles requested 10,000 foot and 3,000 horse. According to Chantonnay, Philip had

protestants were superior in cavalry, on open terrain in which this was decisive, and could have won a lightning victory, in which case, it was feared, Philip would invade. This was very far from being a neurosis, since not only had Philip already offered help as long ago as March 1560, at the time of the conspiracy of Amboise, but also again in September 1560[1] when he sent Don Antonio de Toledo to France. Towards the end of 1561, he was making extensive preparations against, he said, all eventualities, and became extremely threatening, so much so that Charles protested to his ambassador, Sébastien de Laubespine, bishop of Limoges, that he was accountable to God, not the King of Spain, and objected to his haughty dictation.[2] Spanish forces again took part in the second and third civil wars.

If the first civil war had done nothing to solve the problem of religion or improve relations with Spain, neither had it improved the position of the crown in relation to the rivalries of the factions, and their efforts to dominate the court and council; only the circumstances of the rivalries had been altered. In the first place, the catholic faction was less clearly identified because the Triumvirate had been disrupted. Navarre, their princely figurehead, had died at the siege of Rouen in October 1562, and the marshal Jacques d'Albon de Saint-André at the battle of Dreux. More important, their leader, the duc de Guise was murdered at Orléans in February 1563, without which the catholics and Spain would have continued the war. It was only the crown

actually offered 30,000 foot and 6,000 horse, which hardly sounds realistic. Condé, *Mémoires*, ii, *Correspondance de Chantonnay*, 38–41, 7 May 1562, Chantonnay to the duchess of Parma.

[1] B.N., Mss. Clairambault, 354, f. 3, 26 March 1559/60, d'Andelot to Montmorency; La Ferrière, *Lettres*, i, 149, two letters [September and October], Catherine to Philip II; *CSPF.*, *1560–1*, p. 345, 10 October 1560, Throckmorton to Elizabeth; de Ruble, *Antoine de Bourbon*, ii, 357–8.

[2] Limoges was a brother of the secretary of state, Claude de Laubespine, Catherine's confidant. Granvelle, *Papiers d'État*, vi, 433, rapport secret de Courteville; *Archivo documental Español, Francia*, iii, 170–1, 15 December 1561, Chantonnay to Philip II; B.N., fr. 15875, ff. 444–5 verso, 26 December 1561, Charles to Limoges.

that wanted peace. According to the English ambassador, Sir Thomas Smith, Chantonnay was held to have been associated with a council in Paris attended by Guise and the papal nuncio and legate at which it was determined that if Catherine succeeded in making peace, they would resist it. Philip also proposed, upon pretext of the victory of Dreux, to send Don Fernando de Toledo, Alva's illegitimate son, to France, to obstruct the conclusion of peace. It is not clear, however, if he arrived. St Sulpice, for his part, sent his secretary, La Mothe-Fénelon, to inform Catherine of the strenuous efforts of Spain to avert peace, in spite of its desirability.[1] Smith further reported a proposal that the pope should declare Guise protector of the Roman Catholic Church: 'by that means he would remain lieutenant and continue in arms and receive money from the pope and others'.[2] Since Smith affirmed that this was known at court and to the protestants, it could, possibly, have been one reason why Guise was assassinated, as it happened next day, and before he had time to take the protestant stronghold of Orléans.[3] In the same letter Smith declared Lorraine to be 'marvellous busy about the emperor, Swiss catholics and German Papist Princes'.[4] The council of Berne reported to Geneva that a number of Spanish had arrived at Genoa 'pour desservir à la practique du pape, Roy Philippe

---

[1] Cabié, *Ambassade en Espagne de St Sulpice*, 112–13, 31 January 1563, St Sulpice to Catherine; 114, 5 February 1562/3, secret letter from St Sulpice to Charles and Catherine; 115–16, 25 February 1563, St Sulpice to Catherine. Jean Ébrard de St Sulpice was a cousin of Lansac, French ambassador at the council of Trent, and of La Mothe-Fénelon, the judicious ambassador in England from 1568–75 who strove to promote the Anjou marriage. He was also a brother-in-law of Gontaut de Biron, joint architect with the seigneur de Malassise of the treaty of Saint-Germain in 1570. These were all moderates and loyalists who supported Catherine.

[2] *CSPF.*, *1563*, p. 142, 17 February 1562/3, Smith to the privy council.

[3] Guise was assassinated by an obscure fellow from Angoulême, Poltrot de Mérey, but there appears to be at least a prima facie case against Condé. Spain, according to St Sulpice, had relied upon Guise to keep the war going in France. Cabié, *Ambassade en Espagne de St Sulpice*, 123, 27 March 1563, secret letter from St Sulpice to Catherine.

[4] *CSPF.*, *1563*, p. 138, 17 February 1563, Smith to the privy council.

duc de Savoie et aultres contre la France'. A captain called Lazare had gone from the Netherlands to recruit forces to hold in Germany pending Philip's orders. Spanish payments to German merchants were being consigned to military expenses.[1] It would, however, be wrong to conclude from this rather nervous protestant source that Philip was committed to an aggressive catholic league, and there was nothing peculiar about the arrival of Spanish troops at Genoa, the normal route to Spanish Milan, and the overland route to the Netherlands. But there is no doubt that such a league was mooted. According to Smith, writing on 12 March, it was 'mutterid' that a Spanish messenger had been 'detrussid' – relieved of his packets, not his clothing – on his way to Italy, and his letters, taken to Lansac, the French ambassador at Trent, revealed a 'practice' for Spain and the emperor to invade France.[2] This, again, represents what the pope and extremists were seeking, rathei than any actual project. It is inconceivable that the Emperor Ferdinand I, who had signed the religious peace of Augsburg in 1555, permitting each prince to determine the religion of his own state, could have been induced, in his old age, to plunge into profitless catholic war in France, and at the behest of the papacy which had done little enough in the past to help him and his brother Charles V to resist the original entrenchment of protestantism in Germany.[3] Nevertheless, it is certain that Philip strongly desired the continuation of civil war in France, which was quite another matter, and that the Spanish-catholic-Guise attitude had not been altered by the war. The supposed 'practice', however, was sound triumvirate policy which, according to the 'treaty', was to embrace the emperor and German and Swiss catholics,

[1] Archives d'État de Genève, P.H. 1716, 22 January 1562/3, the council of Berne to that of Geneva.

[2] Forbes, ii, 356-9, 12 March 1563, Smith to Elizabeth. Louis de Saint-Gelais, seigneur de Lansac, *chevalier d'honneur* to Catherine; after the council of Trent, he went on an important mission to Spain in 1564, where his cousin, St Sulpice was the ambassador.

[3] The Emperor Ferdinand I died on 25 July 1564, and his successor, Maximilian II, was held to be Lutheran. He also, like his father, urged the pope to permit the marriage of priests. *CSPF.*, *1564-5*, p. 216, 3 October 1564, Gurone Bertano to [Cecil] from Rome; Granvelle, *Papiers d'État*, viii, 448, note 1.

and which was said to have been considered at the council of Trent where, Smith alleged, Lorraine had collected money to continue the war.[1]

It is therefore small wonder that Catherine should have laboured for peace 'malgre le ciel et tous les elements',[2] and her success in this respect disrupted catholic policy. But the assassination of the duc de Guise which, in the absence of Lorraine at Trent, enabled Catherine to make peace, was a paradoxical catastrophe which equally guaranteed the renewal of war through the implacable hostility of the Guises for the admiral, whom they maliciously elected to blame for the murder. No one has seriously believed that Coligny was guilty, though he injudiciously admitted his satisfaction. This was doubtless because he had received warnings, so he claimed, of plans against his own life. He also claimed to have sent the Guises warnings during the previous five to six months.[3] As for the Guises, they must surely have made the accusation whether they believed it or not. While they hoped to seduce the captured prince de Condé,[4] who must not, therefore, be inculpated, it was important to ruin the admiral, and this was a way of adapting triumvirate policy to the post-war circumstances,[5] thereby initiating a resounding vendetta which was henceforth to dominate and cripple French internal affairs until the death of Coligny in the massacre.

The vendetta was the most significant new, post-war development, and served to concentrate attention upon Coligny who had become by 1563, if not before, the key figure in French affairs and – with the increasing internationalisation of French conflicts – in European affairs, which he remained until his death. The vendetta enabled the catholics to ignore the treaty and edict

---

[1] *CSPF., 1563*, p. 12, 3 January 1563, Smith to Cecil.

[2] B.N., Mss. fr. 3180, f. 114, 12 December 1562, the secretary Fresne to the duc de Nemours.

[3] Du Bouchet, *Preuves*, 521–2, 22 March 1562/3, Coligny to Catherine. Both claims were true.

[4] B.N., Mss. Italien, 1724, f. 39, 30 April 1563.

[5] This is, more or less, the opinion expressed by Simon Renard in a letter of 6 October 1564, to the duchess of Parma, in *BSHPF*, xxxvi (1887), 640–3.

of peace, by providing a pretext for remaining more or less in arms, a substitute for their plan to do so by declaring the duke protector of the Catholic Church. If Coligny's life had been, in a general sense, in danger since his emergence as a protestant leader and the formation of triumvirate policy in 1561, after 1563 it was far more specifically and continuously threatened. Everyone was well aware of this. Already on 12 March 1563, the English ambassador recorded his anxiety for Coligny's life, 'with Aumale and the Guisians so great about the queen mother making such a brute to ron upon the admirall'.[1]

If the vendetta became the focus of the rivalries from 1563–72, fostering the circumstances of disruption and insecurity from which further hostilities were engendered, it also linked these personal quarrels to the renewed struggle for the control of the council. Indeed, according to Estienne Pasquier, a *parlementaire*, the principal reason for the vendetta was to exclude Coligny from court, and so from the council and access to the king.[2] Thus the Guises threatened Coligny with arms when he sought for the first time to return to court in May 1563,[3] and repeatedly demanded justice against him in the *parlement*,[4] which was once and for all impugned by Coligny on account of its alleged hostility – apart from the fact that events occurring in time of war were automatically amnestied by the peace; this he was prepared to overlook since, to claim amnesty, would be interpreted as an admission of guilt. So, on 16 May, the king evoked the matter to himself and forbade either side to offend the other in any way.[5] After the expedition in September 1563 against the

---

[1] Forbes, ii, 358, 12 March 1563, Smith to Elizabeth.

[2] *Bref discours de tout ce qui a este negotie pour la querelle entre les maisons de Guyse et de Chatillon*, 1564, attributed by the authority D. Thickett to Estienne Pasquier, which makes this the most valuable extant material on the vendetta. Rare pamphlet in the B.N., Paris, L^b 33 129.

[3] *CSPF.*, *1563*, p. 344, 17 May 1563, Middlemore to Cecil. This is precisely what they were to do again in December 1571; B.N., Mss. Italien, 1724, ff. 56–8, 15 May 1563; Pasquier, *Bref Discours*; Delaborde, *Coligny*, ii, 263–5.

[4] The *parlement* of Paris was widely believed to have been corrupted by the Guises. Whether or not this was true, it was certainly strongly catholic.

[5] B.N., Mss. fr. 3193, ff. 51–2, 16 May 1563, arrêt du conseil, printed in Du

English-occupied port of Le Havre, when Coligny remained at Châtillon, the Guises again threatened the peace by going in force to Meulan, where Catherine was dangerously ill following a fall from her horse,[1] and where it was rumoured that if she died, they planned to seize the young king and execute the constable and his family – ugly echoes of the seizure by the Guises of Condé at Orléans in 1560, and of Charles IX himself at Fontainebleau in March 1562. Catherine's extremity grieved and greatly alarmed her supporters because 'en son grand mal on voyait descouvrir de terribles humeurs'. Civil war was indeed very close in the autumn of 1563. It was upon this occasion that Catherine prepared written instructions for Charles who, though only thirteen and very frail, was newly declared of age; no wonder his mother was described as 'le pillier de ce royaulme', standing almost alone between France and her destruction.[2]

Contemptuously ignoring the royal evocation of their case, the Guises again demanded justice in the *parlement*.[3] Only then, according to his own account, did Coligny permit his followers to assemble. The king repeated his evocation, referring the case to the council, but he was powerless to prevent these assemblies of hostile forces, or to impose an effective reconciliation. In a long letter of 8 October to the king, Coligny complained, among other things, of having been warned that the duc d'Aumale,

---

Bouchet, *Preuves*, 537–8; Delaborde, *Coligny*, ii, 270–1. There are various documents relating to this matter in Condé, *Mémoires*, v.

[1] B.N., Mss. Italien, 1724, ff. 135–6 verso, 17 September 1563; 137–40, 23 September 1563; Ibid., 1725, ff. 34–8, 17 September 1563 (vol. 1725 carries the coded despatches relating to the same period as those in 1724); Ibid., 1724, ff. 139–41 verso, 23 September 1563.

[2] Cabié, *Ambassade en Espagne de St Sulpice*, 155, 21 September 1563, Robertet to St Sulpice; 156, 21 September 1563, de Laubespine to St Sulpice; 157, 29 September & 13 October 1563, the bishop of Mâcon – Jean Baptiste Alamanni – to St Sulpice; 165, 13 October 1563, Fourquevaulx to St Sulpice; 171, 1 November 1563, two letters of St Sulpice to Charles IX and Catherine.

[3] B.N., Mss. Italien, 1724, ff. 143-verso, 30 September 1563; f. 145, 30 September 1563; Pasquier, *Bref Discours*, 13–14.

Guise's brother, had sent two gentlemen to kill him.¹ Again in
November the Guises sent a large force to prevent Coligny from
joining the court near Fontainebleau. Upon this occasion he called
their bluff and, well accompanied, went to Paris about 20
November and resumed his place in the council; the Guises lost
face by their nervous withdrawal.² In December they impugned
the jurisdiction of the council in criminal cases, to which Coligny
responded by petitioning for the evocation to stand. So, on
5 January 1564 the king repeated the evocation and suspended
the matter for three years, or during pleasure. At the same time,
though not banished, the parties were licensed to depart and go
home, which would both separate them and deflect the quarrel
from the council.³ The Guises left immediately, making an excuse
of Lorraine's impending arrival from the council of Trent.

The return of Coligny, which might well have lasted longer
than a mere two months, threw Philip into a state of great consternation, particularly in view of the growing audacity, as he
said, of the leading seigneurs in the Netherlands, who were holding suspicious private meetings. He sent Alva copies of Chantonnay's letters, urgently seeking his advice as to what should be
done to protect his territories, and what representations should
be made to Catherine, partly perhaps because he was preparing,
or about to prepare, the instructions for his new ambassador,
Don Francés de Alava.⁴ It was from the duke of Alva that Philip
received the inflexible advice to proceed in general with great

¹ B.N., Mss. fr. 20461, f. 61; Delaborde, *Coligny*, ii, 295 seq.
² Clearly the danger was not exaggerated since Throckmorton reported to
queen Elizabeth on 26 November that an archer of the king's guard had just
been apprehended 'who was minded to have killed the Admiral within the
Court'. *CSPF., 1563*, p. 600, 26 November 1563, Throckmorton to Elizabeth.
³ *Archivo documental Español, Francia*, vi, 27–9, 5 January 1564, *extraits des
registres du conseil privé*; 32, 8 and 10 January 1564, Chantonnay says the decision
was taken on 4 January. B.N., Mss. Italien, 1724, f. 189, 29 December 1563;
ff. 192–3, 12 January 1564; the Venetian, Suriano, refers to this quarrel as
'questo foco soffocato'.
⁴ Granvelle, *Papiers d'État*, vii, 268–74, 14 December 1563, Philip II to Alva;
Archivo documental Español, Francia, vi, 40–7, 12 January 1564, instructions for
Alava.

severity, and particularly against the nobility. Alva had already admitted to the utmost difficulty in controlling his anger upon receipt of despatches from William of Orange and counts Egmont and Horne.[1] This severity was to have the effect of exciting anger and fear and eliciting precisely that huguenot solidarity with the Netherlands that Philip was most anxious to prevent.

Philip was also alarmed by the renewed influence at court of the old constable, Montmorency.[2] Alva, whose crudely violent answer to Philip's letter apparently sought to frighten him into an aggressive fury, expressed the characteristic wish that the constable too had perished with the other *triumvirs*.[3] This could have been partly because Montmorency, together with his sons the marshal François, and Damville – and his Châtillon nephews with whom he was reconciled, there was once again, as previously in 1561, the possibility that they might have provided Catherine with a powerful nucleus of political and indeed also military support, in which individuals were rather united by loyalty, moderation and family ties, than divided by religion. There was a distinct risk, from the catholic and Spanish point of view, that this might have enabled her to prevail against the catholic extremists, in particular Lorraine. In the event, however, Lorraine returned to court at the end of January 1564 and Coligny withdrew[4] because, as the Venetian ambassador observed, when one faction entered court, the other departed.[5] Coligny never again returned other than very briefly, and this proved to be the

[1] Granvelle, *Papiers d'État*, vii, 231, 21 October 1563, Alva to Philip II from Huesca.

[2] Some months later Smith referred to Montmorency's influence at court. *CSPF.*, 1564–5, p. 227, 21 October 1564, Smith to Cecil.

[3] Granvelle, *Papiers d'État*, vii, 275–6, 22 December 1563. Alva said he thought any approach to Catherine a waste of time. Parts of Alava's instructions repeat almost verbatim the advice tendered in this letter, evidence of Alva's influence over Philip.

[4] *Archivo documental Español, Francia*, vi, 73, 23 January 1564, Chantonnay to Philip II. Coligny had gone to Châtillon four days before. Lorraine arrived on 29 January.

[5] B.N., Mss. Italien, 1724, ff. 208–9, 2 March 1564.

beginning both of Lorraine's re-ascendancy over the council, and of the triumph of the catholics.

From this moment on there was to be no real peace, but plentiful reports of Spanish and catholic 'practices', sinister rumours of secret assemblies of foot and horse, and of preparations on both sides for the renewal of civil war.[1] The Venetian ambassador recorded rumours that Philip meant to make war in France,[2] and Chantonnay reported – just when Lorraine arrived – that this was projected for 1564,[3] although Lansac, writing from Spain a little later, said that Philip wanted peace.[4] Furthermore, an agent Bernadino Ferrario, reported from Padua that, as he had already written in three letters, 'the League' continued to make preparations against England.[5] This again was not only papal, but also pure, specific triumvirate policy, as expressed in the 'treaty'. The key to this alarming clamour lies in a report from Christopher Mundt, queen Elizabeth's agent at Strasbourg, that all were anxious about what 'the Pope and plotters at Trent' intended to do; and not the least of these, though he did not say so, was the cardinal of Lorraine.[6] What Lorraine had done, according to Catherine (doubtless upon the information of the French ambassador, Lansac, one of her supporters), was to 'pratiquer' the Spanish prelates 'pour faire requérir que la reine d'Angleterre soit déclarée incapable de tenir le royaume, pour être hors de l'église'. The throne, it was therefore supposed, would devolve upon Mary Stuart, Lorraine's niece, and he suggested to

[1] Sainte-Croix, *Lettres*, 152, 10 January 1564; *CSPF.*, *1564-5*, p. 78, 12 March 1564, Mundt to Gresham; 120-1, 29 April 1564, Throckmorton to Elizabeth; 128, 9 May 1564, Throckmorton to Elizabeth; B.N., Mss. Italien, 1725, ff. 58-9, 4 April 1564; 16 June 1565, cardinal Armagnac to Catherine in the *Revue historique*, ii (1876), 525-6; 10 October 1564, Simon Renard to the duchess of Parma, in the *BSHPF*, xxxvi (1887), 643-6.

[2] B.N., Mss. Italien, 1725, ff. 53-4, 16 January 1564.

[3] *Archivo documental Español, Francia*, vi, 80, 27 January 1564, Chantonnay to Philip II.

[4] B.N., Mss. Italien, 1724, f. 209, 2 March 1564.

[5] *CSPF.*, *1564-5*, p. 13, 14 January 1564, two letters, Bernadino or Bernado Ferrario to Sir John Mason and Cecil.

[6] *CSPF.*, *1564-5*, p. 44, 8 February 1564, Mundt to Cecil.

Catherine that, in order to thwart any Habsburg marriage, she should propose her son Henri duc d'Orléans (better known as Anjou), heir presumptive (aged twelve) as Mary's suitor.[1]

The papacy, therefore, and Lorraine rather than Spain, was the source of all this ferment, in which Philip's name was nevertheless freely employed both by the ill-informed, and because his participation was vital. Smith actually put it to Chantonnay that Spain, Savoy and others were planning a conference at Nice (then in Savoy).[2] Chantonnay denied it, whether because he could hardly do otherwise, or because Philip was unamenable. He was in fact being urged to participate in a meeting somewhere – whether or not in Nice – that Catherine was also to be pressed to attend, and the pope had sent the bishop of Ventimiglia to persuade him thereto.[3] But he paid little attention, and referred rather vaguely to such a meeting as only a distant project.[4] When he finally joined the pope in a 'holy' league, it was not to combat heresy in Europe, but to contain the Turks in the eastern Mediterranean. The pope's inconveniently aggressive policy in northern Europe probably did more to inflame than to diminish his principal problem, the defence of the Netherlands. Alva warned Philip to be careful of appearing to refuse to support the pope and the French in redressing the present troubles – he referred, presumably to religion – but, he added significantly, if Philip did join them, they would place the whole world upon his shoulders, for which even *his* power could not suffice.[5] Granvelle, a little later, did not hedge his opinion with any qualifications, but roundly enumerated the difficulties and disadvantages, and emphasised the expense. Philip was pouring money into a great fleet, and Granvelle was trying to persuade him of the necessity of going to the Netherlands.[6]

[1] Cabié, *Ambassade en Espagne de St Sulpice*, 147–50, 24 August 1563, Catherine to St Sulpice.

[2] *CSPF.*, *1564–5*, p. 15, 15 January 1564, Smith to Cecil.

[3] Granvelle, *Papiers d'État*, vii, 269–70, 14 December 1563, Philip II to Alva; 332, 23 January 1564, Philip II to Granvelle.

[4] Granvelle, *Papiers d'État*, vii, 270, 14 December 1563, Philip II to Alva.

[5] Granvelle, *Papiers d'État*, vii, 284–5, 22 December 1563, Alva to Philip II.

[6] Granvelle, *Papiers d'État*, viii, 34–46, 8 June 1564, Granvelle to Philip II.

Nor did Catherine escape papal pressure in March 1564, when the court was in Lorraine, from a special legate, Rucellai, who urged her to join a holy league for the extirpation of heresy. She and Philip were also both importuned by French extremists to re-open hostilities in France to the same end and, what they seemed to regard as much the same thing, to avenge the duc de Guise.[1] Soon there were even rumours that the king would actually revoke the edict and, in the summer of 1564, the idea was spread about that 'the court' was bent upon two things, one of which was to subject the huguenots to the papists and the pope, and that Philip II and the house of Lorraine would serve this turn.[2] It is to be supposed that the house of Lorraine, if not Philip II, was already serving this turn, as both the edict of January 1562, and the peace of Amboise had been much of Catherine's making, and since she clearly could not relish the implied subjection either to Philip abroad, or to the Guises at home. Such a revocation was indeed what Blaise de Monluc[3] demanded of Catherine and Lorraine in August 1564.[4] But, back in February, he had sent Philip a remarkable memoir[5] in which he proposed a league of all catholic princes, to press the king to publish the decrees of Trent, and all who did not subscribe should be required to leave France within a month. Those who abjured were to be registered, but those who did neither were to be burnt without trial, men, women and children.[6] Such a measure would permit the *gouverneurs* to take up arms and seize protestant property, which is probably what he really wanted. Monluc was a man after Alva's

---

[1] Castelnau, *Mémoires*, 503–5. Doubtless the negotiation of the treaty of Troyes, 11 April 1564, which settled the matter of Le Havre with England, tended to increase the catholic clamour.

[2] *CSPF., 1564–5*, p. 198, 3 September 1564, Smith to Cecil.

[3] Monluc was a gentleman of Gascony, and one of the most influential catholics in Guyenne, rightly suspected of treasonable practices with Spain. P. Courteault, *Blaise de Monluc, historien*, 483–9.

[4] De Ruble, *Monluc, Commentaires*, iv, 357, 11 August 1564, Monluc to Catherine; 359 [August 1564], extract from a letter to Lorraine; 366–7 [27 October 1564], Monluc to Juan Bardaxi; the French render this as Bardachin.

[5] De Ruble, *Monluc, Commentaires*, iv, 317 seq., 8 February 1564.

[6] De Ruble, *Monluc, Commentaires*, iv, 321.

own heart, with whom he collaborated in the pursuit of violent 'remedies' at the time of the interview between the courts of France and Spain at Bayonne in June 1565.

Not only did the protestants fear the revocation of the edict, but the promulgation of another commanding their extermination, according to the report of a provincial synod held at La Ferté-sous-Jouarre from 27 April–1 May 1564, at which representations were received from all over France, and also a communication from no less a person than Théodore de Bèze, Calvin's successor. De Bèze advised the churches to raise money and maintain close contact with those of Flanders – which they apparently did.[1] Catherine, who knew of these proceedings, was probably alarmed and angry. But, in view of her conduct, it is difficult to believe that she seriously intended to abrogate the edict, which she journeyed laboriously round France endeavouring to implement. If the edict of Roussillon made slight modifications, the edict of Amboise itself was formally confirmed at Marseilles on 9 November 1564.[2] Yet Granvelle, for one, received some impression that she had come to realise that only through the restoration of catholicism could the king's authority be restored. On the other hand, he was also prepared to believe that she was only temporising.[3] The state of fear and confusion was such that any impression might be registered and suspicion harboured. Monluc later recalled in a memoir to Philip II[4] that in 1564, before the great court itinerary of 1564–6, the protestants spread a rumour that Catherine and Charles were becoming protestant, but that during the journey she showed how profoundly catholic they were. If this tallies with Granvelle's impression, it is a very different tale from

---

[1] Granvelle, *Papiers d'État*, vii, 528–31; *CSPF., 1564–5*, pp. 119–20.

[2] Declaration of 24 June 1564; Edict of Roussillon, August 1564, Fontanon, *Édits et ordonnances*, iv, 279–81; *CSPF., 1564–5*, p. 241, Smith sent a copy to England; Castelnau, *Mémoires*, 503; Pasquier, *Lettres historiques*, 147–8, 167–71. The court, a vast army covering several miles, set out upon an immense itinerary in April 1564, returning to Saint-Maur-des-Fossés in April 1566.

[3] Granvelle, *Papiers d'État*, viii, 71, 20 June 1564, Granvelle to the duchess of Parma.

[4] De Ruble, *Monluc, Commentaires*, v, 23–5 [June 1565], *Mémoire au Roy d'Espagne*.

a purported fear that she was about to abrogate the edict. Partisans of both confessions freely interpreted everything 'selon leurs passions', as contemporaries said, and France was large enough to contain different rumours in different areas. What Catherine actually *did* was to strive to enforce the edict, to take security precautions[1] and to emphasise by strict, pious and public observances the catholicity of the crown. This was essential if she were to achieve her requested frontier meeting with Philip II during the great itinerary.

Catherine had always desired such a meeting, if not always for the same reasons, and Philip had always been unfavourable, without ever precisely refusing. Catherine had last proposed an interview at Perpignan in September 1562, which the civil war prevented. In November 1563 she was said to be 'tormenting' Philip to agree. Catherine now mingled the request with the hint that perhaps she might subsequently agree to the papal conference. This might be calculated to conciliate French catholic opinion, if it were known, but was she aware that it would not influence Philip?[2] In December 1563, he contented himself with seeking Alva's advice. Alva irreverently dismissed the pope, who could only depose and excommunicate. He similarly despised and distrusted Catherine, 'dont nous connaissons suffisamment les intentions en ce qui concerne les remèdes à employer dans la crise actuelle'. If the huguenots thought her about to abrogate the edict

---

[1] There were many reports of the imminence of new uprisings. See, for example, 10 October 1564, Simon Renard to the duchess of Parma, in *BSHPF.*, xxxvi (1887), 643–6, from Orleans where the king was building a fortress. Renard reported trouble in Touraine, Poitou, Maine and Vendômois, and considerable protestant preparations and, indeed, readiness. 16 June 1565, 28 June 1566 (sic) cardinal Armagnac to Catherine & Charles IX in *Revue historique*, ii (1876), 525–6, 529–30. He reported trouble in Languedoc and Provence.

[2] Catherine had first proposed a meeting with Philip as early as August 1559. *Archivo documental Español, Francia*, i, 51, 22 August 1559, Chantonnay to Philip II; vol. ii, 254 seq., 12 June 1561, Philip II to Chantonnay; vol. iii, 369, 23 February 1562, Chantonnay to Philip II; 388, 28 February 1562, Chantonnay to Philip II; Granvelle, *Papiers d'État*, vii, 256–7, 15 November 1563, Pérez to Granvelle; 269–70, 14 December 1563, Philip II to Alva; 332, 23 January 1564, Philip II to Granvelle; 385, 5 March 1564, Granvelle to the emperor.

of pacification, Alva emphatically did not. But, if Catherine were first to explain her purpose, he did not entirely oppose a private meeting (he meant with her daughter Elizabeth), which might possibly be used to persuade Catherine to change her councillors.[1] He was, however, opposed to a meeting with Philip on account of the inevitably resounding repercussions of such an imposing and dramatic event. This opinion was faithfully transcribed into Alava's instructions. In January 1564, Philip consented in principle to a meeting of the two queens, but he agreed with Alva, and did not want to risk any sensational repercussions, or the precipitation of an invasion of the Netherlands by Germans and protestants who could be excused, if he were to go himself, for suspecting a conspiracy to enforce the decrees of Trent. Clearly he did not appreciate that the presence of the dread and hated Alva would be quite as disturbing as his own.[2]

The potential danger to the Netherlands was neither imaginary nor exaggerated. Even before the first civil war, Chantonnay had reported Coligny to have considerable 'intelligence' in the Netherlands.[3] After the peace of Amboise, d'Assonleville – a Flemish councillor – writing from England to the duchess of Parma on 15 May 1563, claimed to possess details of a definite plan of Coligny's to enter the Netherlands from Champagne, and cause certain towns to revolt. This was allegedly thwarted by the dispute with England over Calais, and the Havre campaign that summer.[4] Certainly Granvelle kept a nervous eye on the movements of returning mercenary forces after the first civil war.[5] It seems more likely, however, that it was the Guise vendetta,

---

[1] This advice was given when the Châtillons were at court. Granvelle, *Papiers d'État*, vii, 284-6, 22 December 1563, Alva to Philip II.

[2] *Archivo documental Español, Francia*, vi, 63-9, 20 January 1564, Philip II to Alava; Granvelle, *Papiers d'État*, vii, 385-6, 5 March 1564, Granvelle to the emperor.

[3] *Archivo documental Español, Francia*, iii, 392, 28 February 1562, Chantonnay to Philip II.

[4] *CSPSp.*, *1558-67*, pp. 326-8, 15 May 1563, d'Assonleville to the duchess of Parma.

[5] Granvelle, *Papiers d'État*, vii, passim.

rather than the war with England (when Coligny was at home) which then frustrated any projects he might have had. If Coligny really entertained this plan, it could have been a powerful additional reason for the vendetta which restricted his liberty.[1] After the synod of La Ferté-sous-Jouarre in April 1564, there were many reports of movements and gatherings and preparations in Picardy and the north, and Granvelle reported that the huguenots were continually urging the protestants in the Netherlands to revolt.[2] Later in the year there were more specific reports of incessant 'practices' and large French assemblies on the frontier, the reinforcement of garrisons in Condé's *gouvernement* of Picardy, and of definite invasion plans. It was said that the comte de Montgommery (who had connections in England) and Jean d'Estrées would be the 'chefs des Huguenots de Flandres', a significant expression, and that 40,000 men were enrolled.[3] The following month the rumours of invasion were denied, and said to be false.[4] These pernicious reports were all manifestations of that general, perilous, gestating fear which, as cardinal Châtillon later declared, brought forth the second civil war.

If these were all reasons why Philip, for his part, feared the effects of a meeting with Catherine, they were also reasons why she desired one with him. Apart from her natural longing to see her daughter, Elizabeth, she had always sought to reap the advantages of the *entente* of Cateau-Cambrésis – 'confirmer et perpétuer cette fraternelle concorde[5]' – in order to preserve the

[1] In this case it is interesting to compare the similar pattern of events in 1571-2 when the Guises assembled in arms to exclude Coligny from court, and from the Netherlands, with those of 1563-4.

[2] Granvelle, *Papiers d'État*, viii, 18, 3 June 1564, Granvelle to the emperor; 35-46, 8 June 1564, Granvelle to Philip II; 395-402, 12 October 1564, Granvelle to Philip II.

[3] Granvelle, *Papiers d'État*, viii, 526, 6 December 1564, president Viglius to Granvelle, (Brussels); 537, 10 December 1564, Viglius to Granvelle; 549-50, 12 December 1564, Morillon to Granvelle.

[4] Granvelle, *Papiers d'État*, viii, 587, 1 January 1565, l'Écuyer Bordey to Granvelle.

[5] Cabié, *Ambassade en Espagne de St Sulpice*, 231-5, c. February 1564, *mémoire de Catherine à St Sulpice*.

crown from the enmity of Spain and subservience to the French extremists. Now, amidst the menacing clamour of 1564, she was necessarily more anxious than ever to reclaim for the crown she strove to defend, any residual Spanish goodwill which, since 1561, had been bestowed upon the catholics who threatened to destroy the kingdom in order to impose their will. This desire to maintain the *entente* in the interests of the crown, and Catherine's anxiety to neutralise Guise activity in Spain was already explicit in the principles formulated for the guidance of St Sulpice, who went as ambassador to Spain early in April 1562, just after the Triumvirate had seized the king and Catherine at Fontainebleau – evidence of her independence of spirit and intrinsic dissociation from them.[1] St Sulpice consequently laboured to 'interrompre les praticques et intelligences qu'aulcuns procuroient en Espaigne, et desjà [in 1562] les y traitoient assez ouvertement'. He also sought to work with Ruy Gómez, prince of Eboli, in order to resist the influence of Alva 'qui estoit par trop passionné en nos troubles' – as Catherine's experience at Bayonne was unhappily about to confirm.[2] When the interview was accorded,[3] Alva informed St Sulpice with overbearing impertinence that it was folly to imagine that France could 'pouvoir parvenir', and remedy the 'maux et périls qui nous environnaient de tous côtés', without Spain. His calculated ambiguities alluded to the military extermination of protestantism with Spanish participation about which, at other times, he was perfectly explicit. For example, he had written to St Sulpice in October 1562 that the 'meilleur remède à la situation était de recourir uniquement aux armes et à la force'. St Sulpice, who was not easily perplexed, ignored the

---

[1] Cabié, *Ambassade en Espagne de St Sulpice*, 17, 10 & 21 May 1562, St Sulpice to Catherine. He reached Madrid on 21 May and had audience on 27 May; Ibid., 18–19.

[2] Cabié, *Ambassade en Espagne de St Sulpice*, 2–7; 406–8, 1562, *informations pour servir à la conduite de St Sulpice*.

[3] Philip II publicly announced the forthcoming interview on 30 January 1565. Cabié, *Ambassade en Espagne de St Sulpice*, 350, 16 February 1564/5, St Sulpice to Catherine.

implications and seized the opportunity to entertain Alva to a vigorous condemnation of the 'auteurs et première cause de nos troubles et les moyens quils cherchaient pour les entretenir et parvenir à leurs *dessaings*, lesquels avaient été connus', and he hoped that they [the authors and the cause] would be 'mis en évidence, à la grande honte et confusion de ceux qui ont été les ministres.' Not content with this, St Sulpice further deprecated the anonymous miscreants' treatment of the queen when she had sought to resolve public affairs through councils and *colloques*, and the avarice, ambition and presumption of those who 'ont mieux aimé renverser tout et troubler ciel et terre pour disposer toutes choses à leur plaisir', which, they were both tacitly aware, included Alva himself.[1]

The despatches of St Sulpice are of particular interest and value because he represented Catherine, whose policy is nowhere more clearly expounded. This was a foretaste of what Alva might expect to hear from Catherine who, not surprisingly, preferred to see Philip himself even, she had written in 1563 after being very ill, for a single hour; then she could die content.[2] If she could only reach some sufficient understanding with *him*, then there would be a limit to how much harm could be inflicted in France without his co-operation. Besides, she had in mind the matter of Charles' marriage, which was important, to Philip as well as herself. Nevertheless, it was a courageous demand, both on account of the genuine dangers of a protestant reaction, which perhaps affected France even more than Spain, and because it exposed her to the most powerful catholic pressure she had yet had to face.

Philip's subsequent version – for consumption in Rome – of the purpose of the interview (15 June–2 July 1565) was to discuss remedies for the problem of religion in France, and the execution of the decrees of Trent. Monluc expressed it more bluntly

[1] Cabié, *Ambassade en Espagne de St Sulpice*, 7–9, memorandum.
[2] Cabié, *Ambassade en Espagne de St Sulpice*, 169–70, 18 October 1563, Catherine to the queen of Spain; 338–9, 22 January 1565, Catherine to St Sulpice.

as the extinction of heresy.[1] What St Sulpice proposed to Philip II was not quite the same: 'chercher les remèdes les plus convenables pour rétablir l'accord dans les affaires de la religion.' In this, he went on to say, 'l'expérience ayant prouvé que la voie des armes a apporté en cela plus de dangers que de profit, ce qu'il importe le plus pour la France, c'est que chaque parti vive en paix sous l'autorité de la reine mère en attendant que le roi son fils arrive à sa majorité . . .'[2] But the primary concern of Spain was not 'ce qu'il importe le plus pour la France', and Alva who, in the event, went in place of Philip, held precise instructions.[3] The Spanish preference was, as it had always been, for the use of force in the implementation of the most severe measures to exterminate protestantism from France.

St Sulpice was careful to warn Catherine that, to judge from what Alva said, 'ils aient délibéré de vous persuader de faire quelque mauvais règlement de vos sujects ou quelque changement en vos édits pour exciter . . . les troubles qui vous coûtent tant d'apaiser ou pour la crainte qu'ils ont d'être bientôt précipités en semblable danger'.[4]

As Alva had fully expected, however, Catherine and the king were implacably opposed to extreme measures.[5] Alva even dispassionately admired the skill with which Catherine anticipated, parried or averted his onslaughts.[6] In default of royal acquiescence and in spite of the crown, he therefore used the opportunity to

[1] 24 August 1565, Philip II to cardinal Pacheco, in Combes, *L'Entrevue de Bayonne*, 39–49; de Ruble, *Monluc, Commentaires*, iv, 361–4 and 365–71, two letters [27 October 1564], Monluc to Bardaxi.

[2] St Sulpice was not speaking juridically; he meant until Charles was old enough to rule. Cabié, *Ambassade en Espagne de St Sulpice*, 366–7, c. 3 April 1564/5, *discours de St Sulpice à Philippe II*.

[3] La Ferrière, 'L'Entrevue de Bayonne', *Revue des questions historiques*, xxxiv (1883), 483, note 2.

[4] Cabié, *Ambassade en Espagne de St Sulpice*, 386–7, 2 and 6 June 1565, *avis à Catherine à son arrivée à Bayonne*.

[5] Granvelle, *Papiers d'État*, vii, 284, seq., 22 December 1563, Alva to Philip II.

[6] Cabié, *Ambassade en Espagne de St Sulpice*, 398–9, 11 August 1565, *mémoire de St Sulpice à la cour de France*.

strengthen his relations with leading French catholics, by whom Catherine was then apparently surrounded, and prepared the ground to act in concert with them. This is precisely what Philip had first threatened, and then done in 1561–2. It is also, more or less, what was to happen again in 1568 and 1570–2, only the circumstances were different when Alva was preoccupied with the revolt in the Netherlands.

Those catholics specifically mentioned by Alva were the duc de Montpensier, the cardinal of Bourbon – whose danger and usefulness was that he relayed everything to Catherine – d'Escars, a former servant of Navarre,[1] d'Avilla and the abbé de Saint-Pierre, the marshal Bourdillon and several others, unnamed.[2] According to Alva, it was they, or some of them, who suggested as one alternative measure, the arrest and imprisonment or execution of five or six of the protestant leaders.[3] Alva does not specify who voiced this proposition, but La Ferrière states that Montpensier's confessor – unnamed – proposed the execution of Condé, Coligny, d'Andelot, La Rochefoucauld (Condé's brother-in-law) and Antoine de Gramont.[4] Just one month later Lorraine, who did not grace the great itinerary, revealed to Granvelle an association of the Guises, Montpensier and others to support catholicism, and enquired whether Philip would participate.[5] This, therefore, points to Lorraine and confirms 'elimination', first apparent in 1560, as the continuing Guise, catholic and Spanish policy.

Catherine's reaction to Alva's insistence upon discussing religion, was to turn the negotiations in two ways. She proceeded, with considerable tenacity, to talk of marriage – always part of

---

[1] D'Escars was alleged to have betrayed Navarre to Spain which, to judge from Philip's approval of him, was evidently true. *Archivo documental Español, Francia*, vi, 46, 12 January 1564, further instructions for Alava.

[2] Granvelle, *Papiers d'État*, ix, 281–93, 15 June 1565, Alva to Philip II; 294–301, 21 June 1565, Alva to Philip II.

[3] Granvelle, *Papiers d'État*, ix, 298, 21 June 1565, Alva to Philip II.

[4] This, of course, had always been Alva's attitude to the Netherlands nobility, and was to be his disastrous policy once he was in command there. Granvelle, *Papiers d'État*, vii, 229 seq., 21 October 1563, Alva to Philip II.

[5] Granvelle, *Papiers d'État*, ix, 399–403, 15 July 1565, Granvelle to Philip II.

her intentions – and, in return for suitable agreements, she proposed an open league with Philip and the emperor (whose daughter she sought for Charles) against the Turks, who were then engaged in the great siege of Malta.¹ This was not unworthy of Spanish attention, since the problem of the Turks was as pressing as that of the Netherlands, and Catherine defiantly received a Turkish ambassador (a Polish nobleman) at Bayonne. Indeed, according to Granvelle, it was openly alleged in the Empire that Catherine was actually responsible for the great siege, which doubtless amused her. It is rather unlikely that Catherine really entertained the league proposition seriously, but it was a skilful move in her battle with Alva. Such a league might have helped to neutralise Spanish and catholic activity in France and who, then, could deny that Catherine took her Christian duties seriously?²

While Alva reported that Catherine firmly resisted his severe propositions for the remedy of religion, there were three other reports that she had agreed to 'something'. One of these was a completely vague letter from Alva to Francesco de Eraso, of 4 July 1565.³ Secondly Granvelle expressed satisfaction that Catherine had been brought to 'prendre . . . les moyens convenables pour remedier aux maux de la religion en France', an innocuous formula in which she had doubtless taken refuge many times. Indeed he went on to say that she had promised to 'faire merveilles,' while refusing any measures likely to lead to a renewal of hostilities. *He therefore did not think she would do anything.* Finally, Philip himself wrote – for Roman edification – that

---

¹ Gachard, *Correspondance de Philippe II*, i, 368, 25 September 1565, Philip II to Granvelle. The emperor, however, had just concluded a six years' truce with the Turks. *CSPF., 1564–5*, p. 356, 5 May–3 June 1565, Smith to Leicester and Cecil.

² Granvelle, *Papiers d'État*, ix, 307, 21 June 1565, Alva to Philip II; 516–17, [September 1565], memorial to Philip II from Catherine; 543–6, 25 September 1565, Philip II to Chantonnay; 549–52, 25 September 1565, Philip II to Alava; 660 seq., 10 November 1565, Polweiller to Granvelle; Gachard, *Correspondance de Philippe II*, i, 368, 25 September 1565, Philip II to Granvelle.

³ Combes, *L'Entrevue de Bayonne*, 15–16, 37–8; Combes appears to have misinterpreted Alava.

Catherine was truly resolved to remedy the matter of religion,[1] precisely what she had always been doing, in her own estimation. But Philip also, if more cautiously, expressed his doubts as to her real intentions; nor did he intimate what the intended 'remedy' was.

Catherine's 'something' could, possibly, have been the expulsion of protestant pastors – one of Alva's explicit proposals which Alava (sic) seemed to be shortly expecting,[2] although he too doubted whether this would be effective. Monluc maintained that Catherine truly intended to issue a pro-catholic edict (similar to the later edict of Saint-Maur, September 1568) if she were sufficiently assured of Spanish help and ultimate success. Perhaps one should allow for the possibility that this was true, though Catherine's conduct is better evidence than what she said to her tormentors in a delicate situation. Monluc's paranoiac nature was singularly open to self-deception, and Catherine could easily have wished to pacify him. Furthermore, she had experience of Spanish help, which was easily enough invoked, but frightened her far more than any opponents. Monluc's memoir does not tally with Alva's more credible reports, nor with Catherine's own declaration before a full meeting of the council on 23 May 1565, immediately before Bayonne, that she was minded to entertain the edict 'to the extremity,' and that whosoever should attempt anything against it, would be reputed traitors.[3] No one in fact knew for certain what Catherine would do; but no one in any position to judge, believed that she would do anything novel. The French secretary of state, Claude de Laubespine, reported categorically that nothing had been concluded.[4] All the available

---

[1] 24 August 1565, Philip II to cardinal Pacheco, printed in Combes, *L'Entrevue de Bayonne*, 17–19, 'resolvio muy de veras a poner remedio a estas cosas de la religion'.

[2] Granvelle, *Papiers d'État*, ix, 451, 8 August 1565, Alava to Chantonnay.

[3] De Ruble, *Monluc, Commentaires*, v, 23–34, June 1565, *Mémoire au Roy d'Espagne*; CSPF., *1564–5*, p. 356, 5 May–3 June 1565, Smith to Leicester and Cecil.

[4] B.N., Mss. fr. 3249, f. 73, 1 July 1565, de Laubespine to marshal Montmorency.

evidence appears to confirm that neither Catherine, Spain nor the extreme French catholics had changed their policy in any way, which is precisely what one would expect. If the meeting achieved nothing more, Catherine had at least seen her daughter – for the last time – and had not been outmanoeuvred by Alva.

The interview at Bayonne was neither the origin of the general notion of a catholic conspiracy – which, it has been seen, dated from before the first civil war – nor of the particular fear of an 'elimination' policy, or assault upon the protestant leaders which, in a general sense, had been extreme catholic policy since 1560, and embraced by the Triumvirate. But the meeting undoubtedly heightened protestant fears of both these things. In April 1565 Coligny is said to have consulted with Jeanne d'Albret, the Queen of Navarre, at Vendôme, 'upon all doubts which may occur against them of the religion by the interview' and, after the meeting, Smith reported in July that they (he did not say precisely who) thought there had been 'some complot betwixt the Pope, the King of Spain, and the Scottish Queen, by their ambassadors, and some say also the Papists of England'.[1] These fears, if mildly hysterical, were also highly explosive because they ensured that the moment revolt broke out in the Netherlands – which by the summer of 1565 was already imminent – those who were threatened, in whatever respect or capacity, by the power of Spain, the reinvigorated papacy and the decrees of Trent, would have this strong supra-national link in common, and would be likely, if they could, to unite in self protection against them.

Any close connections, whether political or religious, between French protestants and dissident elements in the Netherlands, more particularly if combined with any degree of English or German support, was precisely what Philip had primarily feared ever since the almost simultaneous detachment of England from Spain and from Rome, which had rendered it essential for him to keep England and France apart. Indeed, it was largely for fear of the Netherlands that Philip had always been so concerned to 'remedy'

---

[1] *CSPF., 1564–5*, p. 333, 11 April 1565, occurrences in France; 403, – July 1565, Smith to Leicester and Cecil.

the affairs of France. War in the Netherlands for the possession of Flanders, Artois and frontier towns had been traditional French policy, and diversionary war in the Netherlands, which was so soon to develop into a policy of 'transference', had never lacked supporters since the beginning of the troubles; Estienne Pasquier is a notable example. Before the first civil war, Philip had feared that Navarre might unleash war, whether factional or national, in the Netherlands, where he had property to protect. In 1563, when Navarre was dead, this fear became more plausibly focused on Coligny. Only a matter of days after the conclusion of the conference at Bayonne, Granvelle wrote to warn Philip of the progress of Calvinism in the Netherlands, and that Montigny, Coligny's cousin, was corresponding closely with the Châtillons, virtually every week, and in detail. Montigny was said to be thoroughly protestant at heart though, for the moment, he dissimulated.[1] There can be little doubt that such intercourse, largely based on cousinage and the relations between the churches, existed on a much large scale than has yet been disclosed. It was therefore inevitable that Philip should have continued to regard Coligny as a dangerous enemy,[2] not only as perhaps the most distinguished Calvinist in Europe, but as a leader closely connected with an incipient uprising of 'rebels and heretics' in his own dominions.

[1] Granvelle, *Papiers d'État*, ix, 404, 18 July 1565, Granvelle to Philip II. Florent de Montmorency, baron of Montigny, knight of the Fleece and stadtholder of Tournai. He was executed in Spain in 1570.

[2] Coligny had been in command of the French forces after the capture of the constable at Saint-Quentin in 1557, the only time that Philip himself had taken the field. Coligny also opposed the interests of Spain in a variety of colonial enterprises.

III

France and the Netherlands
1566-1568

It was the appointment of the duke of Alva as military governor of the Netherlands, where he arrived in Brussels on 22 August 1567, following the widespread iconoclastic disorders of the summer of 1566, that precipitated the long-expected crisis in France. With this cruel, arch-ally of the extreme French catholics persecuting and punishing with bloody severity their peers, relatives and co-religionists, the huguenots could enjoy no kind of security. Alva's instructions proclaimed that 'doulceur' having failed, he was to assemble an army on the frontier pending Philip's own arrival; they were both to have gone together.[1]

Inevitably, therefore, there arose the fundamental issue between France and Spain, whether or not France, in either a national or a factional sense, would go to war in the Netherlands, and it is the Netherlands which links both the domestic and foreign aspects of the second and third civil wars, and the story of Coligny and the massacre. Strong and persistent rumours of catholic plots, and well-founded fears of continued Spanish support behind the extreme French catholics, had inevitably emphasised the tendencies of their protestant opponents to seek support and co-operation in the Netherlands, whether of the nobility, who were threatened in their persons, property and status, or of specifically Calvinist elements. Conversely, they were equally inclined to provide

[1] Navarrete, *Colección de documentos*, iv, 388–96, 31 January 1567, instructions (French) for Alva. The rest of his instructions, with puzzling contradiction, enjoin the use of 'doulceur', 'benignité' and clemency. *CSPF., 1566–8*, p. 13, 31 January 1566 [/67]. This document, 1567 new style, is calendared in the wrong place. *CSPSp., 1558–67*, pp. 658–61, 21 July 1567, de Silva to Philip II; 680–1, 15 October 1567, Philip II to de Silva.

reciprocal assistance. Notwithstanding a proclamation to the contrary, a number of captains 'from all parts' immediately went in disguise into the Netherlands in August 1566, while huguenot leaders anxiously met together in Paris to consider what they should do.[1] Essential precautions and preparations continued all the summer and following spring. With the departure in April 1567 of William of Orange for his German estates at Dillenburg – where others followed him – to plan his first invasion of the Netherlands, some sort of hostilities became almost inevitable.[2] As early as February William himself had reported formidable Spanish preparations for war. The following month Condé is said to have offered the king – who was scarcely less alarmed than the huguenots by the impending passage of Alva along the eastern frontiers – a massive force of 30,000 foot and 8,000 horse to make war on Spain.[3]

With Catherine's known aversion from war, and Lorraine's increasing control of the council, this offer, if genuine, had no hope of acceptance. Yet it seemed that the only alternative to war in the Netherlands was civil war in France – almost precisely the situation which was to be reproduced in 1572 – since the huguenots would not quietly lie down and wait for the onslaught they had every reason to fear.

The second and third civil wars, (September 1567 to March 1568, and September 1568 to August 1570) must be considered in

[1] *CSPF., 1566–8*, p. 103, 10 July 1566, John Keyle to Cecil (Antwerp); 116, 13 August 1566, Mundt to Cecil (Strasbourg); 119–20, 17 August 1566, Hugh Fitzwilliam to Cecil. Fitzwilliam deputised as English ambassador following the death of Sir Thomas Hoby.

[2] G. van Prinsterer, *Archives ou correspondance*, série i, vol. iii, 26, 2 February 1567, Orange to his brother, count Jean. William endeavoured to reassure Philip that he had gone to attend to domestic affairs which, no doubt, he did. Ibid., 64–5, –April 1567, William of Orange to Philip II; *CSPF., 1566–8*, pp. 209–10, 18 April 1567, intelligence from France; 216, 27 April 1567, advices from Antwerp; 216, 27 April 1567, John Morrall to Gresham; B.N., Mss. fr. 6866, f. 7, 24 January 1567, William of Orange, having failed to answer certain summonses, was already declared guilty of treason.

[3] These figures seem improbably high. Archives d'État de Genève, P.H. 1831, 20 May 1567, La Fromentée to Claude Le Maistre; B.N., Mss. Italien, 1726, f. 126, 28 June 1567.

terms of the devastating dual impact of Alva in the Netherlands and Lorraine in France; a fierce and formidable combination by any standard, which aroused the nobility of both countries and alarmed all protestant Europe. The partial merging of French and Netherland affairs subtly shifted the emphasis of the Spanish and catholic pressure from one extreme 'remedy' to another, namely from a policy of war which, *de facto* more or less existed from 1567, to that of 'elimination', which could be pursued in either war or 'peace'.

Lorraine's growing control of the council led to another new factor of vital importance in the story of the civil wars and the massacre, namely his influence over the king's brother and heir, Henri, duc d'Anjou. This, together with the first flickering signs of independence on the part of Charles IX, and the catholics' exaggeration of Anjou's youthful importance and distinction, bred such jealousy and hatred between them that Catherine feared for Anjou's life. This was also the beginning of a new and catastrophic type of opposition to the crown – later disgracefully developed by Alençon[1] – which, already weak for dynastic reasons – the first fundamental condition giving rise to the civil wars – became still weaker for family ones. From this time should also be dated the beginning, in the wars, of the role of Paris, whose central importance is obvious in relation to the massacre.

The resurgence of Lorraine in France had been quite sufficiently alarming, even without the later arrival of Alva in the Netherlands. An epidemic of rumours, fears, reports, 'practices' and preparations followed his return from Trent in January 1564, and there is evidence that he wasted no time in exerting himself in the council, newly vacated by the Châtillons.[2] Catherine was under no illusions about what to expect. Already the previous summer, while Lorraine was busy at Trent, she had written to her daughter Elizabeth – because she valued her intercession with Philip – of

---

[1] This was ultimately carried to its extreme limits in the seventeenth century by Gaston d'Orléans, brother and, until 1638, heir to Louis XIII.

[2] Smith commented upon their total absence, and that of Condé during all the negotiations of the treaty of Troyes with England. *CSPF.*, *1564–5*, pp. 110–11, 14 April 1564, Smith to Cecil.

Lorraine's 'envie, par heun moyen ou par heun aultre, revenir à manyer les afayres de ce royaume'.[1] His rank, experience and ability lent him every advantage in this and his leadership of the catholics who continued, through him, to pursue their pre-war, triumvirate policy. As archbishop of Rheims, Lorraine also regarded himself as 'légat né', and therefore the principal executor of papal policy. This was evidently apparent and recognised since, the following year, the council of Berne referred approvingly to his efforts in favour of 'l'extreme soulagement de la papaulté en France'.[2] The Guises were importuning Catherine upon the matter of catholic war in France and the Coligny vendetta and, during the summer of 1564, Lorraine made a further determined but unsuccessful attempt to detach Condé from the protestant party,[3] which would have deprived them of the authority of a princely leader.[4] The death of Condé's wife in April 1564 opened up possibilities. One, apparently serious, project was to marry him to Mary queen of Scots. The matter was 'hot', Smith observed in November, and there was 'great stir who shall bear the belle away'.[5] This disrespectful allusion reflected Smith's low opinion

    [1] Cabié, *Ambassade en Espagne de St Sulpice*, 150, 24 August 1563, Catherine to the queen of Spain.

    [2] Archives d'État de Genève, P.H. 1751, 17 March 1564/5, conseil de Berne à ce de Genève.

    [3] Granvelle, *Papiers d'État*, viii, 126–7, 6 July 1564, occurrents in France.

    [4] This had already been attempted in 1562 and again after the peace of Amboise in 1563.

    [5] *CSPF.*, *1564–5*, p. 239, 7 November 1564, Randolph to Leicester (Edinburgh); 243, 13 November 1564, Smith to Cecil (Marseilles); 246, 20 November 1564, Smith to Cecil (Arles). Granvelle thought the Scottish marriage a fable, since it would be of no advantage to Mary. He should, however, have understood that it would be of great advantage to Lorraine, who was together with Condé at Soissons. But he did think that marriage to madame de Guise (widow of François duc de Guise) was an advantageous possibility, and one favoured by Catherine. Granvelle, *Papiers d'État*, viii, 490, 13–15 November 1564, *nouvelles de France*; 504–8, 23 November 1564, Granvelle to Polweiller; 510, 25 November 1564, Granvelle to Mary queen of Scots. In 1565 Condé married a daughter of the duc de Longueville (considered uncertain in religion although his wife was a Guise), queen Mary married Lord Darnley, and madame de Guise the duc de Nemours, who had long been deeply in love with her.

of the Scottish queen, which shortly declined still further. These several activities of Lorraine were clearly described by the catholic Simon Renard in a letter to the duchess of Parma when he passed through France on his way from the Empire to Spain in the early autumn:

'De jour à aultre s'accroist l'inimitié et partialité, par les practiques que meynent ceulx de la maison de Guyse pour venger la mort du feu sgr. de Guyse, pour réinpétrer le crédit qu'ilz ont eu par le passé, sequestrer leurs partigeans, non seullement de la maniance des affaires . . . ains procurer leur ruyne par vengeance publique et criminelle, ce que l'on discouvre de temps à aultre par les propres serviteurs desdites de Guyse qui revèlent à ceulx de la maison de Chastillon les secretz de leur maistre; s'estans trouvé mémoires de ceste substance . . .'[1]

Although Lorraine did not follow the court on its great itinerary, there is no doubt that he made progress of another kind, while Catherine was suitably surrounded by a catholic council. During the journey, Smith advised Cecil from Marseilles in November that all the posts were channelled via Lorraine without whom nothing was done, and Granvelle – with whom Lorraine was forbidden to communicate – commented at the same time upon his activity in affairs of state and his efforts to sustain his credit.[2] Indeed, were it otherwise, he would hardly have been so hounded and hated that he received certain special permission to carry arms. Having entered Paris, thus in arms, the result was such a violent clash with the *gouverneur* marshal Montmorency, in January 1565, that Coligny hurried to his support, and civil war was narrowly averted.[3] Catherine had been warned well

[1] *BSHPF.*, xxxvi (1887), 640, 6 October 1564, Simon Renard to the duchess of Parma. Renard had been summoned by Philip II. There is no reason to doubt his evidence and Châtillon certainly wrote as though he possessed such information.
[2] Granvelle, *Papiers d'État*, viii, 505–6, 23 November 1564, Granvelle to Polweiller; *CSPF.*, *1564–5*, p. 243, 13 November 1564, Smith to Cecil.
[3] B.N., Mss. fr. 3194, f. 86, 30 October 1565, Charles to marshal Montmorency; B.N., Mss. Italien, 1724, f. 247, 30 January 1565; f. 255 verso, 20

before the start of the great itinerary, which was delayed by the
conclusion in April 1564 of the treaty of Troyes with England,
that Chantonnay and his brother Granvelle would seek to re-
ignite the civil wars as soon as the court had departed for the
south.¹ Whether or not they actually did so, their confederate
Lorraine was highly provocative. This may have been partly why,
a few months later, Charles did not think Lorraine could travel
safely across France to the court at Châteaubriant (in Brittany);²
not that this was really anything new. As early as February 1564
Antonio Sarrón, Chantonnay's secretary, had observed when the
court was travelling about Lorraine that the cardinal should be
careful because 'si l'on peult l'on le fera morir'.³

Lorraine was also the centre and occasion of further trouble
when he rejoined the court and council on 2 or 3 January 1566,
at Moulins – where Charles was ill for several months. Intending
to terminate the vendetta between the Guises and Coligny –
which, since the incident in Paris, had been extended to Montmorency – on 29 January Charles declared Coligny innocent of
the murder of the duke.⁴ But, if Charles thought he could dismiss
the matter with a simple *arrêt* in council, he misjudged Lorraine,
who had already contumaciously declared that he would honour

February 1565; vol. 1725, f. 67 cipher; *Archivo documental Español, Francia*, vi,
52-5, 14 January 1564/5. This document is printed in error under 1564, the old
style date; B.N., Mss. fr. 3188, ff. 6-7 verso, 15 January 1564 [/5], Montmorency to Montpensier; ff. 11-verso, 4 February 1564 [/5], Montpensier to
Montmorency.

¹ Cabié, *Ambassade en Espagne de St Sulpice*, 344-5, 4 February 1565, St
Étienne to St Sulpice.

² B.N., Mss. fr. 3194, f. 86, 30 October 1565, Charles IX to marshal Montmorency.

³ Condé, *Mémoires*, ii, *Correspondance de Chantonnay*, 192, 24 February 1564,
Sarrón to—?

⁴ Archives de Chantilly, papiers de Condé, *série* K, iv, f. 134, s.d., contemporary copy of the *arrêt*; B.N., Mss. fr. 3193, f. 31, 31 January 1566, Coligny to
the duchess of Ferrara (Renée de France, a celebrated protestant sympathiser);
Desjardins, *Negs. Tosc.*, iii, 523, 30 January 1566; *CSPF.*, 1566-8, p. 4, 10
January 1566, affairs of France; 5, 12 January 1566, protestation of Coligny;
13, 29 January 1566, decree in council.

no verdict contrary to his liking, and that his brother, Aumale, would seek the admirals' life, a statement which he re-affirmed with haughty insubordination upon the eve of the second civil war. When asked by the queen mother 'whether he would not stand to the arrest (sic *arrêt*) of the Privy Council given for the Admiral's innocency last year [1566] he answered no, and that if there had been 500 arrests he would never let that pass so unrevenged'.[1]

In May and June there were reports of a 'secret practice' to kill the admiral, d'Andelot – who had narrowly escaped an ambush in January – and La Rochefoucauld, by a 'great concourse of people'. Condé himself also complained that there 'were certain persons lying in wait for his life'.[2]

Such incidents were no more than they might confidently expect after Lorraine's majesterially menacing speech – in which he had not scrupled to threaten the king – that he and his family would seek the admiral's death. It will be interesting to note that he was always most threatening when the king was ill, and this was coming very close to a declaration of civil war against Coligny and the huguenots – which Catherine had already declined to make at his behest – and in lofty disdain for the authority, interests and decrees of the crown.[3] These events at Moulins provide one key to the following years, and an assurance of future hostilities at what was supposed to be a grand reconciliation, not only with Coligny but also his cousins, the house of Montmorency. They also provide a particularly clear illustration of the discrepancy between papal and royal policy, even though the latter was always catholic, which inevitably rendered Lorraine more of an enemy than a servant of the crown. This is a distinction of fundamental importance since, with a total

[1] *CSPF.*, *1566–8*, p. 341, 16 September 1567, advertisements out of France.
[2] B.N., Mss. fr. 3193, ff. 52 verso–57 verso, *ce qui se passa à Moulins*, 1566; *CSPF.*, *1566–8*, p. 9, 23 January 1566, Smith to Leicester; 70, 21 May 1566, Sir Thomas Hoby to Cecil; 82–3, 24 May–8 June 1566, Hoby to Leicester and Cecil; B.N., Mss. Italien, 1726, ff. 19 verso–21 verso, 23 May 1566; Desjardins, *Negs. Tosc.*, iii, 525, 2 June 1566.
[3] B.N., Mss. fr. 3193, ff. 52 verso–57 verso, *ce qui se passa à Moulins*, 1566.

disregard for current circumstances, Catherine is habitually discredited with responsibility for everything which emanated from the court.

These dissensions in council, which occupied the whole of January 1566, were followed, in March, by a resounding row between Lorraine and the chancellor[1] over points of interpretation of the edict of Amboise, which de L'Hospital wished to observe, and which he understood well enough having drafted it himself. Lorraine offensively endorsed outright the chancellor's charge that he sought to ruin the protestants, accused him – his social inferior – of always wanting to be 'cock of the dunghill', and declared that he would attend no more councils in the chancellor's presence. De L'Hospital retorted that they could manage quite well without him. De L'Hospital was especially hated by the catholics on account of his support of the protestants, though only, it would appear, according to the law – which was his business.[2]

Lorraine's mounting influence in the council is linked with his vitally important new ascendancy over the young Henri duc d'Anjou, who was beginning to play some part in public affairs. On 12 November 1567, upon the death of the old constable Montmorency, Anjou was formally appointed lieutenant-general[3] and his commission declared that he had already long been *designated* both 'chef de notre conseil' and 'lieutenant-général'. During the great itinerary of 1564–6, Anjou was reported to Granvelle to have remained in Paris as *gouverneur* and lieutenant-general with a council of six seigneurs of whom, to judge from his activity, Lorraine must surely have been one.[4] However this may be – for the report is unconfirmed and Anjou was only thirteen

[1] B.N., Mss. fr. 3951, ff. 100 verso–107 verso, 15 March 1566.

[2] *CSPF.*, *1564–5*, p. 227, 21 October 1564, Smith to Cecil; Granvelle, *Papiers d'État*, viii, 483, 6 November 1564, *nouvelles de France*; 606, 15 January 1565, Granvelle to Polweiller. He reported a rumour that de L'Hospital was dead, and hoped it was true, for the harm that he might yet do. De Ruble, *Monluc, Commentaires*, v, 29, 32, *Mémoire au Roy d'Espagne*.

[3] B.N., Mss. fr. 3951, ff. 118–23, 12 November 1567, Anjou's commission. Montmorency died at the battle of St Denis, 11 November 1567.

[4] Granvelle, *Papiers d'État*, viii, 384, 6 October 1564, Nicole de Savigny, a female agent, to Granvelle.

Albert de Gondi, comte de Retz

Jeanne d'Albret, Queen of Navarre

Pope Pius V

Medallion of pope Gregory XIII, reverse inscribed UGONOTTORUM STRAGES · 1572

in 1564 – upon the occasion of Lorraine's quarrel in council with de L'Hospital, and after they had all complained to the king, it was Anjou who 're-installed' the council which resumed, until Lorraine stormed out 'aussi fasche et ennuyé quil en fut jamais'[1].

Anjou was really the only person of suitable rank who could be promoted. By 1567 he was sixteen, and his advancement could scarcely be opposed. Catherine must certainly have hoped to be able to influence him, whereas she was powerless to influence, still less to control Condé. Since the death of Navarre, the catholics had been without a princely leader whose rank and authority might be held to legitimise their activities and, since the death of Guise, they had lacked a military commander. Lorraine had therefore tried, but failed, to seduce the prince de Condé, whose principal advantage to the catholics would have been the corresponding deprivation of the protestants. As first prince of the blood, Condé had legitimately aspired to the rank and title of lieutenant-general, formerly held by his brother Navarre. But Navarre had done so on account of the regency and, by declaring the king of age in the *parlement* of Rouen in 1563, Catherine had obviated any need for the lieutenancy. Condé had therefore sought instead the reversion of the office of constable but, after the 'incident de Meaux'[2] and the siege of Paris, he could have no further hope of political advancement.

As heir apparent and lieutenant-general to a very sick, and still unmarried king, it might be supposed that Anjou would cherish the interests of the crown. By the same token he was also an obvious focus of attention. To the catholics he possessed the triple advantage of supreme rank, youth and inexperience. Lorraine must inevitably have sought to influence him in council, and the pope determined to acquire and exploit him in war. In offering the king substantial help in October 1567, after the outbreak of the second civil war, the pope dictated his own demanding terms, instructing his nuncio della Torre to advise the king not to trust the Montmorency or the chancellor – Lorraine's great enemies –

[1] B.N., Mss. fr. 3951, f. 107 verso, 16 March 1566.
[2] See p. 59 below.

but to place Anjou in command.[1] He would then, the pope added
to della Torre, have to be guided by catholic captains, which was
precisely what happened when, a month later, the old constable
died and Anjou was promoted. Thus, quite possibly without his
even fully realising it, the young prince lieutenant was induced
in this way to serve the extreme catholic cause. The pope's letter
to della Torre, written on 16 October 1567, nearly a month
before Anjou's formal appointment, proves conclusively that the
weight of catholicism, national and international, was behind
him.

In this way the heir presumptive had also been ensnared as a
French faction leader, which tended to divide him from the
crown, and potentially also from Catherine, although his position
as figurehead or leader elect must not be regarded as an absolute
mutation, but rather as a factor of relative and fluctuating consequence. This acquisition of Anjou was a clever, shrewd and
mischievous endeavour, whose effects could only be neutralised or
averted if Catherine could exert an even stronger influence than
they over the exploited prince; but the odds against her were
very great. In time of war, she had no hope of succeeding and,
during the second and third civil wars, as in the first, she was
obliged to acquiesce in extreme catholic policy.

Thereafter, from the peace of Saint-Germain in August 1570,
Anjou became the unhappy centre of political controversy. On
the one hand he was pressurised to sustain the interests of the
extreme catholics, Rome and Spain, his every action carrying, as
they intended, the authority of the king's lieutenant-general. On
the other hand, Catherine strove to keep him in line with 'royal'
policy. This is most clearly seen in the English marriage negotiation which, though not pursued until the end of 1570, appears
from a rather shadowy mission to England of the confidential
secretary, Villeroy, to have originated in the summer of 1567.[2]

---

[1] Hirschauer, *La Politique de St Pie V*, 101–2, 16 October 1567, the pope to
della Torre.

[2] B.N., Mss. Italien, 1726, f. 132, 12 July 1567. Villeroy also went to Scotland, but failed to obtain an audience with Mary. *CSPSp.*, *1558–67*, p. 656,
5 July 1567, de Silva to Philip II.

With impending war in the Netherlands, where Philip II was still expected,[1] the crown was in danger of war with Spain on the one hand, and some huguenot alliance with England on the other. A dynastic alliance with England, or perhaps more precisely, since Anjou was only sixteen, the existence of a marriage negotiation, might possibly afford some slight protection and strengthen Catherine in her struggle with Lorraine to control both the council and Anjou himself. Villeroy's mission was abortive, but this quiet move towards England, as the storm approached and the troubled affairs of Scotland might incline Elizabeth more favourably towards France, is excellent evidence as to the real and independent nature of Catherine's policy during the events which preceded the outbreak of the second civil war.

Both the approach of Alva towards the Netherlands about the beginning of August 1567, and that of 6,000 Swiss troops towards France – which indicated the general anxiety of the crown – alarmed the huguenots exceedingly, especially as the catholics began to augment their policy of intimidation. Coligny was already remaining firmly at home having 'by secret means deciphered some practice that wholly tended to his confusion'.[2] According to Sir Henry Norris, the English ambassador, Lorraine had gained great ascendancy over the king, about which Catherine was 'nothing pleased knowing his ambition'. Under cover of a frontier progress he was seeking to draw them to his house at La Marche in Lorraine, 'where many secret matters and practices will be treated on touching religion and Scotland'.[3] This was hardly reassuring for the protestants, while the papists were bragging that once Philip and his forces had arrived in the Netherlands, the king would revoke the edict. Furthermore, certain captains were said to have been appointed in Paris and other towns to proceed against the nobility upon charges of

[1] *CSPF.*, *1566–8*, p. 336, 7 September 1567, intelligence from Antwerp.

[2] *CSPF.*, *1566–8*, p. 305, 31 July 1567, Sir Henry Norris to Leicester; 307, 1 August 1567, Norris to Cecil; 311–12, 6 August 1567, captain Cockburn – a spy also known as George Beaumont – to Cecil (Compiègne); La Noue, *Discours*, 678.

[3] *CSPF.*, *1566–8*, pp. 327–8, 23 August 1567, Norris to Elizabeth.

infractions of the edict.[1] 'Their mark is to bring all the noblemen and gentlemen within the danger of the law,' and the attempt, he thought, 'was like to be sudden'.[2] With Charles 'fleeting' about the country, and the Swiss drawing near, 'motions' which Norris thought would 'rekindle some flames of civil commotion', Condé formally complained to Catherine against the king's prospective revocation of the edict which, it appears, was really going to happen.[3] Catherine replied, significantly, that 'as long as she might prevail he should never break it'.[4] But, how long, in these circumstances, might she be expected to prevail, especially as there followed a report of a proclamation requiring an annual confession of faith for all members of the judiciary upon pain of forfeiture of office and derogation of rank?[5]

Meanwhile, since his arrival in the Netherlands, Alva had wasted no time in persecuting the nobles and gentry, and large numbers, chiefly of those who had signed the first petition of the *gueux*, April 1566, fled into France and joined the prince de Condé. The closure of the frontier was of no avail and, within two months, so many people of all conditions had departed that even Alva himself became nervous lest they should combine, and gather help to launch an invasion.[6]

[1] *CSPF., 1566–8*, pp. 327–8, 23 August 1567, Norris to Elizabeth. These related to the circumstances in which nobles might or might not practise the cult in their own houses.

[2] *CSPF., 1566–8*, pp. 327–8, 23 August 1567, Norris to Elizabeth; 328, 23 August 1567, Norris to Cecil.

[3] *CSPF., 1566–8*, p. 340, 15 September 1567, Norris to Cecil. It was thought that very shortly the articles rescinding the edict would be published 'to the overthrow of religion'; 341, 26 September 1567, advertisements from France.

[4] *CSPF., 1566–8*, p. 330, 28 August 1567, Norris to Cecil; 330, 29 August 1567, Norris to Elizabeth.

[5] *CSPF., 1566–8*, p. 331, 30 August 1567, Adolph Blyleven to Gresham; 501, 14 July 1568, Norris to Elizabeth.

[6] Kervyn de Lettenhove, *Relations*, v, 13, 23 September 1567, Clough to Gresham; Lettenhove reports Clough to have said that 4,000 gentlemen had gone into France, whence an invasion was strongly to be feared. This is almost certainly an error for 400. Pp. 23–4, 7 October 1567, Clough to Cecil; *CSPF., 1566–8*, p. 352, 6 & 7 October 1567, Clough to Gresham. Alva virtually obviated the possibility of any accommodation by deciding in council on 9

The dramatic arrest in the Netherlands on 9 September of count Egmont, and Coligny's cousin Horne, could hardly fail to move the huguenots to anger and alarm, especially when this coincided with extreme catholic measures against themselves and a clamourous renewal of the vendetta from Lorraine's house at La Marche, where the king was resident.[1] This was becoming almost standard practice for the raising of forces on both sides, and for which, indeed, they were both prepared. Accordingly, Coligny 'being advertised', replied that he 'therefore needed a better guard for his safety and that he doubted not by the help of his friends to make the duke of Guise recoil'.[2] Thus it was that Norris wrote to the queen, 'the civil wars so long breeding are now openly declared'.[3]

Hostilities began on 26 September 1567 with what is known as the 'entreprise de Meaux'. This was strongly reminiscent of the conspiracy of Amboise, from which one could arguably date the first civil war, being a further instance of tumultuous petitioning, and for the same purpose. It was claimed that the huguenots sought to remove the Guises, and in particular Lorraine, from about the king, thereby also breaking their stranglehold on the council, and with it their constant threat to the edict of Amboise and to the lives of leading protestants, and the livelihood and property of many.[4] So great was their vital, political and religious need to overcome the catholic influence, personified in Lorraine,

---

October to sequester the property of Orange and 'all the guilty' and to expel him and other members from the Order of the Golden Fleece – a dishonour that no gentleman could then be expected to digest. Navarrete, *Colección de documentos*, iv, 452–60, 2 October 1567, Alva to Philip II; 465–6, 4 October 1567, Alva to Philip II; 470–2, 1567, Alva to Philip II. There is some evidence for supposing that the nobles' desire to recover their property was a substantial factor in the revolt which followed.

[1] The court was there on 6 September 1567, but for just how long is not clear. *CSPF.*, *1566–8*, pp. 335–6, Charles and Lorraine both wrote to Elizabeth.

[2] This refers, of course, to Henri duc de Guise, son of the murdered François. *CSPF.*, *1566–8*, p. 341, 16 September 1567, advertisements out of France.

[3] *CSPF.*, *1566–8*, p. 348, 30 September 1567, Norris to Elizabeth.

[4] The 'incident de Meaux' is particularly well analysed by La Noue, *Discours*, 676 seq.

that they took the fatal risk of laying what was in effect – albeit protestant apologists insist not in intention – an ambush for the king. The protestants had experienced to their dreadful cost how effective had been the catholics' 'possession' of the king, initially at the time of Amboise and, more specifically, when the Trium-virate seized him at Fontainebleau in March 1562. The difference was, however, that the catholics could claim to have acted under the authority of Navarre, the lieutenant-general and, although they were well accompanied, their *coup d'état* was not a military operation in the same sense as the 'entreprise de Meaux'. In 1565 Soubise believed that protestant possession of the king was their only peaceful solution. He therefore advocated what was later performed at 'Meaux' – although by 1567 he was dead. But he had stressed that it must be done efficiently or not at all, otherwise it would ruin the state.[1] Soubise was right; again like that of Amboise, the enterprise was betrayed and miscarried, and the protestants incurred the responsibility for having attacked the king and the court, an offence which placed them almost irre-deemably in the wrong and which was subsequently magnified by their siege of the capital city of Paris where the king took refuge. Indeed it was said that, saving his presence, there would have been a massacre of the hated protestants. In 1572, therefore, it may well have been considered that the city was venting an old hatred, and settling an old score, since the massacre could not have occurred in its historic form without the participation of the populace.[2] The Guises, however, against whom it was all directed, just managed to escape from the *coup* at Meaux, according to Petrucci, the Tuscan ambassador, who was there, 'by the grace of God and their good Turkish horses'.[3] Otherwise, had they been secured, the protestants could safely have presented their petition without further molestation of the court. It seems probable that neither the king nor the capital – not to mention Lorraine – ever forgave them for this dual outrage. It was this

[1] Soubise, *Mémoires*, 89–90.
[2] Desjardins, *Negs. Tosc.*, iii, 549, 3 November 1567.
[3] Desjardins, *Negs. Tosc.*, iii, 530–1, 29 September 1567; 534–41, 8 October 1567; Pasquier, *Lettres historiques*, 167–71.

which definitively ruined any prospect of advancement for Condé. Catherine immediately initiated peace negotiations which clearly establishes her independent attitude.¹ But, within a remarkably short time, there were reports of forces about to pour into France from the pope and Spain. The pope also tried to prise help out of the duc de Lorraine and the doge of Venice and importuned Savoy with the facile promise of the grace of God and the praise of men. He had himself sent money to Lorraine and to the duke of Savoy.² By mid-October, counts Meghem and Arenberg were coming from the Netherlands in command of about 4,000 foot and 1,500 horse,³ 'help' which was evidently solicited by Lorraine, since it would scarcely help Catherine's cause of peace, and she is said to have refused Alva's offer of 5,000 foot and 1,500 horse at the time of the 'incident de Meaux'. When, in December, she asked for 2,000 harquebusiers to help the duc d'Aumale intercept the protestants' German mercenaries, he replied that she was too late, and he could not divide his forces. Catherine, with what sounds suspiciously like relief, retorted that she could not then be blamed for making peace.⁴ After escaping from Meaux, Lorraine had wasted little time in sending his chaplain to Alva. He arrived on 14 October and requested him to despatch a man of trust to Lorraine. He sent Esteban de Ibarra but, only three days after the chaplain, Lorraine sent a captain who pressed the duke to help the king – presumably the help that Catherine declined – and, what is more, proposed that if Charles and his brothers were to die, they might advance Philip's claim to the throne of France – notwithstanding the Salic

¹ Desjardins, *Negs. Tosc.*, iii, 531–4, 1 October 1567.
² B.N., Mss. Italien, 1726, f. 158, 24 October 1567; *CSPF.*, *1566–8*, p. 350, ?[September 1567]; Hirschauer, *La Politique de St Pie V*, 98–100, 101–2, two letters of 16 October 1567, the pope to della Torre; De Potter, *Lettres de St Pie V*, 7–8, 18 October 1567, the pope to the doge of Venice; 9–10, 18 October 1567, the pope to the duke of Savoy, 11–12, 16 November 1567, the pope to the duke of Savoy.
³ Kervyn de Lettenhove, *Relations*, v, 29, 19 October 1567, Clough to Gresham; B.N., Mss. Italien, 1726, ff. 149–50 verso, 7 October 1567.
⁴ Gachard, *Notices et extraits*, i, 401–4, 10 December 1567, Alva to Catherine. She had written to him on 4 December.

law, of which he made light.[1] It was not without reason that Catherine had sought to prohibit Lorraine from relations with Philip's servants[2] or that, as Norris had said, she feared his ambition. This treasonable proposition was a very different matter from the defensible repression of rebels and heretics, and evidently astounded even Alva, who imprisoned the captain until the return of his own envoy. As Lorraine was powerful enough to behave in this way, Catherine was obviously no free agent. This, however, was a faithful reflection of papal policy as previously expressed by Pius IV in the autumn of 1561[3] and illustrates the extent to which Lorraine regarded himself as an agent of the papacy and universal catholicism, rather than as a nobleman of France and a servant of the crown.

As the French crown, albeit definitively catholic, was primarily concerned with the interests of the kingdom, it follows that Catherine must inevitably have opposed Lorraine, who was even inclined to alienate the succession, and this is continuously demonstrated by her correspondence and her conduct. Thus, while Catherine strove for peace, the cardinal strove for war. But the catholics' lack, since the death of François duc de Guise, of any outstanding or acknowledged military commander, was perhaps their weakest point. Thus, their failure to sustain the war, combined with Catherine's efforts to restore the peace, enabled moderate members of the council – François duc de Montmorency, Limoges, Jean de Morvillier[4] and the secretary Alluye – to conclude the treaty of Longjumeau after only six months, on 23 March 1568.

[1] Gachard, *Correspondance de Philippe II*, i, 593–4, 1 November 1567, Alva to Philip II; Ranke, *Civil War and Monarchy in France*, i, 344.

[2] Granvelle, *Papiers d'État*, ix, 399–403, 15 July 1565, Granvelle to Philip II.

[3] Susta, *Die Römische Curie*, i, 280, 18 October–December 1561, instructions for the conte Brocado.

[4] Jean de Morvillier had been ambassador to Venice in 1547 and bishop of Orléans 1552–64. He was *garde des sceaux*, 1568–70. De Morvillier was a relative of several of the secretaries of state, a moderate, and a trusted supporter of Catherine.

IV

The Peace of Longjumeau and the French Enterprise of England

THERE CAN rarely have been a more perjured pact than the 'little peace', as it was called, of Longjumeau, a protestant error and a catholic manoeuvre.[1] The ambassadors of Rome and Madrid, resisting each successive series of negotiations, had 'ceased not to exclaim upon the King and Queen, saying that it was impossible to have two religions in one realm without great confusion', and Philip II offered massive financial support which rather reflected his sentiments than his solvency.[2] Lorraine, who had lately 'escaped very hard at Rheims', being fired upon in his coach,[3] never entertained the notion of any proper peace. But a temporary cessation of hostilities would dispel the protestants' current military advantage, alarmingly augmented by their approaching German mercenaries, and enable him to recover the initiative and control the circumstances of war.

So it was faithlessly resolved to make a six months' peace, 'sans tenir aulcune fidelité à gens infidelles' (sic).[4] Two days after its

[1] Fontanon, *Édits et ordonnances*, iv, 289–91, 23 March 1568. Longjumeau repeated the terms of Amboise, 19 March 1563.

[2] *CSPF., 1566–8*, pp. 401–2, 23 January 1568, Norris to Elizabeth. Philip's offer was '1,000,000 of gold'.

[3] *CSPF., 1566–8*, p. 413, 9 February 1568, Norris to Cecil. One of Lorraine's attendants was killed.

[4] PRO/SP 70/105; *CSPF., 1569–71*, pp. 39–40, [February] 1569, relation of actions in France. This immensely important document, which records Lorraine's organisation of the third civil war, is calendared in the wrong place. It is a contemporary copy without date or place and refers to events in France from the beginning of 1568 to August 1569. It is endorsed 'Mons. de La Forest orator to the emperor with his Majesty's answer and a discourse of the cardinal of Lorraine for the overthrow of them of the religion in France'. Jacques

publication there was already 'great appearance of alteration, the peace depending in very perilous terms'. This refers to a nocturnal meeting on 29 March of the most catholic members of the council, 'sworn enemies to the religion wherein was conspired the surprise of Orleans, Soissons, Rochelle and Auxerre,' cities of protestant and strategic importance. This was to be executed by Sansac, Martigues, Chavigny and Brissac, suddenly, while Condé was disarming, and 'so it would be more easy to work their wills of the principals of the religion . . . But this conspiracy was not so secretly kept as wickedly devised, for by 10 o'clock next day, the Cardinal Chatillon had knowledge thereof'.[1] The protestants, Norris added, were afraid of 'some intention against their persons'. There was indeed an 'intention', in a general sense in the first instance, and soon after more specifically. Lorraine also intended that while the protestants dispersed, 'the king' would remain in arms and secure persons at his devotion in all the towns; persons of trust were to be placed in control of all bridges and passes, and offices were to be conferred only upon catholics known to be of their party. After the peace, a secret *mandement* was shown to 'quelques principaulx' of all garrison towns, with instructions to implement against all protestants a policy of persecution and violent vexation, and generally to tax and burden them with 'toutes sortes de charges', so that 'ainsy mal traictez' they would

---

Bochetel, known as La Forest Bochetel, son of the secretary Guillaume Bochetel (d. 1556), brother of Bernadin, bishop of Rennes, and brother-in-law of Catherine de Medici's confidential secretary, Claude de Laubespine (d. 1567), was sent to the emperor early in 1569 (*CSPF.*, *1569–71*, p. 29, 10 February 1569, Norris to Elizabeth), to obstruct a league between the elector of Saxony and other princes, and to further negotiations for the marriage of Charles IX to the emperor's daughter. The document is not a discourse of Lorraine, but some kind of memorandum written in or after August 1569, the latest date to which it refers. The arrangement and chronology of the contents is confused. La Forest was a moderate and a loyalist. The Spanish ambassador in England took him for a protestant, which is possible. This may be regarded as a good source, more especially as it corroborates other evidence. *CSPSp.*, *1568–79*, p. 72, 18 September 1568, de Spes to Philip II; *CSPF.*, *1566–8*, pp. 537–9, 2 September 1568, Norris to Elizabeth.

[1] *CSPF.*, *1566–8*, p. 436, 30 March 1568, Norris to Cecil.

be reduced to abandoning their homes to soldiers or other catholic inhabitants. A memoir, said to have been presented to the queen at the time of the negotiations at Vincennes, which were in January 1568, stressed the need to secure Condé's *gouvernement* of Picardy, on the Netherlands frontier, where he also possessed property. Marshal Cossé was placed in control with forces at his disposal.

Sometime in May Lorraine proceeded to his real intention: Catherine de Medici had fallen seriously ill in April and did not recover for many weeks. Seizing this advantage, Lorraine held a council at which it was determined to 'exterminer les chefs de ladite religion de sorte que pour ledict effect certaines personnaiges furent deputez pour chacun d'eulx particulierement, qui furent depeschez de la court, et desquels on a sceu les noms, qui avoyent charge de surprendre et assassiner les chefs de ladicte religion. Mais parce quils ne furent trouvez a descouvert et quilz en eurent advertissement l'entreprise fut differée'.[1] This represented, more or less, the extended or Bayonne version of the policy of elimination, first apparent in the quasi-judicial attempt against Condé in 1560, as part of the original extermination policy to which La Forest's statement apparently went on to refer.

But, if this murderous catholic purpose was circumstantially deferred in the early summer of 1568, when events in England and the Netherlands in any case urgently commanded Lorraine's attention, it was nevertheless relentlessly pursued over the next four years until the death of Coligny in the massacre. The elimination of the protestant leaders which, owing to their diligence and successful intelligence, failed in May 1568, was only a part of all that Lorraine had in mind. At the same time, according to La Forest, and equally by advantage of the queen's illness, he had forthwith planned (dressé sa partie) to seize the young king, secure the cardinal de Bourbon, the marshal Damville and the city of Paris, and 'executer par tout le Royaume le desseign quils avoient auparavant protecté' (recte projecté).

[1] PRO/SP 70/105.

This presumably refers to the military plans against the protestants of December 1560 and, according to La Forest, was substantiated by fifteen or sixteen witnesses, 'gens d'honneur' of Paris.[1]

Lorraine's designs on the person of the king must be taken seriously, in view of his record. It will be remembered that he was already said to have planned this when Catherine was ill in September 1563. Queen Elizabeth later declared that when she had sent troops to France in the first civil war, it was because she believed the Guises wanted to master the king and govern at their pleasure, and she had a letter, which she retained, from the queen of France telling her so; evidence, incidentally, of Catherine's attitude to the Guises. Their seizure of the king at Fontainebleau in March 1562 bore this out, which was one reason why Condé took up arms.[2]

This political, not to say revolutionary element, already if slightly differently apparent in Lorraine's treasonable approaches to Alva after the 'incident de Meaux', clearly circumscribes the religious content of his policy, and delineates the irreconcilable gulf between himself and Catherine, whose recovery by mid-May averted the seizure of the king.[3] But, if he could not regain possession of the king, he could and did seek to rise upon the established authority and dawning ambition of Anjou. The king, Norris observed, 'having given his brother all the authority that he possibly might, and having no degree whereunto he might aspire but the highest, has shown some tokens of an ambitious heart'.[4] As a result, Lorraine and Anjou began to create a certain division among the catholics which probably accounts for their otherwise puzzling impotence in the second and third civil wars[5] and, perhaps to some extent, for the survival and success of the protestants, especially when one finds such a violent catholic as

[1] PRO/SP 70/105. *CSPF.*, *1566-8*, p. 458, 17 May 1568, Norris to Cecil.
[2] *CSPSp.*, *1568-79*, p. 13, 20 March 1568, de Silva to Philip II.
[3] Norris reported Catherine to have recovered by 17 May. *CSPF.*, *1566-8*, p. 458, 17 May 1568, Norris to Cecil.
[4] *CSPF.*, *1566-8*, p. 439, 8 April 1568, Norris to Elizabeth.
[5] See p. 95.

the Bourbon duc de Montpensier, principal commander of the original extermination project of 1560, protesting against the predictable results of the non observation of the peace.[1] However this may be, on 2 May, the queen being ill, a council was held in her room at which the marshals Montmorency, Damville and Vieilleville made 'certain oppositions' against the lieutenancy of Anjou. While one must remember that, as lieutenant-general, Anjou's military authority superseded their own, Norris reported their 'oppositions' as being to no other end than 'to ruin to the ground the platform of the Cardinal of Lorraine's devices, who hopes to procure the continuance of Monsr. d'Anjou in his lieutenantship and so the principal affairs of this realm again into his hands'.[2] There can be no doubt that not all the court catholics, either then or later, supported Lorraine and the agents of Rome and Madrid, and the nuance must be taken into account. Clearly the arrangement described by Norris was mutually satisfactory to Lorraine, and Anjou 'a cruel enemy against the favourers of religion'. He was reputedly much 'addicted to follow' the cardinal's advice, and ruled 'all things' through his own privy councillors, of whom Lorraine was the principal, even going so far in opposition to his royal brother as to employ his own chancellor to seal 'all such things as the good old Chancellor of the King refuses to seal, who neither for love nor dread would seal anything against the statutes of the realm'; a fine testimony to the rare probity of de L'Hospital, who shortly left office on just such an issue.[3]

This jealous cleavage between Charles and the heir apparent Anjou, directed and sustained by the detested Lorraine, most powerful and probably the richest man in France, added a desperately dangerous new dimension to the already catastrophic weakness of the crown, and the conflict which this engendered goes far to account for the almost indescribable confusion and semi-paralysis of royal policy – if there ever were such a thing – during

[1] *CSPF.*, *1566–8*, p. 453, 12 May 1568, Norris to Elizabeth.
[2] *CSPF.*, *1566–8*, pp. 453–5, 12 May 1568, Norris to Elizabeth.
[3] *CSPF.*, *1566–8*, pp. 453–5, 12 May 1568, two letters from Norris to Elizabeth and Cecil.

the years 1570–2, following the third civil war, which Lorraine precipitated in September 1568.

While from May – when the huguenots proved elusive – until August, when delay was no longer possible, Lorraine temporised in France, developments in the Netherlands and England closely affected protestant affairs on the one hand, and the plans and prospects of Lorraine on the other. These plans, together with the partial fusion, about to occur, of the interests and enmities of the huguenots and insurgents in the Netherlands, led to the inescapable involvement of England in this broadening politico-religious conflict, as well as to the deepening complexity of French and English relations with Spain. Henceforth, England became an essential factor in the evolution of the complicated situation out of which the massacre arose. This was partly because French connections with the Netherlands altered the nature and degree of England's concern in the outcome of the civil wars. Elizabeth could no longer afford to watch from the shore, periodically fishing in troubled waters for the recovery of Calais – not that she ever lost sight of this objective[1] – because she was simultaneously menaced by the power of Spain, and the French catholic faction under Lorraine who again, as in 1559–60, actively became 'a most cruel enemy to the Queen and her country',[2] and who might or might not succeed in swaying the crown of France. These dangers were alarmingly increased by the aggressively catholicising policy of Pius V, 1566–72, formerly the grand inquisitor, behind the cause of Mary Stuart – Lorraine's niece – who fled into England on 19 May 1568. This was an event of fundamental importance profoundly influencing the history

---

[1] Villeroy actually expressed the fear, in February 1569, that Elizabeth was preparing some enterprise against Calais. B.N., Mss. fr. 17528, f. 52 verso, 10 February 1569, Villeroy's 'Estat des affaires'; *CSPSp.*, *1568–79*, p. 15, 20 March 1568, de Silva to Philip II; there is also a good deal of material relating to Calais in the previous volume, 1558–67; *CSPF.*, *1566–8*, p. 535, 29 August 1568, Norris to Cecil. Norris appeared to be expecting someone, who should be 'sufficient', to come to demand Calais, and the third civil war had scarcely begun when, on 2 September 1568, he wrote to Cecil proposing that 'this time' the recovery of Calais should not be 'omitted'; *CSPF.*, *1566–8*, p. 539.

[2] *CSPF.*, *1566–8*, p. 508, 29 July 1568, Norris to Cecil.

of Europe from then until her death in 1587 – nineteen years of tenuous survival which were considerably more remarkable than her ultimate execution.

As a Scottish queen with trouble at home, and especially after her marriage in 1565, Mary's claim to the throne of England was not an imminent threat, particularly in view of the respective pre-occupations of Spain and France. But from May 1568, as an apparently eligible catholic exile, she was immensely dangerous as the focus of internal disaffection – which some believed to be substantial – and external intervention.[1] Lorraine immediately responded to this development. Seeking to lull the huguenots, who were in no wise deceived by his 'honneste languaige', – not that this was clearly audible – he offered Anjou 200,000 francs per annum from the church (which doubtless only he and the pope could do) to sustain catholicism, 'whereto the Pope, the King of Spain and other Papistical Princes have promised all help, in everything that he attempts to the ruin of them of the religion'. Furthermore, he sought to dazzle Anjou with the prospect of bringing the queen of Scots back into France, where he would 'cause her to yield to him' not only 'all her estate that she pretends to have in England', but also, according to Coligny, her undisputed rights to Scotland.[2] Lorraine had been active in Scottish affairs since the murder of lord Darnley (10 February 1567), trying – among other things – to obtain possession of the infant prince James. There were even those who harboured the suspicion that 'the whole affair [Darnley's murder] might have been arranged by those who wished that the queen of Scotland should marry in France'.[3] This may be going rather far, but it throws light on Lorraine's reputation.

[1] Bothwell and Mary's marital status was spuriously argued, although irregularity in this respect was the least of their suspected transgressions. In 1571 it was proposed to annul the marriage upon the grounds that Bothwell had a lawful wife from whom his divorce was invalid. *CSP Rome, 1558–71*, pp. 442–3, 15 July 1571, brief authorising proceedings for a decree of nullity.

[2] *CSPF., 1566–8*, pp. 476–7, 7 June 1568, Norris to Elizabeth; 489–90, 28 June 1568, Norris to Cecil.

[3] *CSPSp., 1558–67*, p. 621, 22 February 1567, de Silva to Philip II.

Lorraine's involvement in Anglo-Scottish affairs represents the beginning of his most far-reaching exertions as arch-priest of the papacy, otherwise styled by Norris 'the minister of mischief', to execute papal policy in France and England.[1] The proposal to rescue Mary was no mere quixotic romanticism – of which Lorraine was probably incapable – but his serious purpose, requiring an operation of war; hence Coligny's urgent, anxious plea that the queen should 'consider hereof in time'.[2] Indeed both a military enterprise and a conspiracy were simultaneously initiated. Early in July Norris believed that great diligence was being 'used to recover the Queen of Scots to be sent into this country', in which an English lord (probably Arundel), the duke of Alva and the Spanish ambassador were all involved, and the baron de la Garde was charged with preparing 'privily' a small fleet of galleys and other vessels.[3]

Norris was summoned out of Paris to Charenton at this time, presumably for secrecy, to be warned by the 'provost marshal' of a plot contrived between Spain, the pope and the French king – which could only mean Lorraine and the French catholics – to murder the queen in favour of Mary. There was mention of an Italian, the agent to whom Alva sent his letters concerning the conspiracy, who was much conversant with the [catholic] earl of Arundel and the Spanish ambassador.[4] Since he submitted some catholic 'scheme' to the pope sometime in the summer of 1568 this agent was almost certainly the rich, notorious Florentine merchant and banker Roberto Ridolphi, secret nuncio in England since 1566. Ridolphi was a kinsman through his mother, Maddalena Gondi, of Lorraine's Italian supporters and associates in France, Albert de Gondi, in 1565 comte de Retz in the right of his wife, traditionally associated with the massacre, and his cousin Jérôme de Gondi.[5]

[1] *CSPF., 1569–71*, p. 193, 25 February 1570, Norris to Cecil.
[2] *CSPF., 1566–8*, p. 477, 7 June 1568, Norris to Elizabeth.
[3] *CSPF., 1566–8*, p. 494, 5 July 1568, Norris to Cecil; 500–1, 14 July 1568, Norris to Elizabeth.
[4] Haynes, *State Papers*, 466, 7 July 1568, Norris to Cecil.
[5] Ridolphi had been in England at least since 1562 and had been secret

Only a week later cardinal Châtillon sent a friend of Coligny, called Menillie, to warn Norris that Lorraine often received letters from 'divers particular persons of England, who mind to make some insurrection'. Sometimes their letters came via Rome (which would tend to compromise Ridolphi) and sometimes by means of the duke of Alva. There were also certain Italians 'who privily practise these devices,' in which none other was trusted in England but the Spanish ambassador.[1] While no one could identify these felons, both Coligny and d'Andelot were adamant that the queen must have 'great regard to herself' on account of Italians sent by Lorraine 'to practise against her'.[2] At the end of July Norris reported that Sébastien de Luxembourg, vicomte de Martigues, *gouverneur* of Brittany, was preparing forces for England, and that the Spanish ambassador, Don Guerau de Spes, a fiery Catalan of small discretion and detested by Alva, was thought to have knowledge of this conspiracy. On his way from Spain to England he had conferred with Lorraine and gone straight on to Alva.[3]

The affairs of England having diverted his attention from ensnaring the huguenots, Lorraine tried, for at least the third time, to increase his own strength and undermine theirs by the seduction of the prince de Condé who, according to his own testimony, was invited by the pope to command this nascent enterprise that his

nuncio since 1566 because the pope had been struggling to get one admitted into England, but had failed. Francis Edwards, *The Marvellous Chance*, 30; J. Susta, *Die Römische Curie*, i, 335–6, 3 January 1562, cardinal Borromeo to cardinal Ferrara (Rome); Cecil Roth, 'Roberto Ridolfi e la sua congiura', *'Rivista Storica degli Archivi Toscani*, ii (1930), 119; *CSP Rome, 1558–71*, p. 302, 18 April 1569 [Ridolphi] to the pope.

[1] *CSPF., 1566–8*, p. 500, 14 July 1568, Norris to Elizabeth; 502, 14 July 1568, Norris to Cecil.

[2] *CSPF., 1566–8*, p. 505, 23 July 1568, Norris to Cecil.

[3] De Spes arrived in Paris on 17 July 1568. He planned to leave for the Netherlands next day, where he was delayed by the absence in Friesland of Alva. He arrived in England on 3 September. *CSPF., 1566–8*, p. 508, 29 July 1568, Norris to Cecil; *CSPSp., 1568–79*, p. 69, 10 July 1568; 69–70, 25 August 1568; 70, 6 September 1568, all from de Spes to Philip II.

nuncio Ridolphi was promoting in England.[1] Condé, to his credit, exploded with 'many hot words,' denouncing Lorraine as an enemy of God, man and the peace of France, who now aimed to 'usurp the throne [of England] by means of a cession on the part of Mary to the king's brother' – Anjou, which could only have meant through the crown matrimonial. That Mary had been his dead brother's wife (now at two more compromising removes) no longer seemed to matter, and the proposal was not unrealistic in view of Philip's former contract with Mary Tudor.[2] Condé's refusal to command an enterprise against England, their only foreign hope, drew him and the protestants closer to Elizabeth, who was beholden at least to Coligny and Châtillon for much intelligence relating to her mortal danger.

But, if Lorraine contrived to threaten the life and throne of the Queen of England, he was scarcely less menacing in France. How he supposed that he could ever accomplish the marriage of the duc d'Anjou, heir apparent, without the co-operation of the crown, can hardly be explained, unless by the fact that from July to September Charles IX – whose throne he had already proposed to Spain, and whose person he had already threatened – was very seriously ill.[3] Everything however, as in 1562, was interrupted by the civil war, which began in September, and in October Mary was imprisoned in England.

The counter proposal to marry Anjou to queen Elizabeth, already quietly broached in 1567 when Elizabeth sent the earl of Sussex to renew her negotiation with the archduke Charles,[4] was therefore partly revived to block the Marian plan (ironically a much more suitable match), and partly to detach Anjou from

---

[1] Ridolphi was anxious that the enterprise should be in the name of the pope in order to obviate Franco-Spanish rivalry. He was not an astute politician.

[2] Haynes, *State Papers*, 473–5, 6 October 1568, Condé's instructions for M. de Cavaignes, in extenso, and calendared in *HMC Hatfield*, i, 364–5; *CSPF., 1566–8*, pp. 473–5, 4 June 1568, Norris to Elizabeth.

[3] The allegation was not only reported by Norris, but also in the memorandum of La Forest. *CSPF., 1566–8*, p. 458, 17 May 1568, Norris to Cecil; PRO/SP 70/105.

[4] *CSPSp., 1558–67*, pp. 644–6, 14 June 1567; 652, 26 June 1567; 654–6, 5 July 1567, all from de Silva to Philip II.

Lorraine and undermine the cardinal's power. In this respect the interests of the crown coincided with those of the protestants, against whom it was shortly obliged to sustain two devastating years of civil war. The proposal appears to have been transmitted from the duc de Montmorency to Norris via two intermediaries, one of them Coligny's friend, Menillie. The negotiation, it was propounded, would be of 'great commodity' even if Elizabeth did not entertain it seriously since, it was hoped, Montmorency 'taking in hand to deal herein shall in such sort creep into credit with Monsieur, as in the end to work the Cardinal of Lorraine out of favour'; no small undertaking.[1] As Montmorency and Lorraine were jointly admitted 'chief of the Privy Council' at the end of June[2] there must clearly have been a major struggle for power at court. This was interrupted by the civil war, which lent Lorraine a great advantage, but accounts for Montmorency's supremacy thereafter when Lorraine was in disgrace.

The proposal was received in England by members of the privy council – did it ever reach the queen? – in the spirit in which it was made. Cecil and the earls of Pembroke and Leicester replied immediately that they did not 'mislike' the overture made by Menillie in the name of Montmorency 'for the diverting of the enterprise intended by the Cardinal of Lorraine,' although they did not see any 'likelihood of the sequel'.[3] This was not surprising since Elizabeth's inauspicious reaction in 1567, not more than partly to please de Silva, was that it would not result in people seeing 'such a comical farce as an old woman leading a child to the church doors'.[4]

Lorraine, to judge from his procedure once the enterprise of England was under way, appears to have regarded the third civil

[1] *CSPF., 1566–8*, p. 487, 23 June 1568, Norris to Cecil.

[2] *CSPF., 1566–8*, p. 490, 28 June 1568, Norris to Cecil.

[3] *CSPF., 1566–8*, p. 490, 28 June 1568, Pembroke, Leicester and Cecil to Norris. The time lag of only five days between these letters, unless there is some mistake, is possible but remarkable, and suggests that they believed in the danger to England.

[4] *CSPSp., 1558–67*, p. 564, 5 July 1567, de Silva to Philip II. The 'farce' was very nearly enacted a little later, but it was always this aspect which distressed Elizabeth.

war as an integral part of his European strategy – at least if he failed to trap his prey – and Condé having hotly declined its high command became the principal target of its French counterpart. Renewed war in France, it was soon apparent, was the only alternative to a huguenot invasion of the Netherlands, which Alva had rightly feared since the publication in April 1568 of the *Justification* of William of Orange and the simultaneous outbreak of hostilities; the first campaign of the great revolt. Following the alarming and dramatic victory of William's impetuous brother, Louis of Nassau at Heiligerlee on 23 May 1568, Alva promptly resorted to the disastrous policy of violence which he had always generally advocated, and had sought at Bayonne to perpetrate in France. On 5 June Egmont, and Coligny's cousin Horne were executed.[1] Egmont and Horne were just two of the more distinguished among sixty who died in three dreadful days in Brussels, whilst hundreds more died elsewhere, and others fled to France.

This outright assault – by a grandee – upon the Netherlands nobility, whose rank should have ensured their immunity from such treatment, inevitably created a fearful impression, both there and in France where the protestant seigneurs had, through their extreme vigilance, so recently evaded a comparable fate at the hands of Lorraine which rendered them, until the ultimate edict of Nantes in 1598, pre-occupied to the point of obsession with the problem of security. In honour as well as interest, the Netherlands outrage demanded action, and it elicited immediate support from the huguenots whose forces began to assemble in Picardy. Mouvans from Dauphiné and Cocqueville from Normandy swiftly prepared to cross the frontier but perished in the attempt at the hands of Montpensier and Cossé.[2] Others, some of whom served William of Orange when he retreated into France in November 1568, lay in waiting near the frontier, probably

[1] P. Geyl, *The Revolt of the Netherlands*, 103 seq.; C. V. Wedgwood, *William the Silent*, 103–6.

[2] Cocqueville was defeated at St Valéry late in July and executed, his head being sent to be set on a pole in Paris. *CSPF., 1566–8*, p. 505, 23 July 1568, 512, 2 August 1568, Norris to Cecil.

because his preparations were still incomplete.[1] But he protested to Schwendi, a councillor of the emperor, in tones of strangulated grief and fury that Alva's barbarous and inhuman cruelty were totally unendurable.[2] Then, in August 1568, upon the point of departure, he concluded a formal treaty of alliance with Condé and Coligny – previously discussed in 1567.[3] It declared that their respective princes were misguided by evil councillors – signifying Alva and Lorraine – who sought to exterminate the true religion, the nobility and other 'gens de bien'. This is interesting tending to show the revolt as partly a defence of class and property, the estates of the dead and outlawed having all been sequestered. Condé also categorically declared just a few weeks later, that the huguenots were obliged, among other things, to protect the nobility.[4] The treaty was one of full, mutual support, specifying that if peace were to ensue in either country, help must be extended to the other. Hostilities therefore could hardly be delayed once William crossed the Netherlands frontier. He was gathering forces at Cologne and hoped to take the field about 8 August, expecting some 7–8,000 Frenchmen to join him.[5]

This, and the position at the end of July 1568 of the enterprise of England, explain why Lorraine chose the month of August for the execution of his deferred *coup* against the protestant leaders, for which he had made continuous preparations since the peace

[1] Among these were Genlis, Morvillier, Renty, Mouy (murdered in 1569), Autricourt, Esternay, Eraquiers and La Persone. G. van Prinsterer, *Archives ou correspondance*, série i, vol. iii, 291–5, 17 September 1568, William of Orange to the duke of Württemberg; 267, 24 July 1568, B. de Malberg to Solaigré (a pseudonym); 291; Gachard, *Correspondance de Guillaume le Taciturne*, iii, p. iv; Kervyn de Lettenhove, *Les Huguenots*, ii, p. 111.

[2] G. van Prinsterer, *Archives ou correspondance*, série i, vol. iii, 244–51, 19 June 1568.

[3] G. van Prinsterer, *Archives ou correspondance*, série i, vol. iii, 282–6, August 1568, *projet d'alliance*.

[4] Haynes, *State Papers*, 473–5, 6 October 1568, instructions from Condé for M. de Cavaignes, in extenso; calendared in *HMC Hatfield*, i, 364–5.

[5] G. van Prinsterer, *Archives ou correspondance*, série i, vol. iii, 257–61, –July 1568, William of Orange to (his brother) Nassau. William's expected invasion of the south-east followed early in September. C. V. Wedgwood, *William the Silent*, 108.

of Longjumeau. Apart from the accumulation of money, Lorraine is reported to have disposed of 'tous estatz et en faict pourveoir expres que bon luy semble'. Thus he is said to have nominated new *baillis* and channelled presumably their business through Jérôme de Gondi, Pellevé, the archbishop of Sens, and one of the secretaries of state, Simon Fizes, baron de Sauve. The despatches of others were to be disregarded.¹ He could also govern to a wide extent through the vice-regal authority and the personnel of Anjou. This is no more than a tantalising glimpse into the means by which Lorraine was able to mount a nation-wide campaign of harrassment and violence against the protestants, in spite of the intentions of the crown to enforce the edict. Indeed the king himself appears to have been intimidated, if we are to believe La Forest, who maintains that he was required to memorise a formula supplied to the *gouverneurs* by which to respond, no doubt in honied words, to protestant complaints.

On the leadership level, these complaints reached a climax in July and early August 1568 with the attempted assassination of Condé, Coligny, d'Andelot and Esternay² who warned the king that they were being deliberately provoked to the limit of endurance. They and others had, for some time, been obliged 'to lie in divers castles, with captains soldiers and gentlemen about them,' and were so placed that there was no river between them, while Esternay, well accompanied, maintained a ford over the Seine to assure communications between Condé and his sequestered *gouvernement* of Picardy,³ where marshal Cossé replaced

¹ PRO/SP 70/105; *CSPF.*, *1566–8*, pp. 537–9, 2 September 1568, Norris to Elizabeth. Norris confirms the point about Fizes and says that Lorraine caused Catherine to suspect the other secretaries. This was doubtless what he hoped, but it is inconceivable that she suspected Claude de Laubespine or Villeroy.

² *CSPF.*, *1566–8*, p. 471, 31 May 1568, articles presented to the French king by the admiral; 494, 5 July 1568, Norris to Cecil; 508–9, 29 July 1568, Norris to Cecil; 511, 31 July 1568, affairs in France; 511 [July] 1568, Norris to the duke of Norfolk; 515–16, 7 August 1568, Norris to Elizabeth; Cecil Papers, iv, ff. 31–4, declaration of the prince de Condé of the cause and manner of his departure from Noyers, 23 August [1568].

³ *CSPF.*, *1566–8*, pp. 487–8, 23 June 1568, Norris to Elizabeth.

him. Since the peace, he had been menaced in his own houses at Muret and Condé and forced to take refuge at Noyers in Burgundy.[1] Coligny also was in peril at Châtillon; on the way to d'Andelot's *château* at Tanlay he was twice menaced and fired on and he too was obliged to join Condé at Noyers.[2] The lieutenant of d'Andelot's company was among those who were murdered with impunity and, according to Norris, more had perished since the 'peace' than had died in the war. Condé and Coligny, he said, had been less exposed in the war, when they were in arms, than in 'peace', '*the which thing was meant when the peace was yet in treaty, as appears by the letters intercepted from the Cardinal of Lorraine to the Duchess of Guise*'.[3]

For this purpose, Lorraine took a number of specific precautions including the despatch of sixteen companies of gendarmes to garrison towns whose commanders had orders to vex, harrass and ravage the protestants in every possible way. Two of the 'best catholics' in every town were to be elected as leaders to fall upon (courir suz) the protestants. As many as possible were to be driven out of the towns, in order to deprive them of shelter and safety, while the nobility were to be immobilised in their homes, 'qui sera la ruine evidente tant d'eulx mesmes que de tout le corps de ladicte religion'. This bears out Condé's claim that it was necessary to protect them. Finally Lorraine took care to control the *passaiges*, meaning bridges, fords and passes, thus rendering communications difficult and dangerous, if not impossible.

'Sur tous ces fondements ledit seigneur cardinal pense avoir surement estably le comble de ses desseigns,' loudly assuring Catherine, close to the king's sick bed, that they were in a position to exterminate the protestants whenever they would, and 'estouffer une semence sy pernicieuse a cest estat sans leur laisser aulcun moyen de cy apres reprendre racine suivant l'exemple

---

[1] Châtillon's *discourse*, 27 September 1568, endorsed by Cecil, printed by Atkinson, *The Cardinal of Châtillon in England*, 93 seq.

[2] Delaborde, *Coligny*, iii, 17–21.

[3] My italics. *CSPF., 1566–8*, p. 516, 7 August 1568, Norris to Elizabeth.

du Roy d'Espaigne.[1] Such a purge of the 'ravening vermin of sectaries and heretics' had already been urged by the nuncio, della Torre, upon his arrival in 1566, and was ill received by the queen with a 'sour countenance'.[2] It was now objected that the protestants were very vigilant. But Lorraine argued that if the leaders were insufficiently guarded they would be caught and, if not, they could be charged with contravention of the edict; if they permitted La Rochelle to be taken, they would be lost, and if they rose to defend it they would be rebels. Thus it was determined to send forces to besiege the town.[3] This decision, probably taken in the first half of August, was altered by the twentieth on account of the preparation of protestant forces in Poitou and Provence and the readiness of William of Orange at Cologne with 15,000 foot and 5,000 horse who, it was feared, might enter Burgundy and join the prince de Condé.[4]

Thus Lorraine fixed upon 25 August, 'ou ... on congnoistroit les choses estre bien disposees en Bourgoigne pour faire ladicte execution'.[5] Lorraine could not afford to wait any longer since there can be little doubt that his policy of violent persecution, and open hostility to the huguenot leaders in time of 'peace', had forced them to prepare for the renewal of war for which there is a great deal of evidence,[6] troop movements being impossible to conceal. The Spanish ambassador in England, Guzmán de Silva, reported to Philip II the arrival on 17 July of a ciphered letter from Condé to Sir Nicholas Throckmorton, erstwhile ambassador in France, of which he claimed to have a copy. The letter, he said, complained of the non-implementation of the treaty for which Condé blamed only the king's ministers, and confided his

[1] PRO/SP 70/105. It is interesting that Norris sent almost all this information to the queen using in places virtually identical wording. *CSPF.*, *1566-8*, pp. 537-9, 2 September 1568, Norris to Elizabeth.

[2] *CSPF.*, *1566-8*, p. 78, 1 June 1566, reception of the pope's nuncio.

[3] PRO/SP 70/105; *CSPF.*, *1566-8*, pp. 537-9, 2 September 1568, Norris to Elizabeth.   [4] *CSPF.*, *1566-8*, p. 526, 20 August 1568, Norris to Leicester.

[5] PRO/SP 70/105.

[6] There is, altogether, a great deal of detailed evidence relating to the origins and outbreak of the third civil war which cannot be analysed or even indicated here.

intention, for these reasons, of taking up arms on 21 July.[1] Norris stated categorically that Lorraine intended to murder the nobility 'so that they will shortly be forced either to yield up their lives or fly to arms'. For whatever combination of reasons however – and William of Orange was delayed in Cologne and had not yet crossed the Netherlands frontier – Condé was still at Noyers when Lorraine prepared to swoop upon him and Coligny. Personally involved in this enterprise were d'Antragues governor of Orléans who was to divert troops going to Orléans; the comte de Retz who had 'douze Italiens en main qui se vantent de faire merveilles,' the seigneur de Rochefort, and des Croissettes'.[2]

More we do not know, except that Condé reported from an intercepted letter that certain seigneurs claimed to have orders to kill the huguenots, and he had learned of a catholic *confrérie* which was arming and inciting the gentry to fall upon the huguenots when plans were ready.[3] Condé and his colleagues received many warnings of troops assembling to seize them, which is why they suddenly fled towards La Rochelle not, at that moment in arms, but with their families on 23 August, just as William of Orange was expected to enter the Netherlands from Cleves, where he had held his general muster.[4] This departure, upon the eve of William's invasion of the Netherlands, effectively placed the onus of the third civil war, which both the crown and the protestants – not least for financial reasons – would gladly have averted, upon Lorraine, for whom the failure of his *coup* left no alternative.

Thus, however dissimilar in detail and domestic origin, the wars in France and the revolt of the Netherlands became, internationally, two aspects of the same struggle. This fusion together

---

[1] *CSPSp.*, *1568–79*, p. 60, 19 July 1568, de Silva to Philip II; 62–3, 31 July 1568, de Silva to Philip II.

[2] PRO/SP 70/105.

[3] Archives de Chantilly, 1213, ff. 15–18, 12 July 1568, Condé to Charles IX; ff. 19–23, 27 July 1568, Condé to Charles IX; Papiers de Condé, *série* i, vol. ii, ff. 231-verso, 30 July 1568, Condé to Charles IX; *BSHPF.*, iv (1856), 329–31, 8 July 1568, d'Andelot to Catherine; *CSPF.*, *1566–8*, p. 498, 11 July 1568, associations made in the provinces; 516, 7 August 1568, Norris to Cecil; 534–5, 29 August 1568, Norris to Elizabeth.

[4] C. V. Wedgwood, *William the Silent*, 108.

with recent events in Scotland, and the presence of queen Mary in England, further intensified the already daunting complexity of Franco-Spanish relations. While the interests of the two crowns were still fundamentally inimical, in August 1568 they nevertheless found themselves to some extent in the same predicament. If Alva was necessarily afraid, both then and later, of a French incursion into the Netherlands, Charles promptly sent the seigneur de Lignerolles to intercede with Philip to prevent an invasion of France by William of Orange.[1] Neither welcomed an invasion of their territories by the other's subjects; nor did they want civil war at home. On the other hand, the co-operation of their dissident subjects could not suffice to unite them, except in outward appearances. Yet the apparent spectacle of French catholics – who held the crown in thrall – co-operating with Spain against the huguenots in France and the nobility – 'rebels and heretics' – in the Netherlands, looked sufficiently like a Franco-Spanish alliance not only to alert some of the German princes, but also to alarm Elizabeth who – among other measures – impounded the Spanish treasure ships in December 1568, just when Alva's ferocious Spanish troops were unpaid and Catherine was reduced to requesting 'help' against the huguenots' mercenaries for whom Condé was pressing England to provide a loan. But if Philip was positively eager to send such help to France, it was not in order to defend the crown, but to protect the Netherlands against the huguenots and support the extreme French catholics.

Philip's support of the French catholics had, until recently, been straightforward and mutually beneficial. But, in this respect also, new complexities had arisen, largely on account of England. After the death of François duc de Guise, a military hero, catholic leadership in France had devolved upon his hated brother Lorraine who, paradoxically, commanded more power and less support. Since the council of Trent, Lorraine represented Rome rather more than Madrid. This did not mean that he was in any

[1] Towards the end of November Orange was reported to be at Cateau-Cambrésis. B.N., Mss. fr. 5783, f. 11, Gassot, *Discours sommaire*; Gachard, *Notices et extraits*, i, 395, October 1568, Philip II to Alva.

way anti-Spanish. He was in clandestine contact with Granvelle, and with Alva to whom he instantly appealed at the time of 'Meaux'. Besides, there could be no such thing as a catholic league, whether formal or implicit, without Spain. But the Spanish had never trusted Lorraine[1] and, while Philip would gladly have seen him destroy the protestant faction in France, he could not, in 1568, unreservedly rejoice in his predominance, on account of his designs to restore England to catholicism by placing his niece Mary queen of Scots upon the throne. This, and the re-catholicising of England, was a resumption of old triumvirate and papal policy, but whose implementation had formerly been dependent upon Spain because the Guises were not in power at court in 1561 when these policies were formed. Besides, it had then been the Spanish heir Don Carlos, who died in July 1568, or, at worst, the archduke Charles of Austria, and not a prince of France who was proposed as Mary's suitor. While Philip still subscribed to the restoration of England to catholicism under Mary's rule, objectives which he categorically stated in instructions to Alva giving him personal discretionary authority to strike if he saw that the iron was hot,[2] he could not safely permit their accomplishment through the agency of France.

Thus, in its political aspects, the vast catholic movement which originated in France and received its impulse from the papacy, was supported by Spain in defence of the Netherlands, and extended to England in favour of Mary queen of Scots for whom the Elizabethan regime might be overturned, with internal catholic assistance, and the country thereby restored to Rome. This, it appears, had been projected in principle, even before the formation of the Triumvirate in 1561. As early as October 1560, the month of Condé's arrest and Navarre's detention at Orléans, Throckmorton wrote that his friend the Venetian ambassador confided his opinion that England's 'state stood now upon making and marring'. This was because the Guise-controlled French

---

[1] St Sulpice, for example, had reported that the Spanish suspected Lorraine's activities at Trent. Cabié, *Ambassade en Espagne de St Sulpice*, 95, 12 November 1562, St Sulpice to Catherine.

[2] *CSPSp.*, *1568–79*, pp. 109–10, 18 February 1569, Philip II to Alva.

government was preparing forces, in co-operation with Spain –
about which Throckmorton supplied military details – 'to pacify
or utterly suppress all schisms, heresy and rebellion in this country
[France]. This done, and the parties for religion clean overthrown,
these Princes have already accorded to convert their powers
towards England . . .'[1] It was to this project, thwarted in December 1560 by the death of Francis II and the Guises' loss of control,
that Spain and the extremists were always striving to return. So
far as England was concerned, the process was considerably
delayed by these events in France, the civil war and the disruption
of the catholic faction whose laborious reconstruction had to await
the return of Lorraine from Trent in 1564. England therefore
gained eight years of comparative immunity until – coinciding
with the Marian crisis – the offensive began in 1568 with the
'practising' of Lorraine to dispose of Elizabeth in civil commotion
and bring Mary to France, and the rather vaguely planned
invasion of England which, it was projected, Alva should
command, after having settled the revolt in Flanders.[2] This is not
surprising, since the plan corresponded fairly closely to his own
advice to Philip II in 1559, to bring Elizabeth to tolerate the
catholics and, with a large force, to establish 'such government as
seemed suitable'. The difference was that he had not then envisaged the simultaneous problems of the revolt of the Netherlands or those which arose from Elizabeth's seizure in December
1568 of the Spanish treasure, which was not a single incident but
an expanding episode with crippling economic consequences,
including a stoppage of vital commerce. This diverted Spanish
attention from queen Mary and religion because Philip actually
feared a 'general collapse of credit and property' and the consequent impossibility of raising a single *real* with which to meet
his commitments.[3]

At this – quite sufficiently advanced – point, therefore, long-
term plans were superseded by events. This was partly because

[1] *CSPF.*, *1560–1*, p. 345, 10 October 1560, Throckmorton to Elizabeth.

[2] *CSPF.*, *1566–8*, pp. 541–2, 6 September 1568, Norris to Cecil.

[3] *CSPSp.*, *1568–79*, p. 149, 10 May 1569, Alva to Philip II; 150, 15 May 1569,
Philip II to Alva.

of the civil war in France, partly because Alva himself steadily opposed what would, in the unfolding circumstances, have been crass military folly, and also because the revolt of the Netherlands was, with nicely calculated assistance, to assume sufficient proportions to preserve the crowns of England and France from the grand design of the papacy, by absorbing the attention and resources of Spain just when the Turks were ceasing to perform this service. Failing the direct invasion of England, however, the process was more covertly and less surely pursued through papal and Spanish agents in touch with catholics and dissident English noblemen and, with Mary in England, the danger was treated by Cecil, Walsingham, Norris and Throckmorton with the deadly gravity it merited. They were necessarily alert, since some rebellion had been expected as early as 1565 'by reason of the dissension which exists with regard to the state of the kingdom'.[1] The following summer Guzmán de Silva had reported at least twice that a rebellion was expected. Northumberland and 'other catholics' excused themselves from attending parliament, which de Silva thought ill advised 'if they have any object they wish to carry'.[2] There was therefore already a smouldering fire, waiting to be fanned into naked flames, whether by Lorraine, de Spes or Ridolphi, and which the last session of parliament (30 September 1566 to 2 January 1567) had done nothing to dampen down, since it aroused the queen's extreme and articulate displeasure against many of the lords.

There was, however, some confusion of purpose, since ambition and cupidity were sharper spurs than piety.[3] The ignoble lords, Norfolk and Arundel, who corresponded in cipher with

[1] *CSPSp.*, *1558–67*, p. 445, 2 July 1565, de Silva to Philip II. The reference appears to be primarily to the problems of the succession, religion and the enmities of the nobility.

[2] *CSPSp.*, *1558–67*, p. 574, 23 August 1566; 581, 21 September 1566, both from de Silva to Philip II. Northumberland changed his mind and attended parliament.

[3] De Spes referred several times to the lords' desire for profit, and Alva sent 6,000 crowns to entertain Norfolk, Arundel and Lumley. *CSPSp.*, *1568–79*, p. 157, 31 May/1 June 1569, summary of two letters from de Spes to Philip II and Alva; 168, 20 June 1569, Alva to Philip II.

de Spes through the agency of Ridolphi, who revived his scheme of 1568,[1] were probably more interested in opposing the power of Cecil – an intolerably successful social upstart, who dominated the council – than in the catholic cause of Mary Stuart, a relatively new element which greatly complicated their own more personal aspirations. According to de Spes, Leicester prevented Norfolk, Arundel and others from achieving the arrest of Cecil no less than three times in the spring of 1569.[2] Unless by 'arrest' they meant waylay, it is not clear how this could be done. On at least one occasion de Spes reported them to have claimed that they hoped to 'turn out the present accursed Government,' of which Cecil was the strength, 'and raise another Catholic one, *bringing the Queen to consent thereto*'.[3] Whether 'vicount Montagu's brother-in-law' (lord Dacre) who made de Spes some unspecified offer, or the 'northern' earl of Northumberland who waited upon him in disguise at 4 o'clock in the morning to declare his devotion to Philip II, were differently motivated, it is hard to tell.[4] It rather appears that they all wanted money,[5] and Philip himself cautioned de Spes against negotiating with such people.[6] Alva, for his part, strongly suspected that Ridolphi was

[1] *CSP Rome, 1558–71*, pp. 302–5, 18 April 1569 [Ridolphi] to the pope. Ridolphi, de Spes and the English lords claimed to see an opportunity of raising the country in the economic distress caused by the stoppage of trade with the Netherlands and Spain but, wise to this, the government worked hard to mitigate the distress. *CSPSp., 1568–79*, pp. 133–7, 12 March 1569, de Spes to Philip II.

[2] *CSPSp., 1568–79*, p. 146, 9 May 1569, de Spes to Philip II; 166, 15 June 1569, de Spes to Philip II.

[3] My italics. *CSPSp., 1568–79*, pp. 110–12, 29 February 1569, de Spes to Alva.

[4] *CSPSp., 1568–79*, p. 83, 6 November 1568, de Spes to Philip II; 96–7, 8 January 1569, de Spes to Philip II. This offer may have related to the idea, which lord Dacre promoted, of marrying Norfolk to Mary. Most of the lords involved were kinsmen and would – in theory at least – all have profited from this prestigious match.

[5] Norfolk and Arundel were 'constantly' importuning de Spes for money. *CSPSp., 1568–79*, pp. 144–9, 9 May 1569, de Spes to Philip II; 152, 23 May 1569, de Spes to Philip II.

[6] *CSPSp., 1568–79*, p. 143, 23 April 1569, de Spes to Philip II.

suborned to deceive de Spes, from whose despatches, he once told Philip, he would gather little light.[1] If the notoriously rich are not readily suborned, Alva was surely correct in his assessment of the general instability of his English supporters.[2] De Spes' suggestion of an effective blockade was much more realistic, were it not that the Spanish had sustained such disastrous naval losses.[3] Elizabeth's relative safety, therefore, lay in the motley incompatibility of her enemies – domestic and foreign – as well as in the superlative capacity of William Cecil who, as principal secretary of state, wielded a more direct and efficient kind of power than that of the turbulent and irresolute landed aristocracy who opposed him. Elizabethan England was saved by the channel and a strong, well-served monarch; otherwise, in spite of England's different social and political structure, these problems of religion, noble factions, control of the council, finance, and an insecure succession were comparable to those concurrently lacerating France and jeopardising her independence. A large part of the contemporary power of Spain, even stretched as she was beyond her capacities, lay in her relative exemption from these problems; her weakness lay in the Netherlands.

Ridolphi is said to have pensioned both the French and Spanish ambassadors who, he wrote in April 1569, 'had as good as disposed their Kings',[4] and to have transmitted considerable sums of papal money to support the rising of the northern earls later that year. Pius V, to whom it was a 'santa congiura', subsequently asserted that it had been instigated by the French ambassador to divert Elizabeth from assisting the huguenots. Clearly this was not more than one constituent element. Ridolphi was arrested in this

---

[1] *CSPSp.*, *1568–79*, p. 149, 10 May 1569, Alva to Philip II.

[2] *CSPSp.*, *1568–79*, pp, 132–3, 10 March 1569, Alva to Philip II.

[3] *CSPSp.*, *1568–79*, pp. 132–3, 10 March 1569, Alva to Philip II; 143–4, 28 April 1569, copy of a memorial to Philip II from merchants concerned with English affairs; 147, 9 May 1569, de Spes to Philip II.

[4] In the case of Spain, at least, this was not true. Philip II was very cautious and Alva was dead against a rupture with England and ordered de Spes not to meddle. *CSPSp.*, *1568–79*, p. 171, 2 July 1569, Alva to de Spes; 215–17, 11 December 1569, Alva to Philip II.

connection. Nothing was proven against him, but he must have
been carefully watched since Elizabeth and Cecil were suspicious
'even of the birds of the air'.¹ It is therefore not surprising that the
so-called Ridolphi plot was never very secret. Indeed Ridolphi,
as an English pensioner sometimes employed by Cecil as an
intermediary, was far too well-known (as well as indiscreet) for
his activities to be secret.²

The northern rising and Ridolphi plot were not two distinct
events, but successive stages of an evolving process which, from
1568, the problem of Mary had rendered as much a part of the
politico-religious struggle of the rest of Europe as the civil wars
in France and the revolt of the Netherlands, both of which also
had their separate, domestic origins. The earl of Leicester, who
was as close in the queen's councils as any man but Cecil, so
'greatly' feared that England, like France, would collapse into
civil war at the beginning of 1569 that he employed an Italian
engineer to fortify his castle at Kenilworth.³

---

¹ *CSP Rome, 1558–71*, p. 303, 18 April 1569 [Ridolphi] to the pope; Girolamo Catena, *Vita del gloriosissimo Papa Pio Quinto*, 74–8; Cecil Roth, 'Roberto
Ridolfi et la sua congiura', *Rivista Storica degli Archivi Toscani*, ii (1930), 120;
De Potter, *Lettres de Saint Pie V*, 133–5, 18 January 1571, the pope to Catherine
de Medici; *CSPSp.*, *1568–79*, p. 136, 12 March 1569, de Spes to Philip II.
² Ridolphi was also a French pensioner, presumably of Lorraine. *CSPSp.*,
1568–79, p. 163, 13 June 1569, Alva to Philip II.
³ *CSPSp.*, *1568–79*, p. 233, 30 January 1570, de Spes to Philip II. This could
also have had something to do with guarding Mary, but that did not invali-
date the fear.

V

Lorraine's War

WHEN TOGETHER with Coligny Condé evaded Lorraine's intended 'elimination' *coup* by leaving Noyers on 23 August 1568 – events which effectively precipitated the third civil war – he was careful to send his secretary, the seigneur de Marchois, to inform the king of his departure and his intentions, which were in no wise to rebel or levy war against the crown.[1] Shortly after, he prepared a further declaration[2] against the 'murders massacres, assassinations, oppressions and violences' which he and his followers had suffered, and pointed out that his journey, virtually unarmed, with three families – women and children – and only 150 persons in all, could not be represented as a rising.[3] Coligny also wrote to Catherine denying that he wished to make war, but complaining bitterly of Lorraine.[4] Their theoretical and moral position, however, made little practical difference; civil war, which they expected, was bound to follow the failure of Lorraine's *coup* and the flight of the leaders whose only hope of safety lay in arms.

Condé, who had several times sent to the royal commanders to inform them of what he was doing, meant to go to the house of his brother-in-law, La Rochefoucauld, but he also had had to flee, from the sieur de Ruffec, to the relative safety of La Rochelle.

[1] B.N., Mss. Cinq Cents Colbert, 24, f. 178, 22 August 1568, Condé to Charles IX. Printed by Aumale, *Histoire des princes de Condé*, ii, 357–8.

[2] Cecil Papers, iv, ff. 31–4, declaration of the prince de Condé of the cause and manner of his departure from Noyers, 23 August [1568]; Archives de Chantilly, papiers de Condé, *série* i, vol. ii, ff. 168–78.

[3] According to Norris, Condé crossed the Loire with 500 horse and six companies of footmen. They may have joined him en route, but it makes little difference. *CSPF., 1566–8*, p. 534, 29 August 1568, Norris to Elizabeth.

[4] Delaborde, *Coligny*, iii, 43–6.

Condé's cousin, the vidame de Chartres, together with the comte de Montgommery and François de La Noue managed to elude Martigues, the guisard *gouverneur* of Brittany, and just escaped across the Loire with 2,000 men.[1] There does not appear to have been any attempt to catch d'Andelot, who was in Brittany, until he assembled forces and other seigneurs at Beaufort in mid-September, but Jeanne d'Albret said that he was to have been taken.[2] Jeanne herself claimed that the sieur de Losses was sent to capture her and her son Henry, but was taken ill, which gave her time. So, late in August, she went to Nérac and, eluding Monluc, no small achievement, escaped across the Dordogne and joined Condé at Cognac on 24 September.[3]

Finally, Coligny's brother, Châtillon, also made a precipitate departure at three hours' notice, having been warned of his danger by some of those detailed to arrest him. From Sénarpont on 5 September 1568 he wrote to the king explaining that he was obliged to leave since his enemies had 'le glaive de la puissance en la main'.[4] Indeed, the pope had long sought to capture the renegade cardinal, 'condemned of schism, and dead towards the law'.[5] This married, protestant, excommunicate, cardinal bishop arrived in England about 8 September where, having previously transmitted information about the conspiracy against queen Elizabeth, he was well received, provided with £100 a month – twelve times the salary of a secretary of state – and given the use of Ham House. He remained, to play an important role as the protestants' ambassador to the queen, the last thing the catholics desired, and was never again to reside in France.[6]

---

[1] Marlet, *Montgommery*, 69; L. de Bastard d'Estang, *Vie de Jean de Ferrières*, 99–100; Amirault, *La Vie de François de La Noue*, 19–22.

[2] De Ruble, *Mémoires et poésies de Jeanne d'Albret*, p. ix. This would be borne out by the fact that a price was later placed on his head.

[3] Roelker, *Queen of Navarre*, 299–301.

[4] B.N., Mss. Cinq Cents Colbert, 24, f. 182, 5 September 1568, Châtillon to Charles IX. Printed by Marlet, *Correspondance d'Odet de Coligny, cardinal de Châtillon*, 89–90.

[5] *CSPF., 1566–8*, p. 402, 23 January 1568, Norris to Elizabeth.

[6] Atkinson, *The Cardinal of Châtillon in England*, 15, 8 September 1568, Châtillon to Elizabeth (Dover); 20, 14 September 1568, Châtillon to Charles IX;

Châtillon described the background to these events since the peace of Longjumeau in a long 'discourse' to William Cecil. This is the most comprehensive account we have of the protestants' complaints of the catholic rejection of the edict including, among other things, its non-publication in certain places, the exclusion of protestants from offices, the obstruction of justice, the destruction of forty-seven churches, numerous specific murders, the death of 4,300 protestants – all of them unpunished – as well as protestant massacres at Meaux and Amiens.[1] Indeed, all the protestant statements, complaints, declarations and apologies conform, and correspond very closely to Lorraine's intentions as recorded by La Forest. In England, William Cecil, writing to Sir Henry Sidney on 12 September also echoed that 'the only rancour and humour of all the mischief [proceeded] from the red hat of Lorraine',[2] and Bernadin Bochetel, bishop of Rennes, brother of the French ambassador, La Forest, who was sent to England a week or two later, there confessed to an intermediary of Walsingham that the whole government of France was in his hands.[3]

This, no doubt, was why Condé's envoy was arrested on 30 August – curious treatment of a prince – and he received no answer to his letter of 22 August. Orders were immediately despatched for the raising of royal forces 'to obtain,' in Condé's eyes, 'by open war against him, what the conspiracy had failed to achieve'.[4]

Catherine, for her part, immediately reacted as she always did, by seeking to negotiate and, on or before 29 August, sent to the prince to 'stay at some place where she may come and confer with him', which some interpreted as a trap, so that Tavannes,

---

CSPSp., *1568–79*, pp. 71–2, 18 September 1568, de Spes to Philip II; 75–7, 9 October 1568, de Spes to Philip II.

[1] Châtillon's *discourse*, 27 September 1568, endorsed by Cecil, printed by Atkinson, *The Cardinal of Châtillon in England*, 93 seq.

[2] Atkinson, *The Cardinal of Châtillon in England*, 18, 12 September 1568, Cecil to Sir Henry Sidney.

[3] *CSPF.*, *1566–8*, p. 553, 24 September 1568, Walsingham to Cecil.

[4] Cecil Papers, iv, ff. 31–4, declaration of the prince de Condé of the cause and manner of his departure from Noyers, 23 August [1568].

the catholic commander in Burgundy, might overtake them.¹
As an unequivocal catholic and lieutenant-general of the duc
d'Aumale in Burgundy, Tavannes has often passed as a guisard.
In fact he was a supporter of Catherine. There is some evidence
that he may have been instrumental in warning Condé of his
impending danger and, in August 1568, he expressed himself to
the king in strictly moderate language about the problem of the
protestants and their rights under the edict.² Tavannes was
promoted marshal in 1571 in recognition of his military services,
principally the battles of Jarnac and Montcontour for which
Anjou received the public acclaim, a distinction which would
hardly have been conferred on a guisard general at the moment
of their disgrace.

Catherine's initiative was immediately stifled by a proclamation
in the king's name, commanding a mobilisation of *gendarmerie* at
Orléans under Anjou, because, it declared, the chiefs of the new
religion had taken up arms. This amounted to a declaration of
war upon rebels.³ Three days later Catherine nevertheless told
Norris that she 'would have no wars', and that the king – who
was still very ill – would reconcile his nobility.⁴ According to an
agent of the cardinal Antoine de Créquy, Charles had recently
vexed the extremists by imploring Catherine 'presque a jointes
mains', to preserve peace and the edict, to avert the ruin of his
kingdom and the destruction of his people.⁵ In this report
Catherine is shown as tending to favour the extremists, which
probably represents her habitual prevarication in their presence,
on account of her pre-occupation with the Spanish danger. That
this was no insubstantial spectre was shortly borne out by the

¹ *CSPF., 1566–8*, p. 534, 29 August 1568, Norris to Elizabeth.
² B.N., Mss. fr. 15547, f. 282, 20 August 1568. Tavannes to Charles IX,
Dijon; printed by Gigon, *La Troisième guerre de religion*, 385–7. The whole
question of what happened in Burgundy is too big and complex to be included
here.
³ *CSPF., 1566–8*, p. 537, 1 September 1568, proclamation by Charles IX.
⁴ *CSPF., 1566–8*, pp. 541–2, 6 September 1568, Norris to Cecil.
⁵ *CSPF., 1566–8*, pp. 525–6, 9 August 1568, the agent of the cardinal de
Créquy to his master.

report of Jules Gassot (chief clerk of the secretary Alluye and later of Villeroy) that upon the entry of William of Orange into Picardy on 17 November 1568, 'il n'avoit tenu qu'au Roy que le duc d'Alve ne fust entré . . . avec toutes les forces du Roy Catholique'.[1] This was still his policy and advice the following summer, unless the catholics prevailed, which it was hoped they might, after the battle of Jarnac. 'Your Majesty,' he wrote to Philip II, 'should allow me to enter the field with all the forces I have, and as many more as I can get'. Then, having first settled France, 'we can . . . stipulate that your Majesty should be allowed a free hand in England and to marry the queen of Scotland to whomsoever you please'.[2]

That Catherine, and possibly also the king, opposed Lorraine's determination to make war is further supported by his thundering row in the council, on 19 September, with the loyal chancellor, de L'Hospital, who refused to seal orders for the alienation of church property to be used against the protestants and resisted the pope's demand for the revocation of the edict of Longjumeau. De L'Hospital, who maintained that this would lead to war and a German invasion, was saved by the intervention of Montmorency from physical assault at the hands of the apoplectically angry cardinal. But his extremist support in the council was nevertheless sufficient to carry the revocation of the edict, the catholics' long-avowed intention, and its replacement on 28 September by that of Saint-Maur. Consequently de L'Hospital wasted no time in withdrawing to his property at Vignay, where the secretary Brulart went to request his surrender of the seals on 7 October, the day after Anjou had taken the field.[3]

The edict of Saint-Maur, a remarkable document, may be regarded as Lorraine's justification and apology. It chiefly consists of a long, partisan preamble rehearsing, from the extreme

---

[1] B.N., Mss. fr. 5783, f. 22; La Ferrière, 'La Troisième guerre civile et la paix de Saint-Germain, 1568–70', *Revue des questions historiques*, xli (1887), 85.

[2] *CSPSp.*, *1568–79*, p. 159, 1 June 1569, Alva to Philip II.

[3] Baguenauld de Puchesse, *Jean de Morvillier*, 209; Fontanon, *Édits et ordonnances*, iv, 292–4. Other edicts followed depriving protestants of all state, judicial and financial offices. *CSPF.*, *1566–8*, p. 583, 14 and 16 December 1568.

catholic point of view, all the troubles in France since the death of Henry II, while the edict proper, which follows, was very simple. It revoked that of Longjumeau by means of the prohibition of all but the catholic religion, and ordered the expulsion of all protestant ministers within two weeks; precisely what Monluc had proposed before Bayonne. These things, which Catherine could neither have done nor willingly permitted, proclaim the height of Lorraine's power and his ultimate triumph over the council. Norris drew a nice distinction in this respect when, in a letter to Cecil, he referred not to the crown, the king or to Catherine, but to 'the leaders of this Court'.[1] Catherine's resistance, and dissociation from Lorraine is sufficiently illustrated by his disgrace in 1570, when the return of peace, which he again opposed, restored to her some freedom of action. Upon the very date of its registration, 11 August, Norris wrote to Elizabeth: 'her [Catherine's] cruel enemy the Cardinal of Lorraine is not admitted to the Council'.[2]

The revocation of the edict, though symbolically oppressive, made little practical difference at the end of September since the protestants had been making preparations all the month, and had wasted no time in appealing to England where they were well represented by Châtillon, and Condé's envoy Arnold de Cavaignes, who was thoroughly instructed and sufficiently authorised to negotiate a loan and other help, which he did.[3] Elizabeth, for her part, was sufficiently persuaded of the danger to England to show her hand with uncharacteristic speed and clarity. Thus, without any delay, she required Norris to declare

[1] *CSPF.*, *1566–8*, p. 533, 27 August 1568, Norris to Cecil.
[2] *CSPF.*, *1569–71*, p. 314, 11 August 1570, Norris to Elizabeth.
[3] By January 1569 there were said to be 6,000 English troops in Brittany. *CSPDom.*, *1547–80*, p. 318, September 1568, memoir of Cecil; *CSPF.*, *1566–8*, p. 544, 9 September 1568, Norris to Cecil; 562, 5 October 1568, Throckmorton to Pembroke, Leicester and Cecil; 573, 6 November 1568, munitions for Condé; *CSPF.*, *1569–71*, p. 19, 22 January 1569, occurrents in France; *CSPSp.*, *1568–1579*, pp. 72–5, 24 September 1568, de Spes to Philip II; 75–7, 9 October 1568, de Spes to Philip II; 78–80, 23 October 1568, de Spes to Philip II; 82–3, 6 November 1568, de Spes to Philip II; *HMC Hatfield*, xiii, 89, 6 November 1568.

to the king and council that she had taken no part in the last troubles, but that if she interfered now, it was on account of 'the duty due to her subjects, the friendship she has for the king, and the preservation of her own estate'.[1] Norris, who was requested to withdraw from the council, was 'credibly informed' that Lorraine forthwith 'praised God that the Queen of England had declared war for the religion,' – which was not precisely accurate – since she would thereby lose the favour of Philip II and the emperor who would be 'very glad to follow the enterprise against England, and for that the natural of the English is not willingly to suffer a prince stranger, *it would be meet to begin the war by some of their own nobility who have already means thereto, and the affairs troubled it would be easy to send forces into that country'*.[2] Only ten days before, Norris had reported as a 'certain agreement' that, if Alva were successful in the Netherlands, he would 'forthwith invade England'. If, in fact, there was nothing certain about it, it was still essential that neither he should be suffered to succeed in the Netherlands, nor the cardinal of Lorraine in France. The inevitable corollary therefore, was to support the huguenots and William of Orange which, while avoiding war with France or Spain, presented problems.

Elizabeth's declaration was immediately answered by the despatch to England of Bernadin Bochetel, bishop of Rennes, who was initially received by an intermediary of Walsingham, which was not flattering.[3] The agent elicited that Rennes would seek to persuade the queen of the faithful observation of the edict in France and that Condé had no cause to take up arms. Elizabeth, however, was already aware – as she stated in her reply to Rennes – that 'sundry bands and forces [had] gathered in sundry corners of the realm, reported to have been collected to have

---

[1] *CSPF., 1566–8*, p. 545 [10 September] 1568, message delivered by Sir Henry Norris to the French king.

[2] *CSPF., 1566–8*, p. 548, 15 September 1568, Norris to Elizabeth.

[3] *CSPF., 1566–8*, p. 548, 15 September 1568, Norris to Elizabeth; *CSPSp., 1568–79*, pp. 72–5, 24 September 1568, de Spes to Philip II. Rennes arrived on 21 September. His mission may also have had something to do with the first trial of Mary queen of Scots.

destroyed divers of the principals of the religion reformed'.[1] Rennes would also seek to discredit Châtillon (whose escape was a catholic disaster), and dispel the influence of those that 'went about to breed suspicion in the Queen of England of some evil attempt meant against her by the French King'. Walsingham's friend replied that Elizabeth harboured no suspicions of the French king, having 'sure advertisement that the practice should come from the Pope and the Cardinal of Lorraine', and by 'contrarying him in heat,' caused Rennes to divulge that 'all men who seemed to be, were not contented, which one day would break forth'; also that the queen of Scots did not lack friends to redress her wrongs'.[2]

Officially Rennes had charge to declare 'how strange and full of ambiguity' Norris' speech had been, and to administer an insolent admonition against favouring disobedient subjects, whose disease was very contagious.[3] To spread this contagion was, evidently, part of Rennes' purpose. About the time of his departure, Norris had sent word that one in his company had letters to the queen of Scots and 'other papists' there – meaning England – 'of whose delivery [Mary] it is very necessary to take heed'.[4] After Rennes' return in October, it was also said that in reality he had gone 'to practise with some there' and promised 12,000 crowns 'either to destroy this queen [Elizabeth]' or 'to raise up some sedition' about the end of October. This, according to one informant, was equally directed against the life of the earl of Murray, protestant regent of Scotland.[5] The report, however, is not substantiated.

Basically Elizabeth's position was simple, as she later explained to de Spes: she had never declared herself against the king and queen of France, but the house of Guise 'which now ruled', were her enemies, while the Châtillons were her friends.[6] In this

---

[1] *CSPF.*, *1566–8*, p. 558, 30 September 1568, the queen's answer to the bishop of Rennes.

[2] *CSPF.*, *1566–8*, pp. 552–3, 24 September 1568, Walsingham to Cecil.

[3] *CSPF.*, *1566–8*, p. 555, 28 September 1568, the bishop of Rennes' embassy.

[4] *CSPF.*, *1566–8*, p. 550, 18 September 1568, Norris to Cecil.

[5] *CSPF.*, *1566–8*, p. 567, 22 October 1568, Norris to Cecil.

[6] *CSPSp.*, *1568–79*, pp. 88–90, 18 December 1568, de Spes to Philip II.

respect she had a good deal in common with the French crown, which was reflected in their relatively cordial relations after the civil war in which she had sustained the huguenots. Her point of view was made abundantly clear to Charles and Catherine[1] who themselves entered the third civil war divided from Lorraine, and more subtly from Anjou, heir to the throne and, as lieutenant-general, the commander-in-chief. Lorraine and Anjou were themselves divided from three of the four marshals, Montmorency, his brother Damville, and Vieilleville who refused to serve, and from the moderate Gontaut de Biron, colonel-general of the infantry. Even within their own ranks, Aumale and his step-father Nemours were militarily paralysed by mutual jealousy.[2]

When hostilities began in October, it can hardly be doubted that Lorraine did not relinquish his plans against England and may even have intended simultaneous war in England and France, in which religion, and the crowns of England, Scotland, and conceivably also France itself, were at stake. Great as Lorraine's catholic achievements were, this was altogether more than he could hope to direct and control, especially without adequate military leadership, and events proved considerably less impressive; the imprisonment of Mary in England, the abortive northern rising and the rather unsuccessful third civil war in France. Yet, apart from the excellence of his opponents' intelligence, the unscheduled complication which scrambled his grand design, was the revolt of the Netherlands. Whether or not that of the Moriscos in southern Spain, which pre-occupied Philip for two years from December 1568, was to be accounted an advantage or a hindrance, is doubtful. But, if Philip II had gone to the Netherlands, as had been projected in 1567 and the spring of 1568, there is no doubt that Spain would clearly have superseded France, and dominated Europe.[3]

[1] Norris categorically stated the position. *CSPF.*, *1566-8*, p. 566, 22 October 1568, Norris to Elizabeth.

[2] PRO/SP 70/105; B.N., Mss. fr. 17528, f. 69 verso, Villeroy's 'Estat des affaires'.

[3] *CSPSp.*, *1558-67*, p. 661, 21 July 1567, de Silva to Philip II; 680-1, 15 October 1567, Philip II to de Silva.

The recently enhanced solidarity between the Netherlands and the huguenots meant that civil war in France no longer more than partly served Philip's purpose; though he may have been relieved to see William of Orange occupied in France in the summer of 1569. It is true that civil war was still most effective in distorting and neutralising the independent policy of the French crown which, if undisturbed, consistently refused to employ extreme measures against the protestants, preferring peace, moderation and the edicts of limited toleration. Furthermore, if it no longer served to defend the Netherlands, whence he could ill afford to divert his resources to help the French catholics, it did – just – preclude, both an 'enterprise of England', which could have resulted in his loss of the catholic leadership of Europe, and any formal Anglo-French alliance. From the moment that civil war was only partially effective as an instrument of Spanish control in France, the 'elimination' of the huguenot leaders, long advocated by Alva, became the only propitious alternative.

For Lorraine also the situation might still have been radically improved if only he could capture the elusive leaders and, in September, before the outbreak of formal hostilities, Norris reported continued daily preparations 'for the surprise of the Prince and the Admiral, and others of the nobility'. But, failing their physical apprehension, they might still be felled by stealth, and Norris was told of no less than fifty Italians said to have received 1,000 crowns each to 'empoison wine, wells, and other victuals to the destruction of the Prince of Condé and the Admiral'. Doubtless they included those of de Retz, who had already promised marvels in Burgundy.[1] Thus, for multiple reasons, and by one means or another, it seems clear that the protestant leaders were not intended to survive the third civil war; Condé and d'Andelot did not.

There is some uncertainty about the circumstances of Condé's death, which occurred on the day of the battle of Jarnac, 13 March 1569, the first of two pitched battles and catholic victories.

---

[1] *CSPF., 1566-8*, p. 558, 30 September 1568, Norris to Cecil. These seem very large figures but rather suggest exaggeration than fabrication.

It is generally agreed that Condé was captured when his horse was killed and Desormeaux (following J. de Serres, Brantôme, Le Laboureur, de Thou and Mézeray) states that once his identity was known, he was shot by one Joseph Antoine de Montesquiou, a former *sénéchal* of Béarn, and the captain of Anjou's Swiss guard. Desormeaux further claims that Montesquiou and other favourites of Anjou had orders to kill Condé whenever opportunity occurred. It has also been denied that there is any evidence for the Montesquiou story. But S.-C. Gigon, demolishing his own point, says the assertion was made in a letter of 18 April [1569] – for which he gives no reference – from the princes and Coligny to the protestant princes of Germany, and there is no obvious reason why they should have invented this. The point is of some interest in so far as Montesquiou appears to have belonged to a branch of the Monluc family. An entry in the *State Papers Foreign* indicates that Condé was 'killed after he was taken by Martigues and others, who were expressly sent for that purpose by the duc d'Anjou, and so was his body mangled after he was dead'. This is the most plausible account, since it was Martigues, the guisard *gouverneur* of Brittany, who had begun preparations for an expedition against England – which now sustained Condé – and had, as part of Lorraine's *coup*, been assigned to catch the vidame de Chartres, Montgommery, La Noue and possibly also d'Andelot, though this is not clear. It is quite likely that Montesquiou was among 'the others' mentioned, and could well have fired the shot. Villeroy, in his discreet 'Estat des affaires', only said that Condé was murdered, shot in the back of the head and his body disrespectfully removed upon a she ass.[1]

Condé's elimination potentially altered the civil war situation by depriving the protestants of their prince. The war, which

---

[1] B.N., Mss. fr. 17528, ff. 77 verso, 20 March 1569; *CSPF.*, *1569–71*, p. 45, 13 March 1569, the battle of Jarnac; Desormeaux, *Histoire de la maison de Bourbon*, iv, 340–2; Gigon, *La Troisième guerre civile*, 370–2; Whitehead, *Gaspard de Coligny*, 206, note 3 gives the different versions and sources. In February 1567 Montgommery, whose wife was English, asked permission to bring his family to England to secure them from Martigues. *CSPSp.*, *1558–67*, p. 619, 17 February 1567, de Silva to Philip II.

Catherine had never wanted, was increasingly difficult to sustain on account of the indigence of the crown and the divisions of the high command, and it appears that an effort was made in March 1569 to end hostilities by splintering the protestant party. The court was isolated at Metz where Catherine lay seriously ill from February to April. Soon after the news of Jarnac was received – a week later – at 11 p.m. on 20 March, an edict was issued against Coligny.[1] It is not clear whether this was an 'arrêt de mort', or whether it merely relieved him of his office of admiral, which was conferred upon the marquis de Villars, while the duc de Longueville, Condé's father-in-law, but also a kinsman of the Guises, received the prince's *gouvernement* of Picardy. About 26 March the secretary Alluye was despatched from court to Anjou to congratulate him upon his victory, and to convey an edict of amnesty to all those who had served Condé if they returned home after swearing never again to bear arms against the king. Furthermore, Alluye was to extend to Condé's widow a warm invitation to court, by which means, it was hoped, her son Henry, would be removed from Coligny's influence.[2] This was the beginning of another aspect of the massacre story, the struggle to obtain control of the next generation of princes, Henri prince de Condé and Henry King of Navarre.

Before any news of Alluye's mission can have reached the court – especially as he went home and died – Alava, the Spanish ambassador, sent Philip II a remarkable report on 7 April of an audience with the queen.[3] Alava expressed dissatisfaction with the military failure to follow up the victory of Jarnac, which could have been a reference to the proffered amnesty. Catherine, he said, was afraid for Anjou. Whether this meant that he might die in battle, at the hands of an assassin in revenge for Condé, or that Charles was jealous of his mounting reputation, or whether it was an extemporaneous excuse one cannot tell. Alava went on to say

---

[1] B.N., Mss. fr. 17528, ff. 75–6, 20 March 1569, Villeroy's 'Estat des affaires'; Boulé, *Catherine de Médicis et Coligny*, 51, dates the edict 19 March.

[2] B.N., Mss. fr. 17528, f. 77 verso, Villeroy's 'Estat des affaires'; Mss. Italien, 1727, f. 14 verso, 30 March 1569.

[3] Printed by P. de Vaissière, *De Quelques assassins*, 97–9.

that Catherine enquired what more she could do. He replied, 'qu'on sonne donc le glas,' [sound the death knell] à l'amiral, d'Andelot et La Rochefoucauld' – in other words continue the process of elimination. This was pure papal, as well as Spanish policy. Pius V, who received from Anjou the banners of Jarnac, immediately wrote to Charles praising God for the death of Condé, and urging him to proceed with the destruction of the remaining enemies, 'pour arracher entièrement toutes les racines . . . Car à moins de les avoir radicalement extirpées, on les verra repousser de nouveau'. He must therefore eschew 'aucun respect humain en faveur des personnes ou des choses'.[1]

Besides 'elimination', Alava also pressed that some effort be made to detach from the huguenots the duchess of Vendôme – as the Spanish contemptuously styled Jeanne d'Albret, Queen of Navarre. As a sovereign princess she had rank; perhaps even more important, her son Henry of Navarre had become, after the royal brothers, first prince of the blood and, at fifteen and a half, his possession was becoming crucial – as that of his father had been. Alava reports Catherine to have replied that not three days before, she had promised 50,000 *écus* for the death of the admiral, and 20–30,000 for the two others – d'Andelot and La Rochefoucauld – adding that for seven years 'nous étions résolus à en venir là, et certains nous en empechèrent'. This is interesting since it was precisely seven years before, in March 1562, that Coligny first complained of an assault upon his life and, according to the protestant Soubise, it was Catherine herself who had prevented this. Alava went on to claim that Catherine even said, 'qui charger du coup?' whereupon he proposed the violent Monluc – for 100,000 *écus*, twice the market price. Monluc was one of those reported by Alva at the time of Bayonne to be in favour of the policy of elimination, and was notorious for his murderous suppression of Guyenne.

This despatch raises several problems. In the first place it is unclear whether the sum of 50,000 *écus* for Coligny's death,

---

[1] De Potter, *Lettres de St Pie V*, 36–8, 28 March 1569, the pope to Charles IX; 62, 26 April 1569, the pope to Anjou.

mentioned by Alava, was contained in the *arrêt* of March, or whether it was secretly offered in March or April before being publicly proclaimed in September, Coligny having survived.[1] Furthermore, the despatch appears to be the only evidence that a price was ever offered for La Rochefoucauld and d'Andelot.

D'Andelot died at Saintes a month later on 7 May 1569, according to the Venetian ambassador, of a fever, when he should have gone to meet the German mercenaries commanded by the duc des Deux-Ponts.[2] 'Advices from France', dated 10 May and received in England, reported that appearances suggested poison; fever and poison are not mutually exclusive, and the Venetian ambassador would not have been the first to shout murder. The Spanish ambassador also heard from the English court that d'Andelot had been poisoned, it was said by a Florentine – one of *the* Italians? – who sought a reward from the King of France. According to the report, Coligny and La Rochefoucauld were also to have died, but survived an illness.[3] The idea was certainly put about, since Norris reported to Cecil on 27 May 'here is a great bruit arisen, by means of an Italian who has vaunted that he has empoisoned M. d'Andelot and boasted that he made the Admiral and him drink both of one cup'. 'Long ago,' Norris added, 'I gave you to understand . . . that some Italians were sent abroad well waged to work the like enterprises'.[4] In mid-June, however, he reported that Alençon – in Paris – had received letters from the king that the admiral had caused to be 'drawn asunder' at Saintes a gentleman from Anjou's camp who, 'under pretence of service, being entertained by d'Andelot, poisoned him, suborned hereunto by M. Martigues'. If d'Andelot

[1] Delaborde, *Coligny*, iii, 148 mentions two *arrêts* of 19 and 23 March 1569 against cardinal Châtillon, but none against Coligny. As Coligny was frequently referred to as Châtillon, it seems likely that this is an error. *CSPF.*, *1569–71*, p. 102, 27 July 1569, Norris to Cecil. Norris said the *parlement* of Paris was minded to publish the admiral's 'attainder'.

[2] *CSPF.*, *1569–71*, p. 70, 10 May 1569; B.N., Mss. Italien, 1727, f. 31, 20 May 1569; Desjardins, *Negs. Tosc.*, iii, 589–90, 9 June 1569.

[3] Kervyn de Lettenhove, *Relations*, v, 396, 1 June 1569, de Spes to Alva.

[4] *CSPF.*, *1566–8*, p. 558, 30 September 1568, Norris to Cecil; Ibid., *1569–71*, pp. 78–9, 27 May 1569, Norris to Cecil.

might perfectly well have died of a camp fever, it is interesting to note that Coligny was also very ill at the same time, and Châtillon is reported to have told the elector Palatine that his brother was poisoned. That Martigues should have contrived the death of both Condé and d'Andelot is inherently probable, beyond which one cannot go.[1]

Alava's despatch of 7 April 1569 also raises the problem of Catherine's attitude to the huguenot leaders, since he certainly shows her apparently acceding to extreme catholic policy, which happened, ostensibly, in each period of war. Her judicious replies to Alava are not, however, evidence that she supported his policy of elimination which, as the Spanish themselves were liable to complain, she had had ample opportunity to accomplish. In January 1568, during the second civil war, she had resolutely refused to surrender up cardinal Châtillon, then within her grasp, to cardinal Santa Croce, who demanded him in the name of the pope, in whose eyes he was an outlaw.[2] But she was bound to avoid the humiliation of openly admitting to Alava that the crown was constrained to perform, or submit to, the will of Lorraine – from whom at least her own political divorce is clearly established. Having been gravely ill for a good two months, she herself is unlikely to have played any effective part in recent affairs at all. To aggravate the Spanish was potentially dangerous when Orange was no longer engaging Alva in the Netherlands, and her reply had also to be fit for repetition to Philip II since he could assist or impede the proposed marriage of Charles IX – dynastically imperative – to a daughter of the emperor. Catherine's steadfast consistency, indeed her astounding pertinacity in the pursuit of peace and reconciliation have never been queried, and the death of the protestant leaders could only have left her even more disastrously in the power of Lorraine, who was not above threatening the crown. There is therefore no reason to suppose that her temporising answers to the detested Spanish ambassador – upon whose recall she later insisted – represented

[1] *CSPF., 1569–71*, p. 88, 14 June 1569, Norris to Cecil; Atkinson, *The Cardinal of Châtillon in England*, 86.

[2] *CSPF., 1566–8*, p. 402, 23 January 1568, Norris to Elizabeth.

any change of policy on her part, but rather a calculated statement of what Lorraine, 'who now rules both King and subjects', had most recently done in the name of Charles. In fact it will be seen that what she really had in mind were the English and Bourbon marriages, Anjou to queen Elizabeth, and Marguerite to Navarre.[1]

With or without this price already on is head, Coligny was present at the siege of Poitiers from June to September 1569, and on 18 July Norris reported to Cecil from Orléans that a captain Hays, an 'Almain' was despatched hence – he does not say when – 'to seek by empoisoning to destroy the Admiral, and has the same entertainment that others aforetime had for the like'.[2] This is rather a positive statement and, if he was referring to the 'well waged' Italians, rumoured to have poisoned d'Andelot when Coligny also was very ill, then one is bound to consider carefully whether d'Andelot's 'camp fever' was not assisted.

Writing not long after, on 8 August, to Philip II,[3] Alava said that his secretary had omitted to report his last audience in which he told Charles and Catherine that he had in his house a well-informed German who had arrived from the admiral's camp. When he added that the German knew 'qu'on tramait la mort de l'Amiral', he claims to have been hustled into an empty room – he does not say who by – in which he was informed that 'good news' was momentarily expected. Enquiring if Germans were to accomplish this, he received no reply. It is not clear whether this corroborates Norris' report, or refers to something different.

There is, furthermore, an authenticated incident, which could be quite a separate matter, of a *valet de chambre* of Coligny, Dominique d'Albe, who was captured on his way to the duc des Deaux-Ponts by one of Anjou's captains of the guard, Hardouin de Villiers, seigneur de la Rivière-Puytaillé. Albe therefore showed his letters to Catherine, Anjou and Lorraine and – for a consideration – revealed what he knew of the German's plans –

[1] *CSPF.*, *1569–71*, p. 47, 15 March 1569, Norris to Cecil. See Chapter VI.
[2] *CSPF.*, *1569–71*, p. 96, 18 July 1569, Norris to Cecil.
[3] Printed by P. de Vaissière, *De Quelques assassins*, 100–1.

meaning the military plans of Zweibrücken, whom the French called Deux-Ponts and the English Bipont. La Rivière is then said to have suborned him to seek to poison Coligny, whom he rejoined at the siege of Poitiers. But Coligny, suspecting the length of his absence, arrested him, whereupon he confessed and was executed on 20 September 1569 at Faye-la-Vineuse.[1] This account – which is rather precise for a fabrication – is interesting in that, like the allegations relating to Condé, it points to the entourage of Anjou, who had supplied him with a passport dated 30 August 1569 from Plessis-les-Tours.[2] Coligny's suspicion of Albe is supported by the publication, a week before, on 13 September 1569 of an 'arrêt de mort' against him, placing a price of 50,000 *écus* upon his head – precisely the sum mentioned by Alava in April. Coligny, declared to be the principal author of rebellion, was condemned to the loss of rank, property and offices, and to be executed in the place de Grève in Paris or, in his absence, to be hanged in effigy. According to Delaborde, a further *arrêt* was issued on 28 September promising the reward to anyone who killed Coligny, whether French or foreign, together with a free pardon if he were guilty of other, like offences.[3] Pope Pius V, praising Charles for having this 'homme détestable et exécrable, si tant est quil doive être appelé homme,' condemned by 'une sentence équitable' of the *parlement*, went on to declare that, 'en persécutant l'ennemi le plus acharné de la religion catholique, vous aves honoré Dieu lui-même, à la face de tout l'univers catholique . . .' After a long, fulsome paean of praise, the pope added superfluously, 'Nous donnnerons volontiers . . .

[1] Delaborde, *Coligny*, iii, appendix 22, pp. 565–7, *jugement rendu contre Dominique d'Albe par un conseil de guerre, 20 septembre 1569.*

[2] Albe was paid and received a white powder which is said to have been subsequently analysed.

[3] B.N., Mss. fr. 5812, ff. 105–6, *arrest contre Admiral de Chastillon, 3 septembre 1569.* This is a seventeenth-century copy and the date is probably an error for 13; Mss. fr. 5549, ff. 57 bis, 13 September 1569, *arrest de la Cour de Parlement contre Colligny.* Delaborde, *Coligny*, iii, 145–7, *arrêt* of 13 September 1569. There were several reports that this edict was reissued in October and December, but they are not well attested.

à cette belle action, tout l'éclat qui lui est dû,' and urged Charles to continue the just war against the 'infâmes hérétiques'.[1] This was the spirit of the reformed papacy of Pius V – former inquisitor general of christendom, and canonised in 1712 – which then inflamed the politico-religious struggle in Europe. According to Castelnau, the same fate was proclaimed for the comte de Montgommery, and the vidame de Chartres who was in England and consequently stayed there.[2]

It is not clear whether the September 'arrêt de mort' against Coligny was a re-issue or something new, but he was again reported to be seriously ill after the second pitched battle of the war, Montcontour, on 3 October.[3] On 9 October Alava wrote to the duke of Alva that a man had come that day to the queen claiming to have murdered the seigneur de Mouy, Coligny's first lieutenant, one of the protestant captains who had served under William of Orange, retreated with him into France and been present at the siege of Poitiers. The man, Charles de Louviers, seigneur de Maurevert, further said, according to Alava, that he was one of those who had been at the admiral's camp 'pour y tuer les chefs par ordre du Roi'. The next day Norris similarly wrote to Cecil and Leicester that a soldier had informed the king that since the battle of Montcontour he had shot M. de Mouy. He further said that there was a 'complot' of six soldiers, 'everyone choosing his man of the chiefest of the Admiral's company to slay him.' According to de Vaissière, though this is not in the *Calendar of State Papers*, Maurevert added that it was he who had chosen to kill the admiral, but circumstances had prevented him. Norris concluded that 'nothing will more [endanger] the admiral's safety than the 50,000 crowns which the Parisians have decreed

---

[1] De Potter, *Lettres de Saint Pie V*, 74–6, 12 October 1569, the pope to Charles IX. Letters could take up to three weeks to reach Rome. This response was therefore immediate.

[2] Castelnau, *Mémoires*, 545; L. de Bastard d'Estang, *Vie de Jean de Ferrières*, 109–10.

[3] G. van Prinsterer, *Archives ou correspondance*, série i, vol. iii, 324.

[4] Printed by P. de Vaissière, *De Quelques assassins*, 102–3, 9 October 1569, Alava to Alva.

to him who shall murder him'.[1] By Parisians he meant, presumably, the *parlement*. These reports must be substantially correct since Charles immediately wrote from Tours to his brother Alençon in Paris requiring him to reward Maurevert with the 'collier' of the Order of Saint-Michel (so low had this erstwhile distinction fallen) and 'quelque honneste présent, selon ses mérites'. He is also said to have received an abbey *in commendam*, which points to the patronage of Lorraine.[2]

The last of the reports in this series, which again comes from Norris, is interesting in that attempts to obtain control of the young princes, Navarre and Condé having failed, they too became candidates for death and, in January 1570, three men were said to have been despatched from 'Cologne' (Coulonges) to seek, by all means, to destroy both them and the admiral.[3] The timing of this attempt is interesting in that it coincided pretty closely – whether by accident or design – with the murder on 23 January 1570 of the earl of Murray, protestant regent of Scotland. This, inevitably, was followed by a crisis in which Lorraine was striving to intervene, if he could only be free to do so. By this time the military failure of the civil war was becoming evident, and peace negotiations were already in hand. Yet, as well as the two young princes, Coligny in France and Châtillon in England, and other valiant lieutenants like La Rochefoucauld and Montgommery who were among those originally sought, had all survived.

[1] *CSPF., 1569–71*, p. 130, 10 October 1569, Norris to Leicester and Cecil; Jeanne d'Albret also declared the existence of such a plot, Ibid., 145, 24 November 1569, Jeanne d'Albret to Navarre and Condé.

[2] B.N., Mss. fr. 10191, f. 26, 10 October 1569, Charles to Alençon; printed by P. de Vaissière, *De Quelques assassins*, 112–13.

[3] *CSPF., 1569–71*, p. 174, 27 January 1570, Norris to Elizabeth. Coulonges-sur-l'Autize is north of Niort, Deux-Sèvres.

VI

The Treaty of Saint-Germain
August 1570

LORRAINE'S WAR, the only alternative to an invasion of the Netherlands and the immediate result of his failure to capture the protestant leaders, was a disaster, both for his purposes at home and abroad, and for his own career. It had been relatively easy to force the crown into war, but impossible to ensure its successful prosecution. In spite of his influence over Anjou, Lorraine, who was not a soldier, did not control the high command, nor could even he – skilled as he was – secure the necessary money. For the protestants, however, it was less disastrous than the hopeless 'peace', since they could only emerge – if at all – with better terms, affording some material security and realistic hope of enforcing another edict. This third war – bitter, ruinous and cruel – altered the nature of the struggle in France which had, hitherto, been relatively chivalrous and, never again until 1629, did the protestants fully submit to otherwise defenceless dependence upon the law.

If Lorraine's war ended by thwarting his domestic policy, it also precluded his enterprise of England – at a propitious time of turmoil and confusion, and while Philip II was still relatively pre-occupied with the Moriscos, the Turks, and the tortuous troubles over the impounded treasure, which received priority in Alva's English policy. This enterprise of England, projected in the summer of 1568 – when the huguenot leaders should have died – was nevertheless confirmed by Lorraine as part of his intentions at the outbreak of civil war in September. It therefore ensured that the third civil war was not only a huguenot struggle for survival, but also an English war against Lorraine and all that he represented and threatened. For this reason the war, and more important, the peace were profoundly affected by the affairs of England from which the fortunes of France were now inseparable.

The story of the peace of Saint-Germain dates from the beginning of the war, which Catherine initially attempted to extinguish, and illustrates the attitudes and policies of those concerned. The first peace move, after Catherine's *démarche*, came in January 1569 when it was proposed in council that Condé – who had been deprived of Picardy – should have the *gouvernement* of Saintonge, and leave to assist Orange in the Netherlands.[1] This proposal echoes the protestant position of August 1568, and reveals the idea of 'transference' as inherent in their thinking, their predicament and their commitments. It was inevitably rejected since no one at court wanted either to make or to risk war with Spain. The civil war therefore proceeded, while Catherine lay gravely ill at Metz and, to the satisfaction of the catholics, Anjou won the victory of Jarnac on 13 March, at which Condé was captured and murdered, a deed for which there was no word or gesture of admonition. It was after Jarnac that Alava put pressure on Catherine to follow up the victory, and urged the assassination of Coligny, d'Andelot and La Rochefoucauld, without which the death of Condé alone would be of small advantage. His principal contribution had been his rank, which was equally well supplied by that of his nephew Henry of Navarre, now first prince of the blood. Alava therefore also sought the detachment of his mother, Jeanne d'Albret. While Catherine answered him with misleading prevarications, her idea of detaching Jeanne was to propose the marriage of her daughter Marguerite to Henry of Navarre – the Bourbon marriage – which became the basis of her policy of peace and reconciliation.[2]

Alava's proposals in April 1569 were principally intended to enable Lorraine to proceed with the enterprise of England, for which there were naval preparations in Normandy under Martigues, an active promoter of the elimination policy.[3] Alava was fiercely supported by the pope who intended, when France

[1] CSPF., 1569–71, pp. 7–8, 10 January 1569, Norris to Cecil.
[2] CSPF., 1569–71, p. 83, 3 June 1569, Norris to Elizabeth; Delaborde, *Coligny*, iii, 171.   [3] CSPF., 1569–71, p. 81, 31 May 1569, Mundt to Cecil.

was settled in this butcherly fashion, to interdict England, 'giving
the same as a prey to M. d'Anjou'.[1] At the same time, however,
as receiving secret warning that the enterprise was actively in
hand, Norris also reported two visits from an intermediary,
La Mantra, renewing the English suit made by François duc de
Montmorency on behalf of Anjou.[2] As this could not possibly
have been done without the support of Catherine, if not also of
Charles himself, it is evidence that she and other moderates not
only rejected the extreme catholic policy towards the huguenots
but also, it would appear, the enterprise of England. This was a
policy in which Charles – if not Catherine, who never promoted
war – could, conceivably, have agreed with Lorraine, and the
English enterprise was arguably less dangerous than the protestant
proposal to transfer the war to the Netherlands.

Thus, while the catholic extremists hounded the protestant
leaders in preparation for the French enterprise of England, the
idea of peace was already in the air.[3] This was opposed by Spain
who, in spite of many reports of preparations for war, was
cautiously unenthusiastic about the enterprise, and greatly feared
a settlement in France. It was just at this time that Alva proposed
to simplify the issues by invading France – if things turned out
badly there – and think about England later.[4] Philip could hardly
have wanted Alva to leave the Netherlands, but he hastened to
send a grandee, the duke of Negeres, to France to obstruct both
peace and the Bourbon marriage by proposing the King of
Portugal for Marguerite.[5]

'Things', in fact, were turning out very badly, since Anjou
himself called for some pacification, his camp being decimated
by famine and sickness – one reason for not following up his
victory – and in July 1569 Coligny, significantly through the

[1] *CSPF., 1569–71*, pp. 83–4, 3 June 1569, Norris to Cecil.

[2] *CSPF., 1569–71*, pp. 66–7, 28 April 1569, Norris to Cecil.

[3] Spain was probably more interested at this time in the rebellion in Ireland,
which was certainly a more realistic approach. *CSPSp., 1568–79*, pp. 217–18,
16 December 1569, Philip II to Alva.

[4] *CSPSp., 1568–79*, pp. 159–60, 1 June 1569, Alva to Philip II.

[5] *CSPF., 1569–71*, pp. 94–5, 9 July 1569, Norris to Cecil.

agency of Montmorency, presented the king with a long petition in favour of civil peace.[1] Basically the petition requested the free and universal exercise of religion, with guarantees (sûretés). But it also strongly condemned the king's enemies, and their own, who had 'bien sceu industrieusement et subtilement divertir l'orage et la tempeste qui estoit ès Pays-Bas, pour la faire retourner et tomber sur vostre couronne et sur vostre royaume'. Charles should therefore consider whether to let the opposing French armies meet in a battle which would benefit neither victor nor vanquished or, 'les employer ensemble pour . . . le bien de vos affaires . . . et par ce moyen renvoyer l'orage et la tempeste au lieu dont elle est venue'. Though obscurely worded, for the most part, the petition is, however, quite clear in proposing 'transference' of the war to the Netherlands as an alternative to civil war, an obtuse and obsolete representation of French affairs. While civil war had, in effect, if not inevitably, averted an invasion of the Netherlands, such an invasion could hardly be undertaken as an alternative to civil war without the catholic co-operation which the king was powerless to command. France was too deeply divided for so simple a solution.

This long-winded document was neither diplomatic nor realistic; indeed it was singularly unfortunate, as it happened, in view of Alva's frame of mind – which was probably unknown – and the presence in France of the Spanish duke of Negeres – which was probably common knowledge. Without going any further, Charles could not, at that moment, safely even consider the religious demand. The matter was therefore dropped; Anjou was quietened with the county of Maine and the reversion of Auvergne – which belonged to Catherine – and, between July and September the extremists renewed their efforts to catch or despatch Coligny.

The war, however, was becoming increasingly difficult to sustain and the battle on Montcontour, 3 October, was just such a pyrrhic – catholic – victory as Coligny had predicted, and from

[1] *CSPF.*, *1569-71*, pp. 94-5, 9 July 1569, Norris to Cecil; Delaborde, *Coligny*, iii, app. xxi, 560-5.

which the protestant leaders again escaped alive. Appalling conditions and the onset of winter brought rumours of peace for which negotiations began in November.[1] By December the protestants had drafted articles and the principal negotiators on both sides were already involved, Charles de Téligny and Jean de Lafin, seigneur de Beauvais Lanocle for the protestants, and Gontaut de Biron and Henri de Mesmes seigneur de Malassise – both moderates – for the crown.[2] The 'crown' certainly represented Catherine, whose supporters were negotiating. Just where Charles stood it is difficult, as ever, to ascertain. Lorraine cannot have wanted peace, upon the basis of any articles proposed by the huguenots, whose defeat in battle had altered nothing and whose seemingly charmed lives continued to evade his traps. But he certainly wanted some alteration in France, and no doubt some way out of an embarrassing stalemate, because events in England were beginning to command attention.

Some time in September – when Coligny was scheduled to die against a reward of 50,000 *écus* – in England the northern earls had agreed upon a plan to liberate Mary queen of Scots, and the duke of Norfolk had departed to the country to avoid arrest and to make preparations.[3] Norfolk, however, either lost his nerve, or disagreed with his kinsmen; he is reported to have wanted to get Cecil arrested before taking up arms. Either way, he unwisely returned to London and, on 11 October – just one week after Montcontour which looked like a catastrophic defeat of Coligny in France – Norfolk was sent to the Tower.[4] Arundel and Lumley were also arrested, and Pembroke detained.

[1] B.N., Mss. Italien, 1727, f. 90, 15 October 1569; f. 95, 9 November 1569; f. 103, 19 December 1569; f. 105, 1 January 1570; f. 109 verso, 13 January 1570; Desjardins, *Negs. Tosc.*, iii, 604, 13 November 1569; 604, 20 November 1569; 605, 6 December 1569; 607, 27 December 1569.

[2] *CSPF.*, *1569–71*, p. 159, December 1569, articles for the pacification of France; Delaborde, *Coligny*, iii, 172 seq.

[3] *CSPSp.*, *1568–79*, p. 195, 22 September 1569, de Spes to Philip II; 196–7, 27 September 1569, de Spes to Philip II; 197–8, 30 September 1569, de Spes to Philip II.

[4] Given fair winds, a week was long enough for the news to reach England; it would be interesting to know if there were any connection here. *CSPSp.*,

The northern earls of Cumberland, Westmorland and North-umberland, however, proceeded alone, took up arms, entered Durham and intended to rescue Mary. Thus Norris reported on 10 December, that Charles who had indicated his willingness to make peace, would go to Bordeaux 'and take order for ships into Scotland which, Martigues had said, would be within a month. Lorraine's intention was to garrison Dumbarton in the Firth of Clyde, and seek possession of the young prince James.[1] Although the bungled rising temporarily petered out in January, the situation was, if anything, more dangerous than ever, since Westmorland was at liberty in Mary's castle of Dumbarton and, failed by their friends, the humiliated lords were industriously seeking foreign help. Early in January, Elizabeth herself, in declaring the rebellion suppressed, admitted that they claimed to be expecting help from France and Flanders.[2] The French ambassador had appealed for help to de Spes – who actually had orders not to meddle – and lord Montagu and his son-in-law Southampton had attempted to leave for the Netherlands, but were thwarted by bad weather.[3] Philip II was not, in fact, overmuch inclined to help these lords, doubting 'their daring to undertake the enterprise, or that they can succeed in it if they do'.[4] He referred, presumably to the liberation of Mary. On the other hand, he did not want to find himself excluded, if anything effective were achieved, in which, it was always to be feared – if not precisely expected – the French might assist them. In effect,

---

1568–79, pp. 198–200, 8 October 1569, de Spes to Philip II; 200–1, 14 October 1569, de Spes to Philip II.

[1] *CSPF.*, *1569–71*, p. 149, 10 December 1569, Norris to Cecil.

[2] *CSPF.*, *1569–71*, p. 167, 5 January 1570, Elizabeth to Norris.

[3] *CSPF.*, *1569–71*, p. 212, [March] 1570, intelligence from Spain. Sir Francis Englefield, a well-known catholic exile, confirmed that they and Cumberland's son and heir, had long since been expected. They also had a Portuguese merchant/agent working for them in Portugal, with the Spanish ambassador there, Don Fernando Carillo. *CSPSp.*, *1568–79*, pp. 213–14, 1 December 1569, de Spes to Alva; 218–19, 18 December 1569, de Spes to Philip II; 224, 26 December 1569, Philip II to de Spes.

[4] *CSPSp.*, *1568–79*, p. 224, 26 December 1569, Philip II to de Spes.

Norris heard of a 'treaty lately sent hither to the King out of England' and esteemed that 'both here and there they are very maliciously bent against Her Majesty and the quiet of England'.[1]

Partly for these reasons and partly because they could not trust the court at which Lorraine prevailed, the huguenots were in no hurry to make peace. Besides, Charles de Téligny had excused himself from returning to court after Christmas 1569 having narrowly escaped capture while travelling with a royal safe-conduct.[2] When he did return to court near Angers on 24 January – just one day after the murder in Scotland of the regent Murray – he warned Norris that Rambouillet was being sent to promise help to the English rebels. He also learnt from Mont-morency and marshal Vieilleville that Lorraine was preparing in Normandy six great vessels with 3,000 harquebusiers 'to invade England at the first Spring'.[3] This, in fact, was no real secret, since 'they blaze abroad with open mouth this their enterprise into England' but provided 'peace be had here'.[4] There were, however, other ways of achieving this than by granting freedom of religion all over France, and it was precisely then that Norris reported a further attempt to murder not only Coligny but this time the young princes Navarre and Condé as well.[5] Failing this, it was worth trying to bribe the huguenots with the offer of all their articles if, as Anjou enquired of Téligny, 'they would swear to follow and assist him in conquering England'. Téligny is reported to have replied that 'he did not find how with good conscience and a regard to their own safety it might be granted, but that if the King pleased to invade Flanders . . . he should see their readiness, skill, and courage most evidently'.[6]

Elizabeth, for whom the crisis was still mounting, was gravely dependent upon the huguenots early in 1570. 'If the bottom of

[1] *CSPF.*, *1569–71*, p. 164, 2 January 1570, Norris to Cecil.

[2] *CSPF.*, *1569–71*, p. 174, 27 January 1570, Norris to Elizabeth. Téligny married Coligny's daughter, Louise, in 1571.

[3] *CSPF.*, *1569–71*, pp. 174–5, 27 January 1570, Norris to Elizabeth.

[4] *CSPF.*, *1569–71*, p. 176, 27 January 1570, Norris to Cecil.

[5] *CSPF.*, *1569–71*, p. 174, 27 January 1570, Norris to Elizabeth.

[6] *CSPF.*, *1569–71*, p. 174, 27 January 1570, Norris to Elizabeth.

the late rebellion [in England] be searched,' Norris wrote to Cecil, he would find 'the spring head to come from hence or from Flanders.[1] Norris was not entirely correct in his estimate of Spain's attitude to England, though he had every reason to suspect what he did, especially as Alva's brother-in-law, Don Pedro Mandrik, had arrived in France on the last day of January.[2] Anyway, with or without Spain, the danger was quite sufficient since the six ships in Normandy were only a beginning. There was now news of seven at Bordeaux, seven at Newhaven and five at Dieppe to transport an army under Philippe Strozzi.[3] This, like the plan for 1568, evidently also involved the removal of the queen, which was indeed rather obviously essential to her replacement by Mary. Thus Norris – who was among those who believed in Lorraine's implication in the remarkably opportune death of Murray – now sent warning that the cardinal had 'straightways devised to send four to attempt the like to Her Majesty'. One of these was thought to be a disfigured rogue named Villenus who had been imprisoned in La Rochelle for conspiring to kill Condé. He had escaped with one Badcheko, an intimate of 'Baptistis'.[4] Giovanni Baptista was an agent of Lorraine, but as he ended up with rewards in England, he must either have been a double agent, or have altered his allegiance. Much was secretly known about these and other agents and the excommunication of Elizabeth on 5 February 1570, in the midst of this crisis, permitted any catholic to murder her, not only with moral impunity, but with papal benediction. Nor was the pope only morally involved. He had given 600,000 ducats to help the English catholics and induced the rich duke of Florence – whom he created grand duke of Tuscany – to produce another 200,000.[5]

[1] *CSPF.*, *1569–71*, p. 182, 5 February 1570, Norris to Cecil.

[2] *CSPF.*, *1569–71*, p. 184, 9 February 1570, Norris to Elizabeth.

[3] *CSPF.*, *1569–71*, pp. 181–2, 5 February 1570, Norris to Elizabeth.

[4] *CSPF.*, *1569–71*, p. 193, 25 February 1570, Norris to Cecil; 196–7, 1 March 1570, Norris to Cecil; p. 200, 9 March 1570, two letters from Norris to Cecil; *HMC Hatfield*, ii, 143, 319; xiii, 505.

[5] *CSPF.*, *1569–71*, p. 199, 8 March 1570, Robert Hogan or Huggins to Leicester; 209–10, 28 March 1570; Hogan to Norris. Hogan was an English spy who had served in the butlery of Don Carlos and, after his death, the pantry

The 'Pope's Holiness,' had also, according to intelligence from Spain, commended the 'Lords of the North' to Philip II and requested him to help them. They themselves had made similar appeals in response to which Alva was said to have commission to assist them.[1] It appears from a report of John Marsh, a servant of Cecil in the Netherlands – who warned Cecil himself and Nicholas Bacon to 'go abroad well fenced' – that Philip had ordered Alva to give the English lords all the help he could, but secretly.[2] This did not necessarily amount to much, or alter anything, since Alva had already disposed of total discretionary powers for the past year.[3] He did not, however, intend to run the risk of using them. Besides, he was ill and pressing his recall which was already requested in March 1569.[4] Philip, however, had recently won a notable victory over the Turks at Galera and the Morisco war was almost over. It was therefore inevitably wondered whether he would divert his forces to France, or England which, it was agreed, neither he nor France would do without informing the other.[5]

In these perilous circumstances, it was clearly desperately

---

of the prince of Eboli. He was betrayed by his servant Matthew, who considered himself ill-rewarded, to de Spes in England. *CSPSp.*, *1568–79*, p. 247, 18 June 1570, de Spes to Philip II. De Spes later said that Ridolphi had 12,000 crowns from the pope, who would give 100,000 'if these English Earls behave properly'. These vastly lower figures sound more probable but none of them should be assumed to be correct. Ibid., 245, 13 May 1570, de Spes to Philip II.

[1] *CSPF.*, *1569–71*, p. 212 [March] 1570, intelligence from Spain.

[2] *CSPF.*, *1569–71*, p. 216 [11]April 1570, John Marsh [probably to Cecil]; 219–20, 16 April 1570 [Marsh to Cecil]; *CSPSp.*, *1568–79*, p. 240, 25 March 1570, Philip II to de Spes.

[3] *CSPSp.*, *1568–79*, pp. 109–10, 18 February 1569, Philip II to Alva.

[4] This was at first resisted, but Philip II announced the appointment of his successor on 30 June 1570. Gachard, *Correspondance de Philippe II*, ii, 70, 11 March 1569, Alva's secretary Albornoz to Zayas; 134–5, 30 June 1570, Philip II to Alva; *CSPSp.*, *1568–79*, p. 217, 11 December 1569, Alva to Philip II. Alva was absorbed in the Netherlands and his concern with France was from that point of view. He never displayed much interset in the English succession, but only in their vital commercial relations.

[5] *CSPF.*, *1569–71*, p. 204, 16 March 1570, Norris to Cecil.

important to Elizabeth that the French civil war should continue, and this was the principal reason why the treaty of Saint-Germain took, altogether, nearly a year in the making. By early February at the height of the crisis, it appeared to be closer than was really the case. Charles was ill and virtually unarmed, Biron was authorised to make concessions, and the protestants were equally in trouble for lack of aid.[1] Elizabeth responded by offering to mediate in France, a fairly standard means of obstruction, and Châtillon gave out in England that the protestants would never make peace without free (as distinct from conditional) exercise of their religion, with England and the princes of the Empire as guarantors of the treaty; terms which might confidently be expected to take some time to digest.[2] More materially, Elizabeth set about raising 100,000 crowns with which to keep the huguenots in arms. A warrant for half this amount was said to have been handed to Châtillon by 27 March 1570, though it was later alleged that the money, to be transmitted in Germany, was never paid.[3]

But, money or no money, the protestants were perfectly prepared to be exigent, even to the point of outrage. In March they took a leisurely stand upon freedom of religion, and when the deputies returned to court on 24 April they are reported to have demanded Calais and Bordeaux as *places de sûreté*, which caused the king to seize his dagger.[4] In spite of the angry uproar, certain articles had been established by early May as a basis for negotiation – for whose consideration the protestants demanded six weeks; thereafter Lorraine evidently regarded peace as

---

[1] B.N., Mss. Italien, 1727, f. 126 verso, 18 February 1570; f. 130, 26 February 1570; f. 139 verso, 6 March 1570; *CSPF.*, *1569–71*, p. 182, 5 February 1570, Norris to Elizabeth.

[2] *CSPF.*, *1569–71*, p. 190–1, 23 February 1570, instructions for Norris; 200–1, 9 March 1570, Châtillon to Cecil.

[3] *CSPSp.*, *1568–79*, p. 242, 27 March 1570, de Spes to Philip II; 258–9, 1 July 1570, de Spes to Philip II.

[4] Delaborde makes this statement, for which his reference is incomplete. Delaborde, *Coligny*, iii, 201; Desjardins, *Negs. Tosc.*, iii, 623, 22 & 26 April 1570.

inevitable.[1] He had good reasons for thinking so. Apart from the fact that the secretary Villeroy had returned from Germany having concluded negotiations for Charles' marriage to Elizabeth of Austria,[2] Lorraine was fast losing, or had already lost, his vital control of the council. As early as February it was said that nearly all the council wanted peace, no doubt those who were most directly concerned with the waging of war; but this did not go for Lorraine.[3] More significantly, however, two months later the moderate Limoges, a supporter of Catherine, and erstwhile ambassador in Spain, was described as principal councillor.[4] Furthermore, Téligny had been forbidden to negotiate with or in the presence of Lorraine,[5] which came very close to demanding his disgrace as a condition of agreement. Indeed, in a sense, it was an essential pre-condition, though he might have failed in his policies without actually being – as he was in August – excluded from the council. The duc de Guise also fell into disgrace for aspiring to marry Marguerite, who was none too becomingly discreet about being in love with him.[6]

If Lorraine could neither make war, nor dispose of the huguenot leaders, nor condone a pro-protestant peace, nor yet, in those circumstances, proceed with the enterprise of England, then he could not long expect to continue to dominate the council. He was therefore right in presuming that peace must follow, either soon, or a little later.

How this would affect Elizabeth was still uncertain, especially as the news from Spain was of an 'infested malice to England and a vehement presumption of a meaning to invade if opportunity serve'.[7] In May, when the articles were established, Coligny was gravely ill at St-Etienne-de-Forest (Loire) though for once no one

[1] *CSPF.*, *1569–71*, p. 255, 4 May 1570, Lorraine ——?
[2] Sutherland, *The French Secretaries of State*, 170.
[3] B.N., Mss. Italien, 1727, f. 118 verso–19, 6 February 1570.
[4] B.N., Mss. Italien, 1727, f. 144 verso, 6 April 1570.
[5] B.N., Mss. Italien, 1727, ff. 148–verso, 7 April 1570; Delaborde, *Coligny*, iii, 200, n. 1.
[6] *CSPF.*, *1569–71*, p. 291, 9 July 1570, Norris to Elizabeth.
[7] *CSPF.*, *1569–71*, pp. 282–3, June 1570, news from Spain.

said it was poison. This was a genuine reason for delay. Besides, they were not yet satisfied with the religious terms. When he recovered, therefore, the protestants decided to move closer to Paris in order to extract better terms. Thus, while the deputies returned to court with instructions and twenty-nine articles dated 21 June, Coligny precipitated a truce at the beginning of July by occupying La Charité, which commanded the Loire, with an army 'volant' against which marshal Cossé with his force of foot and artillery was helpless; he could not keep up with them.[1]

At this stage, Lorraine virtually recognised defeat by demanding in council that if peace were concluded, open war should be declared upon England, seeing that Elizabeth had supported the rebels, a proposal unworthy of his intelligence since neither the 'rebels' nor those who sought peace with them could be expected to conduct such a war.[2] This also went for the king who, during the course of July 'condescended' to much, 'the necessity of both their cases constraining them thereunto'.[3] So the peace of Saint-Germain was concluded on 4 August and registered by the *parlement* of Paris on the eleventh. 'C'est finir par ou nous devions commencer si nous eussions esté bien sages', was the withering comment of Estienne Pasquier, himself a *parlementaire*; only in war, as in law, one had first of all to be totally ruined.[4]

---

[1] Delaborde, *Coligny*, iii, 213 seq.

[2] *CSPF.*, *1569–71*, p. 274, 20 June 1570, Norris to Elizabeth.

[3] *CSPF.*, *1569–71*, p. 297, 23 July 1570, Norris to Elizabeth.

[4] Pasquier, *Lettres historiques*, 201; Fontanon, *Édits et ordonnances*, iv, 300–4, 11 August 1570. Various different dates for this treaty may be found because it was agreed on 4 August, then drafted, and signed on 8 August and published on 11 August. Charles IX announced it to queen Elizabeth on 4 August. *CSPF.*, *1569–71*, p. 304, 4 August 1570, Charles IX to Elizabeth.

VII

The Aftermath of Peace

WHILE THE king – now aged twenty – was threatened with catholic war if he authorised the cult, and saddled with civil war if he did not, he was necessarily carried on a tide of disaster, unable to manoeuvre. But the failure of the extremists to sustain successful war – which gradually led to their loss of control in the council – and of Alva to invade, ended by breaking this particular deadlock. If there were many contributory reasons why Alva did not invade, it was also debatable how far this would really have served the interests of Spain, since the Netherlands – which would presumably have been in his rear – could not have escaped the conflagration, and even the German princes might well have been smoked out of their habitual lethargy. Such an invasion would, more probably than anything else, have provoked the kind of general war by which Europe was rent in the seventeenth century, but with France in place of Germany as the principal battlefield. Happily Spain did not want general war, which could not occur without her. Ultimately, therefore, as the war was a failure, the conclusion of a treaty could not be resisted; though its implementation might be.

The peace of Saint-Germain necessarily reflected the conditions out of which it arose, and the protestants' long stand – to the salvation of England – for at least satisfactory terms. It represented a total defeat for the policy of general extermination which, by then if not long before, was a physical impossibility. It was therefore quite different from the edict of January and that of Amboise and Longjumeau, and it left the protestants not a vanquished minority, but a power in the state, which could not, henceforth, be disregarded.

The principal clauses related to religion, security, civil and judicial rights, and property. While the protestants had to drop their demand for complete freedom of religion, they obtained special privileges for the nobility in their own houses, and permission to exercise the cult in two – specified – towns per *gouvernement*, and everywhere that it had been publicly held on 1 August 1570. The extent of this important clause is unknown, but it probably included most places with large protestant communities. The security clause, which was something quite new arising from the dangers they had suffered at home, consisted of the cession, for two years, of four *places de sûreté*, as they were called, the strategic and fortified towns of La Rochelle, Cognac, Montauban and La Charité. Besides certain judicial guarantees, the edict provided for the restitution of honours, offices and property – including that of William of Orange, and of Nassau who remained in France – and specified concessions for Jeanne d'Albret, whether in deference to her sovereign status, or to facilitate the Bourbon marriage.

Having been so long delayed, the nature and circumstances of the peace finally proved favourable to Elizabeth, who needed the protestant alliance, but also without prejudice to her relations with the crown, lest the enterprise of England be pursued. There was indeed, still 'great talk of enterprises to be taken in hand, whispered to be into Scotland', but considering that 'the chiefest' about the king were now at least protestant sympathisers, Norris thought the danger had receded, and Elizabeth herself was thinking in terms of calling parliament because of her need for money. But there was still an undeniable risk that Mary might be rescued, there having already been two abortive attempts to do so.[1]

The pros and cons of peace in France as well as war in the Netherlands had been debated during 1570 in England, which served as a kind of protestant headquarters for German, Flemish and French agents and exiles, including the cardinal Châtillon. Châtillon, when consulted in England, indicated that he wanted any treaty and edict to be guaranteed by the queen and the

[1] *CSPF.*, *1569–71*, p. 200, 9 March 1570, Norris to Cecil; 314, 11 August 1570, Norris to Elizabeth; 351, 8 October 1571.

German princes for fear that it would otherwise be violated like the others before it which, among other things, was the cause of his own penurious exile.[1] Elizabeth was sympathetic and also anxious to persuade the king of her 'good meaning towards him', and that she had 'never intended to comfort any of his subjects against him . . . or diminish any parcell of his crown'. But she could not allow the [French] princes to be overthrown by their private enemies so long as they only require of the king the enjoyment of former edicts. She therefore sent over Sir Francis Walsingham – a firm protestant – on a special mission to offer to guarantee the peace provided the king did not 'abridge the same to their misliking whereby they may gather doubtfulness and fear . . .' and to oppose those who sought to 'impeach' or to 'withstand' the accord. At the same time Walsingham was to make it clear to the protestants that the 'special sending of you over . . . was chiefly for their cause'.[2]

Neither Norris, nor Walsingham, sent to obviate the 'infinite discommodities and lamentable mishaps grown to [the king's] estate by denying [the protestants'] reasonable requests' – believed the peace would last, in spite of its protestant nature. If for the moment all was quiet at court because, as Norris recorded with satisfaction, 'the occasioner of all the troubles in this realm is out of credit, and neither haunts the court or [sic] council',[3] peace had not brought 'any firm reconciliation betwixt the nobility so that the original cause and spring of war still continues'.[4]

The chief antagonists all vacated the court, revealing the helplessness of a monarch bereft of the support of the majority

---

[1] Atkinson, *The Cardinal of Châtillon in England*, 68, 72; La Mothe, iii, 256–7, 25 July 1570, La Mothe to Charles IX. According to de Spes, Châtillon was drawing money from piracy. *CSPSp.*, *1568–79*, p. 275, 3 September 1570, de Spes to Philip II.

[2] Digges, 1–5, 11 August 1570, instructions for Walsingham; 5–6, 15 August 1570, Elizabeth to Walsingham. Walsingham returned as resident ambassador at the end of the year. It is interesting to note that Elizabeth's ambassadors to France were all unequivocally protestant; more so, perhaps, than she herself could afford to be.

[3] *CSPF.*, *1569–71*, p. 343, 23 September 1570, Norris to Cecil.

[4] *CSPF.*, *1569–71*, p. 326, 31 August 1570, Norris to Elizabeth.

of his nobility. The huguenot leaders remained in the fortified safety of La Rochelle, represented at court by Bricquemault and Cavaignes, elders of Coligny's generation, and the younger Téligny and his brother-in-law La Noue, who married the widow of the murdered Mouy. Probably there were also others. They were principally supported by François duc de Montmorency, cousin of the count Horne who was executed in the Netherlands and his brother Montigny who perished in Spain. Montmorency was also related through his wife to William's naval commander the comte de la Marck.[1] The protestants, though seemingly fairly strong, were gravely divided among themselves. As Queen of Navarre, Jeanne d'Albret was very vulnerable to Spain; but as a sovereign princess and mother of the first prince of the blood, her interests only partially coincided with those of the huguenots. Furthermore, Coligny, whose life was constantly in danger, and the elders tended to be cautious, putting first the implementation of the edict, while some of the younger leaders, in particular Téligny, Jean de Hangest, Seigneur de Genlis and La Noue, spurred on by the impulsive Louis of Nassau, were rearing to enter the Netherlands. Thus, once William of Orange was ready to invade the Netherlands for the second time, the situation of August 1568 was likely to be repeated; unless the elusive leaders could first be eliminated.

While the protestant leaders eschewed the court, their enemies, the Guises, were in disgrace; sound evidence that the apparent *political* catholicism of the crown and Catherine in the last few years had been a matter of duress. The Guises remained largely excluded from affairs of state for the following two years. Lorraine actually complained to the pope in June 1572 of not having been employed by the king for two years past.[2] He returned to power with the accession of Anjou as Henry III in May 1574, but died seven months later. Their disgrace had the

[1] This relationship was kindly pointed out to me by Miss J. M. Davies.

[2] L. Romier, 'La Saint-Barthélemy . . .', *Revue du XVIᵉ siècle*, i (1913), 548, n. 1, 16 June 1572; Desjardins, *Negs. Tosc.*, iii, 639, 10 August 1570; 640–1, 20 August 1570.

effect of bringing them more forcefully than ever behind the Spanish and catholic pressures, and of causing them to work in devious ways through shady intermediaries in the entourage of Anjou.[1] The extreme catholics were therefore divided from the moderates – who were entirely pacifist – in everything but their opposition to war with Spain, which included any enterprise – however else it might be presented – in the Netherlands.

The Venetian ambassador gives an interesting account of the changes at court as a result of the peace, 'molti mutatione di fortuna et di favori'. Some had risen, some been maintained and others had fallen in status. Among those who had risen, he emphasised Montmorency especially – which could certainly not be cheerfully endured by the Guises – the duc de Longueville, *gouverneur* of Picardy, and a kinsman of both Guise and Condé and, rather curiously, the duc de Nemours, Lorraine's brother-in-law. Finally, in this group, he included the peacemakers, the huguenot Téligny, Biron and Malassise, and François Carnavalet, governor of the duc d'Anjou, who was held to be protestant. The second group consists of moderates, supporters of Catherine, and those named are the cardinal de Bourbon, the chancellor de Morvillier, Limoges, Birague, Lansac and 'altri simili', which means *noblesse de robe*. In the final group the ambassador placed the duc de Montpensier and the whole house of Guise.[2] In August, however, Lorraine appears to have returned to court from Rheims, hopefully no doubt, while the nuncio, no less hopefully, declared that his disgrace appeared to be lessening.[3] But Walsingham said that the king's misliking of the Guises continued, and that he was 'not repaired in credit, neither dealeth he in Government'.[4]

[1] Among these were evidently Villequier, bribed by Lorraine, Lignerolles, Serrat and Cheverny.

[2] B.N., Mss. Italien, 1727, f. 191, 19 August 1570; he does not mention Lorraine's associate the comte de Retz, who probably retained favour, having served in the negotiation of Charles' marriage.

[3] Hirschauer, *La Politique de St Pie V*, 113, 22 August 1570, Frangipani to Rusticucci.

[4] Digges, 8, 29 August 1570, Walsingham to Leicester.

If the peace brought little tranquillity, and the protestants and England doubted that it would last, the catholics and catholic powers resisted it from the start as they had resisted the edicts of January, Amboise and Longjumeau. Charles also had to rebuke very sharply the 'mutinous messieurs of Paris', namely the municipality of the violently catholic capital, and equally the *parlement* which he is said to have assured – with many an oath – that unless they 'turned over another leaf, he will providehim[self] with new Presidents'.[1] In August 1570 the pope expressed the desire to have a papal advocate in the *parlement* of Paris – precisely the sort of hostile influence on the processes of law that the protestants justly feared. The pope had already advised Charles not to make peace when this was rumoured as early as January 1570, and again in April, saying that it would prove a source of even greater troubles. In August 1570 he commanded Lorraine to make every effort 'pour déjouer et pour renverser ces projects de paix' – which is probably why he returned to court – as deplorable, dangerous, and a *coup funeste* on account of its novel and favourable terms.[2] Rusticucci, nuncio in the Empire, condemned it as a 'vituperosa pacificatione' which displeased and distressed the pope – who had spent money on the war – more than anything since his election, and declared its terms to be so pro-protestant that, when first published, they were presumed to be incorrect.[3] Frangipani the nuncio in France declared it a mere truce and 'indegna pace' of universal dissatisfaction, persistently repeating his opinion that it could not last.[4] He also expressed, in this connection, his disapproval of the royal entourage, composed of

[1] Digges, 7–8, 29 August 1570, Walsingham to Leicester; Hirschauer, *La Politique de St Pie V*, 107–8, 19 August 1570, Frangipani to Rusticucci.

[2] De Potter, *Lettres de St Pie V*, 97–100, 29 January 1570, Pius V to Charles IX; 108–12, 23 April 1570, same to same; 116, 14 August 1570, same to Lorraine; 117–20, 14 August 1570, same to cardinal de Bourbon; 121, 23 September 1570, same to same; 125–9, 23 September 1570, same to Lorraine.

[3] Serrano, *Correspondencia diplomatica de S. Pio V*, iv, 41, 25 September 1570, Rusticucci to Castagna, and note 1.

[4] Hirschauer, *La Politique de St Pie V*, 107, 19 August 1570; 114, 30 August 1570; 123, 14 October 1570; 127, 28 October 1570, Frangipani to Rusticucci.

persons 'pieni di interessi, di passioni et dirò anche di bugie',[1] apart from the cardinal de Pellevé, a supporter of Lorraine, and Lorraine himself who was there at that moment.[2] Frangipani hoped Lorraine might recover his former importance, and declared his intention of supporting the cardinal in sustaining a continual catholic pressure on Charles and Catherine, 'oportune et importune'.[3]

Charles, who could not do other than make peace, defended himself as best he might against this holy outcry on the part of those who had forced him into the war initially, and were responsible for his now almost untenable position, to which they themselves were the most vociferous objectors. To the pope's extraordinary nuncio, Bramante, sent to complain and disrupt, Charles claimed that the protestants were strong and had been expecting powerful German help, while he was weak and betrayed by the catholics about him who were more devoted to their own interests and the divisions of France than to the service of God and the king. The despatch points out that the pope should understand that there were, in the kingdom 'più interessi et inimicitie che heresie . . . ne da l'una parte, ne da l'altra'.[4] This conformed pretty much with the regular nuncio Frangipani's own opinion that there was no one at court not moved by material interests and passions, 'vacui di ogni religione'.[5] The religious crisis had long since become an administrative problem for the government, and been absorbed into the conflicts of the nobles. Only fanatics did or could maintain that there was any religious virtue in continuing the civil war. Charles maintained that when he had stabilised the peace, for which he was so strongly censured,

[1] Hirschauer, *La Politique de St Pie V*, 118, 12 September 1570, Frangipani to Rusticucci.

[2] Hirschauer, *La Politique de St Pie V*, 114–16, 30 August 1570, Frangipani to Rusticucci.

[3] Hirschauer, *La Politique de St Pie V*, 116, 2 September 1570, Frangipani to Rusticucci. He did not actually specify Anjou.

[4] Hirschauer, *La Politique de St Pie V*, 139–52, Bramante's parting audience; undated but about the end of 1570 or early 1571.

[5] Hirschauer, *La Politique de St Pie V*, 121, 30 September 1570, Frangipani to Rusticucci.

it would be seen to favour true religion.[1] His diplomatic ambiguity may have given rise to the fear or, in some cases the hope, that the peace concealed, in reality, some treacherous subterfuge, especially since he allegedly went further, employing the sort of sinister insinuations with which Catherine had deflected Alva at Bayonne; not that either Alva or Philip II had been deceived. 'Monsignor nuntio', Frangipani recorded, 'state di bona voglia che noi speramo di tirar questa pace à bono et honorevol termine che il fine comandarà ancho il principio che hoggidi pare cosi malo,' adding mysteriously, 'che son delle cose nel animo che, per poterle fare, non bisogna dirle', always the best way of being non-committal.[2] Frangipani was not in fact deceived by this sort of statement, any more than Alva or Philip II had been. On the contrary, he believed that it was solely 'per aquetar me' [sic]. It could, none the less, be used to sustain the fear, or the hope, that the peace might conceal 'some premeditated snare'.[3] This fear was registered in England whence La Mothe reported that members of the privy council had heard that leading catholics at court openly opposed peace, that Charles never meant to support two religions and that he had very secretly declared this in the *parlement*. It was alleged that he had supported peace to dispose of the huguenot army and to expel foreigners, but that later he would 'otherwise order the affairs of religion'. They also heard that Coligny and others were informed of this, had warned friends in Germany, and 'se tenoient sur leurs gardes'.[4]

If some 'snare' was feared in England, it was naturally hoped for in Rome, whence a policy of elimination continued to be fostered which, in France, was largely channelled into the old Guise/Châtillon vendetta. Michel de la Huguerye, returning from Rome after the war in the suite of Alava's wife, brought with him disturbing reports. From these it appears that the vague words

[1] Hirschauer, *La Politique de St Pie V*, 115, 30 August 1570, Frangipani to Rusticucci.

[2] Hirschauer, *La Politique de St Pie V*, 53, n. 2 and 119, 24 September 1570, Frangipani to Rusticucci.

[3] *CSPF., 1569–71*, p. 355, 2 September 1570, —? to Lord Cobham.

[4] La Mothe, iii, 360–1, 9 November 1570, La Mothe to Charles IX.

employed by Catherine to reassure the nuncio Frangipani, and Bramante, the extraordinary nuncio, gave rise to rumours in Rome that she intended to fell the protestant leaders, and this was retailed by La Huguerye – who was firmly convinced of its truth – to Coligny's lieutenant, Bricquemault, whose service he embraced. Bramante reported cardinal Pellevé to have said that Charles made peace to recover the protestant fortresses and to 'trouver le moyen de se débarrasser des principaux chefs'; also that he meant to bribe someone in the admiral's confidence to murder him and the other leaders.[1] No details were forthcoming and Bramante who, in reality, found Charles unreceptive to papal policy, declared himself regretfully unable to believe this: 'Il discorso mi piace,' he wrote stiffly, 'quantto segua lo effeto'. Pellevé, an extremist, was providing, as usual in the king's name, a rationale of the inevitable treaty in view of Lorraine's inability to sustain the war, and the bribing of assassins allegedly continued. In January 1571, Damville complained of horrible things plotted against him by Lorraine and, at the same time, two men were arrested by Coligny, said to have been hired by the cardinal to murder him.[2] The pope is no more likely to have been deceived than Frangipani or Bramante, since his extreme policy had been steadily resisted ever since his election. But this was not the point. Such murmurings from Rome – so damagingly propagated by the protestant La Huguerye – were maliciously guaranteed to prevent the restoration of confidence, the sole foundation of peace and reconciliation which was to be, both manifestly and explicitly, the policy of the crown.

What else, in his predicament, could Charles IX seek to do? The procedures of war were straightforward, but the problems of peace were tortuous. If Charles could neither defeat his protestant subjects – even if he wished to, which is not established – nor will their disparition, how could he enforce their peace?

[1] Hirschauer, *La Politique de St Pie V*, 132–3 and n. 1, 14 November 1570, Bramante to Rusticucci; 136, 28 November 1570, same to same.

[2] Desjardins, *Negs. Tosc.*, iii, 646, 27 January 1571; 647, 26 January 1571; *CSPF.*, *1569–71*, p. 385, news from France. The undated document has been placed under 1570.

In this they would at least co-operate, but it was also much easier for the catholics to frustrate the peace than to prosecute the war. In this they were still supported by Anjou. Anjou had made 'great suit' that there should be no preaching in his own territory. As a result, he had 'so marvellously won the Catholics, who, as they never omit either poisonings or other treasons to bring their designs to the desired effect, so do the wise greatly doubt lest they will use some desperate attempt against the King to set him up who so favours their cause as never man more'.[1]

Though there had not as yet been any recorded attempts upon the king's life, there were to be two before he died less than four years later, and there was nothing hysterical about this opinion. Walsingham also shared what he called the 'common fear' that Anjou 'can hardly digest to live in the degree of a Subject, having already the reputation of a King'.[2] Whether he was referring to Anjou's exaggerated martial prowess, or to the now receding prospect of his marriage to Mary, is not very clear; probably the latter since he asserted that neither the king nor the country could be safe 'unless he were found some other harborage.'[3] Furthermore, his chances of succeeding to the throne of France were ostensibly diminished by Charles' marriage, already performed by proxy on 27 June, and shortly to be solemnised in France. These fears doubtless sprang from the sinister impressions of an angry row between Charles and Anjou, reported by Petrucci, the Tuscan ambassador, on 10 August, just when peace had been signed and Lorraine disgraced and excluded from the council. Indeed Petrucci – a catholic sympathiser – suspected Guise of having fomented the row upon Lorraine's instigation.[4] The nuncio joyfully made a similar report, since he believed that the catholic cause, in all its aspects, could only triumph through disorders.[5] If the acrimonious relations between Charles and Anjou are

---

[1] *CSPF.*, *1569–71*, pp. 311–12, 9 August 1570, Norris to Leicester.
[2] Digges, 8, 29 August 1570, Walsingham to Leicester.
[3] Digges, 52, 9 March 1571, Walsingham to Leicester.
[4] Desjardins, *Negs. Tosc.*, iii, 639, 10 August 1570.
[5] Hirschauer, *La Politique de St Pie V*, 125–6, 22 October 1570, Frangipani to Rusticucci.

especially stressed by the catholics, who actively fostered them, both Norris and Walsingham considered him to be dangerous. Anjou, not the king, was recognised by all catholic agencies, from the pope down, as their leader and figurehead in France. This bitter cleavage, which increased the weakness of the crown, was all the more serious since, with his authority as lieutenant-general, Anjou was highly susceptible to exploitation by Charles' enemies.

If as Norris feared, Anjou's 'haughty mind' could not be contained within his dukedom,[1] it was just possible that the English marriage – already quietly proposed by Montmorency – might both absorb his ambition and detach him from the extreme catholics, at the same time releasing Charles from his helpless deadlock in France, cornered and disregarded as he was, and endangered from abroad. Thus the English marriage for Anjou, and the Bourbon marriage for Marguerite offered some hope of a basis and means of peace, protection and reconciliation.

The dual marriage plan was politically constructive. But the problem then arose that those inevitably involved included those who favoured a transference of the war to the Netherlands, an old policy based on the inclinations of some, and the assumption of others that war, somewhere, was inevitable. There appear to be several reasons for this assumption: in the first place, there was still the problem of international catholicism, while the issues of the French civil wars remained intractable. There was also the problem of the exiles from the Netherlands, who claimed from the huguenots their treaty rights and sought the restitution of their property, and the martial disposition of the gentry of France who were disinclined to be pacified. In 1567 there had been very large-scale preparations for war, both in France herself and in neighbouring territories, which gravely and imminently threatened to turn the country into the battlefield of Europe.[2] The idea of

---

[1] *CSPF.*, *1569–71*, p. 326, 31 August 1570, Norris to Elizabeth.

[2] The averting of such an international war in France at that time is a big, separate subject. But see, for example, De Potter, *Lettres de St Pie V*, 1–3, 13 October 1567, the pope to Philip II; 4, 16 October 1567, the pope to the duc de Nevers; 9–10, 18 October 1567, the pope to the duke of Savoy; 11–12, 16

transference was explicitly expressed during the peace negotiations after the second civil war at the beginning of 1568: 'If they [the protestants] can come with some good accord [with the king] they mind to join with the prince of Orange against the Spaniards to obtain like liberty of religion'.[1] This naturally commended itself to the exiles in France, and their compatriots plotting in England, as well as to the huguenots. Their alleged intention to join the prince of Orange was evidently true since they had already, in 1567, discussed the treaty of alliance and mutual support concluded in August 1568. While the efforts of the catholics to ambush the huguenot leaders in September 1568 obviated extensive co-operation, nevertheless both the second and the third civil wars were at least partially combined French and Netherlands movements.[2] One may safely assume that Philip's annoyance at the conclusion of peace in 1570, frostily conveyed to the French ambassador,[3] was primarily on account of this threat to the Netherlands, more especially since they then appeared at least outwardly settled, and the Turks had just landed in Cyprus. According to Alva, who hoped to retire, Philip could regard them as 'tout à fait à sa discretion', and he was considering erecting them into a kingdom.[4] After the conclusion of peace, however, Alva expressed the fear that trouble could be expected from France,[5] doubtless because William had always intended to organise a second invasion of the Netherlands. On 10 August 1570, one day before the registration of the treaty of Saint-Germain, William issued a commission appointing Guillain Fiennes, seigneur de Lumbres commander of his fleet.[6] William

November 1567, the pope to the duke of Savoy; 32–5, 6 March 1569, the pope to Charles IX.

[1] *CSPF.*, *1566–8*, p. 397, 15 January 1568, advertisements from Germany.

[2] See, for example, Gachard, *Notices et extraits*, ii, 458 seq.

[3] Serrano, *Correspondencia diplomatica de S. Pie V*, iv, 1–4, 7 September 1570, Castagna to Rusticucci.

[4] Gachard, *Correspondance de Philippe II*, ii, 143, 4 July 1570, Philip II to Alva; 144, 20 July 1570, Alva to Philip II; 145, 9 August 1570, Alva to Philip II.

[5] Gachard, *Notices et extraits*, ii, 496, 502, September, December 1570.

[6] Kervyn de Lettenhove, *Documents inédits du XVIe siècle*, 70–1.

had gone to Germany after the siege of Poitiers in 1569. His brother Louis of Nassau remained in France, based at La Rochelle,[1] and de Lumbres went to England. Their cause was therefore fully represented and actively canvassed in the Netherlands, England, France and the Empire. At the end of 1570 Alva himself sent Philip an intercepted patent dated 25 November 1570 from Dillenburg in the name of Hermann de Ruyter. He was to seek to gain a footing in certain towns in the region of the confluence of the Meuse and the Rhine. An accompanying letter from William reminded the people of his efforts in 1568, which failed at least partly from lack of support, and declared that he was resolved to try again to deliver the Netherlands from the tyranny of Alva.[2]

Transference of the war was, reputedly, what Coligny had always wanted; a statement which is open to serious misinterpretation, and which has obscured the understanding of his later career. Obviously foreign war was generally preferable to civil war, especially when this was accompanied by external intervention. But the Netherlands war that Coligny had always wanted was an extension of the old 'Italian' wars which, latterly, had been pursued in the Netherlands. This was an alternative, not an adjunct to civil war. He, the Guises and all the nobility had, after all, originally fought together against Spain, the traditional enemy, in support – among other things – of the French claim to Flanders and Artois. Coligny himself had been captured at Saint-

---

[1] Hirschauer, *La Politique de St Pie V*, 125, 22 October 1570, Frangipani to Rusticucci.

[2] Gachard, *Correspondance de Philippe II*, ii, 165–6, 29 December 1570, Alva to Philip II. As Alva's successor, the mild duke of Medina Celi, had already been appointed, and Alva only remained *because* of the revolt, this argument seems less than adequate. Similarly, the immense difficulties experienced in contriving the abortive enterprise of 1572 hardly support the theory of an heroic struggle for liberty, nationality, toleration or any other altruistic aspiration. In the first place property had much to do with it. If this is an obvious over simplification, it would probably be more rewarding to consider the revolt in terms of the international fear of Spain and the existence of an embryonic 'protestant' league, from whose undependable support William possibly suffered quite as much as he benefited.

Quentin and imprisoned at Ghent, which he is unlikely to have forgotten. In his petition of July 1569, requesting peace and proposing transference, Coligny made it perfectly clear that it was a *national* war that he had in mind, categorically stating that rather than let the two opposing armies meet in unprofitable conflict in France, the king should employ them together – 'les employer ensemble pour . . . le bien de vos affaires,' which was in the Netherlands. The fact that this was at best naive and at worst insincere, does not alter the point that while it is partly true that he had always wanted transference, he had not, and did not, want it unconditionally. The circumstances of 1570 were unsuitable because there was no question of catholic co-operation, and because he could not, for the same reason, simply abandon the protestants in France. This point of view was clearly stated to Charles IX in July 1570 by La Mothe, his ambassador in England, who was required to canvass opinion among the French protestants there on the subject of both peace and transference. It seems likely that transference was pressed by some of the younger huguenots and friends of Nassau in the making of the peace. In the same letter, La Mothe reported that de Lumbres and others of his country 'font estat par ceste paix, de se retirer en France', on account of their mutual obligation to assist each other, 'quilz ne soyent toutz remiz en leur maysons pour y pourvoir vivre en seurté avec l'exercice de leur religion'.[1] This was a serious predicament, because the treaty obligation was a fact. But, if Coligny could not simply abandon the French protestants in war, neither could he do so in such uncertain peace, and he was in fact to struggle until the day of his death to obtain the execution of the edict. This was what he put first, even to the extent of virtually dividing the party – over which his control was far from absolute – since his own extremists were more enthusiastic about a Netherlands enterprise than they were about peace, security and toleration in France. Furthermore, transference would involve his own return to court which, in the climate of 1570, was unthinkable.

---

[1] La Mothe, iii, 257, 25 July 1570, La Mothe to Charles IX.

Apart from the huguenots, transference was very much in the interests of England, who was vulnerable to the power of Spain and sensitive to events in the Netherlands, but only concerned with the international implications of French domestic quarrels. But, if it would tend to favour England by creating trouble for Spain, and had obvious advantages for the huguenots, transference was far from simple for the catholic Charles IX who had so lately – with whatever reservations – received some troops from Alva and 'support' from other catholic princes, including the pope. Such a shift in royal tactics must necessarily entail the violent opposition of catholics, and a marked risk of hostilities with Spain which would be even more dangerous than her limited support. But, in theory at least, such a divergence just *might* be safely ventured if France were to move significantly closer to England, which the Anjou marriage would achieve. Safety from Spain and the pope, however, by means of a sufficient rapprochement with England was something of a political mirage, sensible, but insubstantial, since Elizabeth was not to be easily ensnared.

VIII

The English Marriage and the Netherlands Enterprise

A RAPPROCHEMENT with England was, politically, the obvious answer to the failure of the Spanish entente of Cateau-Cambrésis. But such a rapprochement was rather more than traditionally difficult on account of England's protestantism, itself the principal cause of her relative detachment from the old Burgundian alliance. It was not, however, a problem to the huguenots, and an English marriage was first proposed – between Elizabeth and Charles – by the prince de Condé to the English ambassador, Sir Thomas Smith, and reported by him to the queen on 1 April 1563.[1] Elizabeth had allied with the huguenots in September 1562, and the proposal was an effort to resolve, in a national and dynastic alliance, the embarrassment of this treaty of Hampton Court, once the first civil war was over. But because it was Calais, and not the huguenot interest that Elizabeth had in mind, Smith replied with his usual wit, that they should first cede the queen what was hers before entering into amity, love or dalliance. More important, perhaps, Coligny also spoke of the matter to his lieutenant Bricquemault, who was going to England on 2 April with articles and conditions – presumably relating to Le Havre and Calais – which Coligny thought the queen would allow. But Elizabeth refused – then as always – to relinquish her pretensions to Calais; and Charles was only thirteen.

The idea, however, was politically sound, and it was revived by Catherine de Medici in November 1564 when the court was at Marseilles, before the celebrated interview at Bayonne in 1565. Elizabeth was then engaged in one of her periodic negotiations

---

[1] *CSPF., 1563*, pp. 262–3, 1 April 1563, Smith to Elizabeth.

with the archduke Charles of Austria, and was in the habit of using one negotiation to fortify another; Catherine was doing the same. A successful outcome would have placed her in a very strong position at Bayonne, strong enough perhaps to outride the catholic storm which would certainly have broken. But time was then against her, both in terms of the impending interview, and because Charles was still too young to marry. She therefore used the interview to further a Habsburg marriage for the king, which undoubtedly had other advantages.[1] It is interesting to note that the English problems raised were those of age, residence and the 'miscontentment of [Elizabeth's] people' but, significantly, not religion. The Spanish ambassador in England confessed his inability to determine who was trying to prevent whom from doing what in these matrimonial matters.[2] Probably in 1565 Elizabeth's real objective was to prevent Mary queen of Scots from becoming contracted to either Charles of Austria or Charles IX, though her marriage to lord Darnley at the end of July was not a welcome solution.

When the idea was revived in 1568, in favour of Anjou, it was, albeit in a different context, again to block a Marian match which, this time, would have been dangerous to England and France alike, because of Anjou's affiliation with the catholic extremists. The proposal was overtaken by the civil war but, in 1570, these elements still obtained. If Elizabeth were contracted to Anjou, Mary, by then a prisoner, could at least not be rescued in his favour. This was also one way of deflecting an enterprise of England, though it could – in extremist as opposed to royalist hands – assume other forms, such as a descent upon Ireland. But, so far as France was concerned, the enterprise really centred on Mary. Besides, the extremists, though very powerful in negative, destructive terms, were unlikely to accomplish any positive enterprise without control of the council. Thus, although the Marian match was not automatically dropped, their loss of power tended to drive them towards greater dependence upon Spain.

[1] *CSPF.*, *1564–5*, pp. 334–7, 15 April 1565, Smith to Elizabeth.
[2] *CSPSp.*, *1558–67*, p. 407, 15 March 1565, de Silva to Philip II.

Whether or not this had anything to do with it, Philip became considerably less cautious and more aggressive in his approach and, from 1571, the ever-impending enterprise of England was predominantly a Spanish threat.[1] This in turn inclined Elizabeth more favourably towards the crown of France. In France the crown badly needed some distraction, and 'harborage', as Walsingham said, for Anjou, some support against the catholic-Spanish-papal pressures by which it was forced towards the protestants, and some safeguard against the protestants' policy of 'transference'.

August 1570 was a time of great perplexity for queen Elizabeth and danger for England where, to judge from some reports – doubtless exaggerated – the fear of foreign invasion was bordering on panic.[2] The corollary to this was first and foremost the preparation of a fleet, but this forced the queen to consider the hazardous ordeal of parliament because of her great need for money.[3] Parliament, however, might be expected to create an undiplomatic clamour about the succession and the queen's marriage. She must therefore have something in hand with which to silence them. Besides, the peace in France alarmed her, since its implications for England were as yet uncertain. So, very likely, did the recent Habsburg marriages of both Philip II and Charles IX. Thus, Elizabeth began to reconsider her severely strained relations with Spain and, among other things, she reopened her fitful marriage negotiations with the archduke Charles of Austria.[4] By 31 August 1570 Sir Henry Cobham was already in the Netherlands on his way to the Empire, allegedly armed with

[1] La Mothe, iii, 299–301, 5 September 1570, La Mothe to Charles IX. La Mothe mentioned the increasing danger to England from Spain.

[2] *CSPSp.*, *1568–79*, p. 256, 30 June 1570, de Guaras to Zayas; 261, 28 July 1570, de Guaras to Zayas; 263, 1 August 1570, de Guaras to Zayas; 268–9, 12 August 1570, de Guaras to Zayas; 269–70, 16 August 1570, de Guaras to Zayas.

[3] La Mothe, iii, 266, 6 August 1570, La Mothe to Charles IX; 300–1, 5 September 1570, La Mothe to Charles IX; *CSPSp.*, *1568–79*, p. 262, 1 August 1570, de Guaras to Zayas; 265–6, 7 August 1570, de Guaras to Zayas; 273, 2 September 1570, de Spes to Philip II.

[4] La Mothe, iii, 289–301, 5 September 1570, La Mothe to Charles IX and Catherine; 358, 9 November 1570, *lettre à part* to Catherine.

sufficient authority and power 'to bind Elizabeth to whatever he may conclude as to the marriage,' though this hardly seems likely.[1]

Unpropitious as Cobham's negotiation may have been, the huguenots could hardly afford to await the outcome in idleness. While the amount of help they received from England could never be described as more than limited, nevertheless the alliance of England was absolutely essential both to them and to their Flemish confederates, and during the war they had all come to regard England as their headquarters and there were obvious naval reasons why they should continue to do so. Thus, already before the treaty of Saint-Germain, in order to impede what would, for the protestants, have been a catastrophic Habsburg alliance, Châtillon, through the agency of the puritan Throckmorton, proposed a marriage between Elizabeth and Henry of Navarre. The matter, however, was not pursued, supposedly on account of Henry's age and size, both of which were inadequate.[2] Whether or not for this reason, since the timing is not clear, the Anjou negotiation appears to have been secretly begun in England with Leicester and Cecil by Jean de Ferrières, the vidame de Chartres, an English pensioner, and was reported by La Mothe to have lasted for three months.[3]

Apart from the intrinsic incapability of the protestants to commit Anjou, the Navarre proposition also reflected both the Flemish and huguenot preference for some *direct*, binding link between themselves and England and, negatively, their dislike of the Bourbon marriage proposal which they suspected and distrusted. If, alternatively, Elizabeth were firmly attached to the French crown, the protestants might be reasonably safe. But if she were attached to them, without or apart from the crown, they might have expected her (probably wrongly) to be more

---

[1] *CSPVen.*, *1558–80*, p. 458, 27 September 1570, Soranzo and Michiel.

[2] Cobham's mission is the reason given by La Mothe, but the timing is uncertain. La Mothe, iii, 358, 9 November 1570, La Mothe to Catherine. La Mothe referred to this just a year later when the idea was revived. Ibid., vol. iv, 224–5, 7 September 1571, La Mothe to Charles IX.

[3] La Mothe, iii, 358, 9 November 1570, La Mothe to Catherine; *CSPF.*, *1566–8*, p. 26, 3 March 1566, the vidame to Elizabeth.

useful, and they would certainly have been more securely independent. The Navarre marriage, however, was hardly practicable and, furthermore, if Elizabeth recoiled from Anjou, a highly sophisticated Renaissance prince, whose personal qualities should be distinguished from his public failures, she could hardly have endured the uncouth, provincial Navarre, even were he not too small and too young.[1] Elizabeth's disinclination to marry has received dubious personal interpretations. But this was, politically, a wise and skilful policy until the problem of Mary's exile in England hurled her, in a different and dangerous sense, into the European maelstrom. Then she recognised the necessity to marry. Her aversion from Anjou and Alençon is sufficiently explained by their unsuitability.

Thus the Anjou marriage negotiation was a combined huguenot-Flemish initiative (though it might equally well have been a royal French one just a little later), and partly in order to deflect Elizabeth from even the residual possibility of a Hapsburg union, which might be expected to have a deleterious effect upon what they believed to be, or hoped would become, her international protestant and Netherlands policy. This dual negotiation enabled Elizabeth to render France in 'quelque jalouzie', and Spain 'encores une plus grande', and thereby to strengthen her position at home, whether against foreign invasion or the calling of parliament.[2]

With the conclusion of peace, the huguenot pursuit of the marriage and the Netherlands enterprise, the focus of political activity began, after further discussions in England, to shift back to France.[3] The vidame appears to have been the first to leave

[1] Guzmán de Silva, the former Spanish ambassador categorically stated that Elizabeth was tall, which is why she objected to a short suitor. Recollecting, no doubt, that Philip II was small she said she had refused him because, at the time, she had 'a great idea not to marry'. *CSPSp.*, *1558–67*, p. 409, 24 March 1565, Guzmán de Silva to Philip II.

[2] La Mothe, iii, 358–9, 9 November 1570, La Mothe *lettre à part* to Catherine.

[3] By 3 September 1570 the vidame had permission to return to France; Châtillon had also requested this; *CSPSp.*, *1568–79*, p. 276, 3 September 1570, de Guaras to Zayas.

England about 21 September, though it is uncertain whether he went home or to Paris; he is likely to have done both. It is also likely that others, such as Cavaignes and Bricquemault, went with him, since they were among those, including Téligny and La Noue, who represented the huguenots at the French court.[1] Châtillon may have awaited the return of Walsingham who had gone – at least ostensibly – to assist the conclusion of peace, and who was back in England by the end of September. However that may be, he appears to have left for Southampton between 5 and 10 October, with the blessing of the English government, since an order of the privy council required John and William Hawkins to transport him in 'the new bark which they have in charge' to La Rochelle or elsewhere.[2] According to de Spes, he had been summoned to La Rochelle by Coligny in order, among other things, to collect the fifth part of their property which they had promised to the King of France.[3] This arouses the suspicion that Charles may, as part of the treaty negotiations, have become involved in some general agreement to help in the Netherlands; though, if so, he had still to be converted to any particular project. Certainly the house of Orange-Nassau had recovered its French property by the terms of the treaty and, according to the nuncio, the protestants were already trying in August to persuade Charles to make count Louis a French pensioner. He declined until July 1571.[4]

De Spes was convinced of an English intention to 'molest' the Netherlands – against which Philip II himself wrote 'notice' – 'believing in this way that they will escape annoyance in their

---

[1] La Mothe, iii, 309–12, 19 September 1570, La Mothe to Charles IX; 325–6, 10 October 1570, La Mothe to Charles IX; *CSPF., 1569–71*, p. 423, 26 March 1571, Walsingham to Burghley. Cecil became lord Burghley on 25 February 1571. The vidame's biographer Bastard de L'Estaing is wrong in saying that he retired to Deux-Sèvres, p. 114; *CSPSp., 1568–79*, p. 279–80, 25 September 1570, de Spes to Philip II.

[2] *HMC Hatfield*, xiii, 101, 5 October 1570.

[3] *CSPSp., 1568–79*, p. 280, 25 September 1570, de Spes to Philip II.

[4] Hirschauer, *La Politique de St Pie V*, 110, 19 August 1570, Frangipani to Rusticucci.

own country',[1] and he reported Châtillon to have told the queen that the enterprise proposed by William of Orange could hardly proceed without money. He also asked La Mothe whether Châtillon had mentioned transferring the war from France to the Netherlands, and whether such a transference was simply a general desire of the protestants, or what he called an 'entreprinse bien preste'. La Mothe does not indicate what he thought.[2] It was obviously on account of the Netherlands' need for money that de Lumbres, William's agent and admiral, had permission from the privy council to amass riches by preying in pirate ships upon Flemish vessels – meaning, presumably, those in Spanish hands.[3] A Flemish and English pirate fleet of forty ships was being sent to join de Lumbres who already had fourteen or fifteen vessels at the Isle of Wight and was expecting others from La Rochelle.[4]

Before Châtillon left England, news had arrived from Henry Cobham from Spires that he had been coolly received by the emperor who witheld any answer concerning the archduke until after the marriage of Charles IX in November.[5] Rumour may well have been more specific, since already by 20 October Catherine in a letter to La Mothe referred to the betrothal of the archduke to his niece, the daughter to the duke of Bavaria.[6] It may, therefore, well be that instead of going to La Rochelle at Coligny's behest, Châtillon hurried straight to Paris to further the Anjou marriage since, in the same letter of 20 October Catherine indicated that he had already put this proposition to Anjou, giving the impression that it could be easily concluded if they wished.[7] Catherine's own wishes were as favourable as

---

[1] *CSPSp., 1568–79*, p. 284, 28 October 1570, de Spes to Philip II.

[2] *CSPSp., 1568–79*, p. 284, 28 October 1570, de Spes to Philip II; La Mothe, iii, 332, 16 October 1570, La Mothe to Charles IX.

[3] *CSPSp., 1568–79*, p. 282, 15 October 1570, de Spes to Philip II.

[4] *CSPSp., 1568–79*, p. 284, 28 October 1570, de Spes to Philip II.

[5] *CSPSp., 1568–79*, p. 283, 15 October 1570, de Spes to Philip II.

[6] La Mothe, vii, 143–7, 20 October 1570, Catherine to La Mothe. Cobham himself said that the betrothal occurred on 22 October. *CSPF., 1569–71*, p. 360, 22 October 1570, Cobham to Cecil.

[7] Catherine wrote from Écouen, a Montmorency residence where she was seriously ill. She appears not to have seen Châtillon himself, but an anonymous

anyone's, but she tended to doubt Elizabeth's intention to marry.

Châtillon had also heard, before leaving England, that all the principal protestants were to assemble at La Charité – a *place de sûreté* – and thereafter meet at La Rochelle in the presence of Jeanne d'Albret.[1] On 22 October Nassau was reported in Paris to be going to La Rochelle and was shortly after said to be expected in England.[2] It is therefore quite possible that they went to La Rochelle together after Châtillon's negotiation in Paris. However, we know nothing for certain about his movements until de Spes reported on 28 November that he was in Leicester's London house.[3] Châtillon left again for Canterbury on 6 December, returning from 'Amptome' about the twentieth.[4] This itinerary suggests that he went to the French court of Villers-Cotterêts and, since he landed at Southampton, possibly returned via La Rochelle.

Circumstances could hardly have been more propitious for Châtillon's negotiation. During his two week's absence in December, three couriers had arrived in England from the Netherlands with letters containing Alva's rejection of Elizabeth's current terms for a settlement of the acrimonious commercial dispute between them, which had persisted since the appropriation of the Spanish treasure ships in December 1568. The privy council was pressing Elizabeth on the subject of this deeply damaging rupture,[5] since England's essential need for commerce

---

third person who had evidently made at least two journeys to visit her. Hirschauer, *La Politique de St Pie V*, 125, 22 October 1570, Frangipani to Rusticucci.

[1] *CSPSp.*, *1568–79*, p. 283, 15 October 1570, de Spes to Philip II.

[2] *CSPSp.*, *1568–79*, p. 284, 28 October 1570, de Spes to Philip II; Hirschauer, *La Politique de St Pie V*, 125, 22 October 1570, Frangipani to Rusticucci.

[3] *CSPSp.*, *1568–79*, pp. 285-6, 28 November 1570, de Spes to Philip II. He does not say when Châtillon returned and his previous recorded letter was of 28 October.

[4] La Mothe, iii, 414, 29 December 1570, La Mothe to Catherine.

[5] La Mothe, iii, 399–402, 13 December 1570, La Mothe to Charles IX; Gachard, *Notices et extraits*, ii, 507, 1 February 1571. Ferrals, the French envoy in the Netherlands, later reported to Charles IX the treaty between Alva and Elizabeth, which *she* then refused to sign. Alva himself had previously reported

with the Netherlands was more important than any *military* reason for avoiding war with Spain. About 10 December also, Cobham returned from the Empire signifying the archduke's termination of their negotiation. Elizabeth can hardly have been surprised, but she made a fine parade of being insulted.[1] More important, however, then her regal chagrin was the fact that thenceforth all Europe knew at least one thing for certain: she would never make a Habsburg marriage. This and Alva's rejection of her proposals could only be countered by a move towards France – including protestant France – especially as there was no loss of face or prestige in turning from the archduke to the duc d'Anjou, heir apparent to the French throne.

Thus lord Buckhurst was appointed, ostensibly to go and congratulate the king upon his marriage, and Walsingham named as resident ambassador, which is some indication of the importance of England's various relations with the French.[2]

Châtillon therefore conferred about Anjou with Leicester and, a few days later a Florentine agent, Guido Cavalcanti[3] arrived from France and broached the matter cautiously via 'ung grand circuyt de bonnes parolles'. But in fact even Elizabeth herself had begun to speak of Anjou, on account of the archduke's engagement. Cavalcanti then put the matter privately to Cecil, who was absent from court on account of illness.[4] As he received it favourably, the next move was for La Mothe, whose position as ambassador was more official, to approach Leicester, with whom

---

the settlement to be far advanced, which Philip II condemned as incompatible with England's plans, among other transgressions, to make Nassau 'head of the pirates'. He may have been thwarted, but he was not deceived by Elizabeth's duplicity. *CSPSp.*, *1568–79*, p. 292, 31 January 1571, Philip II to de Spes.

[1] La Mothe, iii, 424–6, 29 December 1570, La Mothe to Charles IX.

[2] *CSPSp.*, *1568–79*, p. 287, 13 December 1570, 288, 20 December 1570, de Spes to Philip II; La Mothe, iii, 410–20, 29 December 1570, La Mothe to Charles IX and to Catherine.

[3] Cavalcanti was a Florentine pensioner of both England and France like his compatriot Ridolphi, but less well connected and better trusted. *CSPSp.*, *1568–79*, p. 163, 13 June 1569, Alva to Philip II.

[4] La Mothe, iii, 416–20, 29 December 1570, La Mothe to Catherine.

the vidame and Châtillon had first begun, partly perhaps because he was very pro-protestant and had always opposed the Austrian match. Finally, Leicester conducted La Mothe to the queen whereby, at the end of December, the matter 'reached daylight'.[1]

Châtillon, who went to Canterbury at the end of December appears, as a result of these negotiations, to have made another journey to France. However this may be, on or before 18 January 1571, he had an important audience with the queen at which he presented a *lettre de créance* from Charles IX authorising him to treat of the marriage.[2] At the same time, Elizabeth declared her intention to marry, and Châtillon once again left for Canterbury on 24 or 25 January 1571,[3] presumably to conduct the next stage in France. If so, it would appear that the negotiation was brisk. His movements, however, are not clear, and he was still or again in Canterbury when he became ill about a month later.

Châtillon, like Coligny and d'Andelot, had escaped Lorraine's *coup* in 1568. With the return of peace, his influence in England and his relative favour with Catherine were immensely dangerous to the catholics and, on 11 August, the date of the treaty of Saint-Germain, Norris specifically warned him against one Brinon, an agent of Lorraine.[4] When he died at Canterbury on 24 March, it was widely believed, among others by his wife, 'madame la cardinale', and, more significantly, by Walsingham that he had been poisoned. Queen Elizabeth herself was sufficiently disturbed to place his entire household under detention, and to appoint commissioners to report upon an enquiry and autopsy. The result of the autopsy was inconclusive because the liver and lungs were so corrupted as to cause surprise that he had survived so long. On the other hand, he had primarily complained of a

---

[1] La Mothe, iii, 417–20, 29 December 1570, La Mothe to Charles IX.

[2] La Mothe, iii, 438–42, 18 January 1571, La Mothe to Catherine. The whole negotiation was supposed to be deeply secret.

[3] La Mothe, iii, 455, 31 January 1571, La Mothe to Catherine. A letter dated 2 February 1571, Canterbury, from Châtillon to Charles IX is the last we hear of him. *CSPF., 1569–71*, p. 400.

[4] *CSPF., 1569–71*, pp. 314–15, 11 August 1570, Norris to Cecil.

'burning grief at his stomach', and it was precisely the condition of the stomach, 'fretted and pierced through', which was declared symptomatic of the 'operation of poison'. The physicians, who had previously diagnosed an ordinary tertian fever, thought something had been administered when they saw this condition.[1] At the time of his death Châtillon had been seriously ill for a month, since 22 February. Thus the solution could be that, having fallen ill from natural causes, someone took the opportunity and precaution of ensuring that he did not recover. Some accounts allege that he was poisoned by a Basque valet who was arrested as a spy, confessed to the crime, and was executed at La Rochelle two years later. But it appears that the fellow, Vuillin, was tortured, which vitiates his evidence. The vidame de Chartres in a letter to Burghley of 23 March 1573 – some time later – said that two Italians, Pacheco and Pietro Bizarri, confessed to having been suspected of some design against Châtillon.[2]

Whether or not Châtillon was poisoned, his illness and death were highly opportune for the catholics, just as the marriage negotiation had begun to show, as he said, 'quelque fondement'.[3] Indeed, the timing of his death, as Ridolphi was leaving England to plot against Elizabeth in the Netherlands, Rome and Madrid, and frustrate, above all, the Anjou marriage, is not the least suspicious of the circumstances. The cardinal's removal could only be regarded as an inestimable benefit, more particularly since it led to the isolation of Coligny. Just as the catholics had been left in time of war without their general, so the protestants were left in time of 'peace' without their diplomat.

Although, to judge from the surviving evidence – which is sparse – Châtillon was primarily working on the Anjou marriage which at least before the betrothal of the archduke, was the most urgent matter, there is reason to suppose that he also went to La Rochelle, where Nassau and the Flemings were arming

---

[1] Atkinson, *The Cardinal of Châtillon in England*, 82–5. Châtillon was buried in Canterbury cathedral.
[2] Atkinson, *The Cardinal of Châtillon in England*, 88. Pacheco and Bizarri were agents who turn up fairly frequently about this time.
[3] La Mothe, iii, 455, 31 January 1571, La Mothe to Catherine.

'pirate' ships,[1] and that he did not lose sight of the Netherlands enterprise. Upon his return from 'Amptome', towards the end of December 1570, he had questioned La Mothe 'curiously' as to the king's intentions about the observation of the peace of Saint-Germain and whether he did not wish to escape from his subjection to Spain and other princes 'qui tirannisent [la] couronne' – an obvious reference to the Netherlands, by which this could be done.[2]

If Châtillon had indeed visited the French court in December and perhaps again in January 1571, he must have encountered there one Gian Galeazzo Fregoso, an obscure Genoese agent, who seems to have served in several capacities and was engaged at this time in helping to raise money for the Netherlands enterprise. He had been in England, where La Mothe referred to him as a familiar figure, during the summer of 1570, among the group of French and Flemish exiles of which Châtillon was the most distinguished. He was a servant of William of Orange and, possibly by way of reward, in July 1570 was made captain of a ship seized in William's name.[3] Fregoso, like Châtillon himself, evidently left England about the first week in October 1570, and probably went to Florence to seek the support of Cosimo dei Medici, the grand duke of Tuscany – a kinsman of Catherine – whose principal significance lay in his bulging coffers and, at that moment, his disfavour with Spain, who objected to his new title, conferred by the pope. According to La Huguerye, who can be confused and unreliable in matters of chronology, the grand duke sent Fregoso on to the elector Palatine with an offer of 200,000 écus.[4] This figure is unsubstantiated, and poses a problem since he

[1] *CSPSp.*, *1568–79*, p. 289, 9 January 1571, de Spes to Philip II.

[2] Châtillon may have been referring to forty-two articles of complaint against contraventions of the treaty, prepared for submission to the king while the German ambassadors were at court. Charles is said to have ignored them until the ambassadors had gone, when Cavaignes expounded them in council. The timing, however, is uncertain. La Huguerye, *Mémoires*, i, 17; La Mothe, iii, 414–15, 29 December 1570, La Mothe to Catherine.

[3] Desjardins, *Negs. Tosc.*, iii, 648, 8 March 1571; La Mothe, iii, 250, 25 July 1570, La Mothe to Charles IX.

[4] La Huguerye, *Mémoires*, i, 14.

was so recently held to have supported the English earls with the same amount. The Calvinist elector was an old ally of the huguenots and of William, whose Dillenburg estates were close to the Palatinate. The elector had married the widow of count Brederode, a supporter of William, and tended to follow the policy of the elector of Saxony, William's father-in-law.[1] This explains why, as La Huguerye alleged, Fregoso came from Heidelberg when he arrived at the French court at Villers-Cotterêts, presumably in December 1570[2] since the German ambassadors were there,[3] and also La Huguerye himself in the service of Bricquemault. According to La Huguerye, Fregoso's mission was to engage the king in war in the Netherlands, and it

[1] Vogler, 'Le Rôle des électeurs palatins dans les guerres de religion en France, 1559–1592', *Cahiers d'histoire*, x (1965).

[2] Because Fregoso is said to have come to France from Tuscany via the Palatinate, his role has been reversed, and he has been widely represented as an agent of the grand duke seeking to interest Charles in a Netherlands enterprise in order to spite and to distract Philip II, and possibly also the emperor, both of whom, for different reasons, had angrily opposed his new, sovereign status. It is true that the grand duke was conscious of the hostility of Spain, and would therefore be relieved to see her embroiled in the Netherlands. But, to assume from this, as has been done, that the Netherlands project, as it matured in France during 1571, sprang from the initiative of the grand duke of Tuscany, promoted by an obscure Genoese agent, is an absurdity. Even supposing that it were possible for the grand duke to organise an invasion of the Netherlands, one would still have to explain why Petrucci, his ambassador in France, was unaware of his intentions, and why Fregoso was twice sent to Florence to seek his support, which he withheld. The explanation, as one would expect, is that the – or a – Netherlands project proceeded, not from Italy, but from William of Orange, via England. Petrucci himself described Fregoso as a servant of William; so did La Mothe. These misconceptions have been taken from Desjardins, *Deux Années de règne, 1570–1572*, which has been rather slavishly followed, doubtless on account of his good editing of Petrucci's despatches. But used in isolation they are misleading. Desjardins, *Negs. Tosc.*, iii, 648, 8 March 1571; La Mothe, iii, 250, 25 July 1570, La Mothe to Charles IX.

[3] The German ambassadors were at court by 23 December 1570 when Charles was harangued by representatives of the electors of Saxony and Brandenburg, the dukes of Bavaria, Brunswick, Württemberg and Mecklenburg, the landgrave of Hesse and the marquis of Baden. There is no mention of the elector Palatine who was probably represented by Fregoso himself. Goulart, *Mémoires de l'Estat de France sous Charles IX*, i, 24.

is only from this time that the direct indoctrination of Charles IX can actually be traced.[1]

Unfortunately we are dependent, at this stage, upon La Huguerye who is both unreliable, confused and in this instance ignorant. To begin with, he writes of Fregoso as a stranger, whom the protestants did not trust, and whose mission was novel to them and to Nassau, presumably because he took Fregoso to be a servant of the grand duke of Tuscany. Whether or not they trusted Fregoso is another matter, but it is impossible to suppose that he had not been associated in England with the Flemish exiles and the huguenots Cavaignes, Bricquemault, the vidame, La Noue, Téligny and others with whom he arrived to negotiate in France; nor had the Netherlands enterprise, which he promoted there, been conceived in Florence.

Among the huguenot group at court, Téligny was evidently a key figure. It was doubtless during the course of the peace negotiations that he had come close to and won the regard of the king, and since, off and on, they had been associated in this way for so many months, it was natural that Charles should have continued to employ him as his protestant intermediary with Anjou, in the matter of the marriage, with the Tuscan Petrucci, and with Fregoso, Coligny and Nassau. Louis of Nassau, like Téligny, was young and intrepid and must have been a man of considerable magnetism, certainly he later captivated Walsingham. Like the other 'chefs', Nassau was based at La Rochelle at this time, hand in glove with the huguenots, with whom he had served in the third civil war, and no Netherlands enterprise could have proceeded without him. As William's brother and roving ambassador, who had already been personally defeated by Alva,[2] he had a higher stake in the enterprise than anyone else, while remaining unaffected by its complications – sectional, national and international – from which neither Coligny, as effective leader of the huguenots, nor the crown of France could escape.

[1] La Huguerye, *Mémoires*, i, 11–14; *CSPVen.*, *1558–80*, p. 461, 28 December 1570.

[2] Gachard, *Notices et extraits*, ii, 463, 18 July 1568, Ferrals to Charles IX from Groningen.

It was therefore Téligny, Nassau and their supporters who, in the face of mounting opposition most strongly influenced the king, and urged him towards the Netherlands; not the absent Coligny as it has always been assumed. It was they who, together with Fregoso, began to evolve some plan of action – since there was as yet no 'entreprinse preste', as de Spes put it – as well as trying to elicit general support, raise money in Italy, Germany and England, and to arouse enthusiasm.

The timing of events is not clear, but it must have been in January or February that Fregoso pursued his mission to La Rochelle, though one must discount as obvious nonsense what La Huguerye says about his having 'converted' La Noue, Téligny and Nassau. He also says that Fregoso communicated with Nassau through the seigneur de la Prée Taffin, one of the court group of Flemings, and that Coligny was 'informed' separately; we do not know what of.[1] The initial idea appears to have been that they should start by opposing Spain at sea, propositions, La Huguerye says, which Nassau was already able to entertain, there being many ships of William's under the command of de Lumbres, which were landing their prizes near La Rochelle. This was not startlingly original since there is ample evidence that Nassau and his confederates were already fully embarked upon opposing Spain at sea, that renewed conflict in the Netherlands was already brewing, and that Nassau required neither convertion nor inspiration from Florence, though he would certainly have welcomed any ducal contribution, as well as encouragement from Heidelberg and Paris.

In fact a proposal to make Nassau 'head of the pirates' or, more politely, William's commander, 'to the number of thirty-five sail', had already been discussed in England in December 1570.[2] De Lumbres himself appears to have remained in England where William's sea 'beggars' were primarily based, until April 1571, when he sailed from Plymouth with artillery from the Tower

[1] La Huguerye, *Mémoires*, i, 16, 19, 21.

[2] *CSPSp.*, *1568–79*, p. 288, 20 December 1570, de Spes to Philip II; 292, 31 January 1571, Philip II to de Spes.

and a good sum of money.¹ There were, however, reports in January 1571 that the *gueux de mer*² were renewing the war in Flanders, and of a new levy of men in Germany which Elizabeth believed to be in support of Orange. Two months later Walsingham wrote to Cecil that Alva himself had heard that Orange was raising forces in Germany, and La Mothe also wrote in February of talk in England of preparations against the Netherlands in England, France and Denmark.³ The Spanish ambassador claimed not to believe it, but he reiterated his report to Philip II that Nassau was arming at La Rochelle, and had sent a servant to England to summon the corsairs to join him with artillery and stores which the queen was lending him. He estimated that they would have twelve fine ships including one great Venetian ship.⁴ De Spes also heard a few weeks later that Châtillon had sought permission for Nassau to bring certain warships from La Rochelle to join de Lumbres and assist him in holding the channel.⁵ This request was presumably favourably received since Châtillon was then making good progress at court with the marriage negotiation, and Walsingham had been commanded that Nassau, who expressed gratitude for Elizabeth's favours, was not to be hindered in his efforts at La Rochelle.⁶

Still according to La Huguerye, Fregoso evidently went on to hint at the possibility of royal support for something more definite than piracy, arousing Nassau's enthusiasm – if this were

---

¹ Kervyn de Lettenhove, *Relations*, vi, 7, 27 October 1570, de Spes to Alva; La Mothe, iv, 74, 28 April 1571, La Mothe to Charles IX; 103–5, 13 May 1571, La Mothe to Charles IX.

² Gachard, *Notices et extraits*, ii, 502, 30 December 1570, Ferrals to Charles IX. Van den Bergh attacked the area in which he had confiscated property; Ibid., 502, seq.

³ Kervyn de Lettenhove, *Relations*, vi, 32–3, 4 January 1571, John Fitzwilliam to Cecil; La Mothe, iii, 437–8, 18 January 1571, La Mothe to Charles IX; 445, 23 January 1571, La Mothe to Charles IX; 463, 6 February 1571, La Mothe to Charles IX; Digges, 48, 5 March 1570, Walsingham to Cecil.

⁴ *CSPSp.*, *1568–79*, p. 289, 9 January 1571, de Spes to Philip II.

⁵ La Mothe, iii, 464–5, 6 February 1571.

⁶ Kervyn de Lettenhove, *Relations*, vi, 61, 14 February 1571, Nassau to Walsingham, and p. 61, n. 1.

necessary. Thus Nassau is said to have told Fregoso – the procedure appears to be circular – how much he could do for the King of France in the Netherlands, even without his name being mentioned, 'par plusieurs grandes entreprises sur plusieurs places des Pays-Bas tant en la frontière qu'au cœur', provided he would empower the huguenot leaders to perform these exploits by means of those of their followers who were close to the frontier. This may be regarded as substantially true since the 'practising' and capture of important towns is what William had in mind, and indeed in hand, and what was later unsuccessfully attempted.

While Fregoso was still at La Rochelle, Téligny had evidently been working hard on the king. Petrucci said Charles had a longing to be great, and he had heard by 8 March that the king was 'won over'. Charles, in turn, set Téligny to work upon Petrucci, because they hoped his master, the grand duke, would subscribe to their further plans.[1] Talk of a project to make war in Italy was used, and probably embellished, by Téligny to add persuasion to his arguments. Charles, he said, opposed it, but he was 'ardentissimo et resoluto' in the cause of Flanders.

While it is easy to rectify La Huguerye's errors about the origins of the Netherlands enterprise, it is not easy to interpret what he says about Coligny and his relations with Nassau, matters of fundamental importance. The memoir goes on to say that Fregoso made no impression, and that Nassau vainly 'importuned' Coligny, who distrusted the negotiation on account of its source. Distrust there evidently was, but clearly on account of the implications, not the source of the negotiation which was familiar enough. What Coligny necessarily feared was ill-defined involvement with the crown of France, and herein lay his basic, political and personal difference from Nassau, who had no responsibilities in France, but required her material and military help only less than the naval help of England. Whether or not Coligny was really importuned, rather than consulted, this

---

[1] Desjardins, *Negs. Tosc.*, iii, 648, 22 February 1571; 648–52, 8 March 1571; 652, 14 March 1571; 655–7, 19 March 1571.

bypass procedure was hardly reassuring. It becomes clear that he did not give his support to the project, as then proposed, which involved both the leadership and the party generally, and which was forthwith pursued *with* the king and *without* Coligny, to a point of virtual no return. This prevented him from exercising any choice or judgement in the matter, and so, when it was no longer wise or practicable to oppose it, he strove, but failed, to persuade the king to execute the operation properly.

If Coligny, in his absence, was placed in a difficult position, Catherine de Medici also found herself awkwardly involved on account of the increasing interdependence of the Netherlands enterprise, the English marriage and the Bourbon marriage, and the extent to which these projects concerned the same personnel. Peace and general reconciliation, to be achieved through the Bourbon marriage – which it was held would bring the huguenot prince within the royal aegis – were her priorities. For this, she too, besides the Flanders protagonists, required the help of her kinsman the grand duke, whom she hoped might intercede with the pope for the necessary marriage dispensation.[1] While Catherine worked harder than anyone for the English marriage, she was strongly averse from anything which might entail trouble with Spain. The Netherlands enterprise could hardly be expected not to, and Catherine's opposition, or even the absence of her support was necessarily a serious handicap in any major matter. To achieve the Bourbon marriage, she would be ill-advised to antagonise Louis of Nassau, who had, since the peace of Saint-Germain, served Henry's mother Jeanne d'Albret,[2] yet Nassau was necessarily the principal protagonist of the Netherlands enterprise which Catherine was right – it subsequently transpired – in regarding as mortally dangerous. Here, therefore, was a further serious cause of tension at court, and another genuine distinction in policy, but which became difficult to sustain in action, and is now difficult to trace.

[1] Desjardins, *Negs. Tosc.*, iii, 657–61, 23 March 1571.
[2] Gachard, *Notices et extraits*, ii, 351, 12 November 1571, Forquevaulx to Charles IX; 364, 16 January 1572, instructions for Saint-Gouard, French ambassador to Spain.

La Huguerye becomes more than usually confused about events which followed Fregoso's return from La Rochelle between 8 and 14 March 1571. It appears that Charles, having received Nassau's proposals with enthusiasm, immediately sent Fregoso back to Florence – presumably about the Netherlands and the Bourbon marriage – and meanwhile requested Bricquemault to put him into touch with Nassau and to persuade Coligny to co-operate.[1] Thus, it was probably in April, though this is uncertain, that Nassau attended at Téligny's Paris lodging in the rue de Seine, what was evidently an important secret meeting of 'une bonne partye des négociateurs de ces entreprises'.[2] In this way, La Huguerye reveals the presence in Paris of a whole group of Netherlands exiles among whom he names the seigneur d'Eskerder, brother of the sea captain de Lumbres, de Marquette, Vimy de Noyelles, de Famaz – who landed at Brill with the sea beggars in April 1572 – Turqueau, le grand Anthoine (Anthoine Ollivier), the intermediary at La Rochelle La Prée Taffin, and also the comte de Limay who, he says, 'couroit le comté de Zélande pour y négotier des surprises'.[3] At this meeting the associates are said to have planned to deliver into the king's hands the entire frontier of Hainault and Artois. This was hardly something which could be done without even involving the king's name, let alone the hostility of Spain, as Nassau had optimistically and irresponsibly proposed, thereby encouraging the king to persuade himself that he could safely run risks without incurring danger. It appears that specific military plans were discussed in Paris and that the occupation of particular towns or areas was actually assigned to individuals, since we learn only a little later that the specific task of the 'grand Anthoine' was 'sur une ville capitale d'une province'.[4]

Thus, by approximately the end of April 1571, the king had

[1] Desjardins, *Negs. Tosc.*, iii, 655, 19 March 1571; 657–61, 23 March 1571. Fregoso evidently departed almost at once.

[2] Desjardins, *Negs. Tosc.*, iii, 657–61, 23 March 1571; La Huguerye, *Mémoires*, i, 22–4.

[3] La Huguerye, *Mémoires*, i, 24–5.

[4] La Huguerye, *Mémoires*, i, 27.

evidently been persuaded to sanction (it is not clear whether the extent of his commitment was ever defined) a fairly ambitious Netherlands plan, elaborated between Téligny and the protestants at court, a group of refugee gentry from the Netherlands, Louis of Nassau and their liaison agent, Fregoso. In all this Coligny had been passive; at best informed, and at worst importuned. It is clear that he neither approved of, nor consented to, the form the enterprise was taking. It is also clear that, if it were to proceed, the king had need of him.

The protestants, however, were not getting everything their own way. The catholics were making strenuous efforts to dis-unite them, and had equally been putting strong pressures upon the king. Whether or not they knew of the more definite plans developed at La Rochelle and Paris, and canvassed in Florence, a general threat to the Netherlands had long been obvious. They also knew of the particular activities of William of Orange and the increasing audacity of his 'pirates', with the complicity of England,[1] as well as the more easily traversed Anjou negotiation which had, for some weeks past, been the object of their frantic concern.

When Châtillon left for Canterbury in the last week of January, he had expressed the opinion that his negotiation had begun to show 'quelque fondement' but, 'non qu'il y en vît encores nul pour s'y debvoir arrester'.[2] Apart from the fact that La Mothe judged Elizabeth perversely likely to flee when most *recherchée*, the 'arresting' forces were just beginning to marshal their strength, in England as well as in France. In the first place, there was, according to La Mothe, considerable division within the privy council, and what he described as 'une merveilleuse contention,' although the matter was supposed to be secret. In his official despatch, La Mothe himself referred to it in veiled terms such as 'le faict de la petite lettre,' namely a private one *à part* to Catherine. They tended to blame its leakage on the past

---

[1] See, for example, *CSPSp.*, 1568–70, pp. 294–5, 2 March 1571, de Spes to Philip II, in which he refers to the great and dangerous extent of this complicity for which the detailed evidence is considerable.

[2] La Mothe, iii, 455, 31 January 1571, La Mothe to Catherine.

indiscretions of the vidame de Chartres with whom Walsingham declined to deal because he was 'not secret'.[1]

While opposition to the marriage within the council was not necessarily catholic, La Mothe said that the catholic lords and supporters of Mary – most of whom in fact were then elsewhere and not attending the council – were scandalised at this negotiation, conducted by Châtillon to accommodate the needs of the huguenots. He added that the Spanish ambassador and the unnamed papal agent – Ridolphi – had learnt of this factional discontent in England.[2] The only explanation of this otherwise curiously stale observation is that he was referring to what one might call the 'Ridolphi phase' of this continuing factional discontent.

In France, Walsingham who after three weeks, had his first, audience on 25 January 1571[3] shortly after Châtillon's promising *démarche* in England, already saw more opposition than 'fondement' in the matter of the marriage, though he seized upon this early opportunity to send Leicester his requested description of Anjou. He was, he said, esteemed three fingers higher than Walsingham himself, 'in complexion somewhat sallow, his bodie of very good shape, his leg long and small, but reasonably well proportioned; what helps he had to supply any defects of nature, I know not; touching the health of his person, I find the opinion diverse, as I know not what to credit; and for my own part, I

---

[1] De Spes had referred to the matter at least as early as December, and then not as though it were news to him. *CSPSp., 1568–79*, p. 288, 20 December 1570, de Spes to Philip II; La Mothe, iii, 438–42, 18 January 1571, La Mothe, *lettre à part* to Catherine; Digges, 33–4, 16 January 1571, Leicester to Walsingham; *CSPF., 1569–71*, p. 423, 26 March 1571, Walsingham to Burghley.

[2] La Mothe, iii, 438–42, 18 January 1571, La Mothe, *lettre à part* to Catherine; La Mothe referred rather curiously to the English catholics as 'la partie la plus grande, plus noble et plus forte'. Ibid., iii, 448, 23 January 1571, La Mothe, *lettre à part* to Catherine. He was probably impressed by the extent of the disaffection among the upper nobility, very many of whom were kinsmen. But just how catholic they were is another matter; many no more than suited their prospects.

[3] This was at the *château* of Madrid in the Bois de Boulogne. Charles had been away at Chantilly, the principal Montmorency residence.

forbear to be over curious in the search thereof, for divers respects; if all be so well as outwardlie it sheweth, then he is of bodie sound enough. And yet at this present, I did not finde him so well coloured, as I esteemed him to be at my last being here'.[1]

It was upon Anjou that the catholic opposition necessarily centred in France, where the pope, Spain and the 'rest of the confederates' – including, apparently, Lorraine, who had returned from Rheims for the purpose – sought to dissuade him from the English marriage. No longer able to proffer Mary or an Anglo-Scottish enterprise, they proposed instead to make him 'head and chief executioner of the League against the Turk, a thing now newly renewed'.[2] It was also to induce Charles to join the League that, upon pretext of the royal marriage, Bramante the nuncio extraordinary had really come to France,[3] where his hectoring and censorious pronouncements were anything but persuasive.[4] The proposal (if serious) to place Anjou at the head of the League was no by means absurd, since its command was much debated. But Walsingham wittily observed that the League really stretched to 'as many as they repute to be Turks (although better Christians than themselves)' and the king, who seemed very much to 'mislike hereof,' declared that if the matter went forward, 'it behoveth me to make some counter league'. For this purpose he could only turn to Elizabeth who, he supposed with more presumption than logic, would be glad to join him.[5] This, of course, assumes Walsingham's 'catholic' interpretation of Turk; otherwise an anti-Ottoman league might be held to favour England by diverting Philip's attention to the Mediterranean, which it did.

---

[1] Digges, 22–6, 29 January 1571, Norris and Walsingham to Elizabeth; 28–30, 29 January 1571, Walsingham to Leicester. Leicester had in fact requested portraits of both Charles and Anjou, but this was forbidden without licence.

[2] Digges, 26, 28 January 1571, Walsingham to Cecil.

[3] Hirschauer, *La Politique de St Pie V*, 128, 8 November 1570, Bramante to Rusticucci. Bramante arrived three months after the Turks had landed in Cyprus.

[4] Hirschauer, *La Politique de St Pie V*, 139–52, s.d., *c. fin* 1570.

[5] Digges, 26–7, 28 January 1571, Walsingham to Cecil.

Whether or not Anjou aspired to make war on the Turks, Ottoman or otherwise, he announced his refusal of Elizabeth just when she had declared her own intention to marry. It was the mortified Catherine herself, in a secret letter and a great state of consternation, who informed La Mothe of Anjou's obstinate opposition, admitting her inability to budge him, although he was normally obedient. This embarrassment forced her to disclose how much they wished to have 'ce royaulme entre les mains d'un de mes enfans', hardly a realistic conception of marriage with Elizabeth.[1] It was therefore upon this occasion that Catherine first suggested substituting Alençon for his brother. The trouble was that he was both small and disfigured.

It is difficult to determine to what extent Anjou's refusal may have reflected his own sentiments when he saw that the negotiation was serious. Politically, if not personally, it was the most dazzling possible match, except that, as heir presumptive, he was probably reluctant to burn his Gallic boats and leave the country. There would also be serious inconveniences in the union of two reigning monarchs. If his royal prospects were potentially reduced by his brother's recent marriage, Charles was still chronically sick and also, as it happened at the end of January yet again acutely ill with 'a burning Ague', doubtless symptomatic of the consumption which killed him only three years later.[2] Besides, Lorraine, Alva and the Spanish ambassador did not 'stick to use [upon Anjou] many dishonourable arguments . . . and some arguments of danger'.[3] The dishonourable sort were disobliging insinuations about Elizabeth's personal reputation, presumably in reference to the earl of Leicester, whose suit was once more canvassed in

[1] La Mothe, vii, 178–80, 2 February 1571, Catherine to La Mothe. It would be traditional to interpret this as foolish maternal ambition. A better explanation – and there are also others – would appear to be that, whether effective or not, it was the only possible means by which the crown could hope to prevent the foreign policy of England from threatening the interests and safety of France, at the same time exorcising Catherine's continuous and justified fear of war with Spain.

[2] Digges, 28, 28 January 1571, Walsingham to Cecil. Charles fathered an illegitimate son, and one legitimate daughter.

[3] Digges, 43, 18 February 1571, Walsingham to Cecil.

England by the Spanish ambassador; conceivably just what Elizabeth wanted.[1] The Leicester affair could be used and abused, but dishonourable arguments were ill-advised since Alva himself – if not in public – declared Anjou to be entirely absorbed in wenching.[2] The nuncio, for his part, crudely informed Anjou that Elizabeth was a barren heretic, and that as he chiefly aimed at England he could have that with less inconvenience by the sword, which the Guises and Don Francés de Alava made out to be 'a matter of no great consequence, in respect of the intelligence they have there'.[3]

Conversely, this was one good reason why Elizabeth might wish to pursue the Anjou negotiation herself, and she had no intention, if she could help it, of permitting Mary's 'enlargement' from detention in England, whether by release, rescue or escape.[4]

Besides these 'dishonourable arguments', the nuncio was also employing another powerful 'argument of danger': namely to 'draw Anjou,' with large sums of money, into an elaborate scheme for a descent upon Ireland. This was primarily a Spanish enterprise whose success would have profitted her greatly since, with the Spaniards in Ireland, Elizabeth could never have relaxed, nor safely turned away to trouble the Netherlands. Walsingham believed the Guises to be 'great dealers in it', and the matter one of 'great consequency'. Indeed he expressed the urgent hope that Ireland would not be neglected, as Calais had been – a feckless

---

[1] La Mothe, iii, 461, 6 February 1571, La Mothe, *lettre à part* to Catherine.
[2] Kervyn de Lettenhove, *Documents inédits du XVIe siècle*, 135–59, undated. Alva also called him gentle, amiable and weak, which his subsequent career would tend to confirm; hardly a match for queen Elizabeth.
[3] Digges, 36–7, 8 February 1571, Walsingham to Cecil – *CSPF., 1569–71*, p. 403, gives 9 February 1571; Digges, 43, 18 February 1571, Walsingham to Cecil; La Mothe, vii, 178–80, 2 February 1571, Catherine to La Mothe.
[4] There had already been a conspiracy to this purpose in November 1570, which was 'letted' because the ships were not ready, but the intention was not abandoned, as Walsingham reported in June 1571. *CSPF., 1569–71*, pp. 408–9, 23 February 1571, Walsingham to Cecil; 479, 25 June 1571, Walsingham to Burghley.

error which now mattered far more to Elizabeth than ever it had to Marian England.[1]

Thus there were ample pressures upon Anjou both to discourage him from a marriage which was so alarmingly opposed, and to unnerve any sensitive young man of small experience. But his disconcerting refusal did not end the matter, since Catherine could never abandon the struggle against the subversions of the extreme catholic interest at court, and Elizabeth's need of France was never greater. Walsingham – who had no commission to treat of marriage – was strongly in favour, and pressed on Catherine not only the need for amity with England, but also a league with the German princes. At the same time, he urged Leicester to use his influence to expedite the negotiation in England, if no harm were to be done. This entreaty crossed with a letter from the queen providing Walsingham with discretionary power to pursue the marriage, although she rather feared impediment than success, and not unnaturally wanted clarification about Ireland.[2] Walsingham got no response from the Spanish ambassador about Ireland, and told Burghley that he 'never spake with a prouder man or with one more disdainful in countenance and speech,' vowing that he would have nothing to do with him.[3] This postulates some success in the catholic attempts to trouble Anglo-French relations and in March, cardinal Pellevé wrote that Anjou was not willing

[1] Digges, 34–6, 8 February 1571, Walsingham to Cecil; 38, 8 February 1571, Walsingham to Sir Walter Mildmay; 42–3, 18 February 1571, Walsingham to Cecil. Not only was Lorraine said to have returned from Rheims, but the duc de Guise was evidently at court since Petrucci reported him to have created an affray over some trivial exclusion of his page. Desjardins, *Negs. Tosc.*, iii, 657, 19 March 1571. De Spes reported having received news from France that the pope had granted Ireland to Philip II. This, whether true or false, illustrates the current type of excitation of catholics against the queen and, if true, would also be calculated to diminish Philip's anger at the papal elevation of the duke of Florence to grand duke of Tuscany. This was important, since he was struggling to combine the League, for which he needed Spanish support. *CSPSp.*, 1568–79, p. 293, 12 February 1571, de Spes to Philip II.

[2] Digges, 39–40, 11 February 1571, Elizabeth to Walsingham.

[3] Digges, 45–7, 25 February 1571, Walsingham to Burghley.

to marry Elizabeth and that if the Kings of France and Spain 'would accord,' there would be great hope of his marriage to Mary, to which he was well disposed, and by this means the catholics in England might be set free.[1] This was the papal notion sponsored by Ridolphi, and echoes the same naïvety that, once under the papal banner, France and Spain would cease to be rivals and move as one.

But if the active 'accord' of France and Spain was improbable, the catholics' pursuit of Mary still remained a powerful reason why Elizabeth should seek to secure Anjou herself, more particularly since Philip had written to his ambassador about Mary's restoration, and seemed likely to take action. 'Il y est tout prest et tout resolu', wrote La Mothe to Catherine, in a secret memoir of 6 February 1571. He went on to say that the pope had already supplied Alva with money, 'sellon que l'ordre en sera mandé par Ridolfy', who pressed la Mothe – just as Pellevé proposed – that France and Spain should unite in 'that enterprise' – what precisely that was, is not defined.[2] At the same time, ways and means of executing the Spanish enterprise of England were also under discussion in the council in Brussels. It was considered that the least dangerous and expensive procedure would be the secret encouragement of the partisans of the queen of Scots and the catholics.[3] If this was nothing new, and rather less than 'tout pres et tout resolu', they were still 'arguments of danger' for Elizabeth, which doubtless prompted her to question Norris closely about Anjou. Norris, upon Leicester's advice, praised him inordinately, and Elizabeth, now persuaded of the necessity of the marriage, in spite of her aversion, actually proposed a maritime meeting with Anjou, to be arranged during her summer progress. This, she apparently succeeded in persuading

[1] This extract was later sent by Walsingham to Burghley with his letter of 8 October 1571. *CSPF., 1569–71*, p. 545.

[2] La Mothe, iii, 466, 6 February 1571, La Mothe, *lettre à part* to Catherine; *CSPF., 1569–71*, pp. 408–9, 23 February 1571, Walsingham to Cecil; 409, advertisements from France, s.d.n.l.

[3] Gachard, *Correspondance de Philippe II*, ii, 170–1, 23 February 1571, Alva to Philip II.

herself, could be secretly contrived. She could hardly go further to meet him.[1]

If the catholic pressure on Anjou was great, Catherine's could be weighty also, and, in the middle of February, before too much time had elapsed, she informed La Mothe that she had 'persuaded' Anjou.[2] Téligny, Charles' intermediary, who strongly supported the English marriage in the hope of uniting the two crowns in the Netherlands enterprise, complained that he still found Anjou 'si contraire'. Catherine inevitably denied it, though she admitted to lord Buckhurst that there were 'great hinderers'.[3] This meant, among others, her old adversary Lorraine, who went about to persuade Anjou to the Scottish marriage with the help of Ville-quier, one of the unscrupulous intimates by whom Anjou was all too easily swayed, and to whom, for his pains, Lorraine had promised the rich abbey of Fécamp.[4]

There is no evidence, in the midst of this tussle, that Anjou ever had consented to the English marriage. Either the catholics reflected his own private inclinations, or else one is forced to conclude that they proved too strong for him. But, for the moment, whether he was for or against, or merely confused and distraught, he had evidently been 'persuaded' to something; this enabled Catherine to proceed; but the question was how? The presence of Buckhurst, a man of rank, whose mission Châtillon had long-sightedly advised, facilitated this. After having worked extensively with Cavalcanti,[5] Catherine 'encountered'

[1] La Mothe, iv, 9–10, 6 March 1571, La Mothe to Charles IX. Walsingham's discretionary power and Elizabeth's recognition of the need to marry should probably be related to the writ summoning parliament, which was out by 14 February. Digges, 47, 14 February 1571, Leicester to Walsingham.

[2] La Mothe, vii, 183–4, 18 February 1571, Catherine to La Mothe.

[3] La Mothe, vii, 189–93, 2 March 1571, Catherine to La Mothe. *CSPVen.*, *1558–80*, p. 465, 23 February 1571, Contarini to the doge; *CSPF.*, *1569–71*, pp. 409–10, 24 February 1571, Buckhurst to Elizabeth. The timing of the mission of Buckhurst, a man of rank and therefore corresponding authority, who had arrived in Paris by 23 February, is further evidence of Elizabeth's great anxiety, particularly if she had heard of Anjou's humiliating refusal.

[4] *CSPF.*, *1569–71*, pp. 408–9, 23 February 1571, Walsingham to Cecil.

[5] Lord Buckhurst refers to five conferences. *CSPF.*, *1569–71*, pp. 419–20, 16 March 1571, Buckhurst to Elizabeth.

lord Buckhurst 'by accident' in the garden of the Tuileries – her unfinished, uninhabited *château* – on 12 March. It was then decided to send over Paul de Foix who, as a former ambassador, was known and trusted in England.[1] Next day, Buckhurst received eight articles upon which to proceed with the negotiation, and Walsingham, to challenge Lorraine at his own game, shortly advised the use of some 'liberality' to win certain of those about Anjou.[2] In the face of this obdurate determination to continue, the catholics shifted their tactics, and proceeded to devise a series of ever more impossibly demanding religious concessions. This was calculated to cast upon England the blame for their projected breakdown of the negotiation, which they had so far successfully frustrated, but not yet ruptured.

Buckhurst's departure in mid-March with the eight articles must just about have coincided with that of Fregoso to Florence upon the business of the Netherlands and the Bourbon marriage. This resuscitation of the English marriage was followed – almost certainly in April – by the meeting in Téligny's house at which the Netherlands plan was amplified. Thus, all three projects were then under way. This was all the more important in view of the mounting peril of Elizabeth and England, to which none but the catholic extremists could afford to see her succumb. The profound gravity of the situation was expressed by Catherine, who went so far as to declare that upon the outcome of the marriage negotiation, depended the peace of all Europe.

[1] 1561–5.
[2] *CSPF.*, *1569–71*, p. 423, 26 March 1571, Walsingham to Burghley.

IX

The Implications of the
Netherlands Enterprise

UP TO the spring of 1571, the English marriage and the Netherlands enterprise had progressed more or less simultaneously and
the Bourbon marriage was beginning to take form. But during
the summer trouble arose because the three policies ceased to be
sufficiently synchronised. The Bourbon marriage was still only
unilaterally agreed, and the Netherlands plan, which made the
most progress during 1571, became more essentially dependent
upon England, both for military and political reasons, just when
the English marriage negotiations reached the deadlock deliberately contrived by the catholics.

Shortly after lord Buckhurst's departure in mid-March, Anjou,
in spite of having been 'persuaded' by Catherine, alleged that he
was 'like to march . . . in rank with the number of the foresaken',
and so declared that unless he found the answer [on his religious
position] 'direct', he would never 'enter farther into the matter'.
This was clever and devious enough to have proceeded from
Lorraine, since 'direct' was precisely what the answer could never
be,[1] particularly since the English parliament, which opened on
2 April, proved to be most critically preoccupied with religion.
So, for the moment, Elizabeth was circumscribed, paradoxically
in a policy she did not much favour, but had expected parliament
to demand. Subsequently, however, she called the catholic bluff,
and exposed the insincerity of their pious exigence. But for
several months the matter rested in the hands of experts, and

[1] Digges, 67, 2 April 1571, Walsingham to Burghley.

their negotiations on this 'knotty piece of religion' were a veritable *tour de force*.[1]

Awaiting the outcome of Buckhurst's negotiation, and the return of Fregoso from Florence, the court divided on 22 April 1571, and Charles moved away towards Normandy[2] to address himself to the serious business of hunting in which, according to lord Buckhurst, he had developed a 'new manner' chasing after the entire herd of deer with drawn sword and slaughtering every stag.[3] This, in spite of his ill health and the state of his affairs, appears to have been Charles' principal pre-occupation, which is why the court was dispersed until late July, business slow, and the king elusive.

Apart from hunting, the departure for Normandy, and later Brittany, was evidently for the purpose of approaching the protestant and Flemish leaders. The king had not seen Nassau in Paris, presumably on account of the predictable repercussions, and he appears to have been hoping to see Coligny as well; but this was not to be so casually arranged. According to Kervyn de Lettenhove – who is anything but reliable – Charles had discussions with various seigneurs, including Eskeders, brother of the naval commander de Lumbres, at Trie, a *château* belonging to the duc de Longueville who, as *gouverneur* of the frontier province of Picardy, was not unimportant in relation to the enterprise, though his role remains enigmatic.[4] Charles was also in direct touch with William of Orange, and Lettenhove mentions the commencement of a secret correspondence between them, though he only offers one formal letter in evidence.[5] There is no

[1] *CSPF.*, *1569–71*, pp. 435–6, 28 April 1571, Walsingham to Burghley. The evidence on the English marriage negotiations is detailed and voluminous. Only its essentials can be referred to here.

[2] Champion, *Charles IX, la France et le contrôle de l'Espagne*, i, 357.

[3] Desjardins, *Negs. Tosc.*, iii, 665, 26 April 1571; *CSPF.*, *1569–71*, p. 413, 4 March 1571, Buckhurst to Elizabeth.

[4] Kervyn de Lettenhove, *Les Huguenots*, ii, 305. He quotes Simancas K 1522, 13 July 1571, Alava to Alva. Charles appears to have been at Trie in late May and early June, though he could have returned later.

[5] Gachard, *Correspondance de Guillaume le Taciturne*, iii, 35, 10 May 1571, William of Orange to Charles IX; Kervyn de Lettenhove, *Les Huguenots*, ii, 301, no date.

doubt, however, that Charles had become at least deeply involved, if not necessarily heavily committed, and sometime in May, Petrucci reported that war on Spain was held to be agreed. Little, if anything, could be kept truly secret and, during the summer, such rumours steadily increased, while relations with Spain became correspondingly strained.[1] Petrucci inferred, if a little uncertainly, that the agreement on war included the king, who was assured that the enterprise would be easy, lest he were prevailed upon to change his mind and distracted from his current 'umore gagliardo'.[2] Much, it was thought, would be done during the journey to Brittany.   The problems emphasised at this stage were money, and the attitude of Catherine who opposed the journey to Brittany and therefore by implication the Netherlands enterprise, reputedly to be arranged there. Petrucci said it was hoped that she could be prevailed upon.[3]

If Charles and Catherine disagreed over the Netherlands, they were at one in their determination to conclude the Bourbon marriage; nor did they disagree over England, except that Catherine, unlike the king, had a shrewd understanding of Elizabeth's domestic problems and therefore a more realistic conception of her probable reactions. Catherine's ardent promotion of the English marriage must, in a sense, have brought her closer to the huguenots and the Flemings. But it was difficult, if not impossible, to receive their support in terms of England, yet reject them in terms of the Netherlands which, to them, were two aspects of the same thing. To Catherine's predicament about England and the Netherlands there was no specific solution. For the moment she had done all she could about England, and it is

[1] In February there were rumours of 'remuements' in the ever sensitive areas of Flanders and Artois. Gachard, *Notices et extraits*, ii, 332–3, 14 February 1571, Fourquevaulx to Charles IX. Walsingham reported in June daily causes of grievance between France and Spain and, in August, French merchants in Seville and other ports heard that war was 'virtually declared'. Desjardins, *Negs. Tosc.*, iii, 669, 10 May 1571.

[2] '. . . stanno in gelosia che ogni uccello che passa che non interrompa i loro disegni'. Desjardins, *Negs. Tosc.*, iii, 670, 10 May 1571.

[3] Desjardins, *Negs. Tosc.*, iii, 669–74, May 1571; 678, 11 June 1571, Petrucci to François de Medici.

likely, perhaps with the return of Fregoso[1] – about whose generally favourable message we have no details – that she turned her attention to the Bourbon marriage since, by July, it was in 'great forwardness'.[2] Contact with Coligny – since Henry of Navarre was the protestants' titular leader – and with Nassau, who served his mother, was therefore just as essential to Catherine as it was to Charles, for the Bourbon marriage and the Netherlands enterprise alike. Sometime towards mid-June Catherine, together with Anjou, held some secret, and still mysterious meeting in Paris which was evidently communicated to Coligny.[3] Petrucci said she found the protestants very intransigent, demanding their own way precisely.

This appears to postulate some bargaining, though to what extent it affected the edict – which was an administrative matter and not one of policy – possibly Coligny's return to court, the Netherlands, or the Bourbon marriage, it is impossible to determine. The marriage was the most probable topic since Coligny opposed it, and to Nassau it was irrelevant, but together they could probably have prevented, or otherwise frustrated it. Could Catherine now, for the sake of peace and reconciliation, which she envisaged in terms of the Bourbon marriage, be induced to acquiesce in the Netherlands enterprise? The idea had once been mooted – among many others for his future – that Anjou should command such an expedition. This, in itself might, just, be plausible, granted the English marriage.[4] It would have the advantage of a solution to the problem of Anjou, and would render the Netherlands enterprise a national one, thereby greatly reducing the contingent danger from Spain, which is what alienated Catherine. But this danger was an uncertain, fluctuating quantity, nor was it by any means clear that Charles, who was regaled with unrealistic assurances of quick and easy conquests, ever conceived of the Netherlands plan in terms of war with

---

[1] Fregoso returned between 10 & 16 June 1571, Desjardins, *Negs. Tosc.*, iii, 674–7, 7, 10, 16 June 1571.
[2] *CSPF.*, *1569–71*, p. 488, 8 July 1571, Walsingham to Burghley.
[3] Desjardins, *Negs. Tosc.*, iii, 677, 16 June 1571.
[4] Digges, 72–3, 5 April 1571, Walsingham to Burghley.

Spain, even if everyone else did, either because they greatly desired, or greatly feared it. Coligny certainly envisaged the enterprise in terms of war – a national war – with Spain, yet paradoxically so, since it is difficult to imagine him serving under Anjou. This crippling inability to combine a national policy was fundamental to the divisions of the civil wars.

If Charles, unlike Catherine, never fully faced up to the problem of war or peace with Spain, and therefore never decided what to do about it – indeed there is a case for declaring it insoluble – he could never entirely lose sight of it, since the further the two marriages and the Netherlands plan developed, the greater became the catholic opposition which, though variously manifested, represented, above all, the dread power of Spain. Already in January 1571, while the German ambassadors were at court, probably just after the arrival of Fregoso from Florence and perhaps more important, upon the issue of *lettres de créance* to Châtillon to negotiate the Anjou marriage, the young secretary de Laubespine, nephew of the former ambassador, Limoges, was sent on a special mission to Madrid to counter the predictable reaction of Spain.[1] But, since she had always been scrupulously careful to explain things to Philip II, it seems more likely that this represented Catherine's moderate policy executed in Charles' name, as Lorraine's policy had previously been, than any diplomatic demonstration on the part of the king, who was just then becoming fascinated by the risky prospect of the Netherlands. This alternating use of the royal authority by political opponents made Charles IX appear even more wayward than the really was, and it is doubtful, between his youth, his hunting and his ill health, whether he himself played any significant role at all. De Laubespine's comprehensive memoir, dated 7 January 1571 from Villers-Cotterêts, addressed to the ambassador Fourquevaulx to be conveyed to Philip as required, covered different aspects of Franco-Spanish relations, in order to reaffirm the positive, pacific intentions of the king. It strongly condemned the

[1] Gachard, *Notices et extraits*, ii, 325–33, 7 January 1571, *mémoire porté au sieur de Fourquevaulx par de Laubespine*.

wickedness of those who daily and increasingly strove to impair
and disrupt the peace, friendship and good relations between
France and Spain, principally out of villainy and self-seeking.
More specifically, 'Charles' therein complained of Philip's servants in Italy, and in the Netherlands where they had protested
about French garrisons sent into Picardy where it was normal to
maintain them.[1] Doubtless to divert attention from the Netherlands, he referred to the League then being treated in Rome, and
efforts to persuade him to join it. He went so far as to say that he
would do so, if it were serious, but not otherwise. Since France
had recently renewed her alliance with Turkey, this was somewhat less than frank.[2]

The League was finally signed on 20 May, ratified on 25 May
and published in Rome on 1 June.[3] It might therefore claim to be
serious. Other catholic princes were invited to subscribe and,
already before the end of June, the cardinal Santa Croce had
arrived in France ostensibly, if not solely, to express the hope that
Charles would not be the last to enter, although a Turkish
ambassador had arrived soon after, presumably to see that he did
not.[4]

In these circumstances and probably in the face of Catherine's
anxiety about the developing Netherlands enterprise, it is not
surprising that another special envoy, Jérôme de Gondi, cousin

[1] The Spanish ambassador in England had questioned La Mothe on this
subject as early as October 1570. La Mothe, iii, 327–33, 16 October 1570, La
Mothe to Charles IX. In December Ferrals reported to Charles that Philippe de
Noircarmes, stadtholder of Holland and Gilles de Berlaymont had been to the
frontiers to survey them and attend to defences and obtain news from France.
Gachard, *Notices et extraits*, ii, 502–5, 30 December 1570, Ferrals to Charles.

[2] De Laubespine's memoir covered various other matters including the
Portuguese marriage, urged by the catholics for Marguerite, which Charles
said he declined to consider.

[3] Charrière, *Négociations de la France dans le Levant*, iii, 149, 21 May 1571,
Rambouillet to Charles IX; 151, 6 June 1571, same to same; *CSPF., 1569–71*,
p. 463, 1 June 1571, advices from Italy; 483, the Holy League, gives the proportion
of the contributions of the contracting parties.

[4] *CSPF., 1569–71*, p. 480, 28 June 1571, Walsingham to Burghley; Hirschauer, *La Politique de St Pie V*, 157–8, 14 August 1571, Frangipani to Rusticucci.

of de Retz, was sent to Spain. Gondi arrived in Madrid on 22 June partly to complain of the conduct of Alava, the Spanish ambassador, who was universally disliked, and partly to explain away the impending journey to Brittany during which, in the euphemistic words of Fourquevaulx, Coligny, Navarre and Condé might 'se trouver sur vostre chemin pour vous baiser les mains'. The purpose of this, Fourquevaulx proposed to maintain, was 'de voir de les attirer . . . à vous rendre entière obeissance'. In fact no such meeting materialised, so that later in August or early September, Fourquevaulx told Philip that Charles would go to Blois for 'ledict baise mains', stressing the aspects of submission and obedience and adding something also about the suppression of piracy, a major Spanish grievance.[1]

The journey to Brittany remains rather obscure because its objectives were ill defined and its programme ill prepared. It appears, but rather vaguely, that Charles hoped to see Nassau, Coligny and other French and Flemish leaders. But whereas Nassau might be expected to welcome an audience, Coligny had first to be persuaded. Furthermore, while Philip II could not legitimately complain of any meeting with Coligny and the princes, Charles' own subjects, which could never be kept secret because of their necessary entourage, Nassau as a sovereign prince or, to Philip, a hostile Spanish subject, was in a different category. Consequently there was some confusion. As late as 28 June, Walsingham informed Burghley that the voyage into Brittany was 'held for broken'.[2] Just over a week later he wrote that the king had begun to 'like so well' of Coligny, that 'all the adversaries cannot persuade him from sending for him'.[3] While it is certain that Charles did not meet Coligny at this time, Nassau's movements are hard to trace. La Huguerye says that he returned to La Rochelle after the meeting at Téligny's house in

---

[1] Gachard, *Notices et extraits*, ii, 339, 9 July 1571, Fourquevaulx to Charles IX; 342–6, 7 September 1571, Fourquevaulx to Charles IX. Gondi took leave of Philip II on 4 July 1571. Hirschauer, *La Politique de St Pie V*, 152, 2 August 1571, Frangipani to Rusticucci.

[2] *CSPF.*, *1569–71*, p. 480, 28 June 1571, Walsingham to Burghley.

[3] *CSPF.*, *1569–71*, p. 488, 8 July 1571, Walsingham to Burghley.

Paris – perhaps in April or May – leaving the affairs of Flanders in the hands of Bricquemault, La Noue and Téligny in co-operation with Montmorency, serving at the king's request.[1] He also says that it was Nassau whom the king met in deep secrecy on 12 July[2] at the *château* de Lumigny belonging to Mouy's widow, who married La Noue. This combination of circumstances is perfectly plausible. Apart from La Huguerye, our only further knowledge of the conference at Lumigny is derived from a report, addressed to the Spanish ambassador a week later, which does not mention Nassau, whose presence would have been of supreme concern – if it were detected.[3] It does, however, mention an unnamed person. Apart from Nassau, La Huguerye says that Charles, Catherine and Montmorency were there, but not Bricquemault because he disapproved of the [Netherlands] plans, presumably, if this is true, thereby expressing Coligny's opposition. The anonymous report, on the other hand, included Bricquemault and also Biron, Téligny and La Noue. 'Someone' is said to have come with a commission from Jeanne d'Albret, and discussion to have been of the Bourbon marriage, which was already in 'great forwardness'. While the report to Alava does not mention the Netherlands, La Huguerye maintains that 'all' the Netherlands enterprises – whatever this plural usage means – were discussed and demonstrated on a map, but that the 'moyens' were not revealed.[4] In this case the king's role cannot have been determined.

Such garbled evidence is impossible to assess with certainty. Although La Huguerye is not reliable, he *was* in the service of Bricquemault who, whether present or not, is likely to have heard the outcome from Téligny or La Noue. Considering that the two reports are more complementary than contradictory, the most probable interpretation is that the Bourbon marriage and

[1] La Huguerye, *Mémoires*, i, 27.

[2] Kervyn de Lettenhove, *Les Huguenots*, ii, 307 gives 14 July in error.

[3] Kervyn de Lettenhove, *Documents du XVIe siècle*, 133–4, rapport sur la conférence secrète de Lumigny, 19 July 1571. Archives nationales, Simancas, K. 1529, no. 17. Neither Walsingham, who was in Paris, nor Petrucci makes any reference to the meeting at Lumigny.   [4] La Huguerye, *Mémoires*, i, 25.

the Netherlands enterprise were discussed in conjunction, which leads one to suspect, since the protestants opposed the marriage, that agreement to co-operate in obtaining the consent of Jeanne d'Albret and Henry of Navarre was exacted as the price of support for the Netherlands plan. La Huguerye concluded that Charles was favourable to the 'enterprises' – whatever these were – and arranged a further meeting at Fontainebleau.[1] This took place on 28 to 30 July 1571.

Whether or not Nassau had been present at Lumigny, he certainly went to Fontainebleau at the end of July, and in at least intended secrecy. Bricquemault, who La Huguerye said was absent from Lumigny because he disapproved of the plans, could not excuse himself from Fontainebleau because his duty obliged him to follow the court, which was previously dispersed. It must therefore have been he who sent his servant La Huguerye to fetch Nassau from Paris to Fontainebleau. This would tend to suggest that Nassau had gone from Lumigny to Paris, while Charles, at Fontainebleau, was not too far away, because the 'moyens' had not been settled; but one cannot be certain. La Huguerye and Nassau arrived at Fontainebleau at midnight, and Nassau was lodged by the *concierge* so that Charles could see him secretly. There, La Huguerye says, the project was 'si bien pourmené que le roy l'approuva'.[2]

Our best, albeit incomplete, account of what it was that had been approved is derived from Walsingham who was secretly informed by Nassau because, representing England, he was directly concerned. The Fontainebleau plan was much more extensive than any hitherto recorded, amounting to the complete partition of the provinces. France was to receive Flanders and Artois; the Empire Brabant, Guelderland and Luxembourg under the authority of Orange, possibly with the title of elector of Brabant; and England's share was to be Holland and Zeeland. Nassau explained how he had put the Netherlands' history and case to Charles, equally calculated, no doubt, to play upon the protestant sympathies of Walsingham. In beseeching Charles to

[1] La Huguerye, *Mémoires*, i, 25-6.   [2] La Huguerye, *Mémoires*, i, 26.

help them, they had emphasised what a wonderful opportunity this was, and argued that the enterprise was honourable and legitimate. Even more important, he showed that it was both easy and likely to succeed because, religion apart, all the inhabitants were united in hatred of the tyranny they endured. All the towns (here there are two code letters which may indicate certain areas) were ready to receive garrisons in the service of Orange, and other towns on the frontiers would receive forces when they actually approached. On the other hand, Spain had not above 3,000 trustworthy men. With twelve more ships than they already disposed of, they could blockade the channel, and the German princes were willing to co-operate. Charles, for his part, seemed to like this well 'especially if the Q. of England might be brought to be a party'. He therefore wished Nassau to put the matter to the queen, as of his own volition, because, Charles is reported to have said, Elizabeth being lady of the narrow seas, 'I [Charles] weigh not the King of Spain nor all the confederates'. But, Nassau continued, two things had to be provided for: firstly a league with England, and also with Germany – namely certain princes – who would not join without England.[1] The second thing to be provided was, inevitably, money for which Charles intended to tax the clergy up to one year's revenue. Finally, Nassau said that it was not intended to attempt anything before the winter, but to invade the Netherlands in the spring. These great practices, however, were 'staid' upon the outcome of the English negotiation,[2] which was virtually ruptured upon the eve of the conference at Fontainebleau.

During April and May 1571, the diplomats cut so skilfully through the 'knotty piece of religion' as Walsingham had so quaintly put it, that by June the only thing Elizabeth refused was *open* confirmation that, once in England, Anjou would be permitted the private exercise of his religion.[3] It therefore began to look as though the catholics might finally be outwitted, and all problems resolved, whereupon they made ever more frantic

[1] Digges, 123–7, 12 August 1571, Walsingham to Burghley.
[2] Digges, 117, 27 July 1571, Walsingham to Leicester.
[3] La Mothe, iv, 135, 7 June 1571, La Mothe to Catherine.

efforts, in England as well as in France, to frustrate the negotiation. La Mothe wrote of 'tant de contrarietéz par la menée de ceulx qui n'espargnent ny dons, ny promesses ny escuz contantz pour l'interrompre', and Elizabeth was freshly provoked into an agony of indecision and renewed anxiety lest the marriage should result in her personal humiliation.[1] This permitted those who opposed the marriage in France to spread the rumour that she was not sincere.[2]

On the French side, Walsingham also reported 'divers indirect practices of great moment to impeach the marriage', as well as another – presumably the Ridolphi plot – for 'stealing away of the Scottish queen'.[3] Lorraine was urging 'someone of good quality' at court, by all means to 'stay the conclusion of the two marriages for six weeks,' when there would be 'such offers from other places as would stop the proceeding of the same'.[4] So many offers were forthcoming from other places that it is not clear what this referred to. Lorraine was striving to secure Anjou for the Scottish or Portuguese marriage with an annual pension from the clergy of 400,000 *écus*; an insulting proposition, one might have thought, to offer the heir apparent to the throne.[5] It was probably the cardinal legate, Santa Croce, who came upon the business of the Holy League, who revived the old idea that Anjou should assume supreme command of the League, by then already well confided to the far abler Don John of Austria,[6] and La Mothe heard that Anjou had accepted a secret papal commission to exterminate the protestants in France. If, in 1571, this was political nonsense, as a rumour it could still be damaging.[7] Anjou's own, effective contribution, late in July, just when the

---

[1] La Mothe, iv, 165, 9 July 1571, La Mothe to Charles IX.

[2] La Mothe, vii, 232, 8 July 1571, Catherine to La Mothe.

[3] *CSPF.*, *1569–71*, p. 479, 25 June 1571, Walsingham to Burghley; 496, 30 July 1571, Walsingham to Burghley.

[4] *CSPF.*, *1569–71*, p. 480, 28 June 1571, Walsingham to Burghley.

[5] La Mothe, iv, 213–14, 9 August 1571, La Mothe to Catherine; Digges, 119–20, 31 July 1571, Walsingham to Leicester.

[6] Charrière, *Négociations de la France dans le Levant*, iii, 165–7, 8 August 1571, François de Noailles, bishop of Dax to Fizes.

[7] La Mothe, iv, 208–9, 6 August 1571, La Mothe to Catherine.

Netherlands enterprise and Bourbon marriage appear to have been proceeding well, was to stand out for a *public* assurance upon his religion which, it was known, could not be conceded in England without the consent of parliament and would – particularly at that time of plots and plottings, as they said – have put the whole kingdom into a state of combustion.[1] The proposed solution to this, already confidentially suggested by Elizabeth herself to Walsingham on 9 July, was to omit religion altogether from the articles of contract,[2] though just how soon this was known in France is not clear. Catherine admitted to being 'en bien grande peyne', with all the more reason since, according to Walsingham, the French were finally persuaded of Elizabeth's sincerity. But this, in turn explains Anjou's intransigence.[3] Catherine strongly suspected Anjou's intimates Villequier, Lignerolles and Sarret, or possibly all three, of being 'les autheurs de ces fantaisies'. If we could only make sure, she raged to La Mothe, 'je vous asseure quils s'en repentiront';[4] Lignerolles did. Anjou's servants were not, however, the only authors of his fantasies, since the nuncio specifically claimed to have worked very hard to maintain them 'nel suo bon proposito', ensuring that they had their own good reasons – such as the abbey of Fécamp – for wanting to remain in France, their personal self-advancement and interests being the surest foundation upon which to build.[5]

If Catherine could not prevail upon Anjou or against the catholic agents, still less could Charles, who was very angry and reproached his brother for not having used 'some plainess' with him. 'You allege conscience,' Walsingham reported him to have said, 'but I know it is a late pension offered unto you by the

[1] Digges, 118–19, 31 July 1571, Walsingham to Burghley; La Mothe, iv, 189–92, 22 July 1571, La Mothe to Catherine; vol. vii, 234–5, 25 July 1571, Catherine to La Mothe.

[2] Digges, 111–12, 9 July 1571, Elizabeth to Walsingham; La Mothe, iv, 188–92, 22 July 1571, La Mothe to Catherine.

[3] Digges, 119, 31 July 1571, Walsingham to Leicester.

[4] La Mothe, vii, 234–5, 25 July 1571, Catherine to La Mothe.

[5] Hirschauer, *La Politique de St Pie V*, 161–2, 31 August 1571; 157–8, 14 August 1571, Frangipani to Rusticucci.

clergy who would have you still remain here for a champion of the catholic faith.' Charles continued menacingly that he would tolerate no other champion but himself, and, 'seeing you have such a desire to remain here on such respects it behoves me the more narrowly to look to you'. He also vowed that he would deal with the rich clergy and 'the heads' of those who made the offer. Walsingham believed the enmity between them to be so great 'that they cannot refrain half a year from taking arms', which was neither a casual observation, nor the first time he had expressed a comparable opinion.[1] Charles, he said, was loath to have Anjou in France, and Anjou was afraid. Petrucci claimed in June that Anjou was said to have ordered Monluc to raise 400 armed gentlemen for him. Petrucci actually did not believe it but, true or false, the existence of the rumour testifies to the atmosphere, and is interesting in conjunction with Walsingham's apprehensions.[2] There is no doubt as to the truth of this dangerous enmity between Charles and Anjou, which tended to increase and was easily exploited. On this occasion however, in July, Anjou is said to have gone to his study and wept. Walsingham softened a little and declared him a victim, who should be excused, 'being torn in pieces with sundry discourses of those who are hinderers, whose reasons are able to divert one of more years and riper judgement'.[3] Anjou possessed many qualities, but judgement was never one of them and, between the subtlety of the cardinal of Lorraine and the terrible tirades of his mother – who once publicly reduced the intrepid St André to the trembling brink of tears – we may surmise that Walsingham was right.

The machinations of the catholics and the intractability of Anjou had placed Charles and Catherine in a difficult and dangerous position. A severance of relations with England – and when Elizabeth had made every possible concession –

[1] This was doubtless why Charles proposed to tax the clergy to pay for the enterprise, knowing how much they could afford for the suborning of Anjou. *CSPF.*, *1569–71*, pp. 497–8, 30 July 1571, Walsingham to Burghley.

[2] Desjardins, *Negs. Tosc.*, iii, 679, 23 June 1571, Petrucci to Concino.

[3] *CSPF.*, *1569–71*, p. 498, 30 July 1571, Walsingham to Burghley.

was unthinkable, especially as partition, the form of the Netherlands enterprise just approved at Fontainebleau, so unwisely
depended upon the co-operation of England. It was therefore
decided to send over Paul de Foix – a good friend[1] – immediately.

As well as approving Nassau's partition plan at Fontainebleau,
Charles openly declared his intention of proceeding with the
Bourbon marriage, 'affin que, toute diffidence mise soubz le pied,
chacun n'eust aultre dessein que de luy [Charles] faire en ceste
belle entreprise [the Netherlands] ung bon service *incontinent apres
les nopces*'.[2] For this reason, Charles particularly requested the
service and intercession of Nassau – so the count informed La
Huguerye on the way back to Paris – since he and his brother
William of Orange would stand most to gain. Nassau's assent
may be deduced from the fact that he and William both became
French pensioners receiving 2,000 and 1,000 *écus* a month
respectively.[3]

Thus the interdependence of these three ill-conceived projects
is clearly established, as well as the precedence of the Bourbon
marriage – which was supposed to have such remarkable results –
over the Netherlands enterprise.

There might have been reasonable grounds for optimism in
August 1571 – given the success of de Foix's mission – were it
not for the irreconcilable tensions between those concerned with
the execution of the projects. But Charles, Catherine, Coligny
and Nassau were never able to move sufficiently in step, since
neither their fundamental purposes nor their tactics were ever
fully aligned. Charles and Catherine were in agreement upon the
Bourbon marriage and the major point of conflict at court was still

---

[1] Digges, 119–20, 31 July 1571, Walsingham to Leicester.

[2] My italics. La Huguerye, *Mémoires*, i, 26–7.

[3] Kervyn de Lettenhove, *Les Huguenots*, ii, 313, quoting Archives nationales,
Simancas, K. 1522, 1 August 1571, Alava to Alva. Petrucci later reported
Nassau to be receiving 15,000 and then corrected it to 12,000 p.a. Desjardins,
Negs. Tosc., iii, 734, 30 November 1571; 755, 19–30 March 1572. While Alava
received information about the conference at Fontainebleau, neither Petrucci
nor the nuncio recorded anything.

the Netherlands enterprise – with its inevitable Spanish implications – arranged between Nassau and his French confederates and
the king, in the absence of Coligny and without the consent of
Catherine. All her instincts were inevitably to oppose this,
but she nevertheless needed the support of the Nassau group
– as well as Coligny – for her first priority, the Bourbon
marriage.

Since there was no further talk of his changing his mind, it
seems likely that the king had indeed struck some sort of bargain
at Lumigny, to support a Netherlands enterprise in return for the
Bourbon marriage. But there is no evidence that Catherine had
ever consented to this. Besides, there was no need for her to do so
since, in respect of the marriage, she would benefit from such a
bargain in any case. Her position, however, in the summer of
1571, is rather obscure. There is some, not very convincing,
evidence that the protagonists of the Netherlands enterprise
sought to keep her in partial ignorance. But after the meeting at
Fontainebleau Petrucci wrote rather vaguely about Catherine
still being needed to intercede with the grand duke of Tuscany –
presumably for money for the enterprise – and it was decided
that she should be fully 'informed'. Thus, by 10 August, with
the help of Téligny and Fregoso all things were said to have been
'accomodate'.[1] If Catherine was ignorant of anything, it must
have been the details of the partition plan. It is difficult to believe
that she could ever have supported it, either during or after its
formulation. But, as the marriage took precedence, and no
military action was anticipated before the following spring, she
may simply have proceeded with first things first, leaving later
problems to later solutions. Alternatively, she might have seen
the Netherlands project as beyond the scope of her obstruction
(though she rarely abandoned the impossible if it concerned her),
or possibly too dependent upon England to be regarded as
definitive.

But whether or not Catherine had, temporarily, been obliged

---

[1] Desjardins, *Negs. Tosc.*, iii, 686–94, 26–31 July 1571; 694–5, 10 August
1571, both to François de Medici.

to accept the Netherlands enterprise, at Lumigny, Fontainebleau or in August, there was still room for manœuvre since the plan itself was fragile from the start and immediately ran into serious difficulties which might, in her eyes, have tempered its danger and undesirability. In the first place, if we are to believe La Huguerye, it was thought to have been partially betrayed to Alva in the Netherlands, and to the Spanish ambassador Alava, in France, by Anthoine Ollivier, known as 'le grand Anthoine', one of the Flemish 'négociateurs', who was himself scheduled to play an important part in the intended invasion. Anthoine apparently did not deny trading news to Alva, but claimed that he did so only when it was too late to be useful. But, more significantly, in this context, he contrived to open Alava's despatches to discover 'ce qu'ils pouvoit avoir de confidence entre les deux rois à nostre prejudice'. One of these is said to have recounted a discussion between Alava and Charles about the king's dealings with Nassau, and of Charles' reassurances that Alva had nothing to fear.[1] Anthoine and some of the huguenots concluded that they could place no more hope in Charles, and despaired of the 'bon succes des affaires du comte [Nassau] avec le roy'. While it is difficult to see how else Charles could have answered the Spanish ambassador – to whom his affairs were habitually betrayed – probably by Gondi, or de Retz, who was said to be out of favour with the king[2] – it is true that he evidently saw no objection to running with the hare and hunting with the hounds. La Huguerye says that Anthoine offered to sell the whole project to Alva for 10,000 *écus*, and only forbore to do so because Alva refused prepayment. It is therefore not clear how much Alva learnt; certainly that there was now an 'enterprinse preste'. More reliably, Walsingham was aware that the Spanish ambassador possessed information, since Don Francés openly complained of the king's 'secret' conference with Nassau – which Charles denied – and it was Alava who provided Petrucci

[1] La Huguerye, *Mémoires*, i, 27–31, says that this *discours* between Charles and Alava was sent to Coligny.

[2] La Huguerye, *Mémoires*, i, 27–30; Desjardins, *Negs. Tosc.*, iii, 702, 22 August 1571.

and the nuncio with the only information their despatches contain.[1]

Thus, whatever the correct details may be, the Flemings and protestants had grounds for believing that Charles might not be dealing frankly with them – which better politicians would have realised from the start was neither intrinsically probable, nor likely to be possible; also for believing that the Spanish knew something of their intentions. This, no doubt, would not have made much difference, considering what they had known all along, and that a state of war virtually already existed. These considerations probably carried more weight with the Flemings than with Bricquemault, and others who opposed the partition plan, since neither he, nor Coligny whom he represented, is very likely to have trusted the king. La Huguerye, who maintains that his master Bricquemault had only attended at Fontainebleau because he could not in duty decline, recounts a three-day meeting at which Bricquemault played a leading part in seeking to moderate the partition plan. This was in the house of the seigneur de Bourry attended by Téligny, La Noue and all the 'négociateurs'. As usual with La Huguerye, the timing is ignored but, as it can only have been after the partition plan was formulated, it must, presumably, have been in August.[2] All the plans, difficulties and available forces were discussed, in other words the practicability of the plan, and the elderly Bricquemault is said to have commanded attention on account of his military experience. It was propounded that only French forces from Champagne and Picardy, namely the immediate frontier areas, could be used, otherwise secrecy would be impossible. This corresponds to what Fregoso is originally reported to have proposed to Nassau at La Rochelle, and to what was, in fact, attempted in 1572. But as such forces would be insufficient – possibly for the partition project – it was therefore necessary to limit their undertakings. Bricquemault, La Huguerye says, advised them to take only half the designated number of towns, the forces intended for the others going to those

[1] Digges, 121–2, 12 August 1571, Walsingham to Burghley; Hirschauer, *La Politique de St Pie V*, 153–7, 2 August 1571, Frangipani to Rusticucci.
[2] La Huguerye, *Mémoires*, i, 33–5.

which were occupied. Having made this decision, the account continued, the negotiators withdrew to Paris, leaving Bricque-mault to put the revised plan to Montmorency and the king. It seems more likely than not that La Huguerye is substantially accurate in this instance expecially as he adds, which is true, that the king decided to winter at Blois where Coligny was awaited, and that before his arrival Charles would try to settle the Guise vendetta.[1]

Coligny's return to court was becoming urgent for many reasons, but it was not a perfectly simple matter, and it is not clear when he finally agreed to go; one might deduce that it was late in August. Charles, according to La Huguerye, had openly declared at Fontainebleau that he must see Coligny, and would go half way, as far as Blois, to meet him; 'quil ne voulloit entreprendre ung tel [recte une telle] affaire [the Netherlands enterprise] sans luy,' and that he wished to end all discord.[2] If Coligny's return to court was more likely to provoke an uproar, it remained paradoxically true that there could be no general reconciliation without him. Catherine therefore needed him, no less than the king, and she had wasted no time in sending for him.[3] Coligny is reported to have desired a reconciliation with Cather-ine,[4] whether because she opposed the Netherlands project or, more likely, because she alone, since 1560, had done anything to help the protestants, if not for their sake, at least for that of peace, which they both desired in France. It was not the first time that Catherine and Coligny had really needed each other, and their genuine inability to co-operate was one of the disasters of this whole period. Politically they had always had much in common, and Coligny, but for his uncompromising Calvinism, would have been in the loyalist Montmorency tradition. But in spite of their mutual need of each other, the implementation of the edict on the one hand, and the Bourbon marriage on the other, did not

[1] La Huguerye, *Mémoires*, i, 33–5.
[2] La Huguerye, *Mémoires*, i, 27. This testimony may be substantially accepted because it was borne out by subsequent events.
[3] B.N., Mss. fr. 15553, f. 153, 3 August 1571, Coligny to Catherine.
[4] Desjardins, *Negs. Tosc.*, iii, 686, 26–31 July 1571.

then provide them with any common ground, and their opposition to the Netherlands enterprise was a useless, negative agreement for disparate reasons. Catherine could hardly defend the edict to the pope, from whom a marriage dispensation was required, and Coligny opposed the marriage for precisely those reasons which commended it to Catherine. Though he was anxious for peace and reconciliation in France and might not have been averse from strengthening the crown, he could hardly agree, by way of the marriage, to depriving the party of its princely leader, when the catholics boasted of Anjou as theirs. The princes, Navarre and Condé, were young and as likely to be converted themselves as to convert others, which was Catherine's own argument in representing the marriage as a means of restoring catholicism. It is doubtful if she believed this, but it was the obvious aspect to emphasise in sending Fregoso back to Florence to request the grand duke to induce the pope to grant a dispensation, and to favour the return of Coligny to court.[1] Such papal sanction might tend to undermine catholic opposition, but it was neither the kind of argument to which they would readily incline, nor the kind of security that Coligny envisaged. There can be no doubt that Coligny shared the opinion, expressed by La Huguerye, that they would have been far better advised to act alone without the king; but in this they assumed the co-operation of England. La Huguerye even claims to have reproved Nassau for his impetuous lack of judgement, endangering, by his ill-considered actions 'ceux sans lesquels il ne pouvoit rien faire'. This is an uncommonly perspicacious and accurate assessment of Nassau (and indeed of his future conduct also), of the dangerous dilemma in which he had placed Coligny, and of the tragic outcome of the whole affair, both for Coligny, the protestants and for the Netherlands. Not only Nassau, it must be admitted, but also the huguenot extremists had created difficulties by approaching the king over policies involving Coligny and the protestants generally, when it was really England that they required. But it was not *only* England that Nassau required. To

---

[1] Desjardins, *Negs. Tosc.*, iii, 694–8, 10 August 1571.

him the crown of France was only marginally less important than that of England.

The position of Coligny in relation to the court, and the gulf, if not actual breach between himself on the one hand, and Nassau and the extremists on the other, is well illustrated by the Anglo-Bourbon marriage project, which Coligny preferred to the Anjou match, and which was briefly re-explored at this time. The marriage of Navarre to queen Elizabeth would still have had – as in 1570 – the advantages (theoretical) of securing England, of frustrating the Bourbon-Valois marriage and of liberating the protestants from dependence on, and alliance with the crown of France, to which Nassau had so injudiciously committed them. Thus they could have made war in the Netherlands without relying on Charles – who could never be a free agent – and, perhaps above all, Coligny would have had no need to return to court, which he had little enough incentive to do.

If Nassau had endangered and embarrassed Coligny and the protestants, they were certainly not tender in their treatment of him. According to La Huguerye, the negotiations at La Rochelle were conducted by Picheron, a servant of Coligny, Walsingham's secretary Beale, and Nassau. Walsingham's despatches contain no reference to this important matter, the details of which are not well attested, but La Mothe provides independent confirmation that something of the kind did really occur.[1] Beale is said to have charged Nassau with the danger and difficulty of the protestants' position in view of the intelligence between France and Spain – which was neither more nor less than it had been all along – and to have declared that Coligny should not be urged to go to court. To Nassau's lame reply that he had never advised this, Beale retorted that he had, nevertheless, made an important agreement with Charles, who could do nothing *without* Coligny.[2] So Nassau, who had already undertaken to facilitate the Bourbon marriage before his enterprise was launched, was humiliatingly obliged instead to intercede with Jeanne in favour of queen

[1] La Mothe, vii, 241–3, 25 August 1571, Charles to La Mothe; vol. iv, 224–8, 7 September 1571, La Mothe to Charles IX.
[2] La Huguerye, *Mémoires*, i, 56–7.

Elizabeth, and Beale was to put the case in England. Nassau was to bully Jeanne and frighten her about the danger of undertaking the Netherlands enterprise with French 'support', in view of the likely reaction of Spain, to whom her territory was extremely vulnerable, some of it actually located in the Netherlands. Coligny, who believed that she wanted the French marriage, contributed the less than truthful argument that her husband, Anthoine, had been 'perdu' for the sake of his royal lieutenancy, and that she and Henry would now be ruined by her ambition for this marriage. Nassau was also to explain that he and his brother William were bound to seek the help of England but were desperately anxious not, thereby, to forfeit that of the French. Jeanne replied that Charles had promised to support the enterprise *after* the Bourbon marriage, to which Nassau responded that he and the 'négociateurs' could no longer have any faith in France. The explanation of this rather discreditable episode would appear to be threefold. While some of the protestants, including Coligny, had always preferred the English marriage for Navarre, the Anjou match was believed to have collapsed. At the same time, the Anthoine affair had caused alarm and consternation – if not necessarily with Nassau himself – and many of those who cared for his leadership, or his person, were deeply anxious at the perilous prospect of Coligny's return to court; the vendetta, for one thing, could hardly be described as terminated.

Whether or not Jeanne was frightened and deterred, she was certainly not to be stampeded. She was aware that, apart from the personal difficulties, the English marriage would have entailed far-reaching obligations and no advantages for Elizabeth. 'Je doubte,' was her caustic observation, 'qu'elle [Elizabeth] congoist tant les miseres de noz affaires qu'elle n'en vouldroit pas in-commoder ses prospérités'. Jeanne was also wary of gratuitously arousing the anger of Charles and Catherine who, against all odds, had not quite despaired of the Anjou marriage and, how-ever obscure and problematical it might be, it was still in France that she envisaged Henry's future. There was no moving Jeanne, of whom Beale harshly observed that she had done the party even more harm than her late husband Navarre (who in fact had never belonged to it). The real tenor of their thinking, however, is revealed in their relief at having 'au moings gaigné ce point de luy [Nassau] faire tourner le visage vers l'Angleterre pour oster à la France le moyen de se prévaloir des affaires de Flandres'.[1] This is attributed to Beale, Walsingham's secretary and, though it may mirror England's fear of France in the Netherlands, it is still a little difficult to reconcile with Walsingham's advice to Nassau not to rely on receiving English support. On the other hand, no support was reliable, but it still had to be sought. In this respect, those concerned were less than fair to Nassau, who was no defaulter in his approaches to England, desiring her help as much as anyone. But he had no better reason to rely on it, than he had for depending upon that of France.

The failure of the La Rochelle negotiation and the precipitation and political ineptitude of Nassau and Coligny's own extremists, left the huguenots with no alternative solutions. In the words of La Huguerye, they would have to do their best and trust in God. 'Il nous convint passer oultre,' he wrote, 'et audict accord, qui ne sembloit aulcunement sincere en la procédure, et au voyage dudict Sr. admiral'.[2] The 'accord' represented, presumably, the Bourbon marriage followed by one or other version of the Netherlands enterprise, to which they were all committed, together with the king; and the 'voyage' signified Coligny's return to court.

It is not, however, really clear just *why* Coligny was therefore obliged to accept the 'accord', as opposed to remaining inactive in La Rochelle. One must allow that multiple pressures on him were very great, and to refuse the royal summons in time of 'peace' would have been insubordinate, even though his relations with the crown – not to mention those with foreign princes – hardly represented the normal submission of a grand seigneur to the king. He may have been afraid that if he stood aside any longer, his waning control would end in virtual loss of the huguenot leadership, which could only have made confusion worse confounded. He may have seen no other way of trying to

---

[1] La Huguerye, *Mémoires*, i, 88.   [2] La Huguerye, *Mémoires*, i, 89–91.

save the edict, or of fulfilling his treaty obligations to William of Orange. Perhaps, since both the king and Catherine wanted him so much, he gambled on achieving more at court than he was in fact able to do. But whatever the nature of his compulsion, Coligny inclined, and 'se laissa aller au péril évident dont il avoit assez d'advis et d'argumens'.[1]

[1] La Huguerye, *Mémoires*, i, 91.

X

The Return of Coligny
September 1571

THE LONG-DESIRED return of Coligny to court, which he joined at Blois on 12 September 1571[1] escorted by marshal Cossé and otherwise well protected by gentlemen and captains, proved to be a paradoxically dramatic anti-climax, achieving nothing. The decision had not been easily arrived at, and the 'peril' expressed by La Huguerye was not exaggerated. Walsingham, who received orders early in August to go to Blois about 1 September, heard – as one would expect – that there were many 'practices' to overthrow the journey.[2] The protestants' own apprehensive aversion from Coligny's return was fully warranted by the catholics' angry deprecation of the event, doubtless epitomised by Philip II who commented to Alava that the only good reason for summoning Coligny could be to *ensure his arrest and execution.* 'Ce serait,' he wrote, 'un acte de grand mérite et d'honneur', though he did not think Charles possessed, as he said, 'le cœur de la faire'.[3] Coligny's own response, dated 3 August 1571, to Catherine's summons, was to make stipulations about the implementation of the edict, and in particular the removal of

---

[1] Digges, 135, 16 December 1571, Walsingham to Burghley. Pp. 135–6 are missing from some copies of this edition.

[2] Digges, 121–2, 12 August 1571, Walsingham to Burghley.

[3] Champion, *Charles IX, la France et le contrôle de l'Espagne*, i, 405, from Archives nationales, Simancas, K. 1524, 14 September 1571, Philip II to Alva. This is an interesting illustration of Philip's attitude to government, law and the high nobility, considering that any offences of which Coligny might be deemed guilty were amnestied by the peace. The treatment recommended was of course that recently received by Coligny's cousins, Horne and Montigny, as well as Egmont and countless others in the Netherlands.

garrisons from the area of La Rochelle, which had already been conceded.[1]

If the elimination of Coligny, whom they so desperately needed, was manifestly not what Charles or Catherine had in mind, his danger was none the less real, since the protection of their authority was nominal, and there remained the more than vexed question of the vendetta. Strenuous royal efforts had been made to settle this in preparation for Coligny's return. La Huguerye said that during the La Rochelle negotiation, the protestants themselves had responded 'assez froidement,' because their endeavour was partly designed to obviate the need for Coligny's return.[2] Besides, Coligny who utterly denied any complicity in the murder of François duc de Guise, had nothing to concede, and the conduct of the Guises is sufficient indication of their implacable enmity, whether or not they agreed to any polite formula. But, though allegedly in disgrace, they too were needed to implement a policy of reconciliation, and Aumale is said to have been at court. Lorraine, who was not, sent an agent Marmoutiers and, collectively, they were patently in control of Anjou. Their reaction to Coligny's impending return was as menacing as it had always been, since his original expulsion from the council in February 1562, namely preparations to thwart or resist it, given the slightest opportunity. Thus Lorraine organised a disquieting gathering at Joinville.[3] Furthermore, events in Paris, where their influence was always strong, were far from reassuring. The city was in a ferment of religious, partisan hostility over a certain cross, known as the *croix des Gâtines*, recently erected by the catholics to the fury and outrage of the protestants.[4] The incidents themselves are only of interest for the light which they

---

[1] B.N., Mss. fr. 15553, f. 153, 3 August 1571, Coligny to Catherine.

[2] La Huguerye, *Mémoires*, i, 37, 90–1.

[3] Desjardins, *Negs. Tosc.*, iii, 701, 22 August 1571; 706, 19–20 September 1571.

[4] Desjardins, *Negs. Tosc.*, iii, 701, 22 August 1571; Mss. fr. 3188, f. 24, [September] 1571, Nançay to his father, the comte de Bouchage. The *prévôt des marchands* had been ordered to demolish the cross at the request of the huguenots. No one else would obey the order.

throw upon the religious hostility and explosive turbulence of the Parisians a year before the massacre.

Apart from the danger of the vendetta, and in spite of the crown's absolute need of his co-operation, Coligny still had to consider the possibility that he was entering a trap, and there were doubtless many, like La Huguerye, who feared so. No contemporary could be expected to have forgotten the arrest and condemnation of Condé, a prince of the blood, in 1560 from which he had only escaped alive because of the death of Francis II; nor could any huguenot leader forget the more recent efforts to ambush them all in August 1568; an enterprise which Lorraine might well have been preparing to repeat. It is therefore not surprising that Coligny, as Philip II surmised, was astute enough not to quit the protestant citadel of La Rochelle without guarantees, which amounted to a contract. Thus, one of eleven articles agreed before his return, provided for the assurance of his safety in the form of separate and individual written promises submitted to Téligny by the king, Catherine, Anjou, Alençon and all the nobles and marshals; captains of the guard were to receive orders to protect him. By article six, Catherine undertook to do everything she could, not only to enforce the edict – which Charles declared to be the reason for Coligny's return[1] – but also to maintain good relations between him and Charles and his brothers; excellent evidence of Coligny's distrust and misgiving, probably in the first place of Anjou, and of the weakness of the crown. Other articles referred to the edict; the augmentation of Coligny's company of *gens d'armes* to a total of 50, a privilege of princes, and substantial financial concessions, which may, or may not have been honoured.[2]

[1] Desjardins, *Negs. Tosc.*, iii, 704–7, 19–20 September 1571; Douais, *Lettres de Charles IX à M. de Fourquevaulx*, 362–3, 26 September 1571, *mémoire*.

[2] Coligny is said to have been granted 150,000 crowns, an abbey worth 20,000, 100,000 with which to restore Châtillon and certain of the revenues for one year of his late brother the cardinal Châtillon. Desjardins, *Negs. Tosc.*, iii, 698–9, 10 August 1571, Petrucci to François de Medici; 706, 19–20 September 1571; Kervyn de Lettenhove, *Les Huguenots*, ii, 331–2; Champion, *Charles IX, la France et le contrôle de l'Espagne*, i, 373–4.

Persuading Coligny to go to court – to promote the policies he disapproved – may have been a symbol of the royal policy of reconciliation – which alerted all the 'hinderers' but there was, effectively, little that he could do. The enterprise depended upon the co-operation of England, which was problematical to say the least, and upon the Bourbon marriage, which in turn required a dispensation. Jeanne herself had returned to Béarn to take the waters which her chronic ill-health required, apparently intending to return in November; Nassau had gone with her.[1] She had, however, sent the seigneur de Beauvais – who had served her in negotiating the treaty of Saint-Germain – presumably to proceed with the marriage since agreement upon this was announced on 28 September.[2] This conclusion, while essential to the general plan, can have done little to reconcile Coligny and, coming so soon after the acrimonious negotiations at La Rochelle, can only have deepened the cleavage in the huguenot party, just when preparations for action required the maximum co-operation.

Charles hoped to solemnise the marriage as soon as possible, which meant well before the following spring for which the enterprise was scheduled.[3] For this reason, Beauvais and Biron left soon after 20 September to join Jeanne, taking with them the general agreement and draft articles on the nature of the cere-mony, which was complex owing to the impediment of religion.[4] Fregoso, who returned from Florence on 30 September – and was rewarded with a pension of 5,000 francs and the office of

[1] Gachard, *Notices et extraits*, ii, 351, 12 November 1571, Fourquevaulx to Charles IX; Desjardins, *Negs. Tosc.*, iii, 702, 3 September 1571; 731, 28 November 1571.

[2] La Mothe in fact had heard of this in England by 30 September. La Mothe, iv, 245–8, 30 September 1571, La Mothe to Charles IX; Douais, *Lettres de Charles IX à M. de Fourquevaulx*, 360–1, 28 September 1571, Charles IX to Fourquevaulx; Gachard, *Notices et extraits*, ii, 348, 28 September 1571.

[3] Gachard, *Notices et extraits*, ii, 351, 12 October 1571, Charles to Fourque-vaulx.

[4] Digges, 135, 16 September 1571; Walsingham said they were going. Des-jardins, *Negs. Tosc.*, iii, 706–7, 19–20 September 1571; La Mothe, iv, 245, 30 September 1571, La Mothe to Charles IX.

gentleman of the king's chamber[1] – was apparently also sent off in October to fetch Nassau.

Nassau had been pressing Charles 'tres instamment' through the agency of certain protestant leaders – he does not say Coligny – to permit him to reside at court.[2] Charles maintained that he could not honestly refuse this request which Nassau 'solicited' as a German prince. This, no doubt was largely factitious, since the presence of Nassau was essential – more important even than that of Coligny. But it would take some explaining to Philip II, from whom Charles' previous meetings with Nassau were supposed to have been secret. Fourquevaulx, the ambassador in Spain, was therefore instructed to handle this delicately explosive subject and, catching Philip, one must suppose, at his most credulous, to persuade him that if Nassau were received at the court of France, it was not 'pour dresser aucunes entreprinses à son préjudice [Philip II] . . . mais plustost pour le distraire de telle volunté, s'il l'avoit'. Charles wished to know minutely, how Philip reacted.[3] Fourquevaulx did not find that anyone in Spain was anxious to speak about Nassau, so he ventured to observe to Philip that it was given out that certain protestants were pressing Charles to receive him as a German prince to which [therefore] Philip could not take exception. Philip replied dryly that he had no doubt they sought to persuade Charles to do many things 'hors de propos,' and that Orange and Nassau were not normally regarded as German princes even if they did possess land in the Empire. Fourquevaulx continued bravely that if Nassau entered Charles' service, he would be displeased if he engaged in anything prejudicial to Spain, but would rather restrain him therefrom. 'A cella,' Fourquevaulx wrote, 'ledict seigneur m'a respondu, en soubsriant, ne scay quoy, si bas que je ne l'ay peu entendre'.

---

[1] Desjardins, *Negs. Tosc.*, iii, 720, 15 October 1571.

[2] '. . . aucuns des principaulx de la R.P.R. . . . avoir pour agréable son service, et luy permettre de me venir trouver et demeurer . . . en ma court'. Gachard, *Notices et extraits*, ii, 350, 12 October 1571, Charles IX to Fourquevaulx.

[3] Gachard, *Notices et extraits*, ii, 349-51, 12 October 1571, Charles IX to Fourquevaulx.

Philip, he said, was a prince 'qui garde semblables choses en son cœur, sans dire ce qu'il en pense'. He was, however, less reticent on the subject of Coligny and the Anjou negotiation, which affected him somewhat differently – and Fourquevaulx at least did not think that any rupture would ensue on the Spanish side.[1]

Nassau, meanwhile, had left a representative at court to await Elizabeth's answer concerning the Netherlands, as the resolution of that enterprise stood 'upon the expectation of what she will do'.[2] Whether this was the result of the protestants' exhortation at La Rochelle to turn toward England, of Charles' request that Elizabeth might 'be moved' by Nassau to co-operate in the partition plan, or quite simply a matter of liaison, is not clear.[3] But it does illustrate the unconcealed importance attached to the support of England, and thereby the great advantage so in- genuously bestowed upon Elizabeth, enabling her to pursue a villainously flexible foreign policy. After having explained the Netherlands plan to Walsingham, Nassau had asked him plainly whether the queen would join him and Orange; whether upon the assurance of Holland and Zeeland she would lend the neces- sary money; whether she would allow John Hawkins – under- hand – to serve them with certain ships,[4] and license him to supply them with victuals. These were for Strozzi who had a fleet at La Rochelle and, Nassau said, was going to embark about mid-September to 'do some enterprise in Spain'. Finally he wanted permission for 800 Walloons in Rye to go to the Nether- lands. Walsingham told Burghley that he had put count Ludovic 'in no hope of help' from England, and that they should so

---

[1] Gachard, *Notices et extraits*, ii, 351–4, 12 November 1571, Fourquevaulx to Charles IX.

[2] Digges, 135, 16 September 1571, Walsingham to Burghley.

[3] La Huguerye, *Mémoires*, i, 88; Digges, 123–6, 12 August 1571, Walsing- ham to Burghley.

[4] Philip II claimed that a treaty had been signed on his behalf on 10 August 1571 by Fitzwilliam and Feria with John Hawkins to serve him with fifteen ships at Philip's expense. Hawkins, who is said to have been 'covetous in the last degree', was to be 'magnificently' rewarded and pardoned his depredations. Gachard, *Correspondance de Philippe II*, ii, 195–7, 30 August 1571, Philip II to Alva.

'direct their doings that they may stand in no need of England',[1],
This, if doubtfully possible, was also sound advice, and the
contradiction illustrates the intrinsic insecurity of the venture,
especially as Anglo-French relations had never been more tenuous since the beginning of the Anjou negotiation, which had
collapsed in July at least ostensibly upon the 'knotty piece of
religion'.

When de Foix was hurriedly sent to England at the beginning
of August 1571, Charles and Catherine were still thinking in
terms of marriage. Catherine privately informed La Mothe that,
in extremity, she would transfer all her efforts to Alençon, 'qui
ne sera pas si difficile'. In other words, he was neither devout,
nor subject to catholic pressure.[2] The mission of de Foix, who
arrived in England on 12 August and had audience on 15 August,[3]
represents Catherine's final effort to induce Elizabeth to give way
over religion, grant all that the French catholics desired – which,
latterly, had been public assurance of toleration for Anjou – and
clinch the marriage.[4] Catherine knew that this was totally un-
reasonable, and recognised Elizabeth's peculiar and genuine
difficulties. But she believed that Elizabeth did, by then, want the
match, and her capitulation on the 'knotty piece' would cut the
ground from under the French catholics. It was certainly worthy
of one final effort, especially as Catherine must very soon have
learnt that Elizabeth had made coquettish gestures towards La
Mothe which were little short of *risqué*.[5] But Catherine had
evidently misjudged either Anjou, or the hold of others upon
him. According to Walsingham, at this last stage Anjou was
being held in check by his favourite, Lignerolles, although

[1] *CSPF., 1569–71*, p. 506 and 506–8, 12 August 1571, two letters Walsingham to Burghley.

[2] La Mothe, vii, 234–5, 25 July 1571, Catherine to La Mothe.

[3] Kervyn de Lettenhove, *Relations*, vi, 161, 14 August 1571, de Spes to Alva;
Digges, 129 [16 August 1571], Leicester to Burghley. This letter is missing from
some copies.

[4] La Mothe, iv, 238–41, 29 July 1571, instructions for de Foix; vii, 217–21,
19 August 1571, La Mothe to Charles IX.

[5] La Mothe, iv, 200, 31 July 1571, La Mothe to Charles IX; 204, 206, 5
August 1571, La Mothe to Charles IX and to Catherine.

Charles was already said to have evicted two of his principal
supporters – unnamed – at the time of the Fontainebleau row.[1]

If Walsingham had reported the frantic efforts of Lorraine in
France to traverse the English marriage, La Mothe replied that it
was unbelievable 'combien les ministres du Roi d'Espaigne . . .
s'esforcent . . . de donner empeschement à ce propos', seeking
to bribe Elizabeth with offers of excellent conditions of peace in
her quarrel with Spain [over the merchants and ships] if she would
immediately accept the suit of prince Rudolph, the emperor's
son, together with offers of help to gain possession of the little
prince James of Scotland and, by means of gifts, propositions and
promises to members of the privy council, and the queen's ladies
to oppose the match.[2] According to Elizabeth's letter to Walsingham of 2 September, they had juggled with formulas[3] and
struggled hard for a compromise and, if the French accepted her
replies to de Foix, she still meant to proceed, and would receive a
formal embassy. But she thought 'sundry there [would] seek to
provoke the king to a misliking'.[4]

If the catholics were highly successful in frustrating marriage,
they had, however, little power to prevent 'amity' which did
not depend upon the consent of individuals, and was not susceptible to manipulation. Even before de Foix's mission, Walsingham was already thinking in terms of 'straight amity', on account
of the current 'unkindness' between England and Spain,[5] and he
told Leicester they should take 'good hold' on it, if Elizabeth
refused the marriage which her 'staggering state' required;[6] he

[1] La Mothe, iv, 208–10, 6 August 1571, La Mothe to Catherine.

[2] La Mothe, iv, 213, 9 August 1571, La Mothe to Charles IX; 214–16, 12
August 1571, La Mothe to Charles IX; 217–21, 19 August 1571, La Mothe to
Charles IX.

[3] The sort of thing referred to was that Anjou should not be molested from
using any rites 'not repugnant unto the Church of God'. Digges, 130, 2 September 1571, Elizabeth to Walsingham. Only part of this letter appears in some
copies.

[4] Digges, 129–31, 2 September 1571, Elizabeth to Walsingham.

[5] *CSPF.*, *1569–71*, p. 497, 30 July 1571, Walsingham to Burghley; 501,
3 August 1571, Walsingham to Burghley.

[6] Digges, 119, 31 July 1571, Walsingham to Leicester.

referred to the conditions of near insurrection. Walsingham, who saw de Foix at Melun near Fontainebleau before his departure for England, believed him to have a commission to treat of either marriage or amity.[1] Queen Elizabeth apparently also believed this, but de Foix himself denied it, doubtless because there was no mention of amity in his instructions.[2] On the contrary they enjoined him to withdraw 'prudemment' if he failed to conclude the marriage.[3] This will have been to emphasise in his instructions, which were formal, the importance attached to the marriage. But he must have discussed amity with Burghley who drafted a memorandum on the subject and, shortly afterwards, in a letter to Walsingham referred to '*the* treaty of alliance'. To Elizabeth herself de Foix declared that amity would continue and, according to Burghley, had asked the queen to send to France 'someone of credit' to affirm and justify the reasons for her answer and, if the marriage did not take place – they are Burghley's words – 'to enter into *the* treaty of straighter alliance and confederacy'. But when Burghley found that he himself was designated, he dealt 'coldlier therein'.[4] He was a martyr to gout and spoke no foreign language.

Thus, with everything undecided, but fully expecting an envoy 'of credit' to follow him, de Foix returned to court at Blois about 20 September, as Beauvais and Biron were preparing to leave for Béarn. Charles complained to Walsingham that Elizabeth's answer was 'very hard', and hoped the 'envoy of credit' would have authority to qualify it, and to treat of 'other matters'.[5]

[1] *CSPF.*, *1569–71*, p. 502, 3 August 1571, Walsingham to Burghley.

[2] La Mothe, vii, 235–8, 31 July 1571, Charles to La Mothe; *CSPF.*, *1569–71*, p. 501, 1 August 1571, letters of credence for M. de Foix; 502, 3 August 1571, Walsingham to Burghley; 522, 2 September 1571, Elizabeth to Walsingham.

[3] La Mothe, vii, 235–41, 31 July 1571, instructions for de Foix; *CSPF.*, *1569–71*, pp. 513–14, 22 August 1571, considerations for a league with France, in Burghley's hand.

[4] Digges, 129–31, 2 September 1571, Elizabeth to Walsingham; 133–4, 2 September 1571, Burghley to Walsingham.

[5] Digges, 136, 23 September 1571, Walsingham to Burghley. This letter is partly missing from some copies.

Cautious and diplomatic might perhaps have been more accurate than 'very hard' since de Foix, for his part, found Anjou 'so coldly affected to the marriage as he has no hope of the matter'.[1] The nuncio was even then urging upon Rome – possibly on account of the failure of the Ridolphi affair to remove one contracting party – that Anjou ought to be openly supported as the catholic leader – which could only be in opposition to the catholic king – and offered alternative propositions such as a Spanish marriage upon tempting terms – whatever these might be – since his Spanish niece was only a child.[2]

In all this there was no overt mention of the Netherlands, with which de Foix had evidently not been *formally* concerned in England, though it hardly seems possible that the subject was not raised at least with Burghley and Leicester. Upon the arrival of de Foix, Leicester had in fact mentioned good offers for the augmentation of the crown, which rather suggests partition than matrimony,[3] and Burghley had indeed considered the Netherlands enterprise in connection with amity. He tended to think it folly to venture the loss of a kingdom for the sake of conquests else-where, such as the Netherlands; nor did he trust France not to 'fall off'. More important, he was reluctant to provide naval assistance because ships were expensive and, as the wall of England, she could ill-afford to lose them. Besides, the Nether-lands were more important to England, commercially, than they were to France.[4] In practical terms this would mean that he favoured a defensive and not an offensive alliance.

Walsingham, however, was very anxious indeed about this diplomatic intermission – if breach is too strong a term – and the English silence upon the Netherlands. 'Great consultation' on the Netherlands had been held at court between the king, Anjou

[1] *CSPF.*, *1569–71*, p. 538, 26 September 1571, two letters, Walsingham to Burghley.
[2] Hirschauer, *La Politique de St Pie V*, 163, 17 September 1571, Frangipani to Rusticucci.
[3] Digges, 129 [16 August 1571], Leicester to Burghley.
[4] *CSPF.*, *1569–71*, p. 513, 22 August 1571, Burghley's considerations for a league with France.

(presumably as lieutenant-general and therefore commander-in-chief), the four marshals and the admiral. Here again, if somewhat obliquely, one may glimpse the conception of a national undertaking, except that Walsingham does not mention Catherine. There is, however, no better evidence that Anjou, the marshals – apart from Montmorency – or anyone in the council, ever favoured the enterprise, although Walsingham inferred, upon this occasion, that they might be swayed by England. He himself, on the other hand, may have been swayed by the intensity of his anxiety. 'The lets therof,' he continued, 'are two: the expectation of what the queen will do and the lack of money'.[1] Unlike Burghley, who, being in England, saw things from a different angle, Walsingham wished the French might be encouraged to proceed in the enterprise. By joining it, England could prevent France from becoming too great, and take comfort, by deflection of inward troubles, from 'the fire akindling'.[2]

If Walsingham had written those particular words in August, the conference at Blois coincided with the arrest of the duke of Norfolk on 7 September and the crisis in England of the so-called Ridolphi plot which – unlike the northern rising, of which it was the next stage – had the weight of Spain behind it.[3] The Spanish conception of the enterprise of England had developed beyond the cautious conclusions of the Brussels talks early in 1571, and gradually merged with the plans propounded by Ridolphi. Ridolphi arrived in Madrid on 28 June, six days after his kinsman Gondi had come from France; an interesting coincidence. His proposals, as described by Philip II to Alva were, basically, the death of queen Elizabeth, the marriage of Mary to Norfolk and the catholicising of England. The conspirators had requested 6,000 harquebusiers for England and 2,000 each for Scotland and Ireland. They also wanted a further 6,000 men immediately from Alva. Philip determined with uncharacteristic despatch to proceed with this plan as soon as possible, although he declined absolutely

[1] *CSPF.*, *1569–71*, p. 538, 26 September 1571, Walsingham to Burghley.
[2] Digges, 127, 12 August 1571, Walsingham to Leicester.
[3] This, at least, was true in intention, although the timing was hopelessly bungled.

to act in the name of the pope.[1] Alva, who thought Ridolphi a dangerous chatterbox, was horrified at this temerity and analysed some of the risks involved if the enterprise should fail to secure the queen's person. He had no confidence in the duke of Norfolk, in whom he detected neither energy nor courage. He also feared the ineptitude of the Spanish ambassador, de Spes, whom he considered an incompetent fool because, if Elizabeth discovered Philip's involvement, it would drive her into the arms of France, and even, perhaps, of the duc d'Anjou.[2] In spite, or perhaps in a sense because, of the disclosure in England of the plot, of which Philip was informed by de Spes on 23 June and by Alava on 12 July[3] he declared his resolve to spare nothing in furthering what had been begun, considering it his duty before God, so he said, to restore England to catholicism. This motive, however, must not be announced, and, ostensibly the enterprise was to be for the release of Mary, so that neither protestants nor France would have any cause to intervene.[4] Philip therefore sent Alva money, and much more audacious orders, in spite of his unfavourable reaction, and designated his commander, the Florentine Chiapin Vitelli, marquis of Cetona, a curious appointment since his excessive obesity is said to have impeded his mobility.[5]

Alva's initial reaction to Philip's letter of 14 July, had been that Philip could take the responsibility himself, by coming in person to the Netherlands, and his response to Philip's orders of 4 August was positively violent. He declared himself utterly mystified that the king should propose to support conspirators who were bound to fail and would involve him in war. He,

---

[1] Gachard, *Correspondance de Philippe II*, ii, 185–7, 14 July 1571, Philip II to Alva.

[2] Gachard, *Correspondance de Philippe II*, ii, 188, 3 August 1571, Alva to Philip II.

[3] Gachard, *Correspondance de Philippe II*, ii, 191, 4 August 1571, Philip II to Alva.

[4] Gachard, *Correspondance de Philippe II*, ii, 195–7, 30 August 1571, Philip II to Alva.

[5] Gachard, *Correspondance de Philippe II*, ii, 196, 30 August 1571, Philip II to Alva; *CSPSp.*, *1568–79*, p. 191, note; *CSPVen.*, *1558–80*, p. 475, 9 September 1571.

Alva, had no intelligence in England with anyone who could help him, and no information but from spies and fugitives. He discounted de Spes. Furthermore, he objected that he was ordered to make preparations in the ignorance of the council without whom he could do nothing, and he spewed scorn upon Ridolphi who imagined that forces could be raised to capture Elizabeth, release Mary, seize the Tower, and capture the ships in the Thames. This, he stormed, would be impossible with Elizabeth's full co-operation. A few days later he added, for good measure, that Ridolphi had leaked the plan in general and in detail; it was common knowledge among the merchants of Antwerp.[1]

Philip took all this surprisingly calmly, but remained undeterred. On 14 September, two days after the conference had opened at Blois, he wrote to Alva – possibly in view of the religious demands of the 1571 parliament – that if he did not intervene, religion in England would soon be annihilated. He further alleged that whether or not Elizabeth married Anjou or allied with France, she would always be an enemy, poised to do him harm and to profit at his expense, and to such an extent that *the only means of securing the safety of the Netherlands was to overthrow the crown of England*. So he renewed his previous orders.[2] This again was a rather different emphasis from the catholicising of England, and the liberation of Mary. She had complicated the affairs of the disaffected English lords, whose cause or quarrels existed before her flight into England, and even more the weightier problems of Philip II, which persisted after her death in 1587. It was only upon receipt of the news of the arrest of Norfolk that Philip had any misgivings, but even then he re-affirmed that this should not prevent the execution of the enterprise upon the 'first favourable occasion'.[3]

---

[1] Gachard, *Correspondance de Philippe II*, ii, 193-4, 27 August 1571, Alva to Philip II; 197-8, 5 September 1571, Alva to Philip II.

[2] Gachard, *Correspondance de Philippe II*, ii, 198-202, 14 September 1571, Philip II to Alva: '. . . il n'y a d'autre moyen d'assurer le bien et la conservation des Pays-Bas, que le changement de la couronne d'Angleterre'.

[3] Gachard, *Correspondance de Philippe II*, ii, 205, 17 October 1571, Philip II to Alva.

Philip could be almost as obtuse about England as Charles IX about the Netherlands. He envisaged a brief episode, depending upon the outcome of a single battle, with no need for an 'open war'. Neither of them ever elucidated what, if not battles, constituted war.[1]

If Alva had no intention of executing the enterprise, or seeing any occasion as favourable, Philip had other commanders, and his successor, Medina Celi, was about to embark.[2] It can therefore hardly be said that Walsingham was exaggerating the danger to England. Moreover, the traumatic disclosure of the recent conspiracy, with all its menacing ramifications, was swiftly followed by the spectacular victory over the Turks at Lepanto on 7 October 1571, 'ceste tant absolue victoire,' as La Mothe apprehensively described it.[3] Immediate Turkish recovery could not be relied upon to divert Philip from northern Europe and, even though he could hardly have prevailed without the Venetian fleet,[4] Elizabeth, who was not otherwise vulnerable – unless from from Scotland – must necessarily have been impressed by Philip's naval power. Walsingham was also terribly conscious of the weight and strength of the catholic pressure in France, and feared that Charles might actually be forced into some *rapprochement* with Spain through the 'devilish practices of those who seek the utter subversion of the gospel'.[5] Alva had in fact slightly tempered his outburst of 27 August by suggesting to Philip that France just might be induced to co-operate, not in conquering England for Spain, but in dethroning Elizabeth in favour of Mary, in which case, he said, the proposition should be made to France

[1] Gachard, *Correspondance de Philippe II*, ii, 201, 14 September 1571, Philip II to Alva.

[2] This is what Philip said; in fact he was delayed. Gachard, *Correspondance de Philippe II*, ii, 205, 17 October 1571, Philip II to Alva.

[3] La Mothe, iv, 280–1, 10 November 1571, La Mothe to Catherine.

[4] The Venetians are reported to have supplied 109 ships, Spain 55, divided between Spain, Naples and Sicily, and the pope 12. Altogether there were 285 on the side of christendom. Charrière, *Négociations de la France dans le Levant*, iii, 189.

[5] *CSPF., 1569–71*, pp. 538–9, 26 September 1571, Walsingham to Burghley.

by the pope.[1] Ridolphi had proposed from the outset, in 1568, that the enterprise – though it was not then the same version – should be in the name of the pope, in order to obviate Franco-Spanish rivalry. But Philip could never condescend to that, and Alva was only manoeuvring. He added that that would take time, and there would be other opportunities. Philip, for his part, replied that he was opposed to the idea, not least because he distrusted the French.

France and Spain together, as Alva affirmed, might feasibly attack England, just as France and England together might reasonably safely attack the Netherlands (except that this was not what Elizabeth intended). But the inability of any two of these powers to combine against the third produced half a century of seething conflict and the remarkable distinction between battles and war. This, in essence, was the politico-religious struggle of the sixteenth century, in which there came to be so many strands, aspects, and conflicting interests in French, Spanish, English – and papal – policies, as virtually to defy clarification. What happened, in effect, was that Spain, the pope and the French catholics all meddled deeply in Marian plots and the catholicising of England, while Elizabeth sought to divert attention and political activity by manipulating the interests of others in the conflict in the Netherlands, where the policy of everyone concerned was pragmatically guided by their underlying fears; hence the complex confusion.

Walsingham felt that if only negotiations could be kept going with England the protestants, who were devoted to Elizabeth, would continue in credit with Charles. Otherwise he feared that 'the house of Guise are like to bear the sway, who will be as forward in preferring [sic – advancing] the conquest of Ireland and the advancement of their niece [Mary queen of Scots] to the crown of England, as the other side is contrariwise bent to prefer the conquest of Flanders'.[2] Not long after he reported that those who had been having 'great consultations' had resolved upon the

---

[1] Gachard, *Correspondance de Philippe II*, ii, 193–5, 27 August 1571, Alva to Philip II.

[2] *CSPF., 1569–71*, pp. 538–9, 26 September 1571, Walsingham to Burghley.

enterprise of Flanders, possibly through the influence of several Netherlands representatives who, according to Alava, were there.[1] No one tells us just what it was that had been resolved but, without any mention of Coligny, Walsingham went on to say that Catherine and de Morvillier, the chancellor, had 'bred a stay' to see how England was affected, and, a week later, that the enemies of the enterprise persuaded Charles 'not to resolve in that behalf until he may know what Her Majesty will do'. In this case, he was evidently referring to the moderates and supporters of Catherine and not the catholic opposition whose attitude would be unaffected by Elizabeth's intentions.[2]

What Elizabeth would do was, thenceforth, the major problem; and it was never to be resolved. What Elizabeth would do – to which they attached different degrees of importance – and not the traditionally alleged influence of Coligny, also explains the dissension which persisted between Charles and Catherine from then until the massacre in August 1572. In this connection, it is interesting to note the nuncio's observation, while Coligny was still at Blois, that his influence should not be exaggerated, though his ability was to be feared. He did not control all, Frangipani continued, though it would be said that he did; *indeed*, it has been said ever since. Nor, the nuncio added, did he obtain all that he asked for. This is only what one would expect since neither then, nor in 1572, did he carry any weight in the council.[3] Coligny is also alleged by Petrucci to have informed Catherine that he could not act as he chose, since it was the princes who were in command.[4] While the command of the youthful and absent Navarre and Condé was obviously more theoretical than real, it is abundantly

[1] *CSPF.*, *1569–71*, p. 545, 8 October 1571, Walsingham to Burghley; Kervyn de Lettenhove, *Les Huguenots*, ii, 334, Simancas, K.1522, 8 November 1571, Alava to Alva. Alava, who had been recalled, upon the request of the French, had not been at court for sometime. He was temporarily replaced by his allegedly abler secretary, Don Pedro Aiguilon.

[2] *CSPF.*, *1569–71*, pp. 544–5, 8 October 1571, Walsingham to Burghley; 552, 19 October 1571, Walsingham to Burghley.

[3] Hirschauer, *La Politique de St Pie V*, 172, 173 note, 14–15 October 1571, Frangipani to Rusticucci.

[4] Desjardins, *Negs. Tosc.*, iii, 709, 24 September 1571.

clear, both before and after his return to court in September 1571, that Coligny could not control his own extremists – still less Nassau over whom he had no authority – whose injudicious precipitation into the Netherlands imbroglio was shortly to cost him his life, together with many confederates.

Apart from the uncertainty as to what Elizabeth would do, the basic issue of war or peace with Spain could not much longer be evaded. Catherine, therefore, ceased to temporise and had 'bred a stay' in the resolution of the Netherlands enterprise. But Charles, it appears, wanted to fight perhaps, as the Venetian Michiel believed, seeking to emulate Francis I and Henry II. Thus he wished to employ Coligny in the Netherlands in, as it were, 'battles', national battles, glorious, successful and safely immune from undesirable consequences. Having been fed and flattered by facile talk of quick, cheap and easy conquests, he steadily affirmed that he intended no hostility towards Spain, possibly supposing – if he reflected at all – that, like queen Elizabeth, he too could conduct furtive hostilities. But Charles IX was not queen Elizabeth, and France was not an island, and it is not surprising if Catherine saw in this a very serious risk of war with Spain. It is not clear whether she ever conceded that, granted the co-operation of England, the risk was admissible, or whether she suspected that Elizabeth would not relinquish her advantage by committing herself, and so hoped to use the reservation of English support as a means of thwarting so dangerous a policy.

Petrucci, however, reflected early in October that Catherine's firm resolution to maintain peace with Spain was not, paradoxically, without its own dangers, since for decades past the history of France had shown her inability to avoid, for any length of time, either foreign or civil war.[1] In this case, the choice lay between war and war, not war or peace. This was also Coligny's opinion, and France was teetering on the brink of renewed civil war from the moment his return to court was seriously expected. If civil war were the greater calamity, Spanish war was the greater risk and, in the face of this desolate alternative, Catherine's

---

[1] Desjardins, *Negs. Tosc.*, iii, 716–17, 7 October 1571.

reaction was one of pragmatic hesitation, as offering the only, faint hope.

Coligny, on the other hand, clearly opted, as he always had, for foreign war, and it appears to be well substantiated that from this time on, he did everything he could to persuade the king to declare against Spain. The reasons for this may rather be surmised than established.[1] Perhaps because the enterprise had been leaked to Spain, he may have thought, like Philip II himself (who nevertheless deferred it for many years), that war between France and Spain was inevitable.[2] It could certainly have had the advantages of clarifying domestic and foreign relations, of committing Charles definitively, and perhaps inducing him to prosecute the Netherlands enterprise properly. It would also have protected Coligny from the hazard of later repudiation, as well as from Spanish revenge from the Netherlands, or Spanish 'support' of the crown, in the event of further civil war. If there were any choice in the matter it was, after all, more desirable to be behind, rather than against the crown – or the servants of the crown, which was not a military distinction. Apart from this, it may well have been more because he could not afford to see Elizabeth overthrown and England reduced to chaos or restored to Rome, than because he was reluctantly drawn into Nassau's version of the Netherlands enterprise, that Coligny urged the king to declare war against Spain; information which quickly filtered back to Philip from Rome, and doubtless also elsewhere. Elizabeth might steadily decline to assume the role of international protestant champion, but she was still the most powerful counterweight to Philip II. If the enterprise of England – whether predominantly French or Spanish – was temporarily averted by

---

[1] La Mothe, iv, 298, 5 December 1571; 319, 16 December, both from La Mothe to Charles IX; Digges, 153, 6 December 1571, Leicester to Walsingham. Zúñiga, the Spanish ambassador in Rome, reported to Philip II on 16 October 1571 receipt of various letters from France confirming the admiral's pressure on Charles to make war on Spain. Serrano, *Correspondencia diplomatica de S. Pio V*, iv, 485, 16 October 1571, Zúñiga to Philip II.

[2] Gachard, *Correspondance de Philippe II*, ii, 199, 14 September 1571, Philip II to Alva.

the disclosure of the (Ridolphi) conspirators in England, the danger still persisted, and a French declaration against Spain would therefore have been instrumental in protecting both the focal points, England and the Netherlands, in this great struggle for power and security.

Charles, however, was not a free agent, any more than Coligny himself. Only in theory could he make war contrary to the wishes of Anjou, as lieutenant-general, and all the council. Furthermore, he is alleged to have promised at Blois not to undertake war without the knowledge and consent of Catherine who strongly advised him to 'stare in pace ed accomodare il vostro regno, perchè è santo e buono'.[1] Thus nothing had been determined and nothing agreed as a result of Coligny's return to court. On the contrary, there clearly existed a complex, tripartite disagreement between Charles and Catherine, and Coligny who was opposed to each of them on the three major issues, whether as a matter of policy, as in the Bourbon marriage, or as a matter of tactics, in the case of the Netherlands and England.

[1] Desjardins, *Negs. Tosc.*, iii, 712–13, 3 October 1571.

XI

The Catholic Crisis
November–December 1571

WHEN CHARLES left Blois on 18 October 1571, and Coligny on the nineteenth, not to return to court until the following June,[1] everything was in suspense. But Charles did not intend to be away for long because the young princes, Navarre and Condé were to come in about three weeks' time, and Jeanne d'Albret in December.[2] By then it might be known how England was 'affected', since the person 'of credit' requested by de Foix was already expected early in October. But Elizabeth changed her mind, first awaiting the French reactions to de Foix's report, which Charles utterly declined to express before the arrival of the envoy.[3] Thus the negotiations were halted just when the 'two pangs' her majesty lately had showed the need for the French marriage. As for the French themselves, Lepanto made them 'to startle' also, and added to Walsingham's fear that events might 'breed some change' in France and incline the king to 'run one course' with Philip for a time.[4] But, far from denying the urgency of her need, and the desirability of engaging Anjou, even before the battle of Lepanto, Elizabeth had signified that she could be 'content to yield in toleration'. It is not clear to

---

[1] Charles was at Bury near Blois on 18 October. Douais, *Lettres de Charles IX à M. de Fourquevaulx*, 367, 18 October 1571, Charles to Fourquevaulx; Hirschauer, *Correspondance de St Pie V*, 173–4, 17 October 1571, Frangipani to Rusticucci; 174–5, 26–8 October 1571, same to same; Martin, *Journal of Sir Francis Walsingham*, 11.

[2] Desjardins, *Negs. Tosc.*, iii, 719, 11 October 1571; La Mothe, vii, 273, 2 November 1571, Charles to La Mothe.

[3] La Mothe, vii, 253, 27 September 1571, Charles to La Mothe; Digges, 139, 28 September 1571, Burghley to Walsingham.

[4] CSPF., 1569–71, p. 557, 8 November 1571, Walsingham to Burghley and Digges, 149–50.

what formula this refers, and therefore whether it went beyond the omission of religion from the terms of the contract. But Walsingham determined to keep this capitulation to himself unless he saw 'more towardness' in France because – Elizabeth having called the catholics' bluff – he feared the unthinkable diplomatic nightmare in which, 'all being granted' that Anjou desired, he would return an embarrassingly plain refusal.[1]

It was therefore not surprising that Elizabeth should hesitate to send her envoy. Besides, she still, or again, wished to clarify the French attitude to Mary, and to Scotland which had been in a renewed state of crisis since the murder of the regent Lennox on 4 September and his replacement by the earl of Mar.[2] As for Mary, Elizabeth was adamant that she would never release this dangerous enemy who had so recently, as Walsingham said, 'dismembered her Majesties politique body by corruption of sundry of her best qualified Subjects'. Conversely, she would not entertain her execution, which the protestants thought Mary deserved.[3] In mid-November, however, Scotland, Mary and Anjou notwithstanding, Burghley raised with La Mothe the question of close alliance and – since he was ready to leave on 6 December – it cannot have been long after that Elizabeth appointed Sir Thomas Smith, certainly an envoy 'of credit', to go to France to obtain something more substantial than 'dalliance', whether marriage or amity.[4]

---

[1] *CSPF.*, *1569–71*, p. 515, 24 August 1571, reply of the queen to the duke of Anjou's envoys; 544–5, 8 October 1571, Walsingham to Burghley; 551, 19 October 1571, Walsingham to Burghley.

[2] *CSPF.*, *1569–71*, pp. 545–6, 8 October 1571, instructions for Killigrew. Digges, 147 gives 19 October, apparently in error.

[3] Walsingham meant, of course, those of highest rank. Digges, 144, 19 October 1571, Walsingham to Burghley; *CSPF.*, *1569–71*, pp. 581–2, 29 December 1571, Killigrew to Burghley; *1572–4*, p. 35 [3 February] 1572, 'occurrents' in which the protestants are said to have called not merely for Mary's execution, but for her crucifixion; La Mothe, iv, 263–4, 24 October 1571, La Mothe to Charles IX.

[4] Digges, 152, 5 December 1571, Burghley to Walsingham; 153, 6 December 1571, Leicester to Walsingham. La Mothe first mentioned him on 5 December 1571, vol. iv, 298–300, La Mothe to Charles IX.

Through an unnamed third party, probably Coligny's secretary Dupin, Elizabeth assured Coligny of her trust in him
and also of her desire that he should be at court to advise
and assist Sir Thomas Smith, who arrived in France at the end
of December, and reached the court at Amboise about 3 January
1572.[1]

It appears therefore that the two recent 'pangs' caused the
Elizabethan pendulum to swing back from Spain towards the
huguenots, who were at least predictable and reasonably reliable
allies. They were also in possession of the strategically placed
La Rochelle, and were probably more powerful at sea than the
King of France. Thus, towards the end of November, Montgommery, one of their leading lieutenants, was well received by
Elizabeth who 'somewhat opened her mind' to him. Montgommery assured the queen of Coligny's efforts to persuade
Charles to make war on Spain. Elizabeth apparently argued that
as Philip II had not hesitated to foster rebellion in England, she
would not scruple to do the same in the Netherlands.[2] It was this,
and not dominion, which she sought. Thus she was closer to
Coligny than she was to the crown of France, which she did not
wish to buttress, or to Nassau and other supporters of the partition plan, even though Coligny himself had become involved
with the crown and committed to supporting Nassau.

Elizabeth's desire for Coligny's co-operation tends to suggest
that she had already despaired of the Anjou marriage, whose
frustration she rightly attributed to 'ceulx qui de longtemps

[1] Digges, 153–4, 6 December 1571, Leicester to Walsingham; 161, 31
December 1571, Walsingham to Burghley; CSPF., 1572–4, pp. 3–4, 3 January
1572, Smith to Burghley; 8–11, 8 January 1572, Smith and Killigrew to
Elizabeth; 15, 11 January 1572, Walsingham to Burghley; La Mothe, iv, 342–
50, 18 January 1572, La Mothe to Charles and Catherine.
[2] Montgommery had gone to England partly on family business. His
daughter was married to the son of Sir Arthur Champernown, admiral of the
west, a radical in religion. La Mothe, iv, 282–6, 15 November 1571, La Mothe
to Charles IX; 291–3, 26 November 1571, La Mothe to Charles IX; 298–300,
5 December 1571, La Mothe to Charles IX; 317, 22 December 1571, La Mothe
to Charles IX; Digges, 153, 6 December 1571, Leicester to Walsingham; 160,
December 1571 (dated 8 in error), Walsingham to Burghley.

avoient préparé leurs conseils et artiffices contre ce propos'.[1] But these same agencies which, in the weeks before Smith's arrival, brought France to the verge of civil war, effectively excluded Coligny from court. They also did their best to keep Jeanne away, and succeeded in raising turmoil in Paris.

Upon his departure from Blois, Charles maintained that Coligny had gone home 'fort content et satisfaict pour nous venir retrouver . . . que je sois arresté en lieu de séjour,' which meant Blois or Amboise.[2] Charles then proposed to reassemble the court, when the princes arrived, and proceed with his general econciliation, to be based on the Bourbon marriage. Fregoso was the first of the messengers sent from Blois to return from Jeanne. He had found her as trying as everyone else, and told Petrucci that 'l'umore di quella Regina è molto fantastico . . . varia spesso et scappa ad ogni ora'.[3] She hoped and she feared, and she broke off everything for a trifle. Nevertheless, she was still expected to come – according to Biron – in mid-December, although her departure and Henry's had been delayed because he was seriously ill after falling from his horse. In any case, she meant to confer with Charles, Catherine and Marguerite – which she did – before permitting Henry to join her.[4]

Charles, meanwhile, proceeded to summon the Guises – without Lorraine – since the resolution of the vendetta was still fundamental. Indeed, according to the nuncio, Aumale and his nephews Guise and du Maine had been called before the departure from Blois, and their brother-in-law Nevers, was already there.[5] In a letter of 5 November, Lorraine confirmed that his relatives were considering returning to court, but he was going to Rheims,

---

[1] La Mothe, iv, 350-4, 25 January 1572, La Mothe to Charles IX.

[2] La Mothe, vii, 270, 20 October 1571, Charles IX to La Mothe.

[3] Desjardins, *Negs. Tosc.*, iii, 733, 30 November 1571.

[4] Hirschauer, *Correspondance de St Pie V*, 177-8, 23 November 1571, Frangipani to Rusticucci; 178, 27 November 1571, Giorgi, the nuncio's secretary to Rusticucci; *CSPF.*, *1569-71*, p. 569, 3 December 1571, Killigrew, advertisements from France.

[5] Hirschauer, *Correspondance de St Pie V*, 173, 14-15 October 1571, Frangipani to Rusticucci from Blois; *CSPF.*, *1569-71*, p. 569, 3 December 1571, Killigrew, advertisements from France.

'y faire un peu de devoir darcheveque'[1] Apart from Charles'
peripatetic habits, this Guise activity may have been why Coligny
left Blois for Châtillon, which required restoration from the last
civil war. Certainly their reaction to his presence at court had not
been reassuring, and Charles ordered them not to come with
more than their usual suite. This they promised to obey, but
without deprivation since they intended to ensure that Coligny
would not be there.[2] Petrucci also confirmed that the Guises had
been summoned for the purpose of a reconciliation. But for his
part, he could summon no faith in this, or any aspect of the policy.
By no means the most acute of observers, he was clearly sceptical
of Charles' myopic optimism in hoping to patch everything up.
No one obeyed him, nothing improved and there were too many
causes of discord in France where he considered 'le cose . . . sono
molto tenere'.[3] Besides, the indispositions of Charles and Catherine,
which seemed to alternate and with alarming frequency, were
always vulnerable times. Catherine was again seriously ill at the
end of November 1571, and Charles, as usual, was absorbed in
hunting when a grave and mysterious crisis erupted.[4]

This crisis, in Killigrew's words, was 'some practice of the
Catholics who favour Spain'.[5] It was certainly a move against
Coligny, to keep him from court at the risk or the cost of civil
war, and possibly also to murder him if he managed to return.
It also appears, though more obscurely, to have been a positive
move in favour of Anjou, whether as a Gallic sting in Ridolphi's
tail, or as part of the catholics' normal, energetic promotion of
their prince, through whom they sought to frustrate the three
royal policies.

Probably this Guise enterprise, whatever it was, dated at least
from August or September – if not combined during Gondi's

[1] B.N., Mss. fr. 3256, f. 47, 5 November 1571, Lorraine to Secondigny.

[2] *CSPF.*, *1569–71*, p. 559, 12 November 1571.

[3] Desjardins, *Negs. Tosc.*, iii, 726, 19 November 1571; 728, 20 November 1571.

[4] Desjardins, *Negs. Tosc.*, iii, 731, 28 November 1571.

[5] *CSPF.*, *1569–71*, p. 569, 3 December 1571, Killigrew, advertisements from France.

mission to Spain in June, which is possible – when it was publicly
known in France that the English conspiracy was disclosed, when
Coligny's return to court was expected, and the Guises began
their menacing assembly at Joinville. The immediate origin of the
crisis, which broke in mid-November, was the abrupt flight, in
disguise, of the Spanish ambassador Alava, who suddenly 'slipt'
into Flanders, described by the king with an uncharacteristic
flash of sardonic humour as 'une façon nouvelle'.[1]

This 'façon nouvelle', which remains unexplained, should
probably be connected with the interception in Dauphiné of a
packet belonging to the ambassador, from which some 'practice'
was deciphered. Alava, who had been recalled at the end of
August, had in fact been absent for some three months and may
very well have kept in touch with the Guises from the disturbed
city of Paris where their influence was always strong. About the
time of Alava's flight, the Guises entered the city of Troyes in
Champagne, with a large gathering. Since they and Coligny,
who was at Châtillon in Burgundy, were all expected at court,
Coligny had sent to enquire whether he was to take them for
friends or enemies.[2] Also about this time Charles heard news of
some 'brags' of the house of Guise that they would be revenged
upon Coligny which, if certainly not a 'façon nouvelle', was
hardly more propitious than their conduct for the reconciliation
which Charles was hoping to accomplish when the court reassembled.[3] Serious religious disorders in Paris over the *croix des
Gâtines* which was 'plucked down' in the small hours of 20
December also contributed to the sense of general crisis. People
are reported to have rushed about the streets yelling 'let us kill
the Huguenots'. They sacked two houses and, the trouble having
continued all next day, Paris itself was held to be in danger of
destruction, so that the *gouverneur*, Montmorency, shortly after
entered the city with 4–500 horse to restore order and enforce

[1] *CSPF.*, *1569–71*, p. 561, 19 November 1571, Walsingham to Burghley;
La Mothe, vii, 279, 30 November 1571, Charles to La Mothe.
[2] *CSPF.*, *1569–71*, p. 569, 3 December 1571, Killigrew, advertisements from
France; Desjardins, *Negs. Tosc.*, iii, 737–8, 4 December 1571.
[3] *CSPF.*, *1569–71*, p. 576, 17 December 1571, Killigrew to Burghley.

justice.[1] He reported a great increase of Guise followers, who had taken many rooms in different parts of the city and were brewing something among themselves. He learnt of one plan to besiege Coligny in his house in which case he would, it was said, be obliged to assist him, and was making preparations accordingly.

In these circumstances, which looked alarmingly like the approach of civil war, Coligny took the precaution of warning his friends all over France to hold themselves in readiness.[2] This virtually amounted to mobilisation and, only a few weeks later, the protestants were reported to dispose of considerable forces, available at short notice.[3] Coligny told the king that he had alerted his friends on account of the Guise assemblies but, because of his promise at the time of leaving Blois, he had actually gathered no more than twenty-five harquebusiers to defend Châtillon. It would appear, therefore, that he had promised not to take up arms, since he proclaimed that he could otherwise have gone half way to meet the Guises, who were reported to be advancing upon his house. This important, but rather obscure letter of 13 December 1571, insinuated that the Guises would stop at nothing; it contains the remarkable revelations that the king himself had offered to protect Coligny with armed forces (doubtless the meaning of Montmorency's preparations), and that while the Guises were summoned to court, Coligny had now been commanded to remain at home,[4] He agreed, provided he was not dishonoured. There would seem, however, to be something rather more in all this than the habitual Guise efforts to exclude Coligny from court. Killigrew reported that Coligny had secret intelligence from a councillor at court 'to look to

[1] *CSPF.*, *1569–71*, pp. 582–3, 30 December 1571, advertisements from Walsingham; Desjardins, *Negs. Tosc.*, iii, 740–4, 24 December 1571.
[2] B.N., Mss. fr. 3193, f. 25, 13 December 1571, Coligny to Charles IX. Desjardins, *Negs. Tosc.*, iii, 740–3, 24 December 1571.
[3] *CSPF.*, *1572–4*, p. 35 [3 February 1572]; 20,000 foot and 7,000 horse. The cavalry figure sounds very high.
[4] Petrucci was late in reporting this; Desjardins, *Negs. Tosc.*, iii, 744–5, 28–9 December 1571.

himself, for that all is not gold that glisters'[1] – whatever this may refer to – and the Venetian Cavalli, wrote that Saint-Gouard, a kinsman of de Retz and shortly to be sent as ambassador to Spain, was accredited with a plan to destroy Coligny when he returned to court at Amboise in December.[2] It is impossible not to remember, in this connection, Philip's observation that the only good reason for recalling Coligny was to arrest and execute him, and more recently if less well attested, a report that the pope maintained even worse; that the only reason could be 'con disegno di ammazzarlo', which dispensed with preliminary arrest.[3] True or false, such a report still testifies to an atmosphere and climate of opinion. Coligny had survived the conference at Blois, but clearly the crown could not guarantee his safety. He therefore did not return until 6 June 1572 when, no matter how dangerous, particularly in Paris, circumstances finally obliged him to.

These moves against Coligny – established and feared – were one side of the catholic enterprise, but there was evidently also something further involved. On 9 or 10 December, when the Guises were in arms and Coligny unable to leave Châtillon, Lignerolles, one of Anjou's favourites and an instrument of the Guise and Spanish faction, was slain at court, which has always been regarded as a minor historical mystery. Lignerolles had been a servant of the duc de Nemours and involved in the Nemours conspiracy in November 1561 to abduct Anjou, which Sir Nicholas Throckmorton said was also a plot to murder Condé. He had performed a number of catholic missions, was a great supporter of Mary queen of Scots, and a Scottish pensioner.[4] Killigrew described his death as a 'set matter and foul murder', thus precluding any sudden rage or instant quarrel. Lignerolles

---

[1] *CSPF.*, *1569–71*, p. 581, 29 December 1571, Killigrew to Burghley.

[2] Champion, *Charles IX, la France et le contrôle de l'Espagne*, i, 419 seq. Saint-Gouard was a cousin of Claude-Catherine de Clermont, wife of de Retz.

[3] Desjardins, *Negs. Tosc.*, iii, 732, 28 November 1571, anonymous letter from France to François de Médicis.

[4] *CSPF.*, *1561–2*, p. 416, 26 November 1561, Throckmorton to Elizabeth; *1566–8*, pp. 316–17, 12 August 1567, Throckmorton to Elizabeth.

was held to have been the chief 'dissuader' of the English marriage, and Walsingham hoped that his death and the 'Turkish victory' might yield 'new life to the same'.[1] There were, however, other known 'dissuaders', and the timing of his death suggests that there may have been more to it than this. While the English conspiracy, if successful, would have removed one contracting party to the Anjou marriage, and thwarted amity with England, its failure had precisely the opposite effect, namely to render amity, if not marriage, virtually inevitable, and to drive Elizabeth, if not quite directly into the arms of France – which Sir Thomas Smith was shortly expected to manoeuvre – at least perceptibly closer to the huguenots. Some sort of strenuous and extreme catholic reaction was therefore securely predictable.

It was generally known that the plot was disclosed in England in June, before Ridolphi ever reached Madrid, where he is said to have remained until 11 September and then again to have visited France on his way to the Netherlands. According to the bishop of Ross (Mary's ambassador in England, who was arrested in 1571), Ridolphi intended to 'pass into France where he should open the matter to the count de 'Ruseau', an Italian, and nephew to Ridolphi being his sister's son, who is in great credit with the ... council of France'.[2] He is therefore likely to have arrived about a week later, during the conference at Blois and when the arrest of the duke of Norfolk on 7 September, and the final explosion of the plot would have been known in France'. De Foix was, however, then still in England striving to renew the marriage negotiation, and as Walsingham said, the Guises were 'traveling' by all means to break the amity with England. It is more than improbable that Ridolphi did not contact both them and his pro-Spanish Gondi kinsmen. It is interesting that the nuncio chose this juncture – 17 September – to observe that it was time that Anjou should be openly supported as catholic leader, which could

---

[1] *CSPF., 1569–71*, p. 576, 17 December 1571, Killigrew to Burghley from Tours; 583, 31 December 1571, Walsingham to Burghley.

[2] Francis Edwards, *The Marvellous Chance*, 87, 92. Neither this relationship nor the identity of Ruseau is clear.

only be instead of the catholic king, a statement which might have meant a great deal, or merely another expression of opposition to the English marriage.[1] However this may be, Petrucci hinted at some dark secret behind the event and even that Anjou was seeking his brother's throne, the implication therefore being regicide. On the last day of December 1571 the habitually reliable Walsingham reported – though he had no precise information – 'great suspicion' of a new Guise enterprise embracing Anjou, who was also described by Killigrew as 'secretly encouraged' by the Guises.[2] One is bound to wonder whether the concurrent disorders in Guisard Paris, and the expulsion from England in mid-December of the Spanish ambassador, de Spes, for practising to 'alienate the queen's good subjects and to irritate such as be mutable to commit horrible offences,' were all pure coincidences.[3]

There would be nothing incredible about a bid for the throne on the part of Anjou, or in his favour by his increasingly desperate exploiters, either in the light of recent events in Scotland, England and the Netherlands, or previous – and as it transpired subsequent – events in France. Several times already the extreme catholics had shown their readiness to lay hands – though just how violently was not always clear – upon the king[4] and Lorraine had not shrunk from disposing of his crown. Anjou was their ladder to power, in whom they had sown the seeds of a haughty ambition, and already in August 1570 'the wise' had feared they might use 'some desperate attempt to set him up who so favours their cause', more especially since it was thought that he could not 'digest to live in the degree of a Subject having already the reputation of a King'. Very little later, Walsingham also com-

---

[1] Hirschauer, *Correspondance de St Pie V*, 163–4, 17 September 1571, Frangipani to Rusticucci; *CSPVen.*, *1558–80*, p. 480, 9 January 1572.

[2] *CSPF.*, *1569–71*, p. 579, 28 December 1571, Killigrew to Burghley; p. 583, 31 December 1571, Walsingham to Burghley.

[3] *CSPF.*, *1569–71*, p. 573, 14 December 1571, dismissal of the Spanish ambassador; La Mothe, iv, 302, 10 December 1571, La Mothe to Charles IX and 306–12, instructions to Sabran; 312–14, 16 December 1571, La Mothe to Charles IX.

[4] See Chapter IV.

mented that 'there would never grow redress of this realm until they have fewer Kings, and be restored to a monarchy'.[1]

These things, if true, would account for the otherwise insufficiently explained hostility between the royal brothers, which sober reporters regarded as dangerous, and which was shortly to reach such proportions that Catherine went so far as to exile Anjou to the throne of Poland. Furthermore, the existence of such a plot would explain Charles' otherwise rather curious relations with Coligny, and the abnormal offer to defend him in arms, if only the survival of Coligny stood between himself on the one hand and Anjou and the catholics on the other. In such circumstances, Charles could not safely either support or abandon Coligny. This, in turn, would not only provide an additional reason why, from the extreme catholic point of view, the admiral had to die; it would also explain Anjou's *alleged* attitude to the king in August 1572 from whom, according to one account, he feared some violent retribution.

If in all this, nothing is clearly established, there is enough smoke to suggest a fire, and the timing of events at least admits the possibility of a French counterpart to the English conspiracy. In this respect, it is interesting to note that the Spanish 'enterprise of England', as it ultimately materialised in 1588 as the great Armada, was conceived as a dual assault upon England and France who had still, in the eyes of extreme catholics, to be kept apart. Then, paradoxically, it was Anjou himself, as Henry III, who was to be the French victim, tumbled through the agency of the duc de Guise; a truly Shakespearian tragedy which, just a little later, ended in the assassination of them both.

[1] See chapter viii; Digges, 8, 29 August 1570, Walsingham to Leicester; *CSPF.*, *1569–71*, pp. 311–12, 9 August 1571, Norris to Leicester; *1572–4*, p. 18, 17 January 1572, Walsingham to Burghley.

XII

The English Alliance
and the Bourbon Marriage

WHETHER OR not there had actually been a conspiracy *manqué* in favour of Anjou in December 1571, France began the climacteric year of 1572 in a state of perilous disruption. Coligny, the key figure, whose presence was required or desired for their several policies by Charles, Catherine and Nassau, as well as by queen Elizabeth's three ambassadors, Smith, Walsingham and Killigrew, was not only unable to return to court, but was actually commanded, with a surely unprecedented offer of royal protection, to remain at home on account of the threatening conduct of the Guises. For the same reason their own scheduled return was also countermanded, unless they first agreed to a reconciliation. This was the most urgent matter, as Charles specified to Fourquevaulx at the end of December, and he was 'après à les faire tomber d'accord'.[1]

As a result, two councils were held on 31 January and 1 February 1572, to which Guise presented a 'supplication' rejecting the royal settlement pronounced at Moulins in 1566, and desiring redress at the king's hands for the death of his father. This act of insubordination was rightly rejected by the council as a bad precedent. Coligny, for his part, understanding that Guise rejected his disculpation at the hands of the king, asked him to examine Guise, whatever this implied. The matter was therefore again wide open.[2]

---

[1] Douais, *Lettres de Charles IX à M. de Fourquevaulx*, 372–4, 26 December 1571, Charles to Fourquevaulx; Desjardins, *Negs. Tosc.*, iii, 744–5, 28–9 December 1571; 744, 28–9 December 1571; Champion, *Charles IX, la France et le contrôle de l'Espagne*, ii, 14.

[2] *CSPF., 1569–71*, p. 584, s.d., occurrences in France; *1572–4*, pp. 35–6, 31 January & 1 February 1572, news from France.

If this was all a continuation of the old vendetta, it was equally an aspect of the catholics' struggle – which became intense during the months preceding the massacre – to manipulate royal policy and dominate the court. While they were no longer directing policy, as under Lorraine, the crown could still not fully prevail against them without adequate alternative support – and it was becoming obvious that this did not exist – whether from allies abroad, from loyalists at home, or from the huguenots, whose disunited and ill-conducted policies were never fully aligned with the wishes of the crown.

If the Guises were unable to go to court, which happened to be on the Loire, there was nothing to prevent them from going to Paris, where their secret affairs were said to be 'of importance'.[1] Apart from the control of Anjou, these were doubtless to impede the English alliance and the Bourbon marriage.[2] In this the catholics were about to receive renewed support from Rome. It was presumably upon receipt of the news of the September conference at Blois that Don Juan de Zúñiga, the Spanish ambassador in Rome, prevailed upon the pope to send a legate to France to encourage the catholics, whom he then regarded as crestfallen (*caydos*). More specifically, he was to seek to avert the Bourbon marriage, substituting the Portuguese match, and to persuade the king to join the Catholic League. On 16 November the pope had accordingly appointed his nephew, cardinal Alessandrino to perform this office upon his return from Spain and Portugal, where he had gone to explain the purpose of the Holy League. A month later the pope also decided to send Antonio Salviati from Rome.[3]

Salviati arrived ahead of Alessandrino in mid-January, just

---

[1] *CSPF., 1572–4*, p. 18, 17 January 1572, Walsingham to Burghley.

[2] *CSPF., 1572–4*, p. 27–8, 21 January 1572, Killigrew to Burghley.

[3] Charrière, *Négociations de la France dans le Levant*, iii, 150–5, 6 June 1571, Rambouillet to Charles IX; Serrano, *Correspondencia diplomatica de S. Pio V*, iv, 517–18, 12 November 1571, Zúñiga to Philip II; 537, 19 November 1571, Zúñiga to Philip II; 573–7, 16 December 1571, Rusticucci to Alessandrino. Killigrew called him Alexandria and first mentioned him on 28 December 1571, *CSPF., 1569–71*, p. 579.

when Jeanne d'Albret was finally setting out from Nérac, and
the English negotiations had begun. Sir Thomas Smith, who was
already 'in an ague for fear of the failure of his negotiation',[1]
commented with waspish, protestant wit that Salviati 'brings a
holy sword for the king and would bring him into the League,
and a cap [cardinal's] or some other toy for Monsieur from Rome.
The Pope will make him general of the Holy League by land and
will give him a bigger pension in Italy than he has in France. He
will make him Emperor of Constantinople, and then shall the
Duke, by my assent, make the Pope in recompense Caliph of
Baldach [sic Baghdad], hoc est summam Pontificem Babiloniae,
for so he is spiritualiter already'.[2] When Sir Thomas Smith
arrived at court in January 1572,[3] the Anjou marriage had been
in abeyance since the return of de Foix in September 1571. If the
signs were no longer propitious, it had not entirely been abandoned. But its hopelessness quickly became apparent partly, as
Smith said, because Anjou was 'here entangled',[4] by which he
meant with mademoiselle de Châteauneuf, and Catherine described him as 'assottied' in religion. It appears that he already
showed signs of the religious mania which disturbed his later life,
and was fasting 'so precisely' that he grew 'lean and evil coloured'.[5]
Smith, however, was undecided as to whether Anjou was so
'extraordinarily papistically superstitious' for the sake of conscience or ambition, but observed that all his huguenot servants
had transferred to Alençon who, from this time on, hitched his
wagon to the protestant star, and consequently came into conflict
with both his brothers, and to some extent his mother.[6] Smith
also observed that, as the king's lieutenant, Anjou 'governed all'.[7]
and was, in turn, 'altogether governed' by the catholics.[8] His
opinion may have been darkened by the shock of Anjou's final

[1] CSPF., 1572–4, p. 3, 3 January 1572, Smith to Burghley.
[2] CSPF., 1572–4, p. 22, 18 January 1572, Smith to Burghley.
[3] CSPF., 1572–4, p. 3, 3 January 1572, Smith to Burghley.
[4] CSPF., 1572–4, p. 3, 3 January 1572, Smith to Burghley.
[5] CSPF., 1572–4, pp. 8–9, 8 January 1572, Smith and Killigrew to Elizabeth.
[6] CSPF., 1572–4, pp. 11–13, 9 January 1572, Smith to Burghley.
[7] CSPF., 1572–4, pp. 3–4, 3 January 1572, Smith to Burghley.
[8] CSPF., 1572–4, pp. 11–13, 9 January 1572, Smith to Burghley.

demands, dated 7 January, which amounted to the blunt refusal that Walsingham had feared. He had never, he said, seen the king 'in greater chafe', while Catherine 'wept hot tears' – doubtless of rage and outrage – and even the normally articulate Smith himself confessed that he 'wotted not what to say'. What to say to the queen, he carefully left to Burghley.[1]

This, like the exclusion of Coligny from court, was another big catholic triumph, which brought about a new stage in Anglo-French relations, which were never as fully clarified as they might have been by the Anjou marriage. Upon his refusal, Charles and Catherine immediately proposed either the substitution of Alençon, or any other league or amity, and Smith agreed to join with anyone appointed to 'rough hew' the articles of a treaty.[2] Walsingham believed that if the queen, 'proceed ... roundly, she may have what amity she will', because Charles, seeing Anjou so catholic, 'does much suspect false measure' and, like Elizabeth herself, who was seeking to draw closer to Coligny, made 'great account' of him and his followers. Smith therefore urged Burghley to prevent the queen from procrastinating, 'as commonly is her wont'.[3] The question of substituting Alençon for Anjou, now greatly desired by Catherine, could be and was, dealt with at greater leisure. As Walsingham optimistically suggested, if a league were made, Alençon could be sent to ratify it, and thus provide for 'eye contentment' – an improbable eventuality.[4] But, while the French really wanted a close, comprehensive alliance, leading to active co-operation and, failing Anjou, the Alençon match, Elizabeth – if not necessarily the privy council – really preferred a limited, defensive treaty. Defence, in all its different guises was, after all, her principal preoccupation. She had no need to *seek* trouble overseas.

[1] *CSPF.*, 1572–4, p. 11, 7 January 1572, Anjou's demands; 8–11, 8 January 1572, Smith and Killigrew to Elizabeth; 11–13, 9 January 1572, Smith to Burghley.
[2] *CSPF.*, 1572–4, pp. 11–13, 9 January 1572, Smith to Burghley.
[3] *CSPF.*, 1572–4, p. 14, 10 January, Smith to Burghley; 15, 11 January 1572, Walsingham to Burghley.
[4] *CSPF.*, 1572–4, p. 18, 17 January 1572, Walsingham to Burghley.

The 'rough hewing' of articles began on 11 January, without delay, and must therefore have been in progress when Salviati arrived with his Roman blandishments to create Anjou, as Smith caustically proposed, 'Emperor of Constantinople'.[1] Draft articles were sent home on 18 January, while the queen was still digesting Anjou's final demands, which were not intended to be negotiable and which, as we have already seen, Elizabeth rightly attributed to long-term catholic opposition.

At the same time as reopening negotiations with England and clinching the Bourbon marriage, Charles again sought to do what he could to propitiate Spain, availing himself of the opportunity afforded by the departure of Saint-Gouard to succeed Fourquevaulx as his ambassador. This was all the more essential in so far as Alessandrino arrived on 7 February – while the English were awaiting further instructions – and Jeanne d'Albret on the fourteenth. Furthermore, she was accompanied by Nassau, whose presence required some explanation since Philip's reticent muttering about it was not too hard to interpret. For this reason, Saint-Gouard was burdened with the clumsy diplomatic artifice of pretending to try to mediate a reconciliation between Philip and Nassau's brother William of Orange. This was linked to the problem of piracy, since those who wished to operate as pirates tended to join William's forces. Nassau, Saint-Gouard's instructions claim, had sent to inform Charles that he would disarm his brother's ships if Philip would receive them both into his favour, and allow the enjoyment of their property as exiles, since he would not permit them to live in the Netherlands. Nassau, it was said, had requested Charles to intercede for this, and to receive him at court 'affin de y demourer pleige et caution de ce qu'il promet au nom de son frere, pour le desarmement des vaissaulx'. Charles declared that he would consider how else to deal with the problem of pirates, and meanwhile allowed Nassau to accompany Jeanne – to whose suite he belonged – 'pour estre plus asseure de ces offres'.[2] Charles, in fact, had no control over

[1] CSPF., 1572–4, p. 22, 18 January 1572, Smith to Burghley.
[2] Gachard, *Notices et extraits*, ii, 362–4, 16 January 1572, instructions for Saint-Gouard.

Jeanne's servants, or (except for his French pension) over Nassau himself, a sovereign prince, and it is unlikely that either Orange or Nassau was capable of disarming those who subsisted on piracy. This curious proposition had, however, already served its purpose before the Spanish declared it contrary to the service of Philip II.[1]

In order to allow Jeanne d'Albret to arrive first, Alessandrino had been delayed at Bayonne by Saint-Sulpice, sent by the court to meet him. For, whereas her coming had long been awaited and was most earnestly desired, Alessandrino's, a superlative stroke of catholic timing, was grotesquely inconvenient. Jeanne, for a start, who was anxious and perverse, might easily have made it an excuse to withdraw. Alessandrino, however, cunningly took to the post, and so avoided encountering Jeanne by the way, and succeeded in outstripping her.[2] Smith, who was not the least inconvenienced, called him a 'werish man,' who 'looks like a fool'.[3] But, werish or not, Charles still required a dispensation for the marriage which, it was earnestly hoped, was about to be concluded with Jeanne, and a legate at a catholic court had to be correctly received.

In order to avoid meeting Alessandrino – who had just made an offer of 4,000 Spanish troops if the king would break off the Bourbon marriage and make war on the huguenots[4] – Jeanne was met by Catherine, on 15 February, at her favourite *château* of Chenonceaux.[5] Charles had first expected Jeanne early in December, and thereafter about Christmas, but Navarre was ill and she

---

[1] This is interesting in that it draws attention to the Netherlands problems of the nobility in arms, the exiles from the persecution of Alva in 1567–8 and the confiscation of property. Gachard, *Notices et extraits*, ii, 365, 14 April 1572, Saint-Gouard to Charles IX.

[2] Hirschauer, *La Politique de St Pie V*, 181–2, 9 February 1572, Alessandrino to Rusticucci.

[3] *CSPF.*, *1572–4*, p. 36, 8 February 1572, Smith to Burghley.

[4] Desjardins, *Negs. Tosc.*, iii, 748, 14 February 1572; Champion, *Charles IX, la France et le contrôle de l'Espagne*, ii, 20.

[5] *CSPF.*, *1572–4*, pp. 49–50, February 1572, occurrents; Hirschauer, *La Politique de St Pie V*, 182, 19 February 1572, Alessandrino to Rusticucci.

had taken her time.[1] So it was not until mid-January that she finally left Nérac, conceivably encouraged by the presence at court of Smith, as well as Walsingham and Killigrew. It is uncertain when she learnt of the embarrassing mission of Alessandrino, which hardly enhanced her prospects, but she must have known – if this is true – that the protestants had raised forces, estimated at 20,000 foot and 7,000 horse to hold in readiness.[2] If France were really about to erupt into civil war, she would hardly choose to be at court, nor alone and unarmed by the way; she had, after all, to traverse France. Thus, between the rumblings of war, general opposition to the marriage, the Guises, the nuncio, the legate, Salviati and the problem of religion, not to mention her own reservations and changeable disposition, the dice were fairly heavily loaded against her.

The meeting between Jeanne and Catherine – two forceful and antipathetic women who had the misfortune to need each other – was not a success. Jeanne was articulate in her complaints to Henry that, after heavy pressure on her to come, no one was specially anxious to see her.[3] But she wrote this on 21 February, the day that Charles finally refused to join the Catholic League, and Sir Thomas Smith, Walsingham and Killigrew were all received in audience with new instructions and a commission to proceed to the conclusion of a treaty with France.[4] Too much, in fact, was happening all at once, things which conflicted and things which had to be carefully synchronised. Alessandrino, for example, was said to have 'desperata la dispensa', which did nothing to assist the negotiations at Chenonceaux. Salviati hammered home the awful implications of proceeding without one, and

---

[1] Hirschauer, *La Politique de St Pie V*, 178, 27 November 1571, Giorgi to Rusticucci; Desjardins, *Negs. Tosc.*, iii, 733, 30 November 1571; Roelker, *Queen of Navarre*, 363, 368.

[2] *CSPF.*, *1572–4*, p. 35 [3 February 1572], news from France.

[3] Roelker, *Queen of Navarre*, 368–9, 21 February 1572, Jeanne to Henry. The Venetian ambassador reported on 24 February that they had secretly spent two days together. B.N., Mss. Italien, 1727, f. 244 verso, 24 February 1572, Blois.

[4] Digges, 166, 22 February 1572, Walsingham and Smith to Elizabeth; Champion, *La Jeunesse de Henri III*, ii, 27.

Catherine threatened to obtain it from three French archbishops. The matter had long been in hand in Rome and defended on the grounds that Navarre, like his father, would be converted; the marriage was therefore desirable. But Navarre the elder was hardly a satisfactory example, and the pope of course disagreed.[1] There was nothing more to be done, so Alessandrino, having found everything as he expected in 'tanta mala dispositione', left on 25 February with 'no great contentment', and Salviati went with him.[2]

[1] A dispensation had been requested on 19 August 1571. B.N., Mss. fr. 3951, ff. 134–5 verso, 19 January 1572, Charles to Ferrals, ambassador in Rome; Hirschauer, *La Politique de St Pie V*, 77, 80; De Potter, *Lettres de Saint Pie V*, 142–6, 25 January 1572, the pope to Charles IX.

[2] Serrano, *Correspondencia diplomatica de S. Pio V*, iv, 673, 22 February 1572, Alessandrino to Castagna, nuncio in Spain; *CSPF.*, *1572–4*, pp. 49–50 [February 1572], occurrents; Hirschauer, *La Politique de St Pie V*, 89, note 4, gives 24 February 1572.

XIII

The Miscarriage of the Netherlands Enterprise

THE DEPARTURE of Salviati and Alessandrino permitted the crown to concentrate upon its four preoccupations, the English treaty, the Bourbon marriage, the Netherlands enterprise and the resolution of the vendetta. Jeanne was then able to move to court at Blois, on 2 March, accompanied by Nassau.[1] He and Walsingham – who regarded the count as the 'rarest gentleman he had talked withal' since he came to France[2] – played an active part in the Bourbon negotiations. This was obviously, as Jeanne said, because England would only make a treaty with France if the Navarre marriage proceeded[3] and, as Walsingham said, 'upon the success of the Navarre marriage depends the enterprise of Flanders'.[4] This, therefore, was the order of priorities. The intention had been to conclude the English and Bourbon negotiations in 1571, before the enterprise in 1572. But we have seen how the Anjou match was frustrated, and the negotiations virtually lapsed until the arrival of Smith in January. Coligny was effectively excluded from court, and the vendetta magnified rather than resolved. Jeanne, partly hesitant and partly deterred from proceeding with the royal marriage, returned to Béarn, and Henry, upon whom the matter depended, was injured and sick. For these and other reasons, everything was far from complete by the early spring of 1572.

While it is certain that these negotiations were intended to

---

[1] Roelker, *Queen of Navarre*, 370; Desjardins, *Negs. Tosc.*, iii, 751, 4 March 1572.

[2] Digges, 176 [March 1572], Walsingham to Burghley.

[3] Roelker, *Queen of Navarre*, 374.

[4] *CSPF., 1572-4*, p. 60, 19 March 1572, Walsingham to Burghley.

precede the Netherlands enterprise, it is not certain whether there was ever a more specific date for this than the season of 1572. Then, presumably, it was hoped to combine a landing on the west coast with Nassau's invasion from France, and that of Orange from Germany. This was hardly realistic since its successful execution depended upon many and unpredictable factors which no one was in a position to co-ordinate. It is therefore not surprising that the timing of the enterprise should have miscarried. With no co-ordination, it began by staggering from one expedient to another, from which arose the successive crises, or mounting crisis which, in France, culminated in St Bartholomew's night.

Nassau had followed Jeanne to Béarn in August or September 1571, and 'a party' had gone to him in December 1571 to resolve upon the date of the execution of the enterprise of Flanders. Walsingham was actually asked at that time, whether, if this succeeded, and Charles entered all his forces, Elizabeth would send foot to Zeeland, Middelburg being ceded to her.[1] It is quite possible that this is as far as Charles' intentions were formulated; to help Nassau – which, if not exactly specified, does seem to be implied – and thereafter to join him. It also indicates the nature of the hopes which were placed in England, presupposes that someone was going to secure Middelburg, and suggests that the plans of the 'enterprise' were still largely inchoate.

When Nassau came to court, therefore, it was not only as a member of Jeanne's suite and to conclude the marriage – which came first – but also to proceed with preparing the enterprise, and there are some small signs of this being done in March 1572. For example, early in the month artillery was being moved from the Paris arsenal into Picardy.[2] Nassau was also said to be having frequent 'great conference' with the king, who was 'very earnest in the matter, [of Flanders] but the other proceeds both wisely and coldly, and would be glad to leave all things clear here'.[3]

[1] *CSPF.*, *1569-71*, p. 583-4, 31 December 1571, Walsingham to Burghley.
[2] *CSPF.*, *1572-4*, p. 60, 19 March 1572, Walsingham to Burghley; Kervyn de Lettenhove, *Relations*, vi, 346, 20 March 1572, Avis des Pays-Bas.
[3] *CSPF.*, *1572-4*, p. 60, 19 March 1572, Walsingham to Burghley.

It is not obvious who Walsingham meant by 'the other', but it appears from the syntax, and better evidence, to have been Nassau, and almost certainly meant, not that he was suddenly unenthusiastic, but that he was trying to prevent any premature action, which is precisely what was about to happen, with catastrophic results for everyone concerned. This suggests that Nassau feared and was expecting the sea beggars' assault upon Brill – or something of the sort – which occurred on 1 April. This raises the question as to whether an approximate date for the opening of hostilities had ever been agreed, whether Nassau attempted to co-ordinate this with his invasion, which was certainly not ready in March, or whether he intended to issue appropriate instructions when he and Orange were finally ready. A report of de Spes' embassy in England maintained that he had had 'information of the designs against Brill six months before the execution of the project, and had duly advised the duke of Albe at the time'.[1] This would have been about October 1571, when we know for certain that de Spes had informed Alva that some of the inhabitants of neighbouring Sluys had offered to deliver the town to de Lumbres. What is more, Nassau had definitely then been consulted, on account of a quarrel between La Marck and de Lumbres over the command of William's ships, then at Dover. De Lumbres went to France and La Marck received the command.[2] Morillon, the *prévôt* of Brussels, writing on 25 May 1572, referred to Alva's having been warned over three months before ('passez trois mois') and he had also been warned by Vitelli and the Spanish ambassador of everything that occurred in France and 'les conspirations qui y étaient ourdies contre les Pays-Bas'.[3] This timing, three months before late May – suggests that decisions may have been made at Blois in February when

---

[1] *CSPSp., 1568–79*, p. 366. This comes in an interesting document entitled, 'Relation of the Ambassador Don Guerau de Spes respecting English affairs', said to have been among the papers relating to 1571. It is, however, obvious from its contents that it was written about the second week of June 1572.

[2] *CSPSp., 1568–79*, p. 346, 26 October 1571, Guerau de Spes to Philip II; 348, 31 October 1571, Guerau de Spes to Alva.

[3] Granvelle, *Correspondance*, iv, 227–30, 25 May 1572, Morillon to Granvelle.

Jeanne and Nassau were, not actually at court, owing to the inhibiting presence of Salviati and the 'werish' Alessandrino, but nearby. Information relating to the descent upon Brill several months before the event does not, of course, establish that the time had been fixed. But more immediately Sweveghem, Alva's agent in London, informed him on 25 March that La Marck, who was cruising in the region of Dover, actually 'gave out' – thus presumably at least a few days before the report – that he awaited 'compaignyes pour parensemble faire l'entreprinse de la Brielle'. If the Spanish knew this, it is inconceivable that Nassau did not. Besides, Sweveghem had already reported on 21 March that the withdrawal of the 'pirates' from England to La Rochelle had been to join the vessels arming there to intercept the great Spanish fleet which had left Zeeland the previous December and, if Nassau and Coligny did not know what was happening at La Rochelle, it is difficult to imagine who did. These events could account for Nassau's reserve, if it were indeed to him that Walsingham referred as 'the other' on 19 March.[1]

The interception, however, of the returning Netherland's fleet, accomplished on 28 March,[2] was both a golden opportunity and a danger which could not safely be ignored. Had they ignored it, any later attack on Walcheren must have been more difficult, and perhaps even impossible, more especially since Alva was constructing a citadel at Flushing, but had so far neglected to garrison the town.[3]

---

[1] Kervyn de Lettenhove, *Relations*, vi, 347, 21 March 1572, Sweveghem to Courteville. This poses the question as to whether, or to what extent, the timing of the beggars' descent upon Brill was affected by their expulsion from England on 1 March. That document referred to 'freebutters' and very probably never included those holding commissions from William of Orange, although their enemies called them all pirates indiscriminately. Certainly it was not *applied* in respect of William's ships. Ibid., 350–2, 25 March 1572, Sweveghem to Alva.

[2] La Mothe, iv, 427, 14 April 1572, La Mothe to Charles IX.

[3] Granvelle, *Correspondance*, iv, 209, 28 April 1572, Morillon to Granvelle. La Marck had sequestered property in the area, and Frélon, who accompanied him, was the son of a former governor of Brill. *CSPSp.*, *1568–79*, p. 385, 15 April 1572, de Spes to Philip II. The beggars were very probably not well

One can therefore hardly suppose that Nassau and Charles were taken entirely by surprise when the beggars descended upon Brill on 1 April, although this does not dispose of the disaster. Nassau was later reported in Spain to have put his finger to his mouth and declared 'Ah, les sotz, ils se sont trop hastez et ne m'ont pas voullu croire'.[1] This is second-hand evidence, but suggests that he wished or had attempted to restrain them. This was because 'things' were far from being 'clear' in France by 1 April. Catherine and Jeanne, temperamentally poles apart, had been quite unable to agree, and the negotiation had stuck by 19 March – the date of Walsingham's letter referring to ?Nassau's reserve – over the religious details of the wedding ceremony.[2] It was not until late in March that the deadlock was broken by the appointment of four commissioners on each side. Nassau himself, as well as La Noue, were among those who acted for Jeanne[3] and as their interests, unlike hers, were primarily centred in the Netherlands, it is not surprising that the marriage was quickly settled by 4 April, and published on 11 April.[4]

The English negotiation, begun by Smith in January 1572, had been far advanced by the end of February, but its conclusion was delayed, partly by the king's hunting, even at this juncture,[5] as well as by problems relating to Scotland and queen Mary, about whose theatrical career Smith was more amusing than gallant.

---

informed about other aspects of the enterprise, and were in any case highly independent and not notorious for military discipline.

[1] Gachard, *Notices et extraits*, ii, 370, 31 May 1572, Saint-Gouard to Charles IX.

[2] Jeanne complained bitterly to Henry of her treatment at court. B.N., Mss. fr. 3951, f. 148-verso, 8 March 1572; *CSPF.*, *1572–4*, p. 60, 19 March 1572, Walsingham to Burghley.

[3] Groen van Prinsterer, *Archives ou correspondance, série* i, vol. iii, 417; Digges, 184, 29 March 1572, Walsingham to Burghley.

[4] There is a copy of the contract in the Archives de Chantilly, papiers de Condé, *série* i, vol. ii, ff. 60–4 verso. There is more information on this subject in Roelker, *Queen of Navarre* and J.-J.-C. Tauzin, 'Le Mariage de Marguerite de Valois', *Revue des questions historiques*, lxxx (1906), 447–98.

[5] *CSPF.*, *1572–4*, p. 49, 29 February 1572, Smith to Burghley.

Smith, in fact, was angry, fearing that Elizabeth 'would be thought to have no constancy but dalliance and farding off of time', and that they would be discredited.[1] The treaty of Blois, however, quickly followed the completion of the Bourbon marriage negotiation, and was concluded on 19 April.[2]

Even more important to Nassau, however, than the Bourbon marriage and the English treaty was the reconciliation of the vendetta, since the enterprise required the participation of Coligny. At the time of Jeanne's arrival in mid-February, Guise and Coligny were evidently to be ordered to embrace one another ('abbracciare insieme').[3] If this could hardly inspire confidence, there was really nothing else that could be done, and a certain captain Gryllye was sent to Coligny in an effort to obtain a reconciliation.[4] Meanwhile, on 27 March, Charles confirmed the *arrêt* of Moulins, January 1566, declaring Coligny's innocence of the murder of Guise, and Walsingham reported that Coligny's return was shortly expected in 'great hope . . . of compounding of the discord'.[5] Gryllye however was unsuccessful, and these hopes were disappointed. One Nançay, had to try again in May when the young duc de Guise inexplicably ended by consenting, although it is not clear how this was achieved when all previous attempts had failed; unless it could be because Lorraine was absent.[6] It is also possible that he wanted to go to court himself which, at the age of 22 he had barely attended since he was grown up. This, however, did not mean that the dangers of the vendetta were over, because others of the house of Guise, presumably the duke's uncle Aumale, and his mother, madame de Nemours, rejected the settlement because the hated Lorraine

---

[1] Walsingham's secretary Beale, who left on 8 March, had not yet returned by 4 April. Digges, 199, 4 April 1572, Smith and Walsingham to Burghley.

[2] *CSPF.*, *1572–4*, p. 87, 19 April 1572, the treaty of Blois.

[3] Desjardins, *Negs. Tosc.*, iii, 749, 14 February 1572.

[4] *CSPF.*, *1572–4*, pp. 49–50, February 1572, occurrents.

[5] *CSPF.*, *1572–4*, pp. 64–5, 29 March 1572, Walsingham to Burghley; Delaborde, *Coligny*, iii, 380.

[6] B.N., Mss. fr. 3188, f. 27, 5 May 1572, Nançay to his father Bouchage; Desjardins, *Negs. Tosc.*, iii, 771, 28 April 1572; 774, 12 May 1572.

was still excluded from court. Fortunately for everyone, face was saved by the death on 1 May of Pius V, enabling Lorraine to go to Rome, although he had only reached Lyon by 23 May when he received news of the election (on 13 May) of Gregory XIII.[1]

Something therefore had been achieved when the court dispersed around 22 April for some seven weeks, although 'things' could still hardly be described as 'clear': reconciliation of the vendetta was still being urgently pursued. The marriage contract had been concluded, but the dispensation was lacking, not to mention Navarre, although the wedding was optimistically expected quite soon; Petrucci actually said about mid-May.[2] Similarly, if the treaty of Blois provided an opportunity to reopen the English marriage negotiations in favour of Alençon, and could also be expected to disturb Philip II, it was nevertheless purely defensive in character, and did not refer to the Netherlands. Montmorency and de Foix were ready to leave for the ratification of the treaty by 7 May, but only arrived on 13 June with a suite of some 40 persons. The delay arose from the fact that the English were not ready to leave for France. The very serious illness of the queen, and then of Burghley in March and April, followed by the opening of parliament on 8 May, and the execution of the duke of Norfolk on 2 June sufficiently account for that.[3]

It was already three weeks since the landing at Brill on 1 April had precipitated a Netherlands' crisis, and these were not the circumstances in which the enterprise had been projected. This, therefore, was where trouble and divisions began. Walsingham said that Nassau was not 'pryvye' to La Marck's premature descent upon Brill, and was 'very sorrye he began so tymely [sic – soon] but now necessyte forceth them to proceade'. If, by

[1] Romier, 'La Saint-Barthélemy . . .', *Revue du XVIe siècle*, i (1913), 540. Cardinal Pellevé went with him leaving Paris on 17 May, presumably with the knowledge of Nassau's departure for the Netherlands.

[2] Desjardins, *Negs. Tosc.*, iii, 766, 17 April 1572; 668, 22 April 1572.

[3] Digges, 201, 7 May 1572, Walsingham to Burghley; La Mothe, v, 12–19, 17 June 1572, La Mothe to Charles IX.

'pryvye', he meant uninformed, he was almost certainly wrong, but Nassau was clearly not a party to it.[1] William, too, regretted this precipitation, about which he had not been consulted but, the mistake having been made, La Marck must be supported. Thus, on 14 April, he issued a proclamation, from Dillenburg declaring his intention to deliver the inhabitants of the Netherlands from their 'unsupportable exactions, outrages, cruelties and other wrongs inflicted on them by . . . this foreign tyranny'.[2]

Thus the gauntlet was down, and the challenge publicly made. 'Necessyte,' as Walsingham said, was indeed the trouble, and the problem was *how* to 'proceade'. Could the enterprise simply be executed forthwith and, if not, what should be done about it? Meanwhile, with the beggars at Brill, it was essential, if disaster were to be avoided, to prevent Alva from taking Flushing, nautically speaking the strategic key to Flanders and Brabant. That he had not already done so, was a failure on his part which astounded some observers.

For this reason, Nassau initially placed his hopes in queen Elizabeth for the preservation of Flushing, although Walsingham warned him – not for the first time – not to rely on England where things were 'far owt of tune to hope much after any thinges'. Apart from any other thing, Burghley had nearly died, and his indisposition always tended to paralyse English affairs. At the same time, however, Walsingham advised Nassau to use the minimum of Frenchmen in the enterprise, and requested him to wait for fifteen days, 'if he might possiblye', while an answer came, apparently because he was as disinclined as the queen to see the French in Flushing. Charles, however, did promise Nassau 500 men to embark at Dieppe specifically for Flushing, if Elizabeth would not help, and Louis cautiously sent his secretary, who passed through Rouen – the route to Dieppe – on 27 April

[1] Kervyn de Lettenhove, *Relations*, vi, 414, note 1, 22 April 1572, Walsingham to Burghley.

[2] *CSPF.*, 1572–4, p. 81, 14 April 1572, proclamation by the prince of Orange; Granvelle, *Correspondance*, iv, 181, note 1, 25 April 1572, William of Orange to Wesembeek.

to enquire whether they would receive forces there in the name of William of Orange and to inform them that he had ready 5–600 men 'bien en ordre' with ships and munitions.[1]

It transpired that Walsingham was right. For the moment Elizabeth – occupied with parliament – intended no interference, not because she was indifferent to the fate of Flushing which she had no intention of allowing to fall into foreign hands, but because interference was unnecessary. She knew, presumably, that Hawkins and Winter 'were directed' to send a boat to inform the beggars that English ports were open to them. They responded with an offering of Rhine wine, and a letter in Latin from Flushing, which had joined their revolt in favour of William (before the arrival of Nassau's secretary) requesting help and money.[2] Furthermore, count Brederode's illegitimate brother and others were known to be enrolling and arming some 500 men – half of whom had already departed from England by mid-April, and about 1,000 well-armed Walloons had not been prevented from sailing from Harwich to reinforce La Marck.[3]

After the seizure of Brill, Alva wasted no time in sending Adrien d'Ongnyes seigneur de Willerval to France to ascertain Charles' real intentions and to probe his military preparations. Charles was reported to Alva to be assembling ships armed for war at La Rochelle, and Philip II received news from Nantes of a large fleet being fitted out 'sur toute la côte de France', including English ships and some of William's.[4] Furthermore, on 11 April, Charles issued letters patent ordering strongholds and frontier

[1] Kervyn de Lettenhove, *Relations*, vi, 414, note 1, 22 April 1572, Walsingham to Burghley; La Mothe, iv, 427, 14 April 1572, La Mothe to Charles IX; *CSPF.*, *1572–4*, p. 96, 29 April 1572, news from France.

[2] Flushing had been 'very obedient' during the previous troubles. Kervyn de Lettenhove, *Relations*, vi, 384–5, 16 April 1572, Sweveghem to Alva; 391–2, c. 20 April 1572, les gueux to Elizabeth; *CSPSp.*, *1568–79*, p. 385, 15 April 1572, de Spes to Philip II; 386, 26 April 1572, de Spes to Philip II.

[3] Kervyn de Lettenhove, *Relations*, vi, 384–5, 16 April 1572, Sweveghem to Alva; La Mothe, iv, 438, 27 April 1572, La Mothe to Charles IX.

[4] Gachard, *Correspondance de Philippe II*, ii, 239, 5 April 1572, Alva to Philip II; Gachard, *Notices et extraits*, ii, 365–6, 14 April 1572, Saint-Gouard to Charles IX.

towns to lay in supplies of munitions and grain.[1] In informing Philip of the despatch of Willerval, Alva made no mention of Brill, whose loss he brushed aside at the time with a nonchalant 'no es nada', not reporting this for over three weeks hoping, in the meanwhile, to have secured Flushing, and possibly also to receive a reassuring answer from Willerval.[2]

At the same time as seeking to ensure the exclusion of Alva from Flushing, if the beggars were to be properly supported, the opening of hostilities made it essential to create a diversion and, presumably, also to obtain a stronghold just over the largely indefensible French frontier, for which Nassau evidently began to prepare.[3] But, while it was one thing for Charles to have promised, if necessary, minor help for Flushing, the creation of a diversion entailed the departure of Nassau himself. What then was Charles going to do, before the 'enterprise' was ready, or the Bourbon marriage solemnised? Naturally there were strong pressures on him to enter the Netherlands' quarrel. Mondoucet, for example, his agent in the Netherlands, was urging him to profit from the current opportunity to recover Flanders and Artois, in other words to proceed with the enterprise as though it had not miscarried.[4] Téligny had also renewed his periodic entreaties, and there were now many Flemish refugees in France from Alva's tenth penny tax, some of whom went to the court at Blois, where a number of their countrymen – the *bannis* – had long been supporting Nassau's policy, and offered to take up arms if they received help.[5]

[1] B.N., Mss. fr. 15554, f. 52, 11 April 1572; Kervyn de Lettenhove, *Relations*, vi, 386, note 1.

[2] Gachard, *Correspondance de Philippe II*, ii, 238, 3 April 1572, Alva to Philip II; 239, 5 April 1572, Alva to Philip II; 245-7, 26 April 1572, Alva to Philip II; Willerval's instructions were dated 9 April 1572.

[3] La Huguerye, *Mémoires*, i, 102.

[4] Kervyn de Lettenhove, *Relations*, vi, 415, note 1, 22 April 1572, Walsingham to Burghley. This letter had fallen into the hands of a Spanish agent in England who later enclosed it with one of his own dated 24 May to Alva.

[5] Kervyn de Lettenhove, *Documents inédits du XVIe siècle*, 169, 27 April 1572, Charles IX to Nassau; Gachard, *Correspondance de Philippe II*, ii, 215-20, Alva's report on the Netherlands delivered in Madrid on 4 January 1572.

Conversely, there were also strong pressures on Charles to refrain from intervening. The catholics, who were now free to shift their attentions from Anjou to the crown, were doing all they could to 'hinder the Netherlands wars', and those 'of the robe', probably the second-rank councillors in Catherine's entourage, feared that involvement would lead to war with Spain; which was her opinion also. In this, therefore, extremists and moderates agreed, if not for the same reasons, which created a powerful opposition. Walsingham declared that of late there had been 'hard hold for the overthrow of this enterprise', but the king was 'resolute in the matter otherwise it had been quite broken'.[1] Charles had promised Nassau 'what ayde he himself can desyre', which was definitely favourable if not, perhaps, quite precisely what he meant.[2] Petrucci, writing on the same day, said the king had issued orders upon something, which were against the will of the queen, conceivably, since the dates tally, relating to the promised help to Flushing.[3]

It must have been something connected with Charles' resolution in the Netherlands' enterprise which occasioned his row with Catherine; certainly the 'untimely' precipitation of hostilities threw up the problem of war with Spain in new and disquieting circumstances. One must assume that in Nassau's plan, he and his brother William would at least have held the initiative, and that Charles' support presupposed conditions in which he would not be quite unprepared for war with Spain if this should follow upon conflict with Alva. But in April and May 1572, before the enterprise was ready, before the celebration of the Bourbon marriage, the ratification of the English treaty and the completion of the Guise/Châtillon reconciliation, this was emphatically not the case.

Petrucci also insinuates that there was some villainy in the way in which the difference between Charles and his mother was

[1] Digges, 188, 22 April 1572, Walsingham to Burghley.
[2] Kervyn de Lettenhove, *Relations*, vi, 415, note 1, 22 April 1572, Walsingham to Burghley.
[3] Desjardins, *Negs. Tosc.*, iii, 769, 22 April 1572; Kervyn de Lettenhove, *Relations*, vi, 415, note 1, 22 April 1572, Walsingham to Burghley.

exploited. The Netherlands, with its wider Spanish implications, was an issue upon which it was possible to drive a wedge between Charles and Catherine, which would certainly be in the extreme catholic interest, since neither could be powerful alone. Charles was ineffectual without Catherine, and her sole authority was that of the crown. This could only increase its weakness, forcing the king into a position in which, although religion had nothing to do with it, he appeared to be on the protestant side – an error which Catherine had so laboriously avoided in 1562 – and just when he was supplicating the pope for his sister's marriage dispensation. Similarly, through her very well-justified fear of war with Spain, this would drive Catherine, for the fourth time, into the camp of the extreme catholics. One must not, however, exaggerate the differences between Charles and Catherine. He had always been familiar with her attitude to Spain and to war, and they were in complete agreement over their priority policies, the Bourbon marriage and England, whether amity or marriage, upon both of which everything else depended.

If – as is probable – the row between Charles and Catherine stemmed from her opposition to the Netherlands enterprise in the current circumstances of April 1572, it also seems likely that Charles would have preferred its delay. Indeed, it appears from reports of the conference of Fontainebleau in August 1571, that Nassau had agreed to wait until after the marriage. But this had originally been expected at the end of 1571 and was even then still expected quite soon – soon enough not to matter, he may possibly have argued – for it was not then known that Navarre would be unfit to travel before the end of May. The point is explicitly made by La Huguerye who claimed to have urged Nassau to ignore this undertaking, and not to wait. Nassau is alleged to have replied with diplomatic ambiguity that he would 'se laisser conduire à la necessité', which evidently signified agreement. Charles, for his part, might claim to have done the same.[1]

When the court dispersed, after the conclusion of the Bourbon

---

[1] La Huguerye, *Mémoires*, i, 99–100.

marriage contract, and the English treaty at Blois, about 22 April
Nassau went with Jeanne to her city of Vendôme – whence they
might well have conferred with Coligny at Châtillon – before
returning to Paris on 8 May, roughly a month before the king,
who was still hunting about the Loire, but gradually moving
closer to Fontainebleau.[1] After Nassau's departure from Blois,
Charles wrote him a rather cryptic letter from Saint-Léger on
27 April, possibly because the new danger had made it difficult
for him to know what to do. The letter was later seized in the
Netherlands, and, *ex post facto*, inevitably taken as proof of his
implication and bellicose intentions. But it did not commit him
to supporting Nassau then, in April, or even to supporting him at
all in any specified way. In the letter, Charles said that Téligny
had pressed him several times 'd'une manière toute spéciale des
grands moyens qui s'offrent pour faire quelque bonne action en
faveur de la liberté des Pays-Bas qui s'afflige par les Espagnols ce
que de son côté il est bien décidé à faire *dès que les circonstances et
la situation de ses affaires le permettront*'.[2] In the absence of any
definition as to what 'circumstances' and what 'situation' were
envisaged – conceivably after the Bourbon marriage, with the
full, overt support of England, and the co-operation of German
princes, this letter does not *necessarily* mean anything. It could have
been a veiled expression of support; a means of temporising, or a
diplomatic formula of Catherine's to prepare the way for a royal
withdrawal in what was an unforeseen crisis. Perhaps the most
likely interpretation is that it was intended to warn or prepare
Nassau for the precautions that Charles felt obliged to take, since

[1] Charles' movements are not easy to trace: he went to Saint-Léger on or
before 27 April, and to Chambord on 3 May, while Catherine went to Chenonceaux on 5 May. B.N., Mss. fr. 3188, f. 27, 5 May 1572, Nançay to Bouchage. By
13 May they were both at Fontainebleau, considerably nearer Paris. B.N., Mss.
n.a.f., 7731, ff. 45, 59, 18 & 13 (sic) May 1572, Charles and Catherine to
Matignon. About the end of June, Charles was at Saint-Cloud, before returning
to Paris on 7 June.

[2] My italics. Kervyn de Lettenhove, *Documents inédits du XVI*e *siècle*, 169–70.
This is a reconversion from the Spanish translation of the original in Simancas Estado Leg. 551, f. 107; Gachard, *Correspondance de Philippe II*, ii, 269,
note 2.

Louis' departure at that time and in those circumstances did not represent the enterprise as it had been projected, and to which Charles might consider himself committed, but rather an expedient, or emergency holding operation, which might or might not expand into the enterprise proper. In the event, it did not so expand, and this was the essence of the summer's crisis. Thus it was that, with Nassau about to leave for the Netherlands, Charles began to augment his habitual protests of peaceful intentions, constantly belied by his suspicious conduct, with a policy of public disavowals, but accompanied by covert assistance to Nassau and those who followed him. To begin with, Saint-Gouard, his ambassador in Spain, was to deny rumours – attributed to Alva – that Charles had favoured the beggars. So far from having thought of helping them, he was actually diminishing his forces and his frontier garrisons.[1] While Charles naturally represented this as evidence of his peaceful intentions towards Alva, Morillon spelt out to Granvelle that it obviously rendered the same men available for enrolment by Nassau, about whose activities in the province the *gouverneur* Longueville, said Alva had legitimate cause for complaint.[2] It was in fact shortly alleged that men had gone or would go to the Netherlands from the garrisons, which had all been changed, of Calais, Boulogne, Montreuil and Abbéville.[3] At the same time as reducing frontier garrisons, Charles issued a *circulaire* to the *gouverneurs* to restrain his subjects from making war on neighbouring princes, especially Spain, and published in Paris and on the frontiers 'la defense d'aller avec le comte Ludovic', which later enabled him to claim that Frenchmen had departed contrary to his orders.[4] Whether

---

[1] Gachard, *Notices et extraits*, ii, 366, 22 April 1572, Charles to Saint-Gouard; 367, 4 May 1572, Charles to Saint-Gouard.

[2] B.N., Mss. fr. 15554, f. 93, 30 April 1572, Longueville to Charles IX; f. 127 verso, 22 May 1572, Longueville to Charles IX; Gachard, *Notices et extraits*, ii, 367, 4 May 1572, Charles to Saint-Gouard; Granvelle, *Correspondance*, iv, 243, 8 June 1572, Morillon to Granvelle.

[3] Kervyn de Lettenhove, *Relations*, vi, 423, 6 June 1572, de Guaras to Alva.

[4] Gachard, *Notices et extraits*, ii, 367–8, 4 May 1572, Charles to Saint-Gouard; 368, 10 May 1572, Charles to Saint-Gouard.

these orders were secretly countermanded in the case of Picardy, one cannot be sure, but La Huguerye wrote of obtaining certain 'favours' there, by means of express letters to the duc de Longueville.[1]

With Louis' departure evidently so well publicised, Charles chose this moment to return to the subject of disarming William's ships, against which he claimed to have closed his ports, sending Saint-Gouard a written *obligation* from Louis to disarm them. Saint-Gouard, Charles said, should exploit this in Spain as a 'plus grande preuve de ma susdicte intention à l'entretènement de la paix'.[2] While Nassau was in Paris for approximately a week, Fregoso was sent to require him to wait, but only verbal assurances were given.[3] It is of course possible that he was sent by Catherine, or that this was simply a means of obtaining information. Alternatively, if Flushing were not held to be in immediate danger, Charles could, genuinely, have wished or expected that Nassau would wait a little just then. But Alva, who was not idle,[4] could not be expected to attend upon his leisure, and Nassau – it will shortly be seen – evidently had other, bold and pressing reasons for being in a hurry. Thus, there may conceivably have been some element of truth in Charles' complaint to Saint-Gouard, intended for Philip II, that Nassau had abused him.[5]

To Nassau, therefore, it was essential to act immediately if at all. So, undeterred, if not undismayed, he began sending powder, and men in small unarmed groups to Tupigny near Soissons on the Hainault frontier, took leave of Jeanne – as it transpired, for ever – on or about 15 May, and himself reached Tupigny on

---

[1] La Huguerye, *Mémoires*, i, 101.

[2] Morillon reported having heard that if Philip would restore Orange to the enjoyment of his property he would undertake to 'tenir la mer franche et necte et qu'il ne viendroit jamais en ce pays'. Granvelle, *Correspondance*, iv, 179–82, 15 April 1572, Morillon to Granvelle; Gachard, *Notices et extraits*, ii, 368–9, 10 May 1572, Charles to Saint-Gouard.

[3] La Huguerye, *Mémoires*, i, 101–2.

[4] Petrucci reported 'grande apparecchio di guerra' in the Netherlands. Desjardins, *Negs. Tosc.*, iii, 767, 17 April 1572.

[5] Gachard, *Notices et extraits*, ii, 375, 18 June 1572, Charles to Saint-Gouard.

18 May.[1] Fregoso, who had been sent back to Paris a second time, followed him to Tupigny, only to find that he had already crossed the frontier. With him went Mr Morgan, an agent of Walsingham from whom he soon expected news.[2]

Nassau's departure just about coincided with the embarkation from Calais of 'great flocks of Frenchmen' – a Spanish exaggeration – for Flushing and Brill. Furthermore, 150 men from Dieppe were said to have arrived in Flushing before 21 May.[3] It also coincided with the return of Alva's envoy, Willerval, with 'grandes assurances d'amitié', and the despatch to Alva, via Mondoucet, Charles' agent in the Netherlands, of a letter so full of promises that, Alva said, if Charles were not as good as his word, he did not know what he could ever believe.[4] The answer to that was not much, since, if he did not know already, he was very shortly to learn that late in April Mondoucet himself had urged Charles to profit from this opportunity to recover Flanders and Artois.[5]

It was possibly because Charles was apparently seeking to restrain Nassau, as he subsequently sought to restrain Coligny – that Petrucci reported some anxiety – and not for the first time – lest Charles should be induced to change his mind about war with Spain.[6] By this he probably meant more specifically Nassau's plans, or 'battles', than war in any general sense. There is nothing to suggest that Charles had changed his mind, but the circumstances were drastically changed, and it is clear that as he could

[1] Digges, 202, 21 May 1572, Walsingham to Burghley says that Nassau left Paris on 19 May which is probably a misprint for 15 May. La Huguerye, *Mémoires*, i, 104, says he reached Tupigny on 18 May, which seems likely. The exact timing of these movements is impossible to verify, but is not important.

[2] Digges, 202, 21 May 1572, Walsingham to Burghley.

[3] *CSPSp.*, *1568–79*, p. 392, 24 May 1572, de Guaras to Alva. The news to which he referred was dated 19 May. *CSPF.*, *1572–4*, p. 112, 21 May 1572, advertisements from the Low Countries.

[4] Gachard, *Correspondance de Philippe II*, ii, 250, 22 May 1572, Alva to Philip II.

[5] Kervyn de Lettenhove, *Relations*, vi, 415, note 1, 22 April 1572, Walsingham to Burghley.

[6] Desjardins, *Negs. Tosc.*, iii, 670, 10 May 1571.

not restrain Nassau, over whom he had neither authority nor jurisdiction, he made another attempt, which required more skill than he possessed, to run with the hare and hunt with the hounds. A letter which he wrote on 11 May 1572 to François de Noailles, bishop of Dax, ambassador in Constantinople, was considerably more positive than that to Nassau of 27 April. In this letter Charles said: 'Toutes mes fantaisies,' an appropriate word which Catherine would never have used, 'sont bandées pour m'opposer à la grandeur des Espagnols, et je délibère m'y conduire le plus dextrement qu'il me sera possible.' Charles went on to exhort Noailles 'de bien jouer vostre personnage' (the Sultan), because of the restraining Turkish influence on Spanish affairs. Noailles was to inform the great Turk that the fleet which Charles had fitted out, on the pretext of defending his coasts and harbours, was really 'de tenir le Roy Catholique en cervelle,' – which it effectively did – 'et donner hardiesse à ces Gueulx des Pays-Bas de se remuer et entreprendre, ainsy qu'ils ont faict . . .' He concluded by saying that he had clinched the league with England, 'ce qui met les Espagnols en une merveilleuse jalousie,' as did also his intelligence with the princes of Germany.[1] If this was deliberately slanted to accommodate the interests of France in Constantinople, and to revive the vanquished of Lepanto, it was, nevertheless, privately addressed to the ambassador and far exceeded lip service to the Netherlands project. But it does not prove that Charles would not have preferred its execution later in time, and it avoids, unless by implication, the issue of more general war. If, however, Noailles successfully heeded the exhortation to 'bien jouer vostre personnage', this clearly would do as much, if not more, than anything else to keep the enterprise within the category of 'battles', and avert a war with Spain in northern Europe. In an *avis* on the deplorable state of Picardy, the duc de Nevers expressed the opinion at this time, that if the army of the Catholic League were to be engaged against Turkey, then Charles would be safe from invasion for that year. Indeed,

---

[1] Henri de Noailles, *Henri de Valois en Pologne*, i, 9; Kervyn de Lettenhove, *Les Huguenots*, ii, 431–2; Champion, *Charles IX, la France et le contrôle de L'Espagne*, ii, 33 note 1.

there is some evidence to suggest that Charles might even have been banking – or gambling – on just this.[1]

If Charles had really not changed his mind about the enterprise, and had already expressed his willingness to help over Flushing, what else did he actually *do*? The letter to Noailles mentions the fleet – Strozzi's fleet – whose *raison d'être* was the subject of much contemporary speculation, and whose existence – as Charles claimed to have intended – did, effectively, cause Philip II and Alva considerable anxiety.[2] This was not without cause since, according to captain Thomas Morgan, Strozzi did transport some 6,000 men to help Nassau near Brussels in mid-June.[3] It was probably also about this time, or a little before – he does not give the date – that La Huguerye was undertaking Nassau's secret affairs in Paris, soliciting the *mandemens* which, he claims, produced 10,000 francs in Netherlands money and 100 casks of powder from the Paris arsenal.[4] There was also the matter of the garrisons and favours in Picardy. Whatever was happening, there was sufficient to put the *gouverneur* Longueville in 'bien grande peine' lest it should lead to war, possibly for fear of being held responsible for an invasion of France which might well threaten Paris. This had, after all, occurred within living memory.[5]

If Charles was anxious to establish his detachment from Nassau's exploits, Spain was almost equally anxious to be reassured, though not surprisingly she remained unconvinced.

[1] B.N., Mss. n.a.f., 7731, ff. 69–78, 31 May 1572, Nevers' Avis au Roy sur l'Estat des affaires.

[2] Gachard, *Correspondance de Philippe II*, ii, 239, 5 April 1572, Alva to Philip II; 240, 20 April 1572, Philip II to Alva; 250, 22 May 1572, Alva to Philip II; 259, 29 May 1572, Alva to Zúñiga.

[3] Philippe Strozzi was said to have over forty ships in Breton waters with 6,000 men, including 1,500 gentlemen, and he was reported to have left the court at Paris on 8 June for some unknown mission. Hirschauer, *La Politique de St Pie V*, 184–5, 9 June 1572, Frangipani to the pope.

[4] Goulart, *Mémoires de l'Estat de France sous Charles IX*, i (1578), 251, a strongly protestant work, says that Charles gave Nassau some money, munitions and secret commissions.

[5] B.N., Mss. fr. 15554, f. 123, 20 May 1572, Longueville to Charles IX; f. 127 verso, 22 May 1572, Longueville to Charles IX.

The worrying matter of Strozzi's fleet and the English treaty had made Philip nervous and distrustful enough to fear that the seizure of Brill might have been an Anglo-French undertaking. He was greatly exercised by what he called their 'platicas' and 'ligas', since he feared their co-operation as much as Catherine feared war between France and Spain. Of this there was certainly a real danger, if only because Philip II thought so and, according to Saint-Gouard, war was commonly rumoured in Spain.[1] At the end of May he reported on all he had done to erase the suspicions that Charles had assisted the beggars, blaming such talk upon Alva. But the Spanish secretary Zayas spoke 'pis que pendre' of Nassau, and Philip was angry that Charles should have harboured him in France and vouchsafed 'tel crédit et présumption' that he had issued certain commissions – presumably for the raising of men – of which Philip possessed copies.[2] Evidence of ill-faith, if not of more specifically bellicose intentions, reached Alva from all sides. Apart from the warnings he had ignored, there was news by 24 May of the approach of 5,000 men from the frontiers of France towards Avèsnes, east of Cambrai, as well as of other forces being raised in Germany. Just a little later Morillon *prévôt* of Brussels, reported the transfer of money to Strasbourg for troops, and he believed that 'file à file beaucop de François se jectent dedans Monts' (Mons).[3] That this was more probably organised by Nassau or the huguenots than the crown, would

[1] Gachard, *Correspondance de Philippe II*, ii, 200, 14 September 1571, Philip II to Alva; 240, 20 April 1572, Philip II to Alva; Desjardins, *Negs. Tosc.*, iii, 732, 28 November 1571; *CSPF., 1569–71*, p. 569, 3 December 1571, advertisements from France; Serrano, *La Liga de Lepanto*, i, 294–5, 17 May 1572, Philip to Don John; 305–9, 2 June 1572, Philip II to Don Juan de Zúñiga in Rome; Gachard, *Notices et extraits*, ii, 367, 3 May 1572, Saint-Gouard to Charles IX; 369, 21 May 1572, Saint-Gouard to Charles IX.

[2] Gachard, *Notices et extraits*, ii, 370, 31 May 1572, Saint-Gouard to Charles IX.

[3] Gachard, *Correspondance de Philippe II*, ii, 257, 24 May 1572, Alva to Philip II; 259, 29 May 1572, Alva to Zúñiga; 260, 1 June 1572, Alva to Philip II; Desjardins, *Negs. Tosc.*, iii, 782, 31 May 1572; Digges, 204, 29 May 1572, Walsingham to Burghley, two letters; Granvelle, *Correspondance*, iv, 236–44, 8 June 1572, Morillon to Granvelle.

make little difference to the Spanish; they were still offending Frenchmen.

This critical situation suddenly expanded into a crisis with the news that Nassau had captured Valenciennes on 23 May and Mons the day after. Valenciennes was immediately retaken, on 29 May, and garrisoned.[1] But this was not all. The loss of Valenciennes was probably due to over ambition, for it was certainly with more valour than discretion that La Noue, Genlis and 'Buckanans' – presumably Bouchavannes – had forthwith swooped down upon Brussels, in an audacious attempt, by intelligence, to seize the duke of Alva himself. Had this succeeded, it would undeniably have been a brilliant military *coup*, but also a political embarrassment of the first magnitude. The idea was to precipitate a general rebellion in favour of William of Orange, which Alva's central presence in Brussels inhibited, and that the ensuing war would therefore be short. The experience of Valenciennes and Mons, however, tends to suggest an over-optimistic estimation of the disposition of the towns. Besides, a general rising was very unlikely before the arrival of Orange and, the timing having miscarried, Nassau should have contented himself with securing strategic frontier strongholds, and waiting. Apart from their fear of Alva – which the huguenot *coup* was intended to remove – the towns were unlikely to rise because of the impending arrival of his successor, Medina Celi, in whom, according to Alva himself, they placed hope. He arrived at Bruges on 16 June, and Alva shortly after withdrew the abominated tenth penny tax, which had primarily sustained a high fever of opposition. Unlike the exiled nobility, whose property was sequestered, the towns had no interest in war as such, preferring the peaceful pursuit of their industrious lives in acceptable conditions.[2]

[1] Granvelle, *Correspondance*, iv, 227–30, 25 May 1572, Morillon to Granvelle; Digges, 204–5, 29 May 1572, two letters, Walsingham to Burghley and Leicester. Desjardins, *Negs. Tosc.*, iii, 782, 31 May 1572; Gachard, *Correspondance de Philippe II*, ii, 260, 1 June 1572, Alva to Philip II.
[2] B.N., Mss. fr. 15554, f. 208, 22 June 1572, Longueville to Charles IX; Gachard, *Correspondance de Philippe II*, ii, 240, 20 April 1572, Philip to Alva; 263, 24 June 1572, Alva to Philip II.

The Brussels *coup* was almost certainly the reason why Nassau declined to wait, even though no immediate action was essential to divert attention from Flushing. According to Walsingham, Nassau had claimed that he planned to 'give Alva an alarm' within eight days. But as Walsingham did not know what this was to be, it is very unlikely that Charles knew either.[1] It was not only Alva who received an 'alarm'. To give covert help to a foreign prince in a limited enterprise was one thing. But, for French subjects, albeit disavowed, to seek to ambush Philip II's viceroy in his own capital was manifestly *going too far*. If this was not an act of war, it would be difficult to define what was. Charles had been overtaken by events. That he had not sanctioned the assault upon Alva made little difference; distinctions of this kind cannot be sustained. The blame might lie altogether else-where, but he could not escape the responsibility for what these Frenchmen had done. Besides, a short and glorious war might, according to the theory, have restored to France the provinces of Flanders and Artois. It would also have served very well the purposes of William and Nassau. But it would have done nothing substantial to release the civil war tensions in France, the sole justification for foreign adventures.

The *coup* against Alva was either gravely lacking in judgement, or villainously calculated to force Charles' hand; probably the former. But even before this, Alva was already reacting sharply. His communications strongly resembled an ultimatum. Through the Spanish ambassador in France, he demanded from Charles a written assurance that he could remain 'tranquille'; that Charles would ensure that the rebels were not helped by the French fleet – which they were[2] – and that he would majesterially forbid all French subjects to go to the help of rebels in the Netherlands; finally, that he would formally recall all who had already gone. At the same time he cautioned Mondoucet that a rupture would

---

[1] Digges, 204, 29 May 1572, two letters, Walsingham to Burghley; Gran-velle, *Correspondance*, iv, 227-8, Morillon to Granvelle; 229, 29 May 1572, a letter signed D'Yves from Avèsnes referred to the protestants' plans to go to Brussels.

[2] *CSPF.*, *1572-4*, p. 130, 16 June 1572, Morgan to Burghley, from Flushing.

follow if any Frenchmen were discovered among the beggars, even if Charles *had* disavowed them.[1] Their numbers were few, but there were certainly some. At the same time, in a letter probably addressed to the duc de Nevers, Charles rather differently reported Alva to have said that he would regard *any* incursion as a rupture of the peace. This was written immediately upon the receipt in Paris of the news from the Netherlands, including the assault upon Brussels, and clearly states Charles' inevitable fear that Alva was about to open war on him, 'de quoi,' he said, 'je suis en une merveilleuse peine'. This private letter prepared by a confidential secretary, giving orders for the protection of frontiers and fortresses, probably brings us as close as we shall get to the truth about Charles, and tends to suggest that he really was frightened by the repercussions of Nassau's exploits.[2]

To Saint-Gouard Charles confessed that he feared Alva meant to make the events a cause of war while he was armed, the French frontier open, and while Philip had a strong force in Italy.[3] It is true that Alva had already requested a large supply of money and troops from Italy, precisely in case he had to make war on the King of France.[4] After informing Saint-Gouard of these threats, Charles claimed to have decided to do all he could to make his subjects withdraw, to prevent others from leaving and to make exemplary punishment of those who disobeyed. He had also

[1] Gachard, *Correspondance de Philippe II*, ii, 259, 29 May 1572, Alva to Don Diego de Zúñiga, ambassador in Paris. Already by 22 May, before the fall of Mons, Alva had ordered Aiguilon, the Spanish secretary, to demand that Charles should not allow any of his subjects to intervene in the Netherlands. Ibid., 250, 22 May 1572, Alva to Philip II; Navarrete, *Colección de Documentos*, lxxv, 47, Relacion de lo sucedido en los Estados Bajos . . . hasta ultimo de Mayo de 1572; Alva's request that all Frenchmen should be recalled was transmitted to Charles by the ambassador on 26 May. Gachard, *Notices et extraits*, ii, 371–3, 31 May 1572, Charles to Saint-Gouard; B.N., Mss. fr. 15554, f. 180-verso, 12 June 1572, Ferrals – French ambassador in Rome – to Charles IX.

[2] B.N., Mss. fr. 15554, f. 220, 29 May 1572, draft by Villeroy.

[3] Gachard, *Notices et extraits*, ii, 372, 31 May 1572, Charles to Saint-Gouard.

[4] Gachard, *Correspondance de Philippe II*, ii, 257–9, 24 May 1572, Alva to Philip II.

decided to take the precaution of supplying and reinforcing his frontiers, to alert what he enigmatically described as 'mes amys', and to raise a contingent of Swiss troops. This was more than his habitual purveyance to Spain of disavowals. Even before receiving the news of the recapture of Valenciennes, he sounded really anxious. He stressed how very serious war would be, and required Saint-Gouard to obtain all the information he could about reactions and activities in Spain.[1] Longueville did in fact receive corresponding instructions to be careful to enforce peace, to break up armed bands and assemblies and to prevent anyone from crossing to the Netherlands; to what extent these gestures were sincere, it is impossible to tell. Longueville replied that he had issued appropriate orders, but that he disposed of 'aucun moyens' for executing them himself, unless his companies were completed and he was provided with money. Many, he said, were still crossing the frontier, only few had returned, and he himself was quite unable to dispel the suspicion that Charles wanted war. More significant than his instructions to Longueville, Charles also wrote to Bricquemault on 31 May referring to the orders he had given him 'pour faire retourner tous mes subjects qui ont accompagné le comte Ludovicq dedans les pays bas,' adding 'contre mes commandements.[2] Furthermore, Charles both cautioned Orange not to march any troops through France, and wrote to Nassau ordering him to desist from his operations; but the letter was never delivered. As Longueville justly observed, it was already too late; Nassau was too deeply embroiled and so, therefore, was Charles.[3]

Charles ordered Mondoucet to inform Alva of these commands to Longueville, and to express his displeasure at what had occurred. Upon the recapture of Valenciennes, however, documents were

---

[1] Gachard, *Notices et extraits*, ii, 371–3, 31 May 1572, Charles to Saint-Gouard.

[2] B.N., Mss. fr. 15554, f. 1, 31 May 1572, Charles to Bricquemault, rough draft by Villeroy.

[3] B.N., Mss. fr. 15554, f. 145, 31 May 1572, Longueville to Charles IX; 158–9, 5 June 1572, Longueville to Charles IX; Desjardins, *Negs. Tosc.*, iii, 777, 28 May 1572.

taken from Nassau's baggage revealing 'des choses d'une haute importance touchant les ligues tramées avec l'amiral de France, et les discours adressés au roi pour l'engager à envahir les Pays Bas'.[1] Charles, who learnt of this, began to show increasing signs of anxiety. In spite of the many casualties, and the great cruelty inflicted upon the prisoners (who, in these circumstances, were not protected by the laws of war) he unflinchingly declared to Saint-Gouard that he was 'très aise, car ils ont este puniz de leur témérité'. Nor was this simply intended to cover the danger of interception, since he virtually admitted his complicity by observing of the captured documents: 'si on vous en parle par delà, vous asseurerez que ce sont impostures et calumnies n'ayant à la vérité jamais escript aucunes lettres audict conte de ce faict'.[2] Philip II quietly accepted these and other protestations in June, because although he did not believe them, he shrank from being forced into war and, so long as Charles maintained his disavowals, no matter how transparent or dishonourable, there must at least be a limit to the scale of operations in the Netherlands.[3] Whether or not under Charles' auspices, French help did in fact continue to flow into the Netherlands. Strozzi, as we have seen, according to Morgan, transported some 6,000 men to help Louis, which probably corresponded to the 26 companies comprising 6–7,000 men mentioned by Alva to be going to help Mons.[4] Morillon mentioned to Granvelle the presence of twenty-two ensigns in the region of Bohain (Aisne) including many of the *bannis*, gentry exiled by Alva, whose property he had sequestered, and who owed no allegiance to the King of France.[5] Alva also reported the discovery of small, clandestine groups, caught by his reconnaissance

---

[1] Gachard, *Correspondance de Philippe II*, ii, 262, 14 June 1572, Albornoz, Alva's secretary, to Zayas.

[2] Gachard, *Notices et extraits*, ii, 373–4, 6 June 1572, Charles to Saint-Gouard. Albornoz had not, in fact, claimed to possess letters *from* the king, but 'des choses d'une haute importance'.

[3] Gachard, *Notices et extraits*, ii, 374–6, 18 June 1572, Charles to Saint-Gouard; 376–9, 22 June 1572, Longlée to Charles IX; 379–84, 1 July 1572, Saint-Gouard to Charles IX.

[4] *CSPF.*, *1572–4*, p. 130, 16 June 1572, Morgan to Burghley from Flushing.

[5] Granvelle, *Correspondance*, iv, 259, 17 June 1572, Morillon to Granvelle.

cavalry, some members of which were quietly hanged and others taken away and secretly drowned because he and Medina Celi were agreed – despite his ultimatum – that they must avoid any open risk of rupture with France.[1] These small groups could have been those alleged by de Guaras to have gone from the garrisons of Picardy. They could also have been forces of Coligny's which he later admitted had assembled in Champagne (inhospitable Guise country) and filtered – without commissions – into the Netherlands.[2]

For the moment, therefore, Charles was protected by the over-commitment of Spain. But this was not a static situation and it could not survive much deterioration. He and Philip were being steadily forced towards a war which neither of them wanted, by events which neither could control.

[1] Gachard, *Correspondance de Philippe II*, ii, 261, 13 June 1572, Alva to Philip II.
[2] B.N., Mss. fr. 3193, ff. 68–9, 6 August 1572, *Mémoire*; Kervyn de Letten-hove, *Relations*, vi, 432–3, 23 June 1572, de Guaras to Alva.

XIV

The Problem of War or Peace

NASSAU'S INVASION of the Netherlands, the fall of Mons, the fall and recapture of Valenciennes, and the assault upon Alva in Brussels, represent the point at which the long-standing presumption of war turned into the fear and danger of its imminent outbreak. The question therefore arises as to whether, at the first sign of adversity and danger, Charles thought better, or perhaps for the first time realistically, of his general commitment to war, only to find that it was too late. He could temporise, and quite successfully, because Philip was preoccupied; but he could not escape the dilemma. It is possible that he had been deceived by the enthusiastic blandishments of those who sought to embroil him, into thinking of the enterprise uniquely in terms of its brevity and success in ideal circumstances, without considering the alarming weight of opposition which would arise in unfavourable ones. If Nassau and William had insisted, in April, that the beggars, having launched their attack, must be supported in spite of the circumstances, Coligny was equally positive in May that if Nassau were not helped Alva would mop up all opposition within two months. If it gradually became clear that it might take somewhat longer, the point was still valid. Then France would be correspondingly exposed and she, and the huguenots in particular, would stand in grave danger of a war of reprisal.[1]

Charles was therefore faced, from the end of May, with a critically and increasingly dangerous situation that he was incapable of handling. His Netherlands 'policy' was, in fact, the only significant undertaking of his reign which he attempted to conduct himself, and therefore exemplifies most clearly his catastrophic inaptitude for government. So far, he had at least

---

[1] Desjardins, *Negs. Tosc.*, iii, 777–81, 28 May 1572.

tried to be secretive, but Nassau's enterprise was public, and its general implications for France were clear; war, if it came, would involve everyone, and Charles could no longer reserve the matter to himself and the group of Netherlands exiles and young huguenots who followed him, particularly since the court, which had been absent from Paris since April 1571, and dispersed since the last week in April 1572, was finally about to reassemble at the *château* de Madrid in the Bois de Boulogne.[1] Furthermore, the vendetta having been formally composed in May, the young duc de Guise and Coligny were both at court.[2] Coligny returned on 6 June for the first time since October 1571, and well accompanied by 300 horsemen, as Paris was almost as dangerous for him as Rome or Madrid would have been.[3]

The assembling of the court was not on account of the Netherlands crisis, but in order to receive the English admiral, lord Lincoln, who arrived on 8 June for the ratification of the treaty of Blois, and to prepare for the Bourbon marriage, since Navarre was at last on his way from Pau.[4] The business of the English ambassadors in France was largely ceremonial, and there was much feasting and formal entertainment. That of the French in England was more serious, since both the crown and the huguenots – whose cause was supported by the ambassadors Montmorency and de Foix – were suppliants, for material assistance, and for the Alençon marriage.

These issues, however they might be resolved, were inseparably

---

[1] Desjardins, *Negs. Tosc.*, iii, 792, 7 July 1572, Petrucci said the court was arriving that night.

[2] Desjardins, *Negs. Tosc.*, iii, 784, 10 June 1572. Coligny and Henri de Guise, who was only thirteen when his father died, were of different generations and must have been relative strangers.

[3] Hirschauer, *La Politique de St Pie V*, 184, 9 June 1572. At Blois in 1571 Coligny faced only the dangers of the court where any offence against him would have been *lèse-majesté*, not those of the fanatically hostile capital.

[4] The English embassy was there from 8–22 June. Lincoln's instructions, for the most part relating to Scottish affairs, which emphasised the defensive nature of the agreement, were dated 25 May 1572, *CSPF.*, *1572–4*, pp. 114–16; 135, 22 June 1572, Walsingham to Burghley; Hirschauer, *La Politique de St Pie V*, 184, 9 June 1572.

connected with the Netherlands crisis. Ever since the beginning of Charles' reign and the first weeks of Catherine's regency in 1561 before the civil wars, the presence of either the Guises and their partisans, or the Bourbon and Montmorency group had repelled the other. The shadow of Spain had fallen more darkly between them than anything else, and now they were reassembled just when – for the first time since 1559 and on account of the departure of Nassau – France was faced with the supreme issue, which lay behind the Netherlands crisis, namely war or peace with Spain. It is therefore not surprising that the subject should have been passionately debated. But, apart from the presence of the English ambassadors, and possibly the death, on 9 June, of Jeanne d'Albret, it is not clear why the debate should have been delayed until almost the third week in June. Walsingham, writing on 22 June said, 'this day resolution is taken touching Flanders matters, which the Admiral's sickness has caused to hang so long in suspense'. The nuncio also said that Coligny was ill.[1] This is puzzling, since he was active in mid-June in the entertainment of the English embassy. By 'resolution', Walsingham must, presumably, have meant deliberation in council, since the matter was far from having been resolved.

As it survives, the debate consisted of a series of surprisingly academic memoranda or depositions, two of which preceded the return from Mons of the huguenot lieutenant Genlis, which acutely inflamed the Netherlands crisis. The first was prepared by Nevers[2] dated 19 June, and referred to the presence in France of the English admiral Lincoln. It was addressed, not to the king or the council, but to Anjou, presumably as lieutenant-general and therefore commander-in-chief. The second was that of de Morvillier. After the arrival of Genlis, these were followed by three further statements: another memoir of Nevers – which appears not to have been presented – a letter from him dated

---

[1] CSPF., 1572–4, p. 135, 22 June 1572, Walsingham to Burghley; Theiner, *Annales Ecclesiastici*, i, 339, 20 June 1572, Frangipani to cardinal di Como.

[2] Nevers was an Italian, Louis de Gonzague, duc de Nevers in 1565, in the right of his wife Henriette de Clèves, sister of the future duchess of Guise. Nevers is held to have been moderate and loyal.

26 June to the king, the advice of the marshal Tavannes, also requested by the king, and an alleged *discours* of Coligny, which is undated but must belong to this time since it refers to the presence of Genlis.

Nevers had already, at the end of April,[1] declared against war with Spain, primarily for the interesting and significant reason that he feared the monarchy might actually succumb unless reforms were carried through and the country freed from the scourge of foreign troops. In particular he was afraid that war taxation might provoke rebellion. In some places the *taille* had actually ceased and, whereas formerly religion had imposed discipline, now there was only avarice, ambition and vengeance. This theme of the corruption of *mœurs* was no mere verbiage or lip service; it recurs throughout the documentation of the civil wars, the theme of vengeance being added, after 1570, to the earlier ones of avarice and ambition.

In his *discours* of 19 June, Nevers constructed more of an argued case, first setting up what he expected or supposed – sometimes wrongly – to be Coligny's arguments, whether for the sake of disputation or, possibly, because the admiral was ill. According to Nevers, Coligny would claim that the situation in the Netherlands was favourable because they – presumably the beggars – held various towns, while others [such as Flushing] held out against Spanish garrisons; the country was so discontented that the appearance of a French army would elicit a rising and, upon the arrival of Orange, Alva would be outnumbered. The Queen of England could also be expected to help. She would approach the islands and her participation would prevent the arrival of Spanish reinforcements through the channel.

The next point is rather interesting: Coligny, Nevers continued, would not forget to deal with Piedmont and Provence, where the king should make his maximum effort, while for the Netherlands Coligny himself only required simple permission plus the small number of royal frontier forces. This postulates that Coligny

---

[1] B.N., Mss. fr. 3193, ff. 227, 'Discours de Nevers de la paix ou la guerre', April 1572.

was thinking in terms of the desirability of a general war against Spain, in which the king would be occupied elsewhere, at a safe distance from Coligny's area of activity, as opposed to a limited war for the specific purpose of helping the Netherlands to escape from the tyranny of Alva. The results could be the same; but the emphasis is different and, although Coligny did fall back upon the argument that he needed little more than simple permission, he did not – that we know of – discuss Piedmont, Provence or general war factors. Finally, Coligny would claim that money was not an impediment, because little would be needed. In this Nevers was right, but the argument could only possibly be applied to limited war in the Netherlands, and not, as he had anticipated, general war involving the outlying provinces. Nevers went on to advise Anjou to act circumspectly, to avoid both the accusation of causing the king to miss a good opportunity and also the imputation of any 'affection particulliere'. But, passing to military arguments, he said that the number of towns held and of persons in arms were few. They would be afraid of Alva and none showed any signs of seeking help in France. This was followed by the even more cogent point that, if it had ever existed, the great opportunity had passed, with the loss of Valenciennes, the arrival of Alva's successor Medina Celi, and the withdrawal (in June) of the tenth penny. What Nevers did not discuss was the fact that the 'opportunity' having been botched rather than missed, could, in itself, be held to render war inevitable or necessary, even if no longer desirable or profitable. These were separate things. The opportunity argument could, however, at least be sustained, since Morillon, writing to Granvelle on 17 June confessed that the affairs of the Netherlands were in such great disorder 'que je tiens les François ne vouldront lesser eschapper une si belle occasion qu'ils n'ont jamais heu telle', though he did also follow this up by other, contrary considerations.[1] The protestants in fact adopted a middle line; without dropping the opportunity argument, which would probably have been a tactical error, they did stress the necessity.

[1] Granvelle, *Correspondance*, iv, 260, 17 June 1572, the *prévôt* Morillon to Granvelle.

On the subject of England, Nevers made the interesting point that if she were to be relied on, they would have known about it, whereas neither the ambassador, nor the admiral Lincoln, who was there, apparently had any instructions in the matter. War, Nevers concluded, was the worst possible thing for France. It would be dangerous without first holding the principal towns; Alva would be ready before France, and Charles did not even dispose of enough money for ordinary expenses. Besides, Charles might elect to embark upon war but he would be unable to terminate it at will, and it could last seven or eight years. It was in fact generally believed that it would not be short. Charles should also be counselled against the secret sanction of hostilities, because Alva would perceive the intention and resent it. It would be preferable to make open war quickly before he was ready. Nevers did not consider the point that secret permission would be the only way of obtaining the towns without which, he had said, war should be avoided.[1]

The *avis* of de Morvillier, a trusted councillor, which was dated 20 June was requested by the king, and is incomparably the ablest and most interesting of them all, not least on account of his penetrating and accurate assessment of European affairs and, in particular, of the policy of England. In the first place de Morvillier understood the king, and began by stating plainly that although it was a serious matter of doubtful issue, irresolution was as bad as bad counsel, and aroused suspicion in one's neighbours. He declined to discuss the justice or injustice of such a war, and proceeded straight to the questions of 'opportunity', and the expected participation of England; also the points that the German princes would block the transmission of help to Alva, that Orange was bringing considerable forces, and Nassau held Mons. France, he said, considering this side of the argument, was filled with *noblesse* and all kinds of soldiers who must be employed abroad if they were to be restrained from fighting at home. He also mentioned the danger of a war of reprisal.

These, de Morvillier submitted, were arguments which might

---

[1] B.N., Mss. fr. 3950, ff. 84–6 verso, 19 June 1572.

move a wealthy prince bored by long years of peace, but they were ill-founded. The conquest of the Netherlands might be a fine idea but, if not actually impossible, it would not be quickly achieved. While Nevers thought it might entail a seven or eight years' war – the reason for these figures is not clear – de Mor-villier thought it would continue for the whole of Philip's reign which, albeit in the light of later events, would seem the more accurate assessment. He too was concerned about the insufficiency of money, even for ordinary expenses, let alone for a long war; also about the disruption of trade, the oppression of the rural population and the impoverishment of the nobility, whose constraint should be that of discipline under the law. Here speaks the voice of a fearless ex-chancellor, or *garde des sceaux*, who had had the courage to resign in protest against the state of France. It was no argument, he declared with remarkable candour, to claim that a king who could not govern in peace, would be more successful in war.

On the subject of the Netherlands, de Morvillier said that while it was true that they sought deliverance from Alva, it was only individuals who looked for salvation in France – presumably mostly the *bannis*, who were gentry and did not dispose of the towns. People who were moved by present despair would change their minds when conditions improved, which was doubt-less a reference to the abolition of the tenth penny.[1] He developed this important theme in relation to Valenciennes and Mons. Both had been mastered by surprise and intelligence, not consent, and Valenciennes was immediately lost again and garrisoned. The towns, which were primarily interested in commerce, would prefer whomsoever taxed them least, which would not be occupying foreigners. Alva was in a position, de Morvillier said, to seal them off against Orange. As an outlaw, he had nothing to lose, and he would be unable to raise the money he needed. Indeed, this was already, at that moment, delaying his arrival. The towns were afraid of Alva and reluctant to pay.

[1] Gachard, *Correspondance de Philippe II*, ii, 263, 24 June 1572, Alva to Philip II.

Although it was true that the German princes hated Spain, it did not follow that they would either declare open war or be willing to finance one. They were not in the habit of acting with either temerity or prodigality and they had no advantage in the war. This was doubtless a short-term view, and William tried hard to persuade them that his cause was theirs. But it was none the less true that they could not be regarded by France as a safeguard against the dangers of such an enterprise. If the Netherlands towns could not be relied upon to rise, or the German princes to provide much effective help, still less was it advisable to enter into war dependent upon the help of England. About this de Morvillier was either very perceptive or very well informed. The friendship of England, he said, would only last so long as it suited her interests. This may appear quite simple, but in fact English interests were rarely observed and analysed, and all too often assumed to be aligned with those of continental Calvinism. England had concluded the alliance with France, de Morvillier said, as a defence against the conspiracies conceived by the Scottish queen, the duke of Alva (here he was wrong) and English malcontents. It is interesting to remember, in this context, that the instructions of Lincoln, who was still there, were largely concerned with Scotland, a much closer danger than the Netherlands; and it is true that the treaty was only a defensive alliance. It was a mistake, de Morvillier said, to suppose that Elizabeth envisaged the aggrandizement of France; she was uniquely concerned with her own profit and security. This had become clear from the treaty with England for which she did not wish to renounce her defensive agreement with Spain, whereby she could lawfully assist the Netherlands with men and money if France invaded them. The moment war began with Spain, Philip would do everything he could to reassure Elizabeth. For her part, she was afraid, and her kingdom troubled by the uncertainty of her succession. For this reason, she needed peace, *as all her conduct revealed.*[1] Once she saw that France and Spain were at war, she would be freed from the fear of foreign exploitation and of the

---

[1] My italics.

succession problem, and could therefore afford to 'se mettre à la fenestre pour regarder le jeu'. The most, therefore, which could be hoped from England was the continuation of her present goodwill without the renewal of old quarrels.

If, as de Morvillier argued, France should not go to war relying upon English help, when England would merely rest secure in their embroilment, still less should she do so on account of Spanish attitudes. Any conquest in the Netherlands would entail a protracted war with Spain in which she would use Italian forces against Piedmont and naval forces against Provence, and there was no use in making foreign conquests, hard to hold, at the cost of losing parts of France.

De Morvillier thought equally little of the argument, or rather the surmise, that if France did not open war, Spain would. The suppression of the Netherlands would serve to occupy Philip, and Charles would do better to fortify the frontiers. He believed that if France were to keep the peace, so would Spain. This was indeed the case, and could easily then be inferred from the degree of provocation that she had already deigned to overlook. Spain might indicate, de Morvillier continued, that she was 'en grande deffiance,' which was really not without cause. France should therefore desist from provocations, but make preparations. Then, if it should transpire that Spain did really intend war, France would at least not be defenceless. Besides preparing against the eventuality of war and fortifying the frontiers, Charles should strive to restore some unity within France – to be fair, this was the purpose of the Bourbon marriage – some integrity to the administration of justice, and some order to the conduct of other professions, by which he probably meant the finances. These were the things which would render the king respected and redoubtable in the estimation of his neighbours.[1]

These were the arguments being adduced when Genlis arrived in Paris – closely followed by Salviati who returned as nuncio to represent the new pope Gregory XIII. The advent of Genlis to

[1] B.N., Mss. fr. 3177, ff. 120–33, 20 June 1572, 'Avis du seigneur de Morvillier sur le fait des troubles et pretendue conqueste des pays de Flandres', seventeenth-century copy; also in Mss. Dupuy, 753, ff. 149–57 verso, undated copy.

plead for help lent the whole debate great and sudden urgency, since a decision as to whether or not to support him could not be evaded. Nevers prepared a second *discours* dated 26 June, which was apparently never submitted. But he also wrote a letter to the king of the same date.[1] This was primarily concerned with military factors designed to counter the 'opportunity' arguments. France, he said, had neither the men nor the money for what could be a long war, because Alva would be ready first. Nevers believed that Spain was stronger in Milan than anywhere else, that she would spare nothing on the Italian side and could walk over the southern frontiers since the towns of Provence, Languedoc and Guyenne were defensively worthless. This opinion had already been expressed by royal officials.[2]

Most interesting, however, in this second group of depositions was that of Tavannes, one of the few authentic passages in the memoirs which bear his name.[3] As one might expect from a marshal, Tavannes put forward a number of detailed military arguments against making war, from the point of view of a commander who might well have to take responsibility in the field. Thus, to a large extent he agreed with Nevers. But, more interestingly, he also reflected very much the humane and patriotic views of de Morvillier in his concern for France, which confirms his place among the moderates, who supported Catherine. Like Nevers, Tavannes considered that war fiscality would be very dangerous, and that those who had been taxed to suppress protestants at home would object to being taxed again to support them abroad. If this was not quite the measure of the Netherlands enterprise, it was evidently how some people felt

[1] B.N., Mss. fr. 3950, f. 87; f. 89, 26 June 1572, Nevers to Charles IX.
[2] B.N., Mss. 15554, f. 50, 6 April 1572, Aspremont to Charles IX from somewhere near Bayonne, who complained of not having been paid for three years; f. 38, 20 March 1572, to Anjou; Mss. fr. 3158, f. 104, 24 May 1572, Joyeuse to Damville, *gouverneur* of Languedoc.
[3] B.N., Mss. fr. 3950, ff. 93–5, 'Avis de Tavannes', 26 June 1572; Tavannes, *Mémoires*, 376 seq. Gaspard de Saulx-Tavannes left few papers. The memoirs attributed to him were written years later by his son Jean and are a worthless confusion of their two lives.

about it. Indeed, he felt so strongly that war fiscality would be dangerous that he feared it might lead to an accusation of tyranny, that kings were not kings to maintain fortresses, but kings of people by whom they should be loved and obeyed. Then he went on to endorse some of the military arguments of Nevers; in particular he believed that Piedmont would be lost in a month; the Spanish could descend almost immediately upon Dauphiné and Provence. Besides, even if the huguenots did prevail against Alva, the king would then be in their power. This was a point that had greatly worried Catherine in the summer of 1562, when the protestants were relatively much stronger than the catholics in cavalry, in terrain where this would have been decisive. Tavannes then introduced a new argument, that the Netherlands could no longer profit Spain, because in order to control them, Philip would have to ruin them. He therefore came out firmly and clearly in favour of peace: 'maintenons notre reputation envers Dieu et les hommes et la paix avec ung chascun, *surtout avec nostre peuple leur tenant la parolle pour la religion* et reprenons alaine . . . car cest toute la nécessité de ceste couronne et de l'estat'.[1]

Coligny is also held to have contributed a deposition, whether at the time of the council meetings in June, or early in July is not clear. This well-known document was allegedly prepared by Duplessis-Mornay, and published with his *Mémoires et correspondance.*[2] One must, however, seriously question its authenticity since, even allowing for his youthfulness, it falls so far below the quality of thought and penmanship of the accomplished Duplessis-Mornay, and also one would have thought, did less than justice to the cogency of Coligny's case.

The burden of the deposition was that a foreign war was the only remedy for France's domestic ills, a feeble argument which could neither prevail against de Morvillier's penetrating analysis of European politics, nor the huguenots' own plea that war in the Netherlands would be a short, sharp campaign. This 'necessary'

---

[1] My italics.
[2] Duplessis-Mornay, *Mémoires et correspondance,* ii, 20–37, *Discours au Roy Charles IX pour entreprendre la guerre contre l'Espagne es Pays-Bas*; also in B.N., Mss. fr. 23335, ff. 17–35 verso, undated seventeenth-century copy.

war, must be just, easy and useful – rather a curious combination –
and Spanish injuries already sustained rendered it just. This,
however, was only supported by trivial examples of the precedence quarrel variety. A far more telling argument was that
Charles had, already, embarked upon war as effectively as if he
had taken the field in person, since it was known that he had
received, favoured, honoured and 'gratified' Nassau, and other
seigneurs and gentlemen (namely some of the *bannis* and exiles)
at court, and was in touch with Genlis who came to seek substantial assistance in the case. Thus Spain was already bound to
consider France as an enemy. In answer to the financial impediment it was feebly argued that war was prosecuted more with
iron and honour than with wealth, and promptly demolished by
the contradictory assertion that the Spanish forces had not been
paid for three years. The point was not that they did not need to
be paid since, in these circumstances, the dread Alva himself dared
not take them out of garrison.[1] Spain, it was admitted, had a navy,
unlike France, but these were only galleys in the Levant, while
Languedoc was strong and Provence defensible. It is not possible
that Coligny was ignorant of the existence of the Netherlands
fleet, which had been intercepted by the beggars, or that of
Alva's successor even then arriving with Medina Celi on board.
He must also have known that Provence and Languedoc were not
defensible. The probable attitude of other countries – which was
in fact holding Charles in anxious restraint – Scotland, Germany,
Turkey, the Grisons, Venice and the pope, was then briefly
considered, but with the astounding omission of England, which
was perhaps all too glibly assumed to be an ally, and without the
slightest understanding of the complexity of European politics.
The climax of the document appears to be the alleged opportunity
to conduct a swift, easy and just war in the Netherlands, whose
internal divisions would open the gates of the cities to the forces
of France, an argument already sufficiently belied by the presence
and purpose of Genlis.

[1] Gachard, *Correspondance de Philippe II*, ii, 246, 26 April 1572, Alva to
Philip II.

Thus – leaving aside the authenticity or otherwise of this feeble document – only Coligny considered war unavoidable, although these were not the circumstances in which he had advocated it. Charles appears to have dithered, arousing universal anxiety and distrust. The council was unanimously opposed to war, largely for military, financial, and even patriotic reasons. These at least were those recorded. Catherine had always opposed it, and so did Anjou, who was described in the instructions of the new Spanish ambassador, Don Diego de Zúñiga, as being inclined to Philip's service.[1] Coligny was therefore alone.

---

[1] Champion, *Charles IX, la France et le contrôle de l'Espagne*, ii, 33; he quotes Simancas, K. 1529, 31 March 1572.

XV

The Netherlands and the
English Alliance

THESE WERE the arguments being adduced when Genlis – who was among those who had already served William of Orange in 1568[1] – arrived back in Paris from Mons on 23 June 1572. This was doubtless because Alva's son, Don Fadrique de Toledo, had left Brussels on 20 June to invest the city[2] and, despite Strozzi's help, Nassau was not strong enough to survive alone, since neither Coligny nor Orange had arrived. Orange, whose arrangements, for lack of money, seem to have been interminable, did not even leave his German estates at Dillenburg until 29 June, and Alva was known to be raising large forces[3] for a big assault on Mons in mid-August, and 'aull the gentylmen of thys countre to bee redy by 15 of the nexte mounnethe [August]'.[4] Indeed, already before the end of June, Mons was described in England as being surrounded, by forces of Don Fadrique, and Chiapin Vitelli who was to have led the enterprise of England.[5] Nassau therefore urgently wanted someone to divert Alva from trapping him in Mons, and to take Cateau-Cambrésis which lay between him and the frontier.

Nassau's loss of Valenciennes had created the big debate; now

[1] Gachard, *Notices et extraits*, ii, 467, 14 November 1568.

[2] Granvelle, *Correspondance*, iv, 270, 22 June 1572, Morillon to Granvelle.

[3] Gachard, *Correspondance de Guillaume le Taciturne*, iii, p. xv.

[4] Kervyn de Lettenhove, *Relations*, vi, 436, – July 1572, John Lee to Burghley. Alva in fact quit Brussels on 26 August, after the massacre when he had little more to fear from the southern frontier.

[5] *CSPSp.*, 1568–79, p. 397, 28 June 1572, news from England (Antonio Fogaza to ?Ruy Gómez).

the danger to Mons and the presence of Genlis created a crisis. His arrival and demands, in the last week in June, brought embarrassing publicity to a matter which, hitherto, had at least been shrouded in some mystery, if not successfully cloaked in secrecy. Morillon, it is true, referred to Genlis as having been in disguise, but his return and contact with the king appear to have been generally known in political circles.[1] This placed Coligny in a position which was comparable to that of Nassau in May. He had then departed suddenly and prematurely because, after the assault upon Brill it was essential, if he were ever to go at all. But, for Coligny the problem was greater because, being French unlike Nassau, he had diverse responsibilities in France and his recent return to court was at least in part an act of co-operation in the royal policy of general reconciliation. This cannot and must not be discounted as imaginary since he did, in the end, await the Bourbon marriage, and one of his last known letters was primarily concerned with the implementation of the edict of Saint-Germain, referring only secondarily to his delayed departure for the Netherlands.[2]

From the moment of his return on 6 June Coligny had begun to make strenuous efforts to obtain permission to ride off to the Netherlands before Alva was ready; but Charles firmly refused.[3] Then, when he heard of the mounting siege, he began to raise three forces, one under the marquis de Rethel, and Lescat who were to traverse Lorraine with 3,000 foot and 1,000 horse and join Orange before he crossed the Meuse. A second, under Bricquemault, was to conduct 3,500 foot and 600 horse from Picardy to take Cateau-Cambrésis and secure the route between France and Mons, which Coligny himself was to relieve with the main force. At the time of the councils Coligny is alleged to have declared, in the presence of Anjou, the lieutenant-general, that they would have to go alone if Charles did not agree to make

---

[1] Granvelle, *Correspondance*, iv, 319, 20 & 22 July 1572, Morillon to Granvelle.

[2] Dufey, *Massacres de la Saint-Barthélemy*, in *Paris révolutionnaire*, iii, 356–7, 18 August 1572, Coligny to his wife.

[3] Desjardins, *Negs. Tosc.*, iii, 784, 10 June 1572.

war in the Netherlands and that this would result in war in France
because Philip would be revenged upon them.[1]

What then was Charles going to do, in this crisis which called
for a decision, when he was subjected to strong pressure on the
one hand and multiple restraints on the other? Frangipani considered that the trouble had been 'praticate in la botega di detta
Navarra,' namely by Jeanne, and that now she was dead Charles
would not *have* to take part, as he appeared disinclined to do, in
spite of the admiral's importunity.[2] It seems more likely, however,
that the influence was that of Nassau, and that Charles had been
frightened into at least hesitation following the count's departure
in May, by the alarming nature of the Spanish reaction; by a new
version – yet to be discussed – of the old, familiar catholic
pressure; by the unanimous opposition of the council which
included all his military officials and, perhaps not least of all, by
that of Catherine. Catherine resisted the Netherlands policy in
June, as she already had in April and was to do in July, and again
in August. It would appear from Walsingham's reports that she
might have surrendered if assured of the active co-operation of
England, presumably realising how helplessly Charles was
entangled.[3] The trouble, as de Morvillier had so lucidly expounded, was that the co-operation of England could not just
be secured for the desiring, the need, or the asking. Catherine
sought to persuade the nuncio, whose help she needed to obtain
the dispensation, that Charles did not want to support the
protestants,[4] and publicly declared that the king would never
oppose Spain.

Furthermore, if Charles, like Coligny, was also committed to
Nassau – albeit not within a formal treaty – Nassau had been, and
Coligny still was, committed to supporting the Bourbon marriage
for which Navarre arrived in Paris on 8 July in the midst of this

[1] Desjardins, *Negs. Tosc.*, iii, 785, 24 June 1572; 786-7, 26 June 1572.

[2] Theiner, *Annales Ecclesiastici*, i, 339, 20 June 1572, Frangipani to cardinal
di Como.

[3] Digges, 231, 10 August 1572, Walsingham to Smith; 233, 10 August 1572,
Walsingham to Burghley.

[4] Desjardins, *Negs. Tosc.*, iii, 785, 24 June 1572; 786-7, 26 June 1572.

crisis.[1] This marriage was possibly the most definite purpose of Charles' reign. Without it he could never hope to win his mother's support and, until it was accomplished, he could not, or would not, do anything else. If it was no real guarantee of the support of Henry of Navarre, it was the only step he could take towards securing it. Charles therefore was ensnared in a series of predicaments which called for consummate statesmanship, since the issue was not quite yet a straightforward one of war or peace, but fraught with subtleties, beyond his grasp, of interpretation, degree, timing and attendant circumstances.

The first essential, as Navarre arrived, was to restrain Coligny. If Nassau's departure had been serious and compromising enough, Coligny's would be disastrous. It was at least possible, if not convincing, for Charles to disclaim responsibility for the exploits of Nassau, as a foreign prince – although the presence in his forces of such notorious huguenots as Genlis, La Noue, Téligny, Bouchavannes and others was distinctly embarrassing. But he could not plausibly disavow Coligny, a grand seigneur, backed, or perhaps more precisely driven by the strength of the huguenot faction, without either denouncing him as a rebel, which would amount to a declaration of civil war (not to mention a dastardly act of treachery) or else to admitting a loss of control over the affairs of France. Extreme catholics might then be expected to go to the help of Spain and, since fighting could never be confined to the frontier areas and the Netherlands, civil war must follow.

As late as 4 July, Petrucci believed that Charles did not want war, and reported that the debate continued.[2] It was probably therefore in early July that, according to La Huguerye, Charles sent for Coligny via Cavaignes and decided, upon his advice, to send help to the Netherlands; that is to say to continue with his underhand assistance. The nature and extent of this is impossible to ascertain, but both Walsingham and La Huguerye testified to its existence.[3] Considering Coligny's declared intention to go to

---

[1] Desjardins, *Negs. Tosc.*, iii, 792, 7 July 1572.

[2] Desjardins, *Negs. Tosc.*, iii, 788, 4 July 1572.

[3] Digges, 221, 13 July 1572, Walsingham to Burghley; La Huguerye, *Mémoires*, i, 116–17.

the Netherlands, and the opinion recorded by, but certainly not peculiar to Petrucci[1] that the protestants would do as they pleased in any case, it could be argued that Charles was left with no real choice in the matter. By agreeing to underhand assistance, which should take the pressure off Mons, he at least had more hope of restraining Coligny until after the Bourbon marriage which then, at long last seemed imminent, and until they knew more from Montmorency and de Foix, who arrived back just before Navarre on 7 July, about what support they might anticipate from England.[2]

England, to whom Nassau had immediately looked for help in securing Flushing, had always featured largely in his plans, and those of his huguenot supporters, all of them misguidedly seeking to cast Elizabeth in the role of protestant counterpart to Philip II. Orange and Nassau, however, could not operate without at the least her tacit consent, on account of her control of the channel, and the huguenots were naturally more at ease with an English alliance, for all its doubtfulness, than with an even more hazardous French royal, catholic one, which Coligny, for subsequently well-vindicated reasons, had sturdily opposed for as long as possible. Coligny, Orange and Nassau, therefore, had all sought in June to exploit the opportune exchange of embassies for the ratification of the treaty of Blois even before the pressure on Mons and the return of Genlis had exacerbated the crisis. Indeed, it appears, but only from the evidence of these embassies, that there was a project afoot for a further treaty with England to enter together upon war in the Netherlands. Its provenance is not disclosed but, as it could not have originated with Elizabeth, and its purpose was evidently to implement the Netherlands partition plan, it is likely to have been fostered by Montmorency and Coligny, by Nassau,

---

[1] Desjardins, *Negs. Tosc.*, iii, 786, 26 June 1572.

[2] B.M., Mss. Cotton, Vespasian vi, f. 87, 11 July 1572, Montmorency to Elizabeth. He said that he had been in Paris for four days waiting to see the king. He had in fact seen Catherine on 10 July while Charles was hunting. The court had dispersed about 22 April after the conclusion of the Bourbon marriage and the treaty of Blois, reassembled about 7 June to receive the English ambassadors, dispersed again probably after the depositions of 26 June and reassembled on 7 July to receive Navarre, and to hear Montmorency and de Foix.

or all of them – with, or without Charles' consent. This would be
sustained by the fact that Montmorency pursued the matter in
England; in France there is no evidence of any negotiations at the
ambassadorial level.[1]

Among the English embassy, however, were two puritans, Sir
Henry Middlemore, an old acquaintance of Coligny, and cousin
and secretary to Sir Nicholas Throckmorton, former ambassador
to France and Sir Arthur Champernown, father-in-law of the
huguenot lieutenant, Montgommery. On 10 June, before Lincoln
had been received in audience, Middlemore and Champernown
had supper with Coligny. After pronouncing the customary
formalities and expressions of service to the queen, Coligny
'grewe into the matters of Flawnders,' enquiring what Middlemore
had heard. But Middlemore reacted cautiously and told him little.
Coligny then 'toke occasion' to inform Middlemore of all that
'had happenyd latelye there, [in the Netherlands] and wisshyd
somewhat might be donne there joyntlye by the Quenes Majestie
and this Kynge'. Clearly Coligny believed – no doubt correctly –
that if only the Queen of England could be enlisted, Charles
would agree to the war, and Catherine perhaps acquiesce.
Coligny therefore expatiated upon the wealth of Philip II, and the
danger which he represented to England, declaring that his
design, 'in sight of the wisest . . . is to make himselfe monarche of
Christendome, or at the least to rule the same'. It was therefore
necessary to 'brydle that dangerous affection in him'. This,
Coligny said, would never more easily be done than by the
'occasion presently offeryd of the Lowe Countreys so greatly
garboyled.' In the 'enterprisinge' of this, Coligny called for a
'resolute and determinyd order to be sett downe and agreed on
betwixt bothe our Princes' . . . so that 'all good sincere, and trewe
dealynge might be assueryd, all gealousye, suspition and mistrust
taken awaye and avoydyd'. In other words, with a diplomatic
innocence likely to have conjured sardonic smiles in England, he
proposed a formal, offensive treaty. There he 'stayed,' seeking the

---

[1] Ellis, *Original Letters*, 2nd series, iii (ed. London, 1969), 12–22, 18 June 1572,
Smith to Burghley.

opinion of Middlemore who cautiously replied that these were 'matters owt of his reache and far from his acquayntawnce'. But, pressed for a private opinion, he said they desired each prince to 'enjoye his owne' adding, correctly, that England 'colde least lyke that Frawnce shulde commaunde Flawnders'. Coligny denied that this was intended, but rather that Elizabeth should have quite as good a part as the French, 'and so he wolde undertake'. The danger, he went on, 'lay in the protractinge of tyme, in lettynge slipp good occasion, and in so late reasolvinge'.

Leaving the subject of the Netherlands, Coligny urged the desirability of the Alençon match. But Lincoln's instructions did not mention the Netherlands at all, and in the matter of the marriage they were brief and chilling.[1] The result of Coligny's overtures in France were therefore hardly encouraging since Middlemore's replies – though only his private opinion extracted upon a private occasion – indicated sufficiently clearly that England was not inclined to make war.

As one would expect, the French ambassadors, who arrived in England on 13 June, were scarcely more successful. While Coligny did his best in France, de Foix is said to have had special instructions – it is not clear from whom – to represent to Burghley how advisable it would be for France and England to join in war on Flanders, whose territory could then be divided. While Burghley generally cherished the protestants, it is difficult to believe that he really favoured this, since he held no brief for foreign conquests, and Antonio Fogaza, the Portuguese agent from whom the information derives, reported that Leicester and the queen did not 'take it so readily'. He went on to say that this was the matter which Montmorency was to convey to the queen in the admiral's name, but he learnt (whether correctly or otherwise) that Montmorency had done so in the name of his prince. This suggests that he held discretionary powers. It is just possible that this represents a change of policy on the part of Charles IX as a result

---

[1] Ellis, *Original Letters*, 2nd series, iii, 3–11, 17 June 1572, Middlemore to Burghley; *CSPF.*, 1572–4, p. 116, 25 May 1572, instructions for the earl of Lincoln. One should realise that these instructions were prepared before Nassau's exploits in the Netherlands were known in England.

of the Nassau crisis, and the awful menaces of Spain. On the other hand, it might only represent the anxiety of a catholic agent. According to Antonio de Guaras, a Spanish merchant or banker who had long been resident in England, Montmorency spoke especially to Burghley and Leicester; no doubt he approached them all. De Guaras also plainly stated that Nassau took this opportunity to propose the partition plan to the queen, apparently also through Montmorency, though this is not entirely clear.[1] Fogaza's comment was that, so far as he could see, Elizabeth 'did not trust overmuch to these offers and fine words, but wishes to have some sort of security in her hands, thinking of Calais'; nor did he think she had any money for 'a rupture of so much importance'.[2] Fogaza retained his despatch for two days, until 25 June, and added that nothing would be decided before the return of a courier who was sent to France in great haste. This very likely accounts for the first *discours* of Nevers, dated 19 June, and the *avis* of de Morvillier, dated 20 June which was requested by the king. Fogaza reported that the English were arming, but that no fleet could be ready in under six weeks – which meant August – and repeated that the queen was thought to be demanding sureties or hostages before entertaining anything.[3] In this way Elizabeth checked, countered and circumscribed all her moves, giving and withdrawing simultaneously.

The expected reply from France arrived on the night of 25 June – the timing is tight but possible, given fair summer weather – with a letter from Charles to the queen concerning the negotiation of Montmorency and de Foix in his name, about an Anglo-French war in the Netherlands. It is to be supposed that Charles' reply was favourable since, even before the return of Genlis, it appeared that he must soon be forced into open war with Spain, and was therefore anxious that it should not be without the support of England. Such support would go far towards neutralising both the intrinsic danger, and the mounting

[1] Kervyn de Lettenhove, *Relations*, vi, 432, 23 June 1572, de Guaras to Alva.
[2] *CSPSp.*, *1568–79*, p. 395, 23 June 1572, news from England (Antonio de Fogaza to Ruy Gómez).
[3] *CSPSp.*, *1568–79*, p. 396, 23 June 1572, news from England.

opposition in France from all but the most extreme political catholics who must either incline, do nothing, or incur the guilt and odium of *lèse-majesté*. Fogaza gave no further clue as to the attitude taken by Charles in this reply; only that the matter had been 'carried very far, on slight grounds, to her [Elizabeth's] very small advantage'. She went to the council next day and, in the presence of Montmorency and de Foix, announced loudly and emphatically that upon no account would she break with the catholic king. Only a week before this, in his *avis* to the council, de Morvillier had drawn attention to Elizabeth's refusal to renounce her defensive agreement with Spain. Montmorency replied that her intentions were very much changed, since 'M. de Lumay had gone from here with her consent and aid to rob the isle of Brille'. To this the queen agreed, but said it was a 'very different thing,' protesting that she desired to remain friendly with the 'house of Burgundy'. Fogaza went on to say that in the end Montmorency and Burghley finally agreed that if Charles consented to the 'draft treaty,' the queen would do so too. It is difficult to see what this could mean when she herself had so clearly stated that on no account would she break with Spain, but it shows how far the matter had evidently been carried by ministers and ambassadors. For this purpose Montmorency left the next day, presumably taking the draft treaty with him.[1]

The immediate reason for Elizabeth's strongly adverse reaction to the 'offensive' treaty was because on 22 June, that is to say at this same time, Alva had sent her letters from Philip II, delivered by Antonio de Guaras, desiring 'bonne amitié et voisinance'.[2] Already from the time of Smith's arrival in France in January 1572 to negotiate the treaty of Blois – the marriage being in abeyance – Elizabeth had been seeking to draw closer to Spain but, after the dismissal of the Spanish ambassador, Guerau de Spes on 14 December 1571, there had been no suitable person with whom to negotiate. This was not, in itself, a contradiction, because at the time Elizabeth had expressed her willingness to

[1] *CSPSp.*, *1568–79*, p. 396, 27 June 1572, news from England; 397, 28 June 1572, Fogaza to Ruy Gómez.

[2] Kervyn de Lettenhove, *Relations*, vi, 431, 22 June 1572, Alva to Elizabeth.

accept a replacement and also to send an English representative to Spain – a significant olive branch. This was reported by the Venetian ambassador in France, Cavalli, among others, who added that although the English were seeking a closer union with the French, they were, apparently, still prepared to treat with the Spaniards, and did not wish to be considered open enemies of the King of Spain because they did not believe that the friendship of the French was too sure.[1] Here, both Cavalli and de Morvillier identified a basic factor in Anglo-French relations, namely a considerable community of interest thwarted by a fundamental lack of mutual confidence. The combination of France and England was, perhaps, Philip's principal nightmare. Unless Spanish power were truly prodigious, England and France together could surely have prevailed, and yet each was too afraid to take the risk.

Towards the end of March, while Smith was steaming with impatience in France at Elizabeth's delay in concluding the treaty of Blois, Antonio de Guaras informed Alva that according to Burghley Elizabeth and the council were seeking 'un buen acuerdo' with Spain and he, de Guaras, was convinced of England's desire for peace. This is doubtless why Alva did his best to press this on Burghley while the French ambassadors were in England, blaming delays in the negotiation upon the death of Philip's Burgundian (and favourite) secretary, Courteville.[2] Upon receipt of Philip's letters, Elizabeth told de Guaras that 'the Flushing people came daily to offer to deliver the place to her, and if it were to the interests and the wish of his Majesty, she would accept it and hold the town by means of the English who were there . . . with the object of, at once, surrendering the place to the duke of Alba or his representative'.[3] This was typical of Elizabeth's ambivalent attitude, and accounts for the lack of

[1] *CSPVen.*, *1558–80*, p. 480–1, 16 January 1572.
[2] *CSPVen.*, *1558–80*, p. 480, 16 January 1572; Kervyn de Lettenhove, *Relations*, vi, 352–4, 26 March 1572, de Guaras to Alva; 370–3, 11 April 1572, Sweveghem to Alva; 374–6, 11 April 1572, de Guaras to Alva; 432, 23 June 1572, de Guaras to Alva.
[3] *CSPSp.*, *1568–79*, p. 397, 30 June 1572, de Guaras to Alva.

confidence not only between England and France, but equally between England and Spain. The real purpose of the policy of Elizabeth and Burghley, de Guaras informed Alva at the time of the capture of Mons, was 'to deflect the power of Spain from England,' so that if the English wanted peace it was only when they were afraid. Apart from the French alliance, doubtless one reason why Elizabeth sought to draw closer to Spain was that parliament was calling for a declaration of war against her. In the matter of reaching agreement with Spain, Elizabeth had also to reckon with difficulties in the privy council.[1]

The deflection, as de Guaras said, of the power of Spain from England was the whole point of the purely *defensive* French alliance. The conclusion of another, *offensive* one, for the purpose of making war in the Netherlands, might be expected, on the contrary, to attract Spanish hostility. Thus, de Morvillier was clearly correct in his assumption that English friendship could only be relied upon in so far as it was commensurate with her own defence and profit. Why, after all, should England pursue the interests of France, her oldest enemy? He was therefore equally correct in his belief that the aggrandizement of France was no part of Elizabeth's policy. Middlemore had already made this clear to Coligny, who denied any such intention. Small forces were hardly over the French frontier before La Mothe wrote to Charles IX that the English began to fear that these enterprises 'tendent d'impatroniser Vostre Majesté de cest estat, ce qui leur seroit formidable; et ne vouldraient qu'en façon du monde cella succédât, silz n'y participoient'.[2] This was really not accurate, since English 'participation' was actually required for the partition plan. But, if partition countered, in a sense, English fears of the disruption of the balance of power between France and Spain – stressed by Middlemore to Coligny in France – like the offensive treaty, it did nothing to accommodate Elizabeth's principal need to deflect Spanish power from England. This English anxiety may have arisen on account of the appearance of Frenchmen in

[1] Kervyn de Lettenhove, *Relations*, vi, 414–18, 24 May 1572, de Guaras to Alva.

[2] La Mothe, v, 5–8, 5 June 1572, La Mothe to Charles IX.

Flushing on the western seaboard as opposed to Brabant, and help from England, if not exactly English help, flowed steadily into the Netherlands and was greatly increased in July in spite of Elizabeth's negative attitude to the offensive treaty.[1] Certainly Burghley openly conveyed to Walsingham English anxiety lest the maritime parts should fall into French hands. 'We have great cause to bear a jealous countenance thereto,' probably because he saw in Elizabeth a 'lack of disposition to provide the remedy,' and feared that she would let the matter go by default, for there is really no evidence that this was what Charles had in mind and, according to Nassau's partition plan, this area was reserved for England.[2] Indeed it had already been reported by de Guaras to Alva – though he was not quite sure – that the Flemish had actually offered Elizabeth the town of Flushing.[3] It is doubtful if these offers had anything to do with partition, but they certainly played right into Elizabeth's skilful hands by enabling her to secure Flushing, more or less as the French and Nassau were demanding, without, at the same time, further antagonising Spain.

The English attitude both to France and to Spain was quite clearly stated at this time in one of Burghley's celebrated memorials.[4] In this he specified that England must strengthen the people of

[1] For example, Burghley wrote on 21 May, that as many foreigners as wished had been allowed to leave England but if Orange did not follow up this opportunity his cause would never be recoverable thereafter. This was just what Coligny thought. Orange lacked the money to do it, and Burghley was right. Digges, 203, 21 May 1572, Burghley to Walsingham; Kervyn de Letten-hove, *Relations*, vi, 414–18, 24 May 1572, de Guaras to Alva; 418–20, 29 May 1572, de Guaras to Alva; 422–5, 6 June 1572, de Guaras to Alva; La Mothe, iv, 463–4, 28 May 1572, La Mothe to Charles IX. In mid-June there were 500 English, 400 French and 500 Walloons and Flemings at Flushing. Nassau was said to be near Brussels with 4,000 and Strozzi to have brought another 6,000. This tallies with the figure of 10,000 sometimes given. *CSPF.*, *1572–4*, p. 130, 16 June 1572, Morgan to Burghley.

[2] Digges, 212, 6 June 1572, Burghley to Walsingham.

[3] Kervyn de Lettenhove, *Relations*, vi, 418–20, 29 May 1572, de Guaras to Alva. This is likely to have been true since a month later he reported that every day Elizabeth was being offered the town of Flushing. Ibid., 434, 30 June 1572, de Guaras to Alva.

[4] *CSPF.*, *1572–4*, p. 123, 3 June 1572, memorial for Flanders.

Brill and Flushing and other places, and discover their intentions and those of Nassau as well as obtaining intelligence from (nearby catholic) Cologne, which indicates that Nassau's partition plan had not received any general acceptance. The memorial went on to say that if it appeared that Alva could resist the French, both sides should be left alone. This, just as de Morvillier expected, revealed Elizabeth 'à la fenestre pour regarder le jeu'. But, if the French began to possess any part, and especially the maritime parts, 'then it is like they may be too potent neighbours and it will be good to use all convenient means to stay that course'. But Burghley went even further than this: if the French proceed to *seek* the maritime coasts, it were good that Alva were informed secretly of the queen's disposition to help Spain 'by all honourable means,' though he went on to attach prohibitively exacting conditions, such as the reconciliation of the nobility, and deliverance from the inquisition. The best way, Burghley conjectured, would be, 'upon any entry made by the French to demand aid according to former leagues.' In this way the onus would be on Spain, but the vital timing would be English and, with luck the mere intimation of forthcoming mountains and marvels would be sufficient to resolve the danger.

This was high politics at their diabolical best. While this memorial can hardly be interpreted to mean that Elizabeth would really assist Alva to suppress the Netherlands or to defeat the French, it does indicate that she neither intended to permit the French free rein in Flanders, nor to break with Spain on account of the French alliance. In other words, neither France nor Spain could confidently rely upon timely or sufficient help from England, nor could they rest assured of her inactivity. Her intention was to bridle them with uncertainty. This she successfully did, thereby protecting England at the expense of tragedy in France and travail in the Netherlands. France and Spain were no whit more altruistic, but, as de Morvillier predicted, it was the window-gazing queen who won the first round.

The offensive treaty was virtually doomed before the return to France of Montmorency and de Foix. This was not solely on account of the subtler approach of queen Elizabeth, but also because if Charles had ever favoured it – which is uncertain – he did so no longer on account of the multiple restraints upon him. The embassy had therefore made no formal difference, so far as the Netherlands were concerned, and relations with England, though relatively close, continued to be disconcertingly ill-defined. Since the departure for England of Montmorency and de Foix, the Genlis crisis had intervened, and it is uncertain whether their return on 7 July came before or after Charles' decision to provide covert assistance. They appear, however, to have begun work on 10 July with Catherine and Walsingham (while Charles was hunting), and it was not the offensive treaty, but the Alençon marriage which supplied the subject matter of continuing negotiations.[1]

If Charles were either going to make, or become involved in, war with Spain, he still needed to ascertain what was to be the role of England and, if he were unable to support the treaty – primarily desired by Nassau and the huguenots, whose requirements in this respect were straighforward, his most essential need was to clinch the Alençon marriage. This was a more flexible and far-reaching proposition than the treaty, and potentially more advantageous to Elizabeth. As a negotiation, it might serve much the same purpose by substantially restraining Spain, counteracting the worst of the catholic opposition within France, and conciliating the moderates who opposed war for financial and military reasons. Lord Lincoln, in his instructions when he went to France in June, was merely authorised to intimate – which was rather casual – that he had heard the queen say that she was 'not so well used in the other treaty for the Duke of Anjou as was meet . . .' and also that 'the inequality in years cannot but make . . . a full stay'.[2] When, on 13 June, Charles had taken Lincoln to see Catherine who, being ill, received them 'in a wastcote in hir bed,' she asked Smith if Lincoln had 'nothing to speake of the other

---

[1] Digges, 218–19 [2 July 1572], Burghley to Walsingham; 219, 5 July 1572, Burghley to Walsingham; 219–20, 13 July 1572, Walsingham to Burghley; La Mothe, vii, 298–303, 11 & 14 July 1572, Charles to La Mothe.

[2] *CSPF.*, 1572–4, pp. 114–16, 25 May 1572, instructions for the earl of Lincoln.

match,' namely Alençon as opposed to Navarre. Smith replied
nothing 'so far as he could lerne'.[1] This was a disappointment in
France since Montmorency and de Foix had been commissioned
to reopen this negotiation.[2] Elizabeth felt justifiably ill-used in
the matter of the Anjou marriage, though she understood well
enough the nature of the catholic pressure which had traversed it,
even as Catherine understood, in a way which was rare on the
continent, that Elizabeth had to manage both parliament and the
privy council. Elizabeth was therefore unenthusiastic about the
substitution of Anjou's small, pock-marked brother, and – as she
crudely confided to Walsingham just a little later – felt disinclined to 'digest the inconveniences of the same,' if no 'great
commodity' were offered to recompense the absurdity.[3] The
proposition was taken seriously, however, by the privy council,
which favoured the match. Elizabeth therefore proposed a month's
delay to consider the matter and to await the further information
from Montmorency and de Foix after their return to France.
The 'great commodity' was no less than the recovery of Calais
and the re-establishment of the wool staple there which, according to Fogaza, had also been raised in connection with the
offensive treaty.[4] The month's delay had the advantage of
accommodating the council, of entertaining the French in hope
and – perhaps above all – of leaving Elizabeth herself free, *at that
particular moment*, late in June, to bargain with Alva about the
occupation of Flushing.

If Charles was disinclined to face the fundamental issue of war
or peace with Spain, Elizabeth was equally averse from her no
less basic dilemma between the traditional Hapsburg, and a
French alliance; in formal terms – as de Morvillier had pointed
out – she possessed both, at least to some extent. As peace with
Spain would be difficult to sustain within a more clearly defined
French alliance, it could only be obtained at the sacrifice of the
Alençon match – an undeniably dangerous risk. If Elizabeth found

---

[1] Ellis, *Original Letters*, 2nd series, iii, 14–15, 18 June 1572, Smith to Burghley.
[2] La Mothe, v, 12–19, 17 June 1572, La Mothe to Charles IX.
[3] *CSPF.*, *1572–4*, p. 158, 23 July 1572, Elizabeth to Walsingham.
[4] Digges, 218–19 [2 July 1572], Burghley to Walsingham.

the marriage considerably less than irresistible, she was nevertheless reluctantly convinced of its political wisdom – or even necessity. Strong political pressures – including parliament which she could neither easily manage nor lightly ignore, if only for financial reasons, as well as the Ridolphi affair and the victory of Lepanto, all tended to confirm its advisability. But Elizabeth was never impetuous, least of all in expensive matters, and for as long as she could elude joint action with France in the Netherlands, she was likely to delay the marriage. Both were weighty and dangerous issues, best evaded for just so long as ever skill and circumstance permitted.

Thus, the offensive treaty having been discarded or shelved and Catherine having discussed the marriage with Montmorency and de Foix on 10 July, Charles hastened to send Sabran, La Mothe's secretary, back to England. Charles refused to comply with Elizabeth's wish that Alençon should go to England, and the 'compensation' of Calais, even with Alençon as governor for life, was also flatly refused. Instead, Charles reverted to the partition proposal, thereby revealing his disastrous misapprehension of the nature of Elizabeth's foreign policy, and to La Mothe he expressed the wish that Elizabeth 's'embarque avec les Gueux bien avant, et qu'elle se déclare, par ce moyen, ouvertement contre le Roy d'Espagne'. Sabran would explain the reasons why, and also give an account of the arrangements for the Navarre marriage – always Charles' first consideration – which, the letter says, would be in fourteen to eighteen days' time.[1] The inference almost certainly was that, if Elizabeth would agree to declare war upon Spain, Charles would do the same *after* the Bourbon marriage. It was probably also via Sabran that Montmorency, Coligny and de Foix sent long letters to the queen and Burghley saying 'what great things they hope to do,' but *after* the marriage when they 'think they will be able to get the king to agree to anything, as so many of their principal friends will be collected together'. In the meanwhile they urged her to continue to assail the coasts of the Netherlands, whilst they concentrated forces on the land side,

[1] La Mothe, vii, 298–303, 11 & 14 July 1572, Charles to La Mothe.

ready to help Ludovic. This leads one to wonder what verbal assurances might have attended the demise of the treaty; for Elizabeth could be persuaded to *perform* things she would never *contract* to do.[1]

The departure of Sabran either coincided with, or immediately preceded that of Genlis from Paris for Mons. Walsingham said that Genlis left on 12 July with 4,000 foot and 600 horse,[2] although the *prévôt* Morillon, writing from Brussels, said he was still in Paris, in disguise, on 15 July, and that taking leave of the king, Charles 'luy commanda de bien exploicter'.[3] It was because Bricquemault did not want to precede Coligny, who still awaited the marriage, that Genlis had prevailed, and received the command, although he was evidently, and with good reason, regarded as a security risk on account of his impetuous lack of judgement. So he went ahead, a few days after Orange had crossed the Rhine, on 8 July, with the intention of approaching Mons from the north east as soon as he could raise enough money.[4] La Huguerye says that after Genlis' departure Coligny was constantly pressing Charles to let him follow with 'le gros,' estimated at 12,000 foot and 3,000 horse, but that he was always refused until after the Bourbon marriage. Morillon reported from Brussels that there were 8,000 foot and 2,000 horse near Guise; another company near Saint-Dizier, and another in the Vermandois.[5] He was

---

[1] *CSPSp.*, *1568–79*, p. 402, 7 August 1572, intelligence from England; Mondoucet reported from Brussels concentrations of forces on the frontier estimated at 15–1600 horse and 8–10,000 foot; some said more. Gachard, *Notices et extraits*, ii, 517–18, 16 July 1572, Mondoucet to Charles IX.

[2] *CSPF.*, *1572–4*, pp. 145–6, 12 July 1572, Walsingham to Burghley. Petrucci also gave the same number of foot which, he said, echoing the official line, had gone without permission to help Orange who was coming to relieve Nassau at Mons. Desjardins, *Negs. Tosc.*, iii, 798–9, 15 July 1572.

[3] Granvelle, *Correspondance*, iv, 319, 20 & 22 July 1572, Morillon to Granvelle.

[4] G. van Prinsterer, *Archives ou correspondance, série* i, vol. iii, 448; 464–6, 8 July 1572, Orange to Nassau; *CSPF.*, *1572–4*, pp. 145–6, 12 July 1572, Walsingham to Burghley; 154, 18 July 1572, Walsingham to Burghley; La Huguerye, *Mémoires*, i, 110 seq.

[5] Granvelle, *Correspondance*, iv, 301–2, 13 July 1572, Morillon to Granvelle; 308, 16 July 1572, Morillon to Granvelle.

scorchingly critical of Alva's 'no es nada' attitude, as a result of which he had allowed the coastal provinces to fall into the hands of the rebels at the same time as attracting large forces to the southern frontier through his determination to retake Mons, and just when Orange was approaching from across the Rhine. He was really very much afraid that if all those forces, poised on the frontier, should descend upon the Netherlands, they would lose 'tout cest coste'.[1] His fears underline the 'opportunity' argument, and reflect Coligny's point in repeatedly demanding permission to leave with the main force; Alva might then be overthrown but, if he were not, he would be very dangerous.[2] Mondoucet, Charles' agent in Brussels, also thought that military success was feasible provided the French moved quickly.[3] Formally, all these forces were banned from crossing the frontier, and commanded to disperse, which was a part of Charles' policy of public disavowals. These were renewed at the time of Genlis' departure, but Saint-Gouard in Spain was beginning to find Philip II 'encore plus froid que de coustume et fort mélancolicque'.[4]

When Genlis departed about mid-July, Walsingham was as anxious as the French themselves that English support should materialise, and he wrote to Burghley, 'neither may her Majesty, considering those who have gone underhand to Flushing, suffer the cause to be abandoned'.[5] He was well aware how easily 'the cause' could be, if not precisely 'abandoned', at least allowed to fail by default. To begin with, after the return of Lincoln from France, Burghley had written on 5 July of his regrets that 'opinion groweth here of the French King's recoil from the Flanders enterprise,' because 'it breedeth coldness here'.[6] Burghley's letter is vague, and its timing, two weeks before the arrival

[1] Granvelle, *Correspondance*, iv, 30–9, 16 July 1572, Morillon to Granvelle.

[2] Digges, 225, 26 July 1572, Walsingham to Burghley.

[3] Gachard, *Notices et extraits*, ii, 517–18, 16 July 1572, Mondoucet to Charles IX.

[4] Gachard, *Notices et extraits*, ii, 387, 22 July 1572, Saint-Gouard to Charles IX; Granvelle, *Correspondance*, iv, 293–4, 6 or 8 July 1572, Morillon to Granvelle.

[5] *CSPF.*, *1572–4*, pp. 145–6, 12 July 1572, Walsingham to Burghley.

[6] Digges, 219, 5 July 1572, Burghley to Walsingham.

of Sabran on 21 July, makes it difficult to interpret.[1] To what does Charles' recoil refer? It could be his policy of disavowals since the Nassau crisis, but this would really depend upon whether or not he had initially favoured the draft offensive treaty. It is possible that he had not, strongly and publicly advised as he was by everyone but Coligny to avoid war with Spain. Similarly, Lincoln, who left France on 22 June, will have been aware of these strong pressures on Charles. Nor is the nature of the English coldness very plain. It may have arisen because Elizabeth really did not want either the formal treaty, the partition or declared war. Nevertheless, there also appears to have existed, simultaneously like a parallel stream, a basic distrust in Charles' eventual commitment and, if he was afraid of finding himself embarked alone, neither would Elizabeth be talked or tricked into making a unilateral declaration.

On the other hand, Charles' policy, unlike Elizabeth's, was or had been at least in origin aggressive. If he never exactly wanted war with Spain, he did at least at some times, to some extent, and in suitable circumstances, want war in the Netherlands, which was the same thing, but with a different emphasis. But Elizabeth, as de Morvillier had rightly said, needed peace, 'à quoy elle tend comme l'on veoit par toutes ses actions'. Yet again, and paradoxically, one can reason that, undependable as Charles undoubtedly was, he was also 'so far forward as now disguising will not serve'. This was Walsingham's comment on his public prohibitions at the time of the departure of Genlis and Sabran, when Charles was no less anxious than Walsingham himself that Elizabeth should not abandon the cause, but openly declare against Spain, then, while he was unable for domestic and foreign reasons to do so himself.[2]

Thus, if Elizabeth declined to fill, in this way, what others saw as the breach, this was probably less because of her distrust – however real – that Charles would eventually come in, than because it was not necessary for her to do so. Clearly she was not

[1] *CSPSp.*, *1568–79*, p. 402, 7 August 1572, intelligence from England to Alva.

[2] *CSPF.*, *1572–4*, pp. 145–6, 12 July 1572, Walsingham to Burghley.

prepared to shoulder his burdens so long as he might otherwise
be obliged to lighten hers, and she was better placed than he to
avoid or defer the issue of war with Spain in which, from the
agony of his own perplexity, he urgently sought to involve her.

But, if Elizabeth declined to make war on Spain, this did not
meant that she intended to abandon 'the cause'. A steady stream
of help went out from England during the middle of July[1]
but her conception of 'the cause' was somewhat different, and
considerably more complex than that of Walsingham, and her
motives for securing the coastal areas did not correspond very
closely to what he had in mind. If she sent or permitted help,
principally to Flushing and Brill, it was not from the depth of
her concern for 'the cause', whether conceived in terms of
international protestantism or the salvation of the Netherlands
from the tyranny of Alva; still less the restoration to France of
lost provinces. It was rather to exclude Alva, whose military
control of the strategically and commercially vital coastline could
not be permitted by either England or France, and to prevent the
French from doing this for themselves. In securing Flushing and
Brill, Elizabeth both helped to provide for the defence of England,
and for further intervention in the Netherlands if this should
prove to be necessary. It could also be represented as a token of
good faith towards France in sustaining 'the cause'. But, as she
improved her relations with France, Elizabeth sought to propitiate
Spain; and for this purpose Flushing and Brill could be useful as
pawns if, as she proposed to Alva – who was devastatingly criti-
cised for ignoring warnings and failing to garrison Flushing – she
were to hold them in trust *for* the King of Spain.

Whatever Elizabeth may have *said*, or declined to sign, late in
June she was nevertheless planning to launch a considerable offensive. Approximately coinciding with Genlis' return to Hainault,
she had sent Sir Humphrey Gilbert to Flushing followed,

[1] *CSPSp.*, *1568-79*, p. 400, 7 August 1572, intelligence from London to
Alva; *CSPF.*, *1572-4*, p. 155, 20 July 1572, arrival of English forces in the Low
Countries; La Mothe, v, 30-7, 5 July 1572, La Mothe to Charles IX; 40-4,
10 July 1572, La Mothe to Charles IX; 57-61, 20 July 1572, La Mothe to
Charles IX. According to La Mothe there were 2,000 English there.

on 17 July, by captains Chester and Lane, while Pearce went to Brill. Pelham, lieutenant of the ordnance, was to go to Flushing on or soon after 21 July to command the whole force, and he was to be secretly followed by Sir Ralph Sadler, P.C., chancellor of the duchy of Lancaster. Elizabeth, at this point, appears to have had alternative contingency plans. One was a means of extending the expedition, and the other of retrieving it. If it were to be extended, vice-admiral Winter would go with seven of the queen's ships which were being fitted out, and the whole expedition would be commanded by the earl of Warwick (who had commanded at Le Havre in 1562) with the purpose of capturing Middelburg and all the island of Zeeland, thereby controlling communications as far as Bruges and Ghent.[1] Since Elizabeth could no more repudiate the earl of Warwick than Charles could disavow Coligny, it is doubtful whether such an expedition could qualify as 'battles' or, as Elizabeth had put it to Montmorency, 'a very different thing' from a break with the catholic king. It sounds more like the overt action which Charles was then so earnestly requesting, while pleading his own inability to do the same. Yet our informant, Fogaza, declared that they – the English – would not enter into this unless they knew they were going to be supported by France. This brings us full circle to the theme of 'coldness' and distrust, whose disastrous consequences were to be heavily emphasised by Walsingham a week or two later.

The queen's alternative plan involved Pelham and Sadler. They were to inspect the fortifications of Flushing and to inform the queen if it could be strongly held. If not, Pelham was to seek a passport to discuss peace with Alva. If he were inclined to listen, Pelham would turn to Sadler who actually held a commission to agree to a settlement, the re-opening of trade and ports, and the resumption of former commercial privileges. If this could be agreed, then the English would surrender Flushing and other rebel

---

[1] On 7 August 1572, these seven ships were reported to be at Gravesend. *CSPSp.*, *1568–79*, pp. 397–9, 22 July 1572, intelligence from England; 404, 7 August 1572, intelligence from England. There was some disagreement in

places.¹ This does not necessarily mean that Elizabeth really meant to do so. In the first place this commission *could* have been partly to secure them against the atrocious fate of prisoners in an undeclared war.² Besides, such negotiations could easily be interminably extended, or swiftly ruptured by insistence upon impossible conditions. But it was a splendid reinsurance policy while continuing the marriage negotiations with France and, if the French and others were going to occupy Alva's attention in Hainault, then she might profit by the desperately needed resumption of trade, whose severence rendered hostilities with Spain a matter of more than military hazard. Furthermore, she would be covered in this way, against the eventuality of military defeat, by no means improbable, and the move would allow for a maximum flexibility of policy over the next few, obviously critical months. This is a prime example of the way in which Elizabeth manipulated the Netherlands as a regulator of international politics.

The departure of Pelham for the Netherlands was temporarily delayed.³ This was probably on account of the arrival on 20 July of Walsingham's messenger with letters about the marriage, and Charles' attitude to the Netherlands, and the great and dangerous restraints upon him. Next day, La Mothe's secretary, Sabran, arrived to implore Elizabeth to declare against Spain, and to seek to further the Alençon marriage, offering the partition proposal as recompense for what she had so unflatteringly described as the

Flushing between the French and the English; the townsmen evidently preferred the English. Wright, *Queen Elizabeth and her Times*, i, 423–6, 14 July 1572, William Herle to Burghley.

¹ *CSPSp.*, *1568–79*, p. 400, 7 August 1572, intelligence from England to Alva.

² Fogaza reports that Elizabeth attempted to send Portinari, an aged Italian military engineer, who had long been in England. He objected on the grounds that in an undeclared war prisoners were liable to be hanged. Elizabeth laughed and relented, but told him to hold himself in readiness. *CSPSp.*, *1568–79*, p. 399, 22 July 1572, intelligence.

³ *CSPSp.*, *1568–79*, p. 399, 22 July 1572; 400, 7 August 1572, intelligence from England.

'inconvenience' and 'absurdity' of the Alençon match. On the same day, 21 July, one Casimbrot, a secretary of the town of Bruges, also arrived in England representing several German princes, and bearing letters from William of Orange. Orange equally strongly pressed Elizabeth not to desist from supporting the maritime provinces, more especially since the count Palatine and the elector of Brandenburg were ready to come in with forces of foot and horse when they heard that England and France would assail the Netherlands in the west and south. If Elizabeth had ever wanted to join in partitioning the Netherlands, she could have proceeded in July 1572 with at least the minimum of danger and maximum of support. There is no doubt that Alva could have been fairly easily overwhelmed in July or early August had those concerned in the Netherlands' affairs all been shooting at the same mark. But partition, upon the military defeat of Alva, would merely have been grossly provocative, while doing nothing to dispose of the maritime power of Spain, to which England was vulnerable. So it is clear that neither Sabran, Coligny, Orange nor Casimbrot were going to receive any swift, affirmative answers to their several entreaties, before Elizabeth had heard what Pelham and Sadler would report about Flushing, and it was all the easier to delay these affairs since she had departed upon her summer progress and was separated from Burghley, whose absence arrested English transactions.

The prospects, therefore, of England affording a happy issue out of Charles' immediate afflictions, while he felt unable to act himself, were more remote than he showed any signs of having understood. There was, however, no other quarter from which he could seek sufficiently imposing protection from Spain. While Fogaza on the Spanish side, and de Morvillier on the French, clearly understood how Elizabeth was likely to react, Orange, Nassau and Coligny persisted in seeing her as the recent victim of catholic Spain and, as they wished her to be, their great protestant champion. That she had been a victim of Spain was partially true, but they ignored the extent of English dependence upon Spanish commerce, and the fact that an island kingdom had little more than a diversionary advantage in a continental war.

But Coligny, Nassau and Charles all found themselves in a position in which they needed England, thereby handing the queen a notable advantage. It would in no wise serve her purpose to rescue Charles from the predicaments of his inheritance, the consequences of his incompetence, or the alarming pressure of a catholic coalition, so long as he was occupying the attention of Spain.

The old, habitual Spanish catholic pressure, to which Charles' communications with Elizabeth primarily referred, were still the greatest and most alarming restraint upon him, over and above the opposition of the council, the pacific influence of Catherine and the delay of the Bourbon marriage. Catholic pressure had so far failed to thwart this, although the matter of the dispensation – formally desirable but not ultimately indispensable – was still pending, but the catholics had been diabolically skilful in disrupting the Anjou marriage. They could now be expected to employ every weapon to prevent any re-inforcement of Anglo-French relations and, in particular, the royal marriage. Alençon, who was neither lieutenant-general of the kingdom nor heir to the throne, was certainly less dangerous than his brother; and the queen was now manifestly pregnant, which might alter the succession. In the event, the child was a girl, born in October. She died in 1578.[1] Nevertheless, the Alençon marriage would still represent a dangerous dynastic alliance, ignoring religious affiliations – (though Alençon was not very noticeably catholic) which the Spanish and catholic supporters could not passively permit. But, if the pressure had always been strongly applied against the marriages, now all resources were mobilised both to prevent the Netherlands enterprise, in its localised sense, and also the more disastrous, wider war, which was expected to follow. While this was predominantly a renewal of the now historic Franco-Habsburg rivalry, into which the English complication had only recently been injected, such a war was also envisaged in terms of a great ideological, or at least politico-religious struggle of a

---

[1] I am beholden to Miss J. M. Davies for this date.

protestant against a catholic league, which his christian majesty so perversely refused to join. It was in part because these two opposed leagues, while by no means entirely imaginary, were never entirely realised, that a vast international conflagration, though constantly expected, was constantly if narrowly averted until, in altered circumstances, it ultimately materialised as the Thirty Years' War. This was largely because the interests of those on each side were never fully aligned, and none but the disunited Netherlands could really afford to fight.

The grave difficulties created for Charles by this catholic pressure were carefully explained to Elizabeth by Walsingham, who was always a strong sympathiser of Nassau and Coligny. Upon the departure of Genlis he therefore sent a messenger who arrived in England on 20 July to report that, according to the chancellor, Birague, Charles had heard from the emperor 'strongly remonstrating with him for deserting [namely rejecting] the sacred league against a barbarous enemy,' to whom he was allied, and 'for having joined a confederation of enemies of the holy church, urging him very strongly to free himself from such people'. These views were also to be verbally pressed by a 'gentleman' on his way to Spain, by the Venetian ambassador (whose despatches are missing) and, more menacingly by the nuncio, Salviati, who arrived on 24 June for the purpose of bringing the maximum pressure to bear on the king.[1] In spite of repeated efforts to induce him to do so, Charles had never joined the League. France was not vulnerable to Turkey, and the emperor, whose personal and political catholicism was not beyond reproach, was hardly a danger to France, though he might be an adverse influence. Finally there was no such 'confederation' of enemies of the holy church, though Nassau certainly strove for a confederation of the enemies of the King of Spain which, if centred upon catholic France, was really not the same thing. Salviati, however, was an influential and dangerous enemy, and so was Don Diego de Zúñiga, Philip's ambassador in Paris,

[1] *CSPSp.*, *1568–79*, pp. 400–1, 7 August 1572, intelligence from London to Alva.

who demanded the arrest of Genlis and threatened that if war were to be avoided, help for Nassau – just about to be conveyed by Genlis – must be prohibited.[1] It could not safely be assumed that this was an idle threat, and it very likely explains Charles' disavowal measures at the time of Genlis' departure, his ostensible closure of the Picardy frontier,[2] a proclamation recalling French subjects from Mons and forbidding others to go, and the prohibition of the purchase of goods taken at Flushing, upon which Coligny evidently depended, at least to some extent, for his expenses.[3] The Spanish were not deceived by this monotonous bluff, but it suited them not to call it. Philip II, who declared that the French protested their peaceful intentions everywhere, in Vienna, Rome and Madrid, therefore refrained from betraying any sign of his annoyance at Saint-Gouard's reiterated assurances in Madrid; and Mondoucet in Brussels paid Alva in the same coin.[4]

There were also other less obvious but more sinister signs of mounting catholic pressure at this time. De Retz, for instance, whom Charles allegedly detested, was said to be not only very pro-Spanish, and beholden to the King of Spain, but also 'intrigato con i Guisi'.[5] This, in the circumstances, probably meant primarily madame de Nemours, the duke's mother, and Aumale.

[1] Gachard, *Notices et extraits*, ii, 384, 8 July 1572, Charles to Saint-Gouard.

[2] Champion, *Charles IX, la France et le contrôle de l'Espagne*, ii, 79, 8 July 1572; CSPF., 1572–4, pp. 145–6, 12 July 1572, Walsingham to Burghley. Granvelle, *Correspondance*, iv, 293, 6 or 8 July 1572, Morillon to Granvelle.

[3] CSPSp., 1568–79, p. 404, 7 August 1572, intelligence from London to Alva. Coligny is said to have received 150,000 crowns from this source via Louis of Nassau, and Orange to have received 100,000.

[4] Kervyn de Lettenhove, *Les Huguenots*, ii, 488, 8 July 1572, Charles to Saint-Gouard; Gachard, *Correspondance de Philippe II*, ii, 263, 24 June 1572, Alva to Philip II; 266, 30 June 1572, Philip II to Alva; 267, 14 July 1572, Philip II to Alva; 270, 21 July 1572, Philip II to Alva; 271, 2 August 1572, Philip II to Alva. Zúñiga also warned Alva that he thought help would be sent; ibid., 268–9, 18 July 1572, Alva to Philip II.

[5] Desjardins, *Negs. Tosc.*, iii, 787, 26 June 1572. Petrucci had already commented in 1571 upon de Retz' pro-Spanish sentiments, p. 702, 22 August 1571.

De Retz was an intimate of the duke of Savoy who would be important in the event of war and Savoy was not only strongly pro-Spanish, but also a rancorous enemy of Coligny since his marriage, in 1571, to Jacqueline de Montbel, a rich widow of Bourg-en-Bresse, whom the duke had intended for one of his favourites.[1] De Retz's cousin, Jérôme de Gondi was, notoriously, Zúñiga's informant of council affairs, and personally known to Philip II who is reported in August to have encouraged his banking activities by crediting him with 3,000 écus.[2] Philip II was also seeking at this time to tighten his contacts with the Guises, conceivably because Lorraine was away in Rome and, in mid-July approached Alva about the importance of co-operating with them, presumably in order to arrest the nascent enterprise of the Netherlands and consequent war, though this is not specified.[3] Lorraine, perhaps inevitably, was said to be intriguing in Rome, where the grand duke of Tuscany's loan of 100,000 crowns to Alva was allegedly arranged.[4] However this may be, Alva himself admitted to having received a warning from Lorraine (of whom nevertheless, his opinion was most disagreeable) to be on his guard against imminent trouble from France. Lorraine was also suspected of having 'practised' in Rome to obstruct the dispensation, which was crucial since Alva's forces were expected to be ready to invest Mons by mid-August. Until then Philip was alarmingly vulnerable – in his own estimation – to a combination of Netherlands' French, German and English forces, if such collaboration were possible, or were to be achieved in time. Philip, no less then Elizabeth and Charles, tended to exaggerate the danger from abroad; an attribute of fear, as well as a necessary precaution.

There was also another reason why 'the stay of their lingering'

[1] Desjardins, Negs. Tosc., iii, 647, 26 January 1571.
[2] Champion, Charles IX, la France et le contrôle de l'Espagne, ii, 46, 57–8, 10 August 1572.
[3] Gachard, Correspondance de Philippe II, ii, 267–8, 18 July 1572, Alva to Philip II.
[4] CSPF., 1572–4, p. 154, 18 July 1572, Walsingham to Burghley; Desjardins, Negs. Tosc., iii, 789–95, 7 July 1572.

in the Netherlands matter was important to Philip, and also to France between mid-July and mid-August, namely that 'they [the French] wish Don John of Austria onwards on his voyage towards Morea before they make any demonstration to be dealers in the said enterprise'. For this reason they 'made fair weather' with the Spanish ambassador, who pretended to believe them. It should be noted that this observation was made at the time of the departure of Genlis to the Netherlands and Sabran to England.[1] Otherwise, with all the forces intended for the summer campaign against Turkey, Don John could and would have sailed from Messina and fallen upon the undefended provinces of Languedoc and Provence.[2] This was the sanction behind Zúñiga's threats and, while it lasted, the principal danger which Charles had to fear.[3] As early as 17 May – about the time of Nassau's departure – Philip had ordered Don John not to create a godsent opportunity for France by moving the Spanish fleet and forces away from Messina to the Levant.[4] Don John was not convinced of the wisdom of this partly because, by mid-June, most of his supplies and munitions were already in Corfu, and partly for fear that Venice, which had supplied twice as many ships at Lepanto as Spain, might – with or without French mediation – conclude a separate peace with Turkey. This was a serious consideration and one which France had not overlooked.[5] Already at the end of December 1571, Killigrew had reported that Charles was secretly practising in Constantinople to procure peace for the Venetians, and war against Philip 'whereby he might the better proceed with the enterprise of Flanders, to which he is moved by the Prince of

---

[1] *CSPF.*, 1572–4, pp. 145–6, 12 July 1572, Walsingham to Burghley; 154, 18 July 1572, Walsingham to Burghley.

[2] Serrano, *Lepanto*, i, 317–21, 12 June 1572, Don John to Philip II; Granvelle, *Correspondance*, iv, 293, 6 or 8 July 1572, Morillon to Granvelle.

[3] Writing on 16 July from Brussels, Morillon mistakenly believed Don John to have sailed, and was very nervous of the consequences. Granvelle, *Correspondance*, iv, 308–9, 16 July 1572, Morillon to Granvelle.

[4] Serrano, *Lepanto*, i, 294–5, 17 May 1572, Philip II to Don John; 305–9, 2 June 1572, Philip II to Zúñiga in Rome.

[5] Digges, 222–3, 18 July 1572, two letters, Walsingham to Leicester and to Burghley.

Orange and his own Huguenots'.[1] Again, in July 1572, Walsingham alleged that Charles was seeking to mediate between Turkey and Venice, while the Turks tried to bribe Charles to make war on Spain.[2] Don John maintained that, if necessary, he could return fairly quickly, so even his departure did not guarantee the safety of the southern provinces of France, two of which were, in any case, vulnerable also from the mainland of Spain. Don John's delay created tension with the pope, and gave rise to sensational rumours in Rome that Spain meant to declare war on France and therefore, if undesirable in one respect, did serve to sustain the Spanish catholic pressure on Charles.[3]

Philip refused to be overruled by Don John, or directed by the pope because, as he clearly stated, he regarded the trouble at home as much more serious than anything in the Levant. On the other hand, he could ill-afford to risk the collapse of the League, to alienate the pope, or to discourage Venice, upon whose naval contributions he was inconveniently dependent. In this respect, the relationship of Venice to Turkey was not unlike that of England to Spain or, more precisely, the Spanish Netherlands. So, as the size of Philip's Messina fleet exceeded the amount of his obligation, he finally decided to let Don John depart with 64 galleys – enough to meet his undertaking – and to retain the rest; news which was received in Rome with great rejoicing on 25 July.[4]

Philip made the most of this decision magnifying, for papal consumption, his sacrifice for the sake of the League, emphasising the religious aspects of the Netherlands trouble in order to impress upon the pope his christian duty to provide financial assistance for the overthrow of heresy. The big Tuscan loan to Alva, said to have been engineered in Rome, actually pre-dates this letter,

[1] *CSPF., 1569–71*, p. 579, 28 December 1571, Killigrew to Burghley.

[2] Serrano, *Lepanto*, i, 317–21, 12 June 1572, Don John to Philip II.

[3] Serrano, *Lepanto*, i, 348, 26 June 1572, Zúñiga to Philip II.

[4] Serrano, *Lepanto*, i, 363–70, 4 July 1572, Philip II to Don John; ii, 355–6, 22 July 1572, Philip II to Zúñiga; 358–61, 1 August 1572, Zúñiga to Philip II, Rome. Don John arrived in Corfu on 9 August 1572; Ibid., 372–3, 26 August 1572, Don John to Marc Antonio Colonna.

but its theme was probably an habitual Spanish incantation. Philip also applauded the despatch of Salviati, expressly to try to prevent a rupture between France and Spain, albeit more for the preservation of the League than the protection of the Netherlands. Furthermore, Philip II urged Don Juan de Zúñiga in Rome to ensure that the pope sustained his pressure on Charles to keep the peace because, he added menacingly, and in his own hand, if he could not find some way of altering French policy, he would be unable to attend to the affairs of the League.[1] This significant letter, dated 14 July 1572, shows exactly what Philip II was thinking at the time of the departure of Genlis and Sabran and, like the comment of Alva in Brussels on 18 July that the king of France had not yet declared himself – waiting upon events – indicates that the Spanish were constantly, if not daily, expecting war – with or without a declaration. It also sharpens the suspicion that the pope may have been among those who did, very shortly, find a brutally sensational way of altering not only French policy but, in the event, the history of Europe.[2]

These were the reasons for which Charles excused his inaction to Elizabeth, having no alternative but to temporise, while assisting Genlis as covertly as possible. Otherwise he could neither expect to restrain Coligny, nor hope to elicit the support of England, which was never vouchsafed with frank generosity.

[1] '. . . si yo no me aseguro por alguna via de que franceses no lleben el camino que hasta aqui, no podré atender a las cosas de lebante con la voluntad y fuerças que yo deseo'. Serrano, *Lepanto*, ii, 345–8, 14 July 1572, Philip II to Zúñiga; 350–1, a second letter of the same date to Zúñiga; 362–9, 19 August 1572, Zúñiga to Philip II.

[2] Serrano, *Lepanto*, ii, 345–9, 14 July 1572, Philip II to Zúñiga; 350–1, a second letter of the same date to Zúñiga; Gachard, *Correspondance de Philippe II*, ii, 269, 18 July 1572, Alva to Philip II; Champion, *Charles IX, la France et le contrôle de l'Espagne*, ii, 49.

XVI

The Collapse of the Netherlands Enterprise

SINCE, IN mid-July 1572, Alva was not yet in a strong position[1] and Mons could have held out for a short while,[2] the Netherlands enterprise might yet have prospered had Genlis not more than realised the worst apprehensions of those who had doubted his judgement and ability by disobeying his instructions and bungling his assignment. According to La Huguerye at least a dozen messengers were sent to remind him of his orders to seize Cateau-Cambrésis, whereby to ensure communications and facilitate the passage of further forces, and thereafter to approach the prince of Orange via Philippeville to the east. But, instead of taking Cateau-Cambrésis, against his orders he made straight for Mons, where he was hotly received, and overwhelmed with heavy losses on 17 July. Alva claimed that the victory went to his son, Don Fadrique; others that he was a safe league away, 'qui est le milleur corcelet,' Morillon commented with blistering contempt, 'que l'on scauroit avoir'.[3] The whole episode had occupied only a few days, and disrupted all existing calculations, which were based upon a need for time.

[1] Gachard, *Correspondance de Philippe II*, ii, 266–7, 2 July 1572, Alva to Philip II; 268–9, 18 July 1572, Alva to Philip II.

[2] La Huguerye, *Mémoires*, i, 112 seq.

[3] Granvelle, *Correspondance*, iv, 308–18, 16 July 1572, Morillon to Granvelle; 337, 28 July 1572, Morillon to Granvelle; 319, 20 & 22 July 1572, Morillon to Granvelle; Kervyn de Lettenhove, *Les Huguenots*, ii, 493 seq., and *Relations*, vi, 459–60, 18 July 1572, *avis* from Antwerp; *CSPSp.*, *1568–79*, p. 402, 7 August 1572, unsigned letter from London to Alva. According to Orange, Louis reported that 3–400 of Genlis' men had been killed and 4–500 captured. G. van Prinsterer, *Archives ou correspondance*, série i, vol. iii, 485–8, 5 August 1572, Orange to his brother, count Jean. Another report from Antwerp put the dead

The unnecessary defeat of Genlis through his own perversity was not only a disaster for 'the cause', but regenerated, in an even more acute form, the political crisis of the last few weeks, closely affecting, in different ways, Charles, Coligny, Spain and England. It heightened the intensity of Charles' embarrassing predicament, and the urgency of reaching some decisive solution when, for the same reasons, he still needed time. It therefore also intensified his essential need of English help and support – which might have conciliated moderate French opinion – since war with Spain was one long step nearer. Even if Charles made no formal declaration, he could not indefinitely dissociate himself from events around him, and the restraint of Coligny became increasingly difficult. The problems, previously relating to Nassau, who was a foreign prince, and to Genlis who was not socially significant, were now centred upon Coligny, who was neither foreign nor undistinguished. Owing to the seizure of documents from the captured Genlis and the seigneur de Lagny, Charles was now irreversibly implicated and, if and when Coligny led substantial forces into the Netherlands, war with Spain could hardly be avoided. The big problem, therefore, was how to prevent this.

The sands were not completely spent. Three more weeks might yet secure the Bourbon marriage and even, as Charles mistakenly hoped, the support of England, if not also the Alençon marriage. To work fast for these three things and restrain Coligny, was all that Charles could do, while Mondoucet in the Netherlands, and Saint-Gouard in Madrid swiftly sought to minimise the crisis by offering congratulations upon Alva's defeat of Genlis.[1] Philip, and his servants in the Netherlands, passively accepted this for what it was worth.[2] Charles gave orders that any compromising

---

at 1800. *CSPF.*, *1572–4*, p. 153, 18 July 1572, news from Antwerp. The news from Mons might have reached Antwerp by 18 July, but the same document mentions the reactions in Paris, for which there had certainly not been time. Either it was begun on 18 July and completed later, or else the date is an error.

[1] Gachard, *Correspondance de Philippe II*, ii, 268–9, 18 July 1572, Alva to Philip II; 269–70, 19 July 1572, Albornoz to Zayas; 271, 2 August 1572, Philip II to Alva; Kervyn de Lettenhove, *Les Huguenots*, ii, 501.

[2] Gachard, *Correspondance de Philippe II*, ii, 270, 21 July 1572, Philip II to Alva.

documents should be disclaimed as forgeries, when Mondoucet warned him that they were being scrutinised for evidence of his complicity which, it seems, was not lacking.[1] Thus Albornoz, Alva's secretary, writing to the Spanish secretary Zayas, claimed to possess 'une lettre du roi de France qui vous frapperait de stupeur, si vous la voyiez; mais, pour le moment, il convient de n'en rien dire'.[2] According to Gachard, the letter in question was that of 27 April 1572 from Charles to Nassau, which would certainly have seemed much less innocuous or ambiguous in Brussels in July – after the events at Valenciennes and Mons – than textually it was, or had appeared to be in April. One cannot help wondering, however, whether there were not something more specifically incriminating among other papers, allegedly indicating 'lignes et intelligences pour souslever les Pays Bas'. Genlis certainly enhanced this impression, but then he is said to have been tortured. Morillon reported him to be uttering 'merveilles' and, a few days later [qu'il] 'jase comme ung geay'. He had proclaimed, among other things, that Coligny would come with 100,000 men. If no one was likely to believe such a figure, there was every reason to suppose that he would shortly do his redoubtable best. Whether from the documents or from Genlis it was held that the French would relieve Mons and proceed to Brussels, which was plausible since it had already been attempted. According to Morillon, they now anticipated little resistance because the way was prepared by intelligence within the towns. Documents apparently showed that Lille and Tournay had been 'pratiqués' and according to the 'complot', the catholics were to be murdered in each place.[3] This might well be gossip, fear, or hostile bravado but, whether true or false, it was dangerously incendiary.

If, for the moment, as Albornoz said, Charles, should not be

---

[1] Kervyn de Lettenhove, *Les Huguenots*, ii, 499; *Bulletin de la Commission royale d'Histoire*, série ii, vol. iv, 342–3, 12 August 1572, Charles to Mondoucet.

[2] Gachard, *Correspondance de Philippe II*, ii, 269–70, 19 July 1572, Albornoz to Zayas.

[3] Granvelle, *Correspondance*, iv, 328–9, 27 July 1572, Morillon to Granvelle; 339–41, 4 August 1572, Morillon to Granvelle.

accused, this was because Alva was not yet ready; in a sense he was embarrassed by his own premature victory, which events had precipitated. Besides, as Alva said, Charles had not yet declared himself, which was because he was not yet ready either. Alva therefore sent his agent, Gomicourt, to Paris 'to know whether Charles will avowe Genlis' enterprise or not'. In the circumstances, after all his protestations of peace, before the Bourbon marriage, before he knew that Don John had permission to quit Messina, and while the role of England was still ill-defined, Charles, albeit with ever increasing ignominy, could only accept this face-saving opportunity to continue his disavowals.[1]

The defeat and disavowal of Genlis affected Coligny no less than the king. As the only significant spokesman of those who either wanted war, or were convinced of its inevitability, Coligny became the sole focus of political, personal and doctrinal controversy, fear and hatred, thus intensifying the personal danger which had virtually excluded him from Paris and from court since 1562. This was alarmingly emphasised by the violently catholic citizens of Paris – where Coligny then was – who, 'understanding of Genlis' overthrow, conceived souche joye therof as that theye spared not to make open declaration of the same by generall procession bankettes and souche lyke congratulations'.[2] It is hardly surprising, therefore, that the protestants should have felt – as they informed Charles who was at Blois at the end of July and, according to Walsingham, did not answer – that unless their enterprise in the Netherlands succeeded, their cause was desperate. 'If Orange quail,' as Walsingham put it, Charles would be powerless to protect them and maintain his edicts, a royal failure which had already been, for the protestants, a basic issue of the three civil wars. In other words, they were afraid both of the possible turn of events and, more directly of

[1] *CSPF.*, *1572–4*, p. 153, ?18 July 1572, news from Antwerp; La Huguerye, *Mémoires*, i, 126. La Huguerye seems to be alone in saying this specifically, but one can deduce nothing else from Charles' conduct.

[2] Kervyn de Lettenhove, *Relations*, vi, 459–60; *CSPF.*, *1572–4*, p. 153, ?18 July 1572, news from Antwerp.

Alva's revenge if they did not take pre-emptive action by going to William's assistance with adequate royal support.

Coligny was not only anxious about the protestants in France and Orange to whom he was bound by treaty obligations. He was also anxious about the hostage prisoners at Mons who, in view of Charles' disavowals, were liable to execution; anxiety which can only have been increased by the torture of Genlis who confessed – whether truly or otherwise – to holding a royal commission, and the prisoners themselves affirmed that they had acted with the king's assent (*licence*).[1] Coligny evidently proposed to ransom them, at which Alva derisively laughed and requested instructions upon how to treat them, meanwhile following his own naturally cruel propensities.[2] This was why, according to Petrucci, Coligny sent for 'il Gondino' – Jérôme de Gondi, Don Diego's informant – roughly requiring him to find this ambassador and inform him that if he did not obtain the release of the prisoners, he could expect to be murdered in Paris, and no Spaniard would be safe in France.[3] This is not recorded by anyone else and may simply be a loose rendering of an angry message. But, if true, it is important, especially in view of the intention, alleged by Morillon, to murder catholics in the Netherlands' towns, and of the disquieting anti-protestant manifestations in Paris. But, true or false, the mere existence of such reports suggests a mounting tension and atmosphere of impending commotion.

Whether or not Zúñiga, the Spanish ambassador, took the threat seriously, Genlis' defeat, albeit a Spanish victory, paradoxically also intensified the crisis for Spain and her supporters, by increasing the apparent imminence of war both before Alva was ready and just after Don John had been authorised to leave Messina. Don John is likely to have received Philip's letter of

[1] Granvelle, *Correspondance*, iv, 372, 16 August 1572, Morillon to Granvelle.
[2] Desjardins, *Negs. Tosc.*, iii, 800, 31 July 1572; La Huguerye, *Mémoires*, i, 127.
[3] Desjardins, *Negs. Tosc.*, iii, 800, 13 July 1572. Mondoucet tried to obtain better terms for the prisoners. Gachard, *Notices et extraits*, ii, 520, 17 August 1572, Mondoucet to Charles IX.

4 July very close to the time of Genlis' defeat.[1] It was therefore all the more urgent, as Philip had said to his ambassador in Rome, 'to alter French policy'; to thwart the Bourbon marriage; to frustrate co-operation, and especially the dynastic alliance with England, and to restrain Coligny – the one anxiety that Philip and Charles had in common – for once Coligny crossed the frontier, the situation, for both of them, would be beyond control.

It was not difficult for Coligny, who had lived so dangerously for so long, to realise that, in the last resort, his elimination from the scene was the only way of preventing this. The magnitude of the Genlis crisis should therefore not be underestimated.

Philip's personal reaction was, as one might expect, in tune with the extreme measures which – if not always well defined or clearly specified – he had consistently advocated since before the civil wars began. So had the papacy. Upon this occasion Philip informed Rossano, the nuncio in Spain, that the huguenot defeat in the Netherlands was greater than had been represented because many of their most valorous leaders had been killed or captured. Thus, if Charles wished to purge his kingdom of his enemies, *now was the time.* In co-operation with Spain – 'se tenesse intelligenza' – the nuncio continued, the rest of the huguenots could be destroyed, more particularly since the admiral was in Paris where the people were catholic and loyal 'dove potria se volesse facilmente levarselo dinnanzi per sempre'. Philip, the nuncio went on, would then employ all his strength and resources to liberate the kingdom – what he had hoped to do in 1562, and Catherine's lifelong nightmare, which makes sense of the whole of her career – and restore it to its pristine splendour and safety, from which would also proceed the safety of his own. Philip intended, according to the nuncio, that both he himself and Alva should put this invitation to Charles. In other words, he would conquer France, which Alva was always more prepared to undertake than any enterprise in England. As this letter, dated 5 August 1572, was addressed to the cardinal di Como in Italy,

[1] Serrano, *Lepanto*, i, 363–70, 4 July 1572, Philip II to Don John.

it is doubtful, for reasons of timing, if the invitation was ever delivered.[1] But there could be no clearer statement of the extreme political catholic policy, which had advanced from a rather general notion of strong measures in 1560, through the Triumvirate of 1561, to the policy of 'elimination', as expressed at Bayonne, and attempted by Lorraine in 1568. It had long been the policy of Alva, of which Egmont and Horne were the symbols – but by no means the only victims – and the Netherlands' *bannis* the result. It was believed by La Huguerye (though almost certainly in a mistaken form), and had, according to his own testimony, most recently been adopted by Salviati, whose principal mission in France was to avert an invasion of the Netherlands and the outbreak of Franco-Spanish war. This also reflected the unflinching policy of the late Pius V which, if more on account of the League than the Lord, was also sustained by his successor Gregory XIII. This is not to allege that Philip II or even Salviati, who was there, organised either the murder of Coligny – which had so often been attempted before – or the massacre which followed in the rage, panic and heat of an August night. What happened in or to France was of secondary interest to Philip, while the diversion from the Netherlands of the huguenot forces was paramount. Without them Charles could do him little harm, and indeed would no longer be much inclined to harm him at all, since the Netherlands enterprise – if not the revolt – would be totally dissipated.

One possible way, at least of delaying if not diverting these forces, was to obstruct the dispensation for the Bourbon marriage. In this respect every week counted, since Alva was expected to be ready for campaigning by the middle of August. Charles had been given some cause to hope for the dispensation, so he wrote from Blois on 31 July 1572 to Lorraine, who was held to have been 'practising' in Rome since his arrival there on 13 June. Now, encountering a changed attitude, Charles began to suspect that 'quelqu'un n'ait diverty sa dicte saincteté'.[2] Charles also

---

[1] Theiner, *Annales Ecclesiastici*, i, 327-8, 5 August 1572, Rossano to cardinal di Como.

[2] B.N., Mss. fr. 3951, f. 142, 31 July 1572, Charles to Lorraine.

wrote to Ferrals, his ambassador in Rome, protesting against the pope's conditional insistence upon Navarre's conversion. He claimed that the marriage was the only way to 'ramener' Navarre, attach him to the crown, and prevent him from becoming the huguenot 'chef de party'. This was undoubtedly true, at the time, but the argument was superseded by the Netherlands crisis, since to delay the marriage appeared to be the best way of delaying the invasion; but not for much longer. Charles therefore sent Chavigny to Rome, ordered Lorraine to exert himself helpfully, and Ferrals – if the pope remained obdurate – to conduct the cardinals of Lorraine and Ferrara to the pontiff to inform him that he, Charles, would be obliged to take essential measures for the protection of the state, and to proceed with the marriage, which he was fully determined to do. He required Ferrals to expedite Chavigny's return, once he had an answer, and he roundly declared to Lorraine that 'favourable ou non jay resolu et desliberé de passer outre'. Three weeks was about the minimum time in which an answer could be expected from Rome. The fact that the marriage was celebrated only eighteen days later illustrates both the urgency of the timing and, for once, the king's resolution.[1] Charles, of course, was correct in his suspicions: Don Juan de Zúñiga was doing everything in the power of Spain to obstruct the dispensation which Philip, so he told the pope, would regard as a scandal; indeed he marvelled that such a thing could even be discussed.[2]

But, if Philip was primarily concerned about the Netherlands and France, as he had categorically stated to Zúñiga, the pope was primarily concerned about the maintenance of the League. For this reason, though no direct evidence confirms it, he was probably disinclined to risk a definitive breach with France lest Charles' ambassador in Constantinople should succeed in mediating peace

---

[1] Chavigny arrived in Rome on 12 August 1572. Serrano, *Lepanto*, ii, 367, 19 August 1572, Zúñiga to Philip II; B.N., Mss. fr. 3951, ff. 139 verso-42, 31 July 1572, Charles to Ferrals; ff. 39 verso-40 gives the terms which the pope would recognise for Navarre's conversion.

[2] Serrano, *Lepanto*, ii, 362-9, 19 August 1572, Zúñiga to Philip II.

between Venice and the Turk, who was reported to be making large-scale preparations and offering Charles substantial sums to break with Spain. In this respect, however, Franco-Turkish interests no longer coincided, and Turkey like England sought to provide for her own protection by forcing France to fight her battles or otherwise deflect and absorb the dangerous energies of Spain. Peace between Venice and Turkey would be all the more dangerous to the pope since the emperor had already concluded a truce. He therefore no longer assisted the League, within which the pope had hoped to unite the Empire, France and Spain, a quixotic ideal remote from the realities of European politics.

If the restraint of Coligny was, for Charles, the most immediate problem arising from the defeat of Genlis, the major question upon which, in a sense, all else depended, was the response of queen Elizabeth. Thus de Fogaza later informed Alva from London that upon the receipt of the news of Genlis' defeat Charles was closeted with Montmorency for over two hours, and then despatched La Mole to England.[1] La Mole was a servant and favourite of Alençon and to conceal the fact that he was urgently sent by the king on account of the Genlis crisis, it was given out by La Mothe that he came as the duke's representative. Not that his master's marriage was an insignificant part of his mission. Indeed, although he also requested every scrap of news about Elizabeth's attitude to the Netherlands, the marriage was strongly pressed in Charles' letter of 20 July conveyed by La Mole to La Mothe. If only this could be accomplished then, from the Spanish point of view, England would be regarded as gained by France.[2] But Elizabeth used the marriage negotiation to play for time in the matter of the Netherlands. Having imposed her

---

[1] Charles was probably at Montmorency's house at l'Isle-Adam near Pontoise, whence the duke wrote all the operative letters relating to the mission. Charles' personal contribution was purely formal. La Mothe, vii, 303-5, 20 July 1572, Charles to La Mothe; *CSPSp.*, *1568-79*, p. 403, 7 August 1572, intelligence from London; *CSPF.*, *1572-4*, p. 158, 23 July 1572, Montmorency to Elizabeth; B.M., Mss. Cotton Vespasian F. vi, f. 123, 20 July 1572, Charles to Elizabeth; f. 127, 23 July 1572, Montmorency to Burghley.

[2] La Mothe, vii, 303-5, 20 July 1572, Charles to La Mothe.

month's delay, towards the end of June, she had been insisting, about the time of the arrival of Sabran on 21 July (five days before the news in England of Genlis' defeat, and six days before the appearance of La Mole) that she could not accept the disparity of age, and Alençon's diminutive stature and pock-marked face.[1] This may have been true but, more significantly, as we have seen, it did not suit her at that crucial moment either to decide about the marriage or to declare against the King of Spain. Thus she explained to Walsingham in a letter of 23 July that when Montmorency was in England, it was because she had been 'so laboured unto by her Council and by her estates in Parliament for the necessity of her marriage . . . that she [had] yielded to take further consideration of the matter', a euphemistic reference to her month's delay. The fact remained that she could not find herself 'void of doubt and misliking'.[2] But, according to Elizabeth herself, upon the arrival of Sabran (21 July) La Mothe swiftly requested an audience – before she could communicate with Walsingham again – and 'in respect to the desire which she sees in the King and the Queen Mother she has thought convenient to enlarge her answer in some part'.[3] Thus the letter of 23 July was 'stayed', as Elizabeth said. By this, she meant, with calculated equivocation, both communicated and also superseded by another of 27 July, in which she pushed the chamber door slightly ajar. She now allowed that the matter of religion could be settled, but again began to insist upon an interview, gallantly offering, if she thereafter rejected Alençon, to assume 'la plus grande moictie de la honte' while, publicly, they would both proclaim the difficulty to have been religious. Burghley, writing to Walsingham on the same day, clearly stated that Elizabeth 'really found the marriage necessary'; what she minded was the opinion of others.[4] Alençon had already intimated his willingness to go to England but this was not customary, and Charles refused.

[1] La Mothe, v, 57–61, 20 July 1572, La Mothe to Charles IX; Digges, 226–8, 23 July 1572, Elizabeth to Walsingham.
[2] *CSPF.*, 1572–4, pp. 158–9, 23 July 1572, Elizabeth to Walsingham.
[3] *CSPF.*, 1572–4, pp. 159–60, 27 July 1572, Elizabeth to Walsingham.
[4] Digges, 230, 27 July 1572, Burghley to Walsingham.

The French, as La Mothe flamboyantly put it, were unwilling to risk the infliction of 'ung extrême crèvecœur et d'ung perdurable regret'. Catherine, however, was less sensitive to this, and told Walsingham that she would willingly consent 'if she were assured that from it 'there might grow a liklihood of liking'.[1]

During his month at the English court La Mole evidently made real progress since, at the time of his departure, even the cautious Burghley was by no means unhopeful, and made so bold as to write to Alençon albeit 'not accustomed to write to his superiors, being stranger princes'.[2] Even the subject of Calais had evidently been resumed since, according to Alva's agent, de Guaras, it was agreed to establish the wool staple at Calais and Rouen, presumably a compromise upon the demand for Calais by way of 'recompence' for the 'inconvenience' of the marriage.[3] Any concession on Calais indicates an extreme French desire for the marriage, certainly their strongest defence against Spain, and presumably the most promising means of committing Elizabeth to an active Netherlands policy. La Mole's secret and public missions were therefore intimately connected.

It seems probable that Elizabeth had found it 'convenient to enlarge her answer' relating to the marriage, less 'in respect', as she had said, 'of the French desire', most recently conveyed by Sabran, than on account of the receipt in England, on 26 July, of the news of the defeat of Genlis.[4] If this did not exactly create a crisis for Elizabeth, it obliged her to reconsider her Flushing policy, and therefore to recall Pelham and Sadler because, if the French and Spanish were about to occupy each other in Brabant there would be no need for her to commit herself by sending an imposing expedition under the earl of Warwick and admiral Winter with royal ships. Sadler, is said to have landed 'very secretly' near Sandwich on 30 July, followed by Pelham, in

[1] La Mothe, v, 87, 11 August 1572, La Mothe to Charles IX; *CSPF., 1572–4,* p. 167, 10 August 1572, Walsingham to Smith.

[2] *CSPF., 1572–4,* p. 171, 22 August 1572, Burghley to Alençon.

[3] *CSPSp., 1568–79,* p. 409, 30 August 1572, de Guaras to Alva.

[4] This news seems to have taken unusually long to reach England, but there had to be a ship and favourable winds.

disguise, at Gravesend; 'secrets' which were immediately known to La Mothe and Alva's agent in London. Pelham apparently reported that Flushing could not be defended without sending a fleet powerful enough to resist Alva's.[1] Reflecting the anxiety of France, La Mothe expressed this more positively, stating that Flushing *could* be held if Elizabeth would assume its protection. But he encountered suspicions in England that Strozzi meant to take it, with his mysterious fleet, and this, La Mothe said, would alienate (*refroidir*) the English, who did not want the French to operate at all in that quarter of the Netherlands.[2]

Clearly Elizabeth had first to see Pelham and Sadler before receiving either La Mole or one Casimbrot, a representative of La Marck, who also arrived on 27 July, to request men and money as the beggars had obtained an entry into Holland by which stores could be introduced. Elizabeth's relative inaccessibility, while on progress, facilitated this manoeuvring, and Casimbrot went straight to court fifty miles away, and La Mole was obliged to wait.[3] He did, however, see Burghley – probably his best ally – on 28 July very secretly at 11 p.m., 'when all folks were asleep'. He left London for the court on 1 August and had – again very secretly – a nocturnal audience on 3 August in the presence of only La Mothe, Leicester and Smith.[4]

La Mole's secret mission is uniquely reported by de Fogaza. According to him, La Mole was to inform the queen that Charles 'could not openly declare himself in the matter of Flanders *as she desired*, for many reasons', which postulated – but for which we

[1] *CSPSp.*, *1568–79*, p. 402, 7 August 1572, intelligence from London addressed to Alva; La Mothe, v, 76–9, 3 August 1572, La Mothe to Charles IX. Four days between the receipt in England of the news of Genlis' defeat and the arrival of Sadler suggests either that these dates are not quite accurate, or else that Sadler did not wait to be recalled.

[2] *CSPSp.*, *1568–79*, p. 404, 7 August 1572, intelligence from London addressed to Alva; La Mothe, v, 88–9, 11 August 1572, La Mothe to Charles IX.

[3] *CSPSp.*, *1568–79*, p. 402, 7 August 1572, intelligence from London addressed to Alva.

[4] How Alva's agent learnt of this remains a mystery unless he suborned Elizabeth's one lady in waiting. *CSPSp.*, *1568–79*, p. 403, 7 August 1572, intelligence from London addressed to Alva.

have no other evidence – that while Charles had urged Elizabeth
in his letter of 11 & 14 July to declare against Spain, Elizabeth
had been asking him to do the same. If this is true, both requested
what neither was prepared to do first, or trusted the other to do
at all. 'The best and most desirable way of gaining their ends,'
the report continues, thereby revealing the fundamental error of
supposing 'their ends' to be identical, 'would be to proceed in the
same way as heretofore.' This, presumably, meant unofficial aid
in undeclared war. For the moment Charles was against 'any
rash action', being afraid of provoking a league of the pope, the
King of Spain and the Venetians – which in fact already existed –
as well as others, against which he could not defend himself.
Portugal was said to have 12–15,000 men, and Savoy to be fully
armed. He might have added Florence, Triers, Bavaria and
Cologne who, according to Walsingham, were all on the other
side.[1] All this, La Mole is alleged to have urged, must be considered by Charles, 'before any bold step was taken'. The next
day, 4 August (La Mothe gives 5 August), La Mole emerged
publicly and went 'very bravely' to the palace, where he was
received in state as the acknowledged envoy of Alençon.[2]

La Mole's message, as reported by de Fogaza, raises certain
problems because it appears to differ from that of Sabran, by
merely urging that England and France should 'proceed in the
same way as heretofore', without requesting Elizabeth either to
take definitive action or to declare against Spain, though it did
correspond to the message of Sabran in explaining why Charles
could not do so himself. This difference seems improbable and
does not make very good sense since Charles, who so urgently
required Elizabeth's participation on 14 July, needed it even more
desperately a week later. As there is only one report of a mission
intended to be deeply secret, one must query whether it is not
perhaps incomplete or in some way misleading. Whatever the
truth of this, Coligny sent his secretary Dupin at the same time,
bringing letters from himself and Montmorency excusing the

[1] Digges, 225, 26 July 1572, Walsingham to Burghley.
[2] *CSPSp.*, *1568–79*, p. 403, 7 August 1572, intelligence from London
addressed to Alva.

king from openly declaring himself and explaining that they were raising 8,000 *more* foot and 2,000 horse to trouble Alva until Orange arrived. Meanwhile, they proposed to wait until 15 August with 12,000 foot and 4,000 horse. Urging the importance of help from England, they added that Brandenburg and the Palatinate were also sending help to Mons. Thus there was no danger of England's being isolated and, whether or not an open declaration was specifically requested, her definitive help certainly was.[1]

Walsingham, who remained in Paris when the court went to Blois at the end of July, viewed the whole crisis with the utmost gravity. He was most anxious on all accounts – that of England, Orange and Coligny – whose several vital interests he saw as more simply and completely aligned than Elizabeth ever would. To Burghley he urged the essential need of German as well as English support – the Saxon-born Gaspard de Schomberg had in fact already gone from France to seek help, and to persuade the princes, which was difficult, of their common danger.[2] Casimbrot however, had already made known the willingness of certain princes to participate, provided England and France were both committed.[3] Walsingham wrote even more strongly to Leicester after the defeat of Genlis that 'to suffer [Orange] to miscarry knowing our own danger were to lack both policy and magnanimity'. He envisaged Orange as an instrument of God to 'entertain' Spain, without whom 'a dangerous fire ere this time had bin kindled in our own home'. So, in a sense did Elizabeth; but her tactics were more deviously sophisticated, and magnanimity was not among her political virtues.[4] Walsingham also tried to ascertain, but from the non-committal Burghley, who was absent from court, whether Elizabeth would join with Charles if he approached her to that effect. This sounds almost like an effort to revive the 'offensive' treaty proposal, perhaps because there

[1] *CSPSp.*, *1568–79*, p. 403–4, 7 August 1572, intelligence from England addressed to Alva.
[2] Delaborde, *Coligny*, iii, 378.
[3] Digges, 225, 26 July 1572, Walsingham to Burghley.
[4] Digges, 225–6, 26 July 1572, Walsingham to Leicester.

appears, at the end of July or early in August to have been a
general, if rather nebulous assumption that Charles then intended
to make war, apparently on account of the most adamant insistence
of Coligny. But Catherine, who had gone to Châlons to meet her
daughter Claude, duchess of Lorraine, is said to have returned
in a hurry and brought Charles back to Paris where, on or before
6 August, two evidently stormy council meetings were held, at
which Coligny was unanimously opposed, and it was determined
to have nothing to do with war.[1] This decision – and apparent
deflection of royal policy – seems to have been directly related to
a rumour from the Netherlands that Elizabeth meant to recall her
subjects, whereupon the pro-Spanish members of the council had
put Catherine 'in such a fear that the enterprise cannot but
miscarry without the assistance of England, as she with tears had
disswaded the King for the time, who otherwise was very
resolute'. In another letter of the same date, addressed to Leicester,
Walsingham said that Catherine could not 'consent to grow to
any open dealing' without England. Thus, he wrote to Burghley
with grim humour, 'your lordship seeth how the bruit of your
fear there, hath bred fear here; whereof I fear there will follow
fearfull effects'. Fearful they were indeed to be, beyond anything
that Walsingham imagined.[2]

Walsingham's report is the clearest suggestion we have that
Catherine had either consented – as a *pis aller* – been obliged to
consent, or otherwise found herself unable to oppose war, given
the support of England. The reverse, at least, is clear; without
such an assurance her absolute opposition explains why it was
commonly given out in August that the king would not 'meddle';
why Petrucci declared that everything was in confusion, and
Walsingham that everything was in suspense.[3] So it was that,

---

[1] Desjardins, *Negs. Tosc.*, iii, 801, 6 August 1572; Albèri, *Relazioni*, 1st
series, iv, 283–5; Champion, *Charles IX, la France et le contrôle de l'Espagne*,
ii, 53.

[2] Digges, 233, 10 August 1572, Walsingham to Burghley, 233–4, 10 August
1572, Walsingham to Burghley and Leicester.

[3] Desjardins, *Negs. Tosc.*, iii, 801–2, 6 August 1572; Digges, 231, 10 August
1572, Walsingham to Smith. There are errors here in the pagination.

on 9 August, after the stormy council meetings, Charles wrote to La Mothe making more parade than one would have expected, to his own ambassador, of having nothing to do with the war 'bien fort' which was expected in Flanders, and that any French-men who were found there would have made a clandestine escape; a grotesque description indeed, if this were to refer to the departure of Coligny and the huguenot party. On the other hand, he reiterated forcefully his entreaties of mid-July that 'il seroit bien bon pour mes affaires que la Royne d'Angleterre . . . s'y mist de piedz et de mains, et qu'elle pratiquât en Zélande et ez villes qui sont de ce costé là'. La Mothe must do everything possible to foment (eschaufer) Elizabeth into an open declaration.[1] So, whether or not La Mole originally requested this, there was no doubt about the entreaty three weeks later.

Walsingham's urgent pleas to Burghley and Leicester for English co-operation were despatched before the receipt of the rumour that the queen meant to recall her subjects. According to him, Charles had then been 'very forward'. Commissions for the levying of troops in various provinces were ready for sealing, and the king would have 'proceeded to an open dealing', from which Walsingham assured Leicester, England had nothing to fear because pleasure and youth would not suffer Charles 'to take profit of advantages'. Walsingham therefore expressed the hope that the rumour was false, at the same time as writing 'earnestly' to both Burghley and Leicester to 'procure the stay of the revocation'.[2] It was now not only publicly declared – as it had always been – but also generally assumed that, after all, Charles would *not* go to war. This implies a change of policy, whereas there was no practical, material change that Charles could make. He had, in any case, been awaiting the marriage and developments in England, and probably the departure of Don John from Messina, since this was the only diminution of Spanish catholic pressure of which there was any prospect. He had, therefore, never shifted from his policy of disavowals and underhand help.

[1] La Mothe, vii, 14, 9 August 1572, Charles to La Mothe.
[2] Digges, 232–4, 10 August 1572, three letters, Walsingham to Smith, Burghley and Leicester.

The difference was one of degree, that he needed English help more urgently than ever, and the problem of restraining Coligny had become more acutely difficult. Everything possible was already being done to obtain the English marriage, but Charles redoubled his efforts to secure Elizabeth's military support. During La Mole's three weeks at the English court he received three successive couriers directing him to press the queen to break with Spain. Then Charles would 'in such case seek a pretext for doing the same, and would prove his good will in the matter by giving her, within fifteen days after her rupture . . . 200,000 ducats'; the first mention of any acceptable inducement.[1]

The restraint of Coligny was more difficult because he saw no alternative and was therefore fully determined to go to the Netherlands. 'The admiral in this brunt,' Walsingham wrote to Burghley, 'whose mind is invincible . . . doth not now give over.' The danger was such, he continued, that Coligny was 'bound to do what lieth in him to prevent the mischief which threatened'.[2] Already by 11 August Orange, who was at Roermond on the Meuse, had received letters from Coligny, which must have been despatched after the council meetings, by 9 August at the latest, announcing that he would accompany about 12,000 foot and 3,000 horse to his assistance, and warning him – lest the Genlis fiasco were not warning enough – against giving battle before they had joined forces.[3]

Opposed by the unanimous council and the weight of Catherine's influence, Coligny had sought to persuade them of the great danger involved in not helping Orange. But, if he failed to obtain the declaration he wanted, he did, according to Walsingham, obtain something.[4] The clue to what this 'something' was, might lie in a memoir of what Coligny is alleged to have said on

[1] *CSPSp.*, *1568–79*, pp. 411–12, 8 September 1572, intelligence from London.

[2] Digges, 233, 10 August 1572, Walsingham to Burghley; Albèri, *Relazioni*, 1st series, iv, 285.

[3] G. van Prinsterer, *Archives ou correspondance*, série i, vol. iii, 490–1, 11 August 1572, Orange to count Jean.

[4] Digges, 233–4, 10 August 1572, Walsingham to Leicester.

6 August, not in council, but in the king's cabinet.[1] This is an unsigned, contemporary copy of a rather hostile report in which Coligny is held to have intimidated the king. It was perhaps upon this occasion that he issued, or repeated his warning about Orange. According to Petrucci, he showed Catherine letters relating to William's advance which implied that, if not adequately assisted, he might invade France; this in turn would entail war with Spain. A hostile critic might well represent this as intimidation. But, at this stage, the truth itself was intimidating since Catherine and Charles, no less than Coligny, could easily remember that William had already done this once, in 1568, after the failure of his first invasion of the Netherlands. On that occasion, however, Alva was at least theoretically assisting the king. This time he would not be and, militarily speaking, his worst enemies would all be located in France.[2] The memoir goes on to suggest that Coligny sought permission to despatch 4,000 foot and 2,000 horse towards the frontier. He would then do this very quickly – the inference being before the marriage – in order to reinforce Orange and enable him to operate in the Netherlands. William's calculations had, after all, been based upon the expectation of support from the south. This, the memoir maintains in effect, though the point is differently expressed, could shelter like the previous expeditions of Nassau and Genlis under the disavowal policy, which was true – at a stretch – since it could be executed without the departure of Coligny himself.

There is another reason why Coligny might well have urged such a policy, if the memoir of events of 6 August is true. Coligny had never pretended that he could fully control the huguenots, and the history of 1570–2 demonstrates that he could not. In August 1572 they were reacting very threateningly to the ill-treatment of Genlis and the French prisoners in the Netherlands, and the offensive, hostile rejoicing of Paris upon this same account. They were preparing to look to their own, as contemporaries put it, and they had an excellent and disquieting opportunity to do

[1] B.N., Mss. fr. 3193, ff. 68–9, memoir of what Coligny said in the *cabinet du roi* on 6 August 1572.

[2] Desjardins, *Negs. Tosc.*, iii, 802, 9–12 August 1572.

so when they quit Paris *en masse* to attend the marriage on
10 August at Blandy-en-Brie (near Melun) of the young prince
de Condé to his cousin Marie de Clèves, daughter of François duc
de Nevers.[1] They are also said to have threatened to molest the
comte de Retz, to whom they attributed the adverse decision in
council, because he had assured both Zúñiga and Salviati that
such a resolution would be carried.[2] If true, this would not have
been without significantly augmenting the alarming crisis in
which war and peace, and life and death, lay in the balance. As
Florentine protégés of Catherine, the Spanish affiliations of the
Gondi cousins was doubly unfortunate in these circumstances,
making her appear hostile to the huguenots for whom she had
done more than anyone in France to establish a legal settlement.

So it began to look as though the choice no longer lay between
war or peace with Spain, but between foreign or civil war, or
worst of all, the mortally dangerous combination which later
materialised in the reign of Henry IV. It is therefore possible that
interim permission to succour Orange, before it was too late,
was what Coligny had privately obtained after the adverse ruling
in council. Certainly Alva complained, only a few days later, of
the presence of troops on the frontier, and requested Charles to
prohibit them from entering the Netherlands.[3] Such permission
to Coligny would also have afforded a little more time in which
to receive an answer from La Mole, potentially a saving advantage.

If this interpretation is correct – and it cannot be more completely established – it would explain why, in spite of everything –
Coligny delayed his departure for so long – too long as it
transpired – awaiting the Bourbon marriage, and hopefully the
return of La Mole from England. After the marriage celebrated
on 18 August, it is clear that Coligny would go. Writing that day
to his wife, he confided his aversion on personal grounds from
lingering in Paris. This could be a general remark, or a reference
to a warning he is said to have received on 16 or 17 August from
Jean de Mergey and his master La Rochefoucauld, of the intended

---

[1] Aumale, *Histoire des princes de Condé*, ii, 98.
[2] Desjardins, *Negs. Tosc.*, iii, 801, 6 August 1572.
[3] Gachard, *Notices et extraits*, i, 409, 11 August 1572, Alva to Charles IX.

assault upon Coligny's life.[1] According to de Mergey, his informant was a doctor in the service of the duke of Savoy, a
known enemy of Coligny. But, Coligny continued to his wife,
Charles had promised to attend to the complaints of the protestants against the violations of the edict. Oddly enough he does not
mention the Netherlands except to say that he had not got
permission to depart before the next week; the following Monday
was 25 August.[2] Doubtless Coligny's arrangements depended to
some extent upon the king, and Charles, apart from being
engrossed, in honour of the Bourbon wedding, in some of the
most elaborate and untimely celebrations ever mounted by his
mother and the Valois court, still awaited answers from England.

Although Elizabeth was allegedly moving towards a real intention to marry, upon the basis of the articles agreed for Anjou,
she was still, in mid-August, insisting upon an interview. If this
was bluff, it was called by Catherine who, ever adventurous, and
longing – so she told La Mothe – to meet Elizabeth herself,
revived on 21 August Elizabeth's own audacious proposal for a
maritime meeting 'en un beau jour, bien calme' between
Boulogne, Calais and Dover.[3] This insistence upon an interview
took care of delaying the marriage. On the subject of war and
Charles' secret entreaties, bluff and prevarication were more
difficult. La Mole received the reply that Elizabeth was not
satisfied with Charles' procedure. While she had written autograph letters to him, he had not similarly honoured her. They
would therefore have nothing to do with the matter, which was
one of 'great weight', until the king himself wrote and personally
signed all his promises. All they would do was to supply the
coastal provinces with victuals and ammunition; which was
simply what she anyway intended.[4]

This blatantly specious procedural objection was made because

[1] Jean de Mergey, *Mémoires*, 574–5.
[2] Dufey, *La Saint-Barthélemy*, in *Paris révolutionnaire*, iii, 356–7, 18 August
1572, Coligny to his wife.
[3] La Mothe, iv, 9–10, 6 March 1571; vii, 320, 21 August 1572, Catherine to
La Mothe.
[4] *CSPSp.*, *1568–79*, pp. 411–13, 8 September 1572, intelligence to Alva.

Elizabeth was still negotiating with Alva.[1] 'The design of the English,' his agent wrote from London, 'is to support Mons to hold out through the winter and [to] assist the coast places to the end that Orange may there establish his winter quarters.'[2] Consequently Casimbrot – whose mission to obtain help had coincided with La Mole's to obtain rather more – left London on 19 August to return to Orange with bills of exchange for £30,000, advanced by the queen through merchants at Hamburg. This, and other material help which followed in the next few days, was further proof, so the agent declared, of Elizabeth's design to seize and hold Flushing so as to be on a better footing for negotiating with Philip.[3] This was certainly one result of the policy, if not its sole explanation, and de Guaras wrote on the same day that the English court was awaiting the reply of Philip and Alva to their offer to recall the English.[4]

This 'offer' is obscure. It might be an allusion to Elizabeth's proposal to accept Flushing in order to surrender it to Alva, or perhaps to something else which has not come to light. It must, if it really existed, presumably date from the last days of July, after the receipt in England of the news of Genlis' defeat and while La Mole awaited audience. This would have been approximately a week before the rumour of an English revocation of forces reached France, precipitating the crisis there early in August. Smith, however, writing on 22 August – after the departure of Casimbrot bearing financial help – denied the veracity of the rumour: 'indeed as yet there is no revocation neither done nor meant of our men at Flushing or in Flanders, howsoever the brute is made there with you'. But, he continued, 'Alva by letters this last week required they should be revoked, but he is gently

---

[1] Alva is said to have had a considerable secret correspondence with Elizabeth, seized by Philip's secretaries. Certainly he never favoured the enterprise of England although as its prospective commander this is understandable. Tomás González, *Apuntamientos. Memorias de la Real Academia de la Historia*, vii (1832), 370–1.

[2] *CSPSp.*, *1568–79*, pp. 404–5, 19 August 1572, intelligence from London.

[3] *CSPSp.*, *1568–79*, p. 407, 30 August 1572, intelligence from London.

[4] *CSPSp.*, *1568–79*, pp. 408–9, 30 August 1572, de Guaras to Alva.

answered with a dilatory and doubtful answer'.[1] 'Last week' could have referred to any day from Sunday 9 August to Saturday 15 August. Walsingham first referred to the rumour in a letter of 10 August. It is therefore not clear whether the rumour arose from the recall of Sadler and Pelham, from some specific English offer, or whether it preceded a Spanish demand for withdrawal. It could equally well have been fabricated to elicit exactly the restraining effect that it had in France.

With Coligny about to depart, with royal permission, Charles could no longer sustain his policy of disavowals, no longer avoid war, nor yet safely wage it. This was all the more reason for Elizabeth to continue with protracting of time, as they said, simultaneously assuring her hold upon vital strategic positions in the Netherlands, entertaining Alva with diplomatic civilities and, still not definitively committed, assuming her position at the window 'pour regarder le jeu'. Nevertheless, the Bourbon marriage was finally accomplished and, during the week of celebrations, before Coligny's intended departure, Charles had not yet received Elizabeth's frivolous demand for autograph letters, for La Mole was still in England.[2] His policy, therefore, in so far as he can be said to have had one, was not quite yet a failure. Don John had left Messina, and Alva was still in Brussels. Orange was approaching, and it was not without some residual hope of English support and ultimate success – whatever form that might take – that he had finally granted Coligny's long-desired permission to enter the Netherlands sometime in the week beginning 25 August.

[1] Digges, 236–7, 22 August 1572, Smith to Walsingham.
[2] It is not clear whether La Mole left England on 28 or 30 August, probably the former but it does not make any difference. *CSPSp.*, *1568–79*, p. 407, 30 August 1572, intelligence from London; 411–12, 8 September 1572, intelligence from London.

XVII

The Massacre and the Evidence

BY 25 August 1572 Coligny was dead. During the previous nine
or ten years, in which his life had been continually menaced, there
can have been few convenient opportunities for an assassin. In all
that time he had only been at court for a matter of weeks, and
only twice for as long as five weeks together, and he was habitually
well accompanied whether there, in the field, in the stronghold
of La Rochelle or at Châtillon. Why he was so foolhardy that
Friday morning, 22 August, as to be vulnerably ill-surrounded
in the streets of hostile Paris, remains a mystery. Returning from
the Louvre to his lodging nearby in the rue Béthizy, Coligny was
wounded in the right hand and the left arm by shots fired from a
window. These wounds are explained by the fact that he bent
over at the crucial moment to adjust a shoe. It is generally
accepted that the marksman was Maurevert, who had murdered
Mouy in 1569, and reputedly tried to murder the admiral himself,
and that the house – which was an official court lodging – had
some Guisard connection. The details are confused. Upon receipt
of the news, Charles immediately ordered an enquiry.[1] He is also
said to have twice invited Coligny into the Louvre; Coligny declined but wanted the huguenots to evacuate Paris. Either would
have been a sensible, and probably effective precaution. Later in
the day Charles, Catherine and members of the court visited
Coligny in his lodgings. These bare 'facts' command a consensus
of opinion, but there are differing versions of the conversation
between Charles and Coligny, and of what subsequently happened
that day, and on Saturday. It has, however, never been contested
that Coligny finally met his death at the hands of a group of
followers of Henri duc de Guise and his uncle Aumale who,

---

[1] Isambert, *Édits et ordonnances*, xiv, 255, 22 August 1572, no text.

overcoming all resistance, burst into his bedroom in the small hours of Sunday morning and slew him. The initiative, however, at this, second stage, is not normally imputed to the Guises, whose notorious hatred for Coligny is held to have been exploited. The usually reliable Pasquier later recounted how one of the Guise troop, M. de Saissac, personally told him that he had received an express order from the duc d'Anjou 'de faire tuer l'Admiral à quelque prix que ce fust'.[1]

The differences in the versions of what happened after the wounded Coligny returned to his lodgings, largely hinge upon the attitude to, and version of the huguenots' reaction to the assault, and upon who is to be predominantly blamed for the assault, the massacre or both. Between distress, anger and fear, it is obvious that the protestants must have reacted strongly, raging and fulminating threats. Some sources merely indicate their menacing temper; others allege a definite plot, or plan of action against the court, formally prepared at one or two councils. Most of the sources subscribe to an actual plot, but the protestant *Mémoires de l'Estat de France sous Charles IX*[2] records a protestant council on both the Friday, and the Saturday morning, but claims that only justice was demanded 'sans violence ni parolle out-rageuse'. The point, however, is not of basic importance as emotions had been running high since the Genlis fiasco and violence was bound to be feared by the court, and likely to occur. As for what happened at the court, one story is that on Saturday after dinner, which was in the morning, Catherine held a council in the Tuileries garden, at which the idea of multiple murder – namely the policy of elimination – was discussed. But most sources move from Friday afternoon to an evening council on Saturday 23 August at which the king was persuaded by, or in the presence of, various members to agree to the 'elimination' of

---

[1] François Catillac de Saissac – whose name is variously spelt – was a Gascon gentleman and captain who, according to de Thou, had been in the service of the Guises, and accompanied Anjou to Poland. Pasquier, *Lettres historiques*, 362 and 377, n. 6.

[2] Attributed to Simon Goulart, the *Mémoires de l'Estat de France sous Charles IX* were printed in 1577 (s.l.) and in Middelburg in the Netherlands in 1578.

Coligny and others, on account of the immediate danger to the court which their plot or their fury (whichever it was) represented. Arrangements for this were then said to have been made with great rapidity, and executed in the small hours, precipitating a bloody tumult in the city of Paris which, according to some versions was organised, and to others spontaneous.

Nobody whose written word remains knew clearly what had happened upon either occasion – the assault or the massacre – and contemporaries were stunned, confused and frightened, and expressed their opinions, as people do, according to their passions and predilections. The episode was one of emotional explosion after which satisfaction and stupefaction and the nature of the repercussions mattered considerably more than the *truth* of what had happened. As immediate comment was neither informed nor objective, and polemical purposes have governed the subsequent literature of St Bartholomew, the only solution is to analyse the more serious evidence. The extreme protestant account, which embodies the rather tedious theory of premeditation on the part of the crown, prevailed until about 1837. Thereafter the tide turned in favour of a version more acceptable to the restored monarchy and premeditation was gradually discredited. It is therefore hardly surprising that the entire historiography of the subject, which has been outlined by Professor Butterfield, should reveal not merely 'a residuum of loose ends,' as he says, but utter confusion.[1]

This protestant version is primarily exemplified by the *Mémoires de l'Estat de France*, in which the protestants argued that the purpose of the peace of Saint-Germain, ending the third civil war in 1570, had been to dispose of them in a different manner. The catholic extremists, who had always desired violent measures, provided them with grist to this mill, and Catherine's alleged diplomatic utterances to the pope on the subject of the peace are used as evidence of her basic malevolence towards the protestants. Apart from any other consideration, the total inability of the crown to sustain the war is a much simpler

[1] Butterfield, *Man on his Past*, chapter vi.

explanation of the peace. The disgrace of the Guises in August 1570 – the first possible moment – and the continuing absence of Lorraine, is ignored, as well as the fact that the original edict of January 1562, and the subsequent edicts of pacification permitting the protestants a degree of toleration, owed more to Catherine's realistic influence than to any other individual. The need of both Charles and Catherine for protestant support, and that of Coligny in particular is circumvented, because after the massacre the Netherlands enterprise and the Bourbon marriage can themselves be represented as stratagems to ensnare the protestants. Such arguments cannot be reconciled with a long-term analysis of royal policy and Franco-Spanish relations, and reveal the basically polemical nature of the work. But, in the absence of any such detailed study, the idea of premeditation arrested historians for a very long time. This was partly because they treated the massacre as an isolated outrage, and partly because they were inexplicably obsessed by the criminal approach. But, more seriously, premeditation became confused with the extreme catholic and Spanish policy of violent remedies in general, and 'elimination' in particular, and the evidence relating to the policy of elimination was mistaken for premeditation. It is very likely that 'elimination' really had a great deal to do with what happened. But if, in some ways, comparable, it was nevertheless not at all the same thing as the premeditation of the massacre – meaning the whole complex of events – in its historic form. Above all 'elimination', as the policy of the ultramontane, pro-Spanish extremists had been continuously and steadfastly resisted by the catholic crown to which the premeditation was attributed. Thus there existed both a confusion of ideas, and a transposition of evidence.

Because the *Mémoires de l'Estat de France* is one of the few relatively full accounts, it has been constantly quarried and indeed, it does contain much valid information. Apart, however, from its manifestly partisan nature, it needs the most careful handling because it gives few dates, and the chronology is badly confused. It also contains factual inaccuracies and, most misleading in this context, about the movements of Coligny. This is extremely important since the *Mémoires* is one of the principal origins of the traditional belief in Coligny's predominant influence over the king, which is claimed by the protestants as a matter of prestige, and propounded by catholics as a fatal grievance against him. The fallacy of this assertion, whether as a boast or an accusation, is clear from the detailed history of the years 1570–2. Coligny returned to court on 12 September 1571 for five weeks. The *Mémoires*, and various secondary works which follow them, say that he then went to court again in November 1571, withdrew in March 1572 when Alessandrino arrived, and returned for the third time when Jeanne went to court with Nassau. In fact Coligny did not return to court in November 1571, on account of the menacing attitude of the Guises, or at any time in 1572 until 6 June; and it was in February, not March that Alessandrino had arrived. In May 1572 Coligny is said, in the *Mémoires*, to have remained at court, high in favour; in other words exercising influence over the king. This is a complete fabrication since the court was dispersed from the last week in April until 7 June, and Coligny was at home.[1] June, it has been seen, was occupied by the entertainment of the English embassy, after which the court again dispersed. It would indeed be difficult to demonstrate Coligny's influence over the king in July, when his most urgent, desperate advice was steadily rejected – to the ultimate undoing of Charles IX – and in August, the month of the Bourbon marriages, because of preparations and the most extensive and lavish celebrations, affairs of state were virtually in abeyance. The king was awaiting news from England and, even in the week after the marriage, Coligny was concentrating on matters related to the edict of Saint-Germain.

The *Mémoires* attribute the origin of the assault upon Coligny to the king, Catherine, Anjou and leading members of the council – here said to be three separate councils which all co-operated for this purpose. The final assassination plot is held to have been arranged by them three weeks before the Bourbon wedding. This is another complete fabrication, since the court

---

[1] Goulart, *Mémoires de l'Estat de France*, 84 verso–5, 207 verso, 216; on 27 May 1572 Coligny wrote to Burghley from his home at Châtillon, Wright, *Queen Elizabeth and her Times*, i, 422–3.

was dispersed in the latter part of July with Charles on the Loire, whence he worked to obtain the dispensation, and Catherine was away in the east of France meeting Claude de Lorraine. This is therefore a potentially useful work, but with great reservations, and most certainly not a pure spring to be imbibed without analysis of its contents.

The *De Furoribus Gallicis*[1] is another protestant source which has also been widely used. This, far from maintaining that Coligny latterly controlled the king or directed his affairs, states disapprovingly that 'by reason of nightly riotous sitting-up' – namely the marriage celebrations – the admiral could not 'have access to the king's speech, nor entrance to deal in weighty matters'. These were the complaints of the churches about infractions of the edict, with which he was showered immediately before his departure.[2] Even on 22 August, the day of the assault, when Coligny attended a council meeting in the Louvre, it was, according to this account, in the absence of the king. Without accusing anyone of the assault, apart from indicating the Guise connections of the house which was used and the persons said to have been involved, the *De Furoribus* is, as one would expect, another principal source for the incrimination of Catherine, as well as the treachery of Charles. The subsequent massacre is attributed to her sole determination to seize this 'notable opportunity', without any pretext of a protestant plot. It is later denied, in the tract, that such a plot could have been possible in Paris since, it is said, the king was well guarded. Where, as in *De Furoribus*, the events of the 24 August are attributed chiefly or solely to Catherine, we find the story of the Friday afternoon Tuileries council. In this version the garden council was attended by Anjou, Nevers, Tavannes and de Retz, as well as by Charles himself, who is not usually brought in before the Saturday night council in the Louvre, here omitted. There follows a confusion over timing – not infrequently reproduced in secondary works without either comment or explanation – and the narrative moves straight to the

---

[1] Varamundus – pseudonym – *De Furoribus Gallicis*, published in Scotland in 1573.

[2] *De Furoribus*, 345–6.

events of the Saturday night, under the direction of Guise, as though they had occurred that same Friday night. *De Furoribus* is also the chief source for much of the more lurid and oft-repeated trivia about the escape and pursuit of the marksman; about the king hurling down his tennis racket upon receipt of the news, and also of the butcherly obscenities perpetrated upon the body of the admiral, whose head, we are told, was despatched to Rome.

Among the predominantly catholic sources, the only two pamphlets of any real interest and significance are the *Vera et Brevis Descriptio Tumultus Postremi Gallici Lutetiani*, published in Latin in Cracow in 1573,[1] and the *Discours du Roy Henri III à un personnage d'honneur*, otherwise known as the *Version du duc d'Anjou*.[2] There are also other much less important pamphlets, such as Camillo Capilupi's *Lo stratagemma di Carlo IX* (1572), and *Le Tocsain contre les autheurs du massacre de France*, published in Rheims in 1578.[3]

Confusion has arisen between the *Vera et Brevis Descriptio*, and the *Discours du Roy Henri III à un personnage d'honneur* because the former was published in Latin in Cracow in 1573 when Anjou was king of Poland, and the latter specifically claims to be his version. This controversy has been adequately disposed of in Monod's article and need not be rehearsed. It is, in any case, purely academic. It is quite possible, indeed probable, that neither version emanated from Anjou; they are different, and serve different purposes. Both must be assessed with critical care and neither should ever have been used as a straightforward source from which to pad out a narrative. By gleaning every separate detail without critical consideration of its context, one can fabricate a fairly solid account, or variable accounts, but which

[1] This has been printed in French and analysed by Henri Monod, 'La Saint-Barthélemy. Version du duc d'Anjou', *BSHPF.*, 58 (1909). Monod argues that this was the real Anjou version, and not the one that bears that title.

[2] The *Discours* has been published with the *Mémoires* of Nicolas de Neufville, seigneur de Villeroy, secretary of state, which themselves throw no light at all on the massacre although he was at court. Petitot, *Collection des mémoires*, série i, vol. xliv.

[3] Cimber et Danjou, *Archives curieuses*, série i, vol. vii, 3-76, 409-71.

have no more than a gambler's chance of hitting upon the truth. It is not surprising to find that the central purpose of the *Vera et Brevis Descriptio*, intended for Polish consumption, is to disculpate their French king from any part in the massacre, either because he *was* genuinely implicated, was believed to be so, or because as lieutenant-general he was so close to the crown as to have been tarnished by the royal assumption of responsibility in a declaration of 26 August. In this account, the assault was blamed upon the house of Guise, and the massacre upon the council, on account of a rather vaguely expressed protestant danger. It is claimed that Anjou walked out of the Saturday night council in the Louvre, and that nothing thereafter could persuade him to return. This disculpation reveals the partisan purpose, which the rest of the document must therefore necessarily sustain. On the other hand, it was evidently written by someone who knew a good deal about the truth, and it presents considerable difficulties. It is likely to remain controversial, and should only be used – with proper identification – in the consideration of hypotheses and not offered as part of supposedly authentic accounts of what happened.

The *Vera et Brevis Desciptio* is interesting in that it discusses the origins of the civil wars, attributing them to the youth of the king and the rivalry of the nobility. This is preliminary to blaming the Guises – in other words the vendetta – for the assault on Coligny. Further to this theme the document describes two quarrels at court, not recorded elsewhere, which is highly improbable, if they were true, since Coligny's infrequent presence at court invariably made ambassadorial news. The first quarrel was between Coligny and Nevers (Guise's brother-in-law) in 1571. The king comes well out of this by composing the quarrel instead of allowing Nevers to kill Coligny. But the fact that the king did not wish Coligny dead in 1571, when he could do nothing without him, hardly requires labouring, and there is no prima facie reason to assume that, had they fought – which was illegal – it would not have been Coligny who killed Nevers. A further quarrel is then recounted between Coligny and Guise while the king was at table, by inference about the time of the

Bourbon marriage in August. This leads up to a consequent assault upon Coligny at the instigation of Guise. It goes on to describe a tremendous protestant clamour for the arrest of Guise, followed by a huguenot conspiracy to invade the Louvre to kill, not the king, but all the Guises and their partisans. The Guises are more generally said to have moved out of the Louvre, because it was filled with protestants. The king, however, became afraid, believing that he too must be in danger, and sent for Anjou to explain a plan which had therefore already been formulated by the council before his arrival. Thus, one is to deduce that the innocent Anjou was presented with a *fait accompli*. This carries little conviction, since it is hardly likely that Anjou, as heir presumptive and lieutenant-general, would not have been present from the start of such a momentous session. Monod commented that 'l'isolement de ce témoignage d'innocence est un puissant indice qu'il émane du coupable'. While this may be questionable, Anjou must, nevertheless, be accounted a principal suspect, because of his affiliation with the extreme political catholics.

Perhaps in order to shield Anjou, the document is rather vague about what actually happened, except that Guise personally is said to have killed the admiral, and the massacre – meaning the municipal tumult – to have occurred *without* the consent of the king. The former is improbable and the latter almost certainly true.

The *Discours du Roy Henri III*, although alleged to have been dictated in Cracow – when Henry was duc d'Anjou and not yet Henry III – was unknown before 1623. This date, together with the paradoxical fact that the *Discours* is the principal source for the incrimination of Anjou himself, are the main reasons why its authenticity is usually denied. The theory is that it was fabricated later in order to exonerate de Retz, the most widely accused of any individual. This idea has sinister possibilities considering that de Retz accompanied Henry to Poland and therefore, presumably, knew of the *Vera et Brevis Descriptio*, if it were indeed composed in Cracow. This, it will be remembered, incriminated the Guises and the council in general and not de Retz or other individuals. Both he and Anjou, however, were among the extreme political catholics and his subsequent career was greatly advanced by Henry III. De Retz, one could go on to postulate further, might equally well have been responsible for both versions; but it must be emphasised that no one knows.

Thus, whereas the *Vera et Brevis Descriptio* disculpates Anjou and, as far as possible, the crown, the *Discours du Roy Henri III* incriminates himself, as Anjou, and explicitly disculpates de Retz. Since both accounts cannot therefore be true, it follows from this alone that neither can be reliably quoted as fact, although both have constantly been used. The *Discours* is one of the most quoted of all accounts, and is the principal source for the incrimination of Catherine, as well as Anjou, in conjunction, initially, with madame de Nemours. Petrucci reported on 23 July that madame de Nemours (mother of the duc de Guise) was working hard with Catherine, who was engaged in some secret negotiation through de Retz and Salviati for a Spanish marriage for Anjou. De Retz, he had already explained, was 'obbligato al Re di Spagna' and 'intrigato con i Guisi'.[1] If Catherine really were engaged in such negotiations at that moment, this was doubtless in an effort to support Charles' disavowal policy in the face of Genlis' exploits, to entertain Spain in a harmless and civil matter and probably also to disconcert queen Elizabeth. The marriage story was not an invention, and a few weeks later Salviati reported such a negotiation with the Spanish ambassador.[2] The principal objection to an account which incriminates Anjou and Catherine in about equal proportions in the initial assault upon Coligny, is that although they were both strongly averse from war with Spain, their policies were otherwise opposed, and Catherine needed Coligny at least as much for the reconciliation she sought to achieve in France, as she might be held to need his removal to avert the war she feared with Spain. However, in the *Discours*, Coligny is said to have had frequent conferences with the king, and this and the nuncio Salviati are the sources for his supposedly rough and hostile manners and disagreeable conduct which rendered him

[1] Desjardins, *Negs. Tosc.*, iii, 787, 26 June 1572; 799, 23 July 1572.
[2] Theiner, *Annales Ecclesiastici*, i, 332, 1 October 1572, Salviati to cardinal di Como.

unacceptable in court, especially to Anjou and Catherine. It is also, to some extent, one of the sources for his alleged influence over the king, less on account of the conferences to which the passage refers, than because he is here said to have turned the king against Anjou and Catherine, the inference, presumably, being because they both opposed war with Spain. But there was little to be gained from this, since Charles and Anjou had notoriously been quarrelling for a long time past, and Catherine was the principal supporter of the English policy and the edict of Saint-Germain.

Because Coligny is said to have turned Charles against Catherine, the fatuous 'maternal jealousy' theory is derived from the *Discours*, from which it has so frequently been argued that Catherine consequently resolved to murder Coligny. In the *Discours*, however, the malicious influence of Coligny is not erected in order to level an outstandingly foolish accusation at Catherine, but to support the subsequent statement that Charles, in silent fury, menaced Anjou with his dagger, 'd'une façon si animeuse' that Anjou beat a hasty – and, one would have thought, ignominious – retreat. Thereupon, it is said, he went to see Catherine, and they decided to be rid of Coligny, and so sought the help of madame de Nemours. Considering Charles' apparently psychopathic nature, and his known hatred for Anjou, it is perfectly possible that he threatened his brother. They had had menacing rows before, and without the intervention of Coligny. This seems a very feeble story or, at the least, incomplete. It would be interesting to know where madame de Nemours may have been, since Salviati reported on 22 August that she was pregnant, indisposed, and had quit the capital; but he does not say exactly when.[1] According to the *Discours*, Catherine, Anjou and madame de Nemours are then said to have sent for 'Montravel'. This is either an unusually odd rendering, or a very poor recollection of Maurevert. It is, however, definitely Maurevert who is intended, since the text specifies the murderer of Mouy. The

---

[1] Theiner, *Annales Ecclesiastici*, i, 328, 22 August 1572, Salviati to cardinal di Como.

inculpation of Maurevert is about the most constant element in the different versions, and one reason why it is essential to allow for the possibility of a coincidental assault, since he could well have been biding his time, with tragic consequences for the protestants, the king, and for France.

It is in this version that on the Friday afternoon, during the royal visit to Coligny, Anjou and Catherine are said to have become terrified by the number of sinister, menacing huguenot gentlemen who began to mill about them, while Coligny is said to have lectured Charles, who was bullied into repeating the conversation, about having surrendered his power and authority into the hands of Catherine and Anjou. Since this was precisely the period of his reign in which he displayed a maximum of independence, and Catherine and Coligny needed each other, this is not very convincing. The point, however, is that Catherine and Anjou were as offended by this conversation as they were frightened by the glowering huguenot gentry, and therefore decided next morning – Saturday – that whatever happened Coligny must die. For this it was essential to enlist the king. So they went to his study after dinner, which means around midday. The *Discours* records no huguenot council for the development of a plot, and no Tuileries council (on Friday) held by Catherine. Having gone to the king, he then sent for Nevers, Tavannes, de Retz and Birague 'pour avoir seulement leurs avis *des moyens* que nous tiendrions à l'exécution [of Coligny], laquelle nous avions desjà arrestée, ma mère et moy'. Thus, whereas in the *Vera et Brevis Descriptio*, Anjou is presented with a *fait accompli* by the council, in the *Discours* he and Catherine present the council with a predetermined resolution. Catherine, it says, urged upon Charles that he would soon be alone between two great parties – the predicament of the crown since 1560 – but a single stroke could avert that as the protestants' designs would expire with Coligny. They had not, previously, died with Condé, and it is not credible that Catherine could have been so silly. The first to give counsel agreed – although they had supposedly only been consulted on the means – but de Retz disappointed them. Although the admiral was his enemy, the text says, he did not wish to be avenged in this manner, from which dishonour and distrust would result. It is claimed that he made a great impression, but that no one else supported him, and the others prevailed upon the king, 'passant bien plus outre et plus criminellement'. The *Discours* together with the memoirs of Tavannes, are the sources of the towering rage in which Charles is then alleged to have stormed that if they wanted to kill the admiral, they could kill all the huguenots in France, before slamming out of his study.

Thus the *Discours* places responsibility for the original assault, and the further decision to dispose of Coligny, fully and solely upon Anjou and Catherine (for curiously slight, if not frivolous reasons, when much better ones were to hand), and on Charles for what followed. The part played by de Retz and singled out for comment, is notably innocent, honourable and magnanimous. But de Retz was not that sort of man, and that he should have rejected an anti-huguenot policy acceptable to Nevers, Tavannes and Birague, all of them moderates, is not plausible. Besides, if there were any two men at court who shared the same opinions, they were surely de Retz and Anjou, in the absence of Lorraine the principal catholic extremists.

The *Discours* then proceeds to practical arrangements, beginning with the municipality and assigning individuals to despatch individuals, designating Guise to murder Coligny. It is this account which claims that Anjou and Catherine were horror stricken at the last moment by the implications of impending events, only to find that it was too late to arrest them.

If it were true that de Retz later fabricated this account, then he might have attributed his own culpability either to Anjou or to Catherine. Charles is alleged to have loathed de Retz, and the huguenots, it will be remembered, were reported by Petrucci to have threatened about two weeks before to molest him. Everything we know for certain about de Retz makes him the strongest of all individual suspects, but he could not, even so, have operated alone. Anjou was capable of action when sufficiently aroused, and certainly susceptible to influence. As a catholic extremist, de Retz had long been associated with Anjou and, in the different capacity of Florentine *protégé*, he had also long been associated with Catherine. If neither de Retz nor Anjou was well placed to influence the king, it is also difficult to argue that Catherine had lost her influence over the king, on account of Coligny, and also that she persuaded Charles to consent to the policy of 'elimination,' which they had always both opposed. Yet while it was Anjou and Catherine who were said to have presented the king and councillors with their violent resolution, the *Discours* states rather vaguely that it was 'they', presumably those present apart from de Retz, who persuaded the king.

Camillo Capilupi's *Lo stratagemma di Carlo IX* was written and published immediately after the massacre. His underlying theme is indicated by his title. He asserts the influence of Coligny at court, attributing to him the initiative both in the negotiations with England and the Netherlands enterprise, which it has already been established was not the case. The only other point worth noting, is that Capilupi alleges the existence of a protestant plot *before* the August assault upon Coligny. The same point is made by Claude Haton, a priest of Provins. This simply takes a catholic exoneration of the crown one step further back, and is illustrative of the ignorant irrelevance of much of the commentary since the actual circumstances – both domestic and foreign – make nonsense of this assertion.

Le Tocsain was another later work, not published until 1578. It is less partisan than some, but distinctly confused. In general it appears to echo the *Mémoires de l'Estat de France*. It does, however, make the potentially significant point that de Retz received 25–30,000 *écus* to prevent the Netherlands enterprise. This, if it could be verified, would provide the clue to the assault, and would fit well with the Guisard connections of the house and marksman, and the implication by some authors of madame de Nemours. Furthermore, de Retz, with his banking connections, easily could have been quietly credited with a large sum of money. One can only speculate, however, where it would have come from; possibly Florence at the instigation of Savoy, but there is no sign that Petrucci knew anything about it. Brantôme, who usually passes as a gossip, but contains much valuable material states, rather baldly, that de Retz was the chief author of the massacre, and his name has perhaps been more widely associated with the event than that of any other individual councillor.[1]

The principal memoirs connected with the massacre are those of Gaspard de Saulx, seigneur de Tavannes, though there are also others with a little bearing on the subject such as the protestant Jean de Mergey, a servant of La Rochefoucauld, the catholic Claude Haton already mentioned, and Marguerite de Valois, who was in the Louvre at the time. Memoirs are notoriously unreliable as source material and those of Tavannes are frequently and correctly stated to be so. Nevertheless they have been more widely quoted than probably any others, often without annotation.

The *Mémoires* of Tavannes are more than usually unreliable because they were written in the seventeenth century by his son Jean, who jumbled his own life with that of his father, with predictable distortions of chronology. For example, the battle of Lepanto, October 1571, is placed between a discussion which appears to relate to July 1572 and a long digression, followed by a reversion to June 1572, although no dates are given. Jean de Tavannes is described by the editor as being proud, vain, complaining and hyperbolical. His father died in 1573, leaving very few papers, and his son received only a pension and none of his offices. Jean was therefore violently anti-Catherine, and became an extreme *ligueur*. Probably for this reason he was not employed by Henry IV or Louis XIII either. So he composed the so-called *Mémoires* of his father in a perverse spirit of anger and revenge. There is practically nothing in them which came from Tavannes himself, but it is interesting to note that his genuine *avis*, submitted to the council in June 1572 and included in the *Mémoires*, is quite different in style and tone from other parts of the text. Tavannes, far from having been violently anti-Catherine like his son, was a catholic moderate like herself, and just when the Guises were disgraced he was rewarded for his services in the third civil war with a – supernumerary – office of marshal. Because of the

---

[1] Brantôme, *Œuvres*, iv, 301. D'Aubigny also incriminates de Retz, adding that everyone interpreted the event 'selon sa passion'. *Histoire universelle*, iii, 304–5.

victories of Jarnac and Montcontour Tavannes is represented as a violent enemy of Coligny. They certainly were opponents, but there is no impartial evidence of personal enmity, and in Coligny, half a Montmorency, there was much of the loyalist *manqué*. In other words, only their religions divided them which in practice was rarely disastrous where other factors did not intervene. As one would expect, therefore, these *Mémoires* chiefly incriminate Catherine, and in strongly emotive language, but without any suggestion of premeditation, which is denied.

'La jalousie du gouvernement de son fils et de l'Estat, ambition demesurée, enflamme, brusle la Royne dehors et dedans, et tient conseil de se defaire de l'Admiral.

Le Roy chasseur va à Montpipeau; [Tavannes is alone in saying so; without a date] la Royne y court; enfermée en un cabinet avec luy, elle fond en larmes, dit: "Je n'eusse pensé que, pour avoir pris tant de peine à vous eslever, vous avoir conservé la coronne que les Huguenots et Catholiques vous vouloient oster, apres m'estre sacrifiée pour vous et encouru tant d'hazard, que m'eussiez voulu donner recompense si miserable. Vous vous cachez de moy, qui suis votre mere, pour prendre conseil de vos ennemis; vous vous ostez de mes bras qui vous ont conservé, pour vous appuyer des leurs qui vous ont voulu assassiner. Je sçay que vous tenez des conseils secrets avec l'Admiral; [they had not recently been in the same place if this refers, as it would appear, to early August] vous desirez vous plonger en la guerre d'Espagne inconsidérement, pour mettre votre royaume, vous et nos personnes, en proye de ceux de la religion. Si je suis si malhereuse, avant que voir cela donnez moy congé de me retirer au lieu de ma naissance, et esloigner de vous vostre frere, qui se peut nommer infortuné d'avoir employé sa vie pour conserver la vostre . . ." '[1]

Was there, one is tempted to enquire, a stenographer behind the arras, and how does one reconcile this boundless ambition with a request for permission to retire to Florence? This histrionic

[1] Tavannes, *Mémoires*, 385-6.

rubbish has been woven into the fabric of history and sanctioned by time and repetition. Coligny is said to have informed Charles – there is no indication as to when – that he must limit Catherine's power and get rid of Anjou, and Gondi (by whom Tavannes usually means de Retz) and the secretary Fizes are said to have told her this.

Catherine is therefore said to have turned to Anjou, and together with two unnamed councillors they resolved upon the death of Coligny. These four then applied to Guise, behind whose enmity for Coligny they proposed to hide. Catherine, Jean de Tavannes' real aversion, is therefore presented in the worst possible light. After the assault it is she and de Retz together who are said to have 'enraged' the king – an item which reappears in almost every secondary account – violent anger being one of his peculiar vices. Then everything is held to have been arranged by a council of six, Catherine, Anjou, Tavannes, Nevers, de Retz and Birague. Guise and Aumale are conspicuously absent from this list. Tavannes alone is held to have been responsible for saving Navarre – then reigning as Henry IV when the *Mémoires* were written; furthermore, 'le seul sieur de Tavannes a les mains nettes'. De Retz is represented as having been very extreme, and suspected of having coveted huguenot offices – presumably that of admiral. This may doubtless be explained by the fact that it was de Retz who subsequently received Tavannes' important offices of marshal, and *gouverneur* of Provence which his son Jean resented.

Marguerite de Valois also strongly incriminated de Retz, who was sent to Charles, according to her, on the Saturday evening, and persuaded him of the necessity of the massacre, meaning, most likely, only of Coligny and the huguenot leaders. This, she said, was upon the advice of Anjou and Guise, and presumably de Retz himself, if he undertook the mission. Marguerite also said that de Retz told Charles that Catherine had been implicated in the original assault, but whether to strengthen his argument, to lessen his own guilt or for what reason, is not clear.[1]

[1] Marguerite de Valois, *Mémoires*, 408–9.

The interest of the *Mémoires* of the protestant Jean de Mergey, a servant of La Rochefoucauld, lies in his statement that Coligny received a warning five or six days in advance. The warning came from one Textor, minister of Verteuil, through de Mergey's wife. Textor, it is said, had heard of this from his brother, who was doctor to the duke of Savoy. While this, if true, by no means establishes the implication of Savoy, the point is, nevertheless, of interest since Petrucci strongly advanced the possibility and the duke of Savoy regarded Coligny as a personal enemy.

Many contemporary memoirs pass over the massacre altogether, for example Villeroy, Villars, de Vieilleville, Cheverny and Nevers, and the diplomatic sources are abnormally thin. These consist of a few despatches each from the nuncio Salviati, and the Tuscan Petrucci. Together with his despatches there is an anonymous account attributed to an Italian physician Cavriana who himself later served as the Tuscan ambassador and wrote many despatches of high quality. This, so far as it goes, is probably the best of all the sources. The despatches of the two Venetians, Cavalli and Michiel, are missing, but their *Relazioni* are frequently cited in this connection. Alva's representative, Gomicourt, wrote what is usually known as Alva's account, which amounts to extremely little, and Olaegui, secretary to the Spanish ambassador, was immediately sent to Spain where he dictated a report to the secretary Gabriel de Zayas. The *Calendars of State Papers Foreign* contain disappointingly little and nothing of interest, doubtless because on 3 September Walsingham sent home 'a bearer' – very likely William Faunt – 'thoroughly instructed, . . . able to render a very good account of what he has seen'. Burghley could guess, Walsingham said – and so can we – why he forbore 'to afford many lines'.[1]

Perhaps the most controversial among the ambassadorial reports are those of the nuncio Salviati. His evidence, contained in five letters of 22, 24, 27 August, 2 and 22 September is confused, inconclusive and slightly contradictory.[2] The first of his letters relates to the assault on 22 August which, via circumstantial

---

[1] *CSPF.*, 1572–4, p. 173, 3 September 1572, Walsingham to Burghley.
[2] Theiner, *Annales Ecclesiastici*, i, 328–32, all addressed to cardinal di Como

evidence, he linked with the Guises, without specifically incriminating anyone. His laconic comment was that everything would
be disrupted and altered. Thus, at that time, he showed no signs
of possessing inside information, but only what was publicly
known. On 24 August, however, he claims to have known that
Coligny would no longer be tolerated, but that when, in recent
days, he had declared that he soon hoped to send some good news,
he would never have believed the tenth part of what he then
witnessed – namely the massacre. There is nothing definite here,
for everyone knew that Coligny was in constant, mortal danger
in Paris. Apart from these enigmatic remarks, and some reporting
on the night's events, Salviati only says that since the original
assault on Coligny the huguenots had been extremely menacing
(sempre parlato et trattato arrogantissimamente), particularly La
Rochefoucauld and Téligny who had dealt insolently with the
queen (dissero alla Regina parole troppo insolenti).

The next letter, of 27 August, is primarily concerned with the
religious situation. The queen, he said, eventually intended to
revoke the edict [of Saint-Germain] and to restore the observance
of catholicism. She did not think that anyone could any longer
reasonably doubt this, now that they [their majesties] had executed
the admiral and others, as she had previously explained to him
at Blois at the time of the negotiation of the Bourbon marriage
(February 1572) and other matters of current importance (the
English alliance) to the veracity of which he would testify before
God and the world.

> 'Qual Regina in progresso di tempo intende poi non solo di
> rivocare tal editto, ma per mezzo della giustitia di restituir la
> fede Cattolica nell'antica osservanza, parendogli che nessuno
> ne debba dubitare adesso, che hanno fatto morire l'Armiraglio
> con tanti altri huomini di valore, conforme ai raggionamenti
> altre volte havuti con esso meco essendo a Bles, et trattando
> del Parentato di Navarra, et dell'altre cose che correvano in
> quei tempi, il che essendo vero, ne posso rendere testimonianza,
> e a Nostro Signore e a tutto il mondo.'

While punctuation would appear to indicate that what had been discussed at Blois was the revocation of the edict and the restoration of France to catholicism, the letter could, possibly, be held to contain a slight innuendo that the death of the admiral might also have been discussed at Blois. As this had long been papal and catholic policy, at least since 1563, and the pope had allegedly written in November 1571 that the only possible purpose in permitting the admiral's return to court could be to destroy him, it is indeed likely that this was propounded by his extraordinary agents at Blois in February.[1] If so, Salviati was probably seeking a little personal credit by suggesting that he had been instrumental in provoking this portentous event, which the pope so warmly acclaimed. But the extreme dissatisfaction of Alessandrino at the time of his departure from Blois on 25 February 1572 precludes the possibility of any such decision having been taken.

It was obvious, following the declaration of 26 August by which the crown sought to secure the catholic advantages of the massacre, that Catherine should represent it to Salviati and hence to the pope as evidence of her long-term intention to restore catholicism, as he constantly demanded. The purpose of Salviati and cardinal Alessandrino in going to Blois in February 1572, had been to induce the king to join the Holy League and to frustrate the Bourbon marriage, in favour of a Portuguese match. The argument in favour of a Bourbon marriage and its dispensation, was as a means of attaching to the crown and converting to the faith the young princes, Navarre and Condé, thereby restoring peace to France, and France herself to catholicism. Thus, the marriage accomplished (albeit without the dispensation), the princes constrained to abjure, and the protestant leaders dead, it was easy – if ultimately disparaging – to maintain that this had been sincere. It was the obvious case for the crown to put to the pope.

It was not until 2 September that Salviati even claimed to have any *information*, although as late as 22 September he said there

[1] According to de Retz' biographer, this was also discussed early in 1572 at the house of his cousin Gondi at St Cloud. H. de Pommerol, *Albert de Gondi, maréchal de Retz*, 60.

were many versions of what had happened. In other words it was never generally known, even among the extreme catholics, and there was no consensus of opinion among contemporaries. On 2 September Salviati wrote that while the admiral had been at court he had gained such ascendancy over the king that he virtually disposed of everything as he wished. Either this was believed by Coligny's enemies or else it was propounded to explain whatever version of the subsequent events they subscribed to, since it has already been shown that there were very few days in August during which he *could* have been with the king, that he had met with Charles' stubborn opposition, that he was obliged to delay his departure until 25 August at the earliest, and that, on account of the marriages of Condé and Navarre and the dilatory tactics of queen Elizabeth, affairs of state were largely in abeyance. According to Salviati, this alleged predominance of Coligny offended de Morvillier, de Retz (a curious mixture) and others, and aroused the great jealousy (gelosia) of the queen, inaccurately described as 'madama la Regente'. But, in his letter of 22 September, he put not 'gelosia' but 'diffidenza', which is different. They – the queen and the councillors – therefore approached madame de Nemours and decided to dispose of Coligny. He included Anjou in the initial project, but not the king. The death of Coligny and his followers on 24 August he attributed to the danger implicit in the huguenot reaction, though he did not allege an actual plot. Finally, on 22 September, Salviati maintained that Catherine distrusted Coligny (venendo in diffidenza) and a few days before the event determined with madame de Nemours, Guise and Anjou – this time omitting de Retz – to have him shot. But such evidence, written a month after the public assumption by the crown of responsibility, is of little value. Salviati is therefore a major source for the incrimination of Catherine and Anjou, and also for the jealousy theory, although he used the words 'gelosia' and 'diffidenza' indifferently. He has also been used as evidence for premeditation, which involves distorting the texts of his letters.

Petrucci, writing on 23 August, gives a good impression of the fear and disorientation which followed the assault upon Coligny.

Neither then nor after the massacre did he claim to possess other than general information, and frankly stated that there were various opinions; some blamed the Guises and some enigmatically 'the palace'; others believed that the assault had been concerted by Lorraine with Savoy, de Retz and, rather vaguely, Spanish ministers. De Retz, he pointed out, was 'intrinsichissimo' with the duke of Savoy whose sister-in-law, madame de Dampierre, sent frequent information from the court to Savoy whenever anything adverse to the huguenots arose, because the duke held Coligny to be a personal enemy. Savoy was said by the Venetian, Cavalli, to be entirely Spanish.[1] The day after the massacre Petrucci reported that it was said to be on account of a protestant plot, but without confirming the opinion himself. Even at the end of August he only wrote that de Morvillier had wept in the council, and that he himself did not believe in any premeditation. The *gouverneurs* were being sent to their posts for fear of a nationwide furore. Coligny, he said, had wanted the huguenots to evacuate Paris, leaving only his son-in-law, Téligny with him, but they had refused. He himself would then have been safe and the rest could, presumably, have gone to the Netherlands. Coligny was not mortally wounded, the report continued, and this would certainly have been the most sensible plan; nothing vital need have been lost. This, if true – and it rings true – shows how little control Coligny exercised, and thus why he should, in the first place, have been forced by his own extremists into adopting an ill-conceived policy of which he disapproved, and manoeuvred into a catastrophically untenable position. This inability to control his followers is specifically stated, in Cavriana's account, to have been declared by Coligny himself. Petrucci concluded by saying that Anjou was 'sospeso' uttering barely a hundred words a day and, once again he feared a dangerous rift between the prince and the king.[2]

The anonymous account dated 27 August published by Desardins with Petrucci's despatches, and attributed to the Mantuan

[1] Desjardins, *Negs. Tosc.*, iii, 804–8, 23 August 1572; Albèri, *Relazioni*, 1st series, iv, 268.

[2] Desjardins, *Negs. Tosc.*, iii, 832, 31 August 1572.

physician Cavriana is the fullest, most interesting and measured of first-hand accounts.[1] Cavriana had no partisan purpose and clearly said that no one knew for certain what had happened. After stating what was generally known about the circumstances of the assault, he said that everyone was considering their own affairs and making various judgements. Some thought it was Guise, others blamed Lorraine, but 'i piu sobrii et savii' believed it was the handiwork of Anjou. Others said madame de Nemours, by means of a master of the royal household whose brother was majordomo to the cardinal Pellevé, from whose lodging the shot was fired. The question of ownership or occupation of the house seems to be generally confused, but the mention of Pellevé is interesting. He was an extreme political catholic and a strong 'eliminationist', absent in Rome with Lorraine.

After the assault, Cavriana says, almost the whole court visited Coligny, who is here said to have told the king that whatever happened it was absolutely essential that he should open war on Spain. The principal reason for this was not hatred of Spain, but to avert a civil war in France, far worse than ever before, because Coligny could no longer restrain the nobles, who were determined to fight (la quale non voleva altri che l'armi). Among all the unverifiable reports, this makes incomparably better sense, in so desperate an emergency, than allegations of conspiratorial whisperings about the influence of different members of the royal family. War or peace with Spain was, after all, the core and focus of the crisis and, if the report is true, represents an implicit recognition on the part of Coligny that this was why he had been assaulted.

Cavriana goes on to say that the huguenots, who were lodged about the admiral, began to discuss the form of their revenge. Téligny is said to have taken the lead in this, which is likely since he had promoted the Netherlands enterprise and represented the protestants at court since the peace of Saint-Germain. Several times he asked someone whom Cavriana described as 'un

[1] Desjardins, *Negs. Tosc.*, iii, 812–22, 27 August 1572, anonymous, possibly Cavriana to Concini.

gentilissimo amico nostro' (and presumably the writer's informant), to signify to the queen that he would do everything in his
power to avenge in arms this attempted assassination, if justice
were not done, fuming and threatening death and extermination.
He alerted the protestant churches and prepared to bring a contingent of cavalry into Paris, to arrive on 26 August which, together
with those already there, would number 4,000. This force, would
then seize the Louvre and kill everyone who had counselled,
assisted or promoted the assault, nominating certain individuals
to specific tasks. Thus Piles was to guard the entrance; Monino
to murder Guise, and Bricquemault Nevers. It was very much to
be feared that they would not even spare the royal family on
account of their fear of Anjou and Catherine. This, Cavriana said,
was practicable because of the numbers of protestants, estimated
at at least eighty, in the service of Navarre and Condé and
including Piles and Monino, who were already in the Louvre.

It is interesting to note that this is a cross between reports of a
dangerously menacing protestant attitude, and an actual protestant plot. Cavriana was not sure whether it was true, as some said,
that the actual plan of campaign had been revealed by Bouchavannes, or whether their threats alone had terrorised the court.
In Cavriana's account the nocturnal council in the Louvre on
Saturday 23 August consisted of Guise, Nevers, Montpensier,
Tavannes, de Retz, Birague, de Morvillier and others. The
participation of Anjou upon such an occasion is probably assumed.
He also records the moving collapse of de Morvillier, a keeper
who had surrendered the seals because he could not wield them
with integrity. Cavriana says that Catherine claimed to have
received three separate letters of warning that the huguenots had
resolved to kill herself, the king and indeed all the court. He does
not mention the municipality, but merely says that the seigneurs
took up arms, and refers to the popular tumult and the rejoicing
of the people of Paris. The court, he concluded – not only Anjou –
was thunderstruck by what had happened, and unable to recover any composure. The Spanish were jubilant, and he prayed
God they would not wax too great at the cost of French
blood.

The Venetians, Michiel and Cavalli,[1] must be mentioned, because they are normally and rightly held to be an excellent source. But, in this case, it is abundantly clear that they were as ignorant as everyone else. Michiel blamed Catherine and Anjou for the assault on the admiral, but his colleague Cavalli, who was also there, did not. They both attributed much influence to Coligny over the king, apparently referring to the month of August, but at the same time saying that after the defeat of Genlis Charles depended upon Catherine.

The brief paper known as Alva's account, sent by his agent in France, Gomicourt, on 28 August, is remarkably ill-informed, and adds nothing of the slightest interest except that he, like Cavriana, mentions an intended gathering of 4,000 huguenots. But he also says that the court had not four hours to spare, which does not make sense. He reports the marquis (sic) de Retz as being one of the dead, and clearly had no grasp whatever of French affairs.[2]

The last of the diplomatic documents to be considered is the report dictated in Spain by Olaegui[3] secretary to Zúñiga the Spanish ambassador in France. The report is very thin and quickly establishes that Zúñiga knew no more than anyone else. After describing in some detail the assault on the admiral, the escape and pursuit of the assassin, Olaegui mentions unselectively the king *or* (sic) Anjou, Guise and Aumaule, *or* Alva as having instigated the deed. He goes on to describe the royal visit to Coligny, attributing to Charles and Coligny a childish argument about which of them could raise the greater number of men. He then represents protestant threats as coming from the prince de Condé in the Louvre. That night, Olaegui continued, Charles went to bed early and rose again at 10 p.m., to send for the

---

[1] Albèri, *Relazioni*, 1st series, iv.

[2] This, roughly was the opinion of Gachard, who published the account in the *Bulletins de l'Académie royale de Belgique*, ix (1842), 560-7. It is interesting to note that Morillon, the *prévôt* of Brussels expressed his astonishment in a letter to Granvelle that Alva should be so ill-informed; he meant in a general sense. Granvelle, *Correspondance*, iv, p. 318, c. 16 July 1572, Morillon to Granvelle.

[3] *Bulletins de l'Académie royale de Belgique*, xvi (1849), 235-57.

former *prévôt des marchands* to prepare for trouble in the city, to begin when they heard the alarm. 'That night' would appear to refer to Friday, but what follows refers to Saturday 23 August. This confusion of timing has been reproduced in various places. After writing about the killings, in which Guise personally is said to have killed Coligny, Olaegui says that Charles went to the *parlement* on Tuesday 27 August and revoked the edict of Saint-Germain, restoring the previous one [of Saint-Maur 1568]. In fact he went to the *parlement* on Tuesday 26 August, and he confirmed the edict of Saint-Germain. The rest of the account refers to the events of Olaegui's journey, except to add that there were not more protestants on the frontiers of Champagne than Alva could easily slaughter.

XVIII

The Meaning of the Massacre

THE POVERTY, confusion and partiality of this evidence relating to the massacre is incontestable, and no individual role can be adequately established. The comte de Retz, in conjunction with Anjou, is the most commonly incriminated and, in view of the ignorance of Salviati, Zúñiga and Petrucci, and the absence of Lorraine, de Retz is the most *likely* person in France to have promoted another assault upon the admiral, and for the pro-Spanish purpose of preventing an invasion of the Netherlands. One should, however, beware of deducing from the circumstances that the last and most notorious of all attempts upon Coligny's life was *necessarily* an immediate consequence of the international situation.[1] This cannot be fully substantiated and dramatic and consequential coincidences do occur. The most likely explanation is a remarkable concurrence of external and internal, or European and civil-war pressures with more individual animosities. But the mystery remains, and it must be emphasised that *no definite assertion is justifiable*, so far as the assault is concerned.

It would, however, be difficult to avoid the conclusion that the court – not to be more specific – together with a group of leading councillors, adopted the catholic policy of elimination as an emergency measure in fear and desperation during the night of 23–24 August. An item in Isambert dated 22–23 August, but

---

[1] J. H. Huizinga quotes a telling anecdote from Michelet: 'Years after the Revolution, a young man asked the old Merlin of Thionville why he helped to condemn Robespierre. The old man kept silent, but seemed to be groping for words. Suddenly he rose up and said with a violent gesture: "Robespierre . . . Robespierre! If only you had seen his green eyes, you, too, would surely have condemned him." His green eyes.' Huizinga, *Dutch Civilisation in the Seventeenth Century*, 233.

minus the text which is lost, runs as follows: 'Ordre royal délibéré en conseil privé où assistaient la reine mère, les deux frères du roi, et plusieurs conseillers intimes qui ordonne le massacre de la Saint-Barthélemy.'[1] Further evidence makes it morally certain that this should be interpreted to mean the huguenot leaders. The *Régistres des délibérations du bureau de la ville de Paris*, which must be regarded as a good source, record precautions against disorders in the capital, beginning on the Friday morning after the assault upon Coligny.[2] The various city guards were to be mobilised, powder guarded and the gates watched. It is further recorded that the *prévôt des marchands* was summoned to the Louvre late on the Saturday night to the emergency council meeting. There he was informed by the king that the protestants meant to 's'élever par conspiration' against himself and the state, and to disturb Paris. The *prévôt* was therefore to close all the gates, seize the keys, and let no one pass. He was to chain up the boats on the river, and mobilise all the municipal guards. He was to place all the artillery of Paris before the hôtel de ville, to close the nearby boulevard des Célestins, and to guard other points such as the tour de Nesle to the east of Paris on the river.

One does not know what passed by word of mouth. If such measures might have been employed to facilitate a massacre, this is highly improbable, not least because of its peril. More convincing, however, than security measures, is the evidence that Charles sought to arrest the massacre, together with the reports of Cavriana and Petrucci that the court and Anjou were shocked and stupefied by what had happened. This understandable condition appears to have been reflected in the immediate reactions of the crown, which were not consistent. Writing to La Mothe in England on 22 and 24 August, Charles blamed both the assault and the massacre upon the Guises and the vendetta, the simplest explanation and one which was widely assumed.

[1] Isambert, *Édits et ordonnances*, xiv, 256.
[2] François Bonardot, *Registres des délibérations du bureau de la ville de Paris*, vii, 9 seq. These minutes are reprinted in Cimber et Danjou, *Archives curieuses*, série i, vol. vii, 211–29.

Then, on 26 August, Charles sent Mondoucet in the Netherlands an account of the assault on Coligny, after which he again said that in order to forestall the 'si pernicieuse entreprise' of the protestants, he had been obliged to permit and assist the Guises to strike down the admiral, which they did, together with all his adherents. Among the dead were Téligny and La Rochefoucauld. Cavaignes and Bricquemault were executed in October; La Noue was in the Netherlands, and the vidame and Montgommery escaped to England. But to Mondoucet Charles explained that the death of the leaders had been accompanied by a popular disturbance, as a result of which many other protestants also perished.[1] This is borne out by Salviati who maintains that the murder of Coligny and the huguenot leaders began at 2 a.m., and that the city then rose in arms against all huguenots. He appears to be alone in recording that the king had issued an edict at 3 a.m. on 24 August ordering the cessation of killing and sacking, in which case the crown had taken corrective action the *moment* the popular tumult became apparent.[2] One may query Salviati's timing, but he is rather unlikely to have invented the edict. Furthermore, the Paris *Régistres* record that the *quarteniers* received orders, dated 24 August, to command the 'bourgeois, manans et habitans' to disarm and go home. One could, of course, precipitate a tumult and then countermand it, but one cannot take the argument any further.

Apart from this evidence, there is no reason to suppose that the crown was responsible for the massacre, in the popular sense which, by its intrinsic nature, might perhaps be unleashed but scarcely organised. Paris had for years past been seething with riotous, sectarian turbulence and manifest hatred. There had been violent trouble over the *croix des Gâtines*, between August and the night of 20 December 1571, when the populace sacked two

[1] *Bulletin de la Commission royale d'histoire*, série ii, vol. iv (1852), 334–6, 26 August 1572, Charles to Mondoucet.

[2] Theiner, *Annales Ecclesiastici*, i, 328–9, 24 August 1572, Salviati to cardinal di Como; Isambert, *Édits et ordonnances*, xiv, 256, indicates, without the text, such an edict dated 25 August 1572. The timing of the night's events is confused. The alarm is variously said to have sounded at 12, 1, 3 and 4 a.m.

protestant houses and raced about the streets yelling for the blood of the huguenots. Order had had to be restored by the *gouverneur*, François de Montmorency, with 4–500 horse.[1] If this temper persisted in the capital, it is not surprising that a massacre should have broken out when Paris was abnormally filled with unwelcome huguenots and rough Gascon types who appeared as boorish foreigners in the Ile-de-France. Besides, it is to be supposed, if it cannot be demonstrated, that Parisians had not so quickly forgiven and forgotten the siege of their city in 1567, during the second civil war. The massacre in Paris shows the continuation of violent religious antipathy at a popular level, whereas no contemporary ever suggested that religion, as such, had anything directly to do with the death of the admiral and his principal followers.

It is therefore reasonable to suppose that the measures commanded on the Saturday night were intended both to facilitate the elimination of the huguenot leaders and to prevent them from acting themselves. According to the *prévôt*, they had gone so far as to convey to the king 'quelques propos haultains et souvans en menasses'. This is imprecise, and it is very unlikely that anyone ever clearly knew what to expect. But, whether or not they were organised under Téligny's leadership, it is certain that they were furiously enraged against the government which had failed, yet again, to protect them and their leader within the law. At the least, ferocious *ad hoc* disorders must be anticipated, if not a military attack by Téligny's 4,000 cavalry, or both. This could not possibly be disregarded as an idle threat, since it was exactly the number of horse that Coligny had informed queen Elizabeth would be ready to invade the Netherlands by 15 August. Furthermore, there were also 12,000 foot not very far away'[2] A possible plan of campaign, said to involve 4,000 horse, in Paris, in arms and against the king, that was countered by pre-emptive

---

[1] Desjardins, *Negs. Tosc.*, iii, 701, 22 August 1571; B.N., Mss. fr. 3188, f. 24, 29 September [1571], Nançay to his father the comte de Bouchage; *CSPF.*, 1569–71, p. 579, 28 December 1571, Killigrew to Burghley; 582–3, 30 December 1571, Walsingham, advertisements.

[2] See p. 306.

action on the part of the court, which could not sanely retire for the night awaiting events, should not be seen in terms of murder and massacre. This was war: the catastrophic, ruinous, fourth civil war, which Coligny had feared and repeatedly predicted, and whichever party – the court or the huguenots – failed to seize the initiative, was very likely to perish.

Thus Charles' letter to Mondoucet was probably pretty close to the truth. But, also on 26 August – the day that Alva left Brussels to march towards Mons – Charles appeared before the *parlement* of Paris and declared that everything had been done upon his orders, and letters patent, probably of the same date, drafted by Villeroy, announced his responsibility for the death of the admiral and 'aultres ses adherans' on account of their conspiracy against the royal family and other members of the court, at the same time as confirming the edict of pacification.[1] Estienne Pasquier, himself a *parlementaire*, also recorded that, 'deux jours après ceste grande execution, le Roy est venu au Parlement & là seant en son lict de Justice a advoué tout ce qui s'estoit passé, comme faict par son exprés commandement'.[2] There appears to have been a further declaration of 28 August which also specifically confirmed the edict but, at the same time, temporarily forbade all assemblies for preaching or any other purpose.[3] It could be this, if accurate, which gave rise to reports that the edict had been revoked. But it is clear from a letter of 24 August 1572 to the *gouverneur* of Burgundy that these documents, which were doubtless very hurriedly drafted, represent a clumsy attempt both to guarantee the edict, and to prevent any local armed gatherings or general rising.[4] The letter of 24 August 1572 to the lieutenant-general in Touraine called for the maintenance of the edict more diligently than ever before, in order to

[1] Institut de France, Fonds Godefroy, 290, f. 25, letters patent, undated draft by Villeroy; Isambert, *Édits et ordonnances*, xiv, 257; La Mothe, vii, 322, 323–5, 22 & 24 August 1572, Charles to La Mothe; Desjardins, *Negs. Tosc.*, iii, 809–11, 27 August 1572, Petrucci to Concini.

[2] Pasquier, *Lettres historiques*, 207.

[3] Isambert, *Édits et ordonnances*, xiv, 257–9, 28 August 1572.

[4] Cimber et Danjou, *Archives curieuses*, série i, vol. vii, 132–5, 24 August 1572, Charles to the *gouverneur* of Burgundy.

prevent any risings in the country. Although everyone was commanded to remain at home – that is to say, not to take the field – there is not otherwise any mention here of the prohibition of either assemblies or preaching.[1] Ambiguous directives, however, could be variously interpreted by those concerned, and variously executed according to the disposition of the *gouverneurs* and local officials.

The items in Isambert tally with the words of Pasquier declaring the king the author of everything that had happened. They do not, however, tally with Villeroy's draft of the letters patent, which only accepted responsibility for the death of the admiral and 'aultres ses adherans', or the letter to Mondoucet in which the massacre was blamed upon the popular disturbance. This is an important distinction, clear in the documents. It is likely to be true, and it is difficult to interpret. Was it a fortuitous result of careless drafting, or did the king originally intend to sustain it? If so, why was the intention so quickly abandoned? While one cannot be sure, the answer may lie in the immediate dangers of the crisis. Charles was probably vainly seeking to confine the inevitable conflagration to the Netherlands, and the assumption of responsibility was not without some political acumen in the circumstances. As the protestants were maddened beyond control, regardless of the true origins of the assault and the massacre, they were no longer a potential source of support. It was therefore both obvious and essential for the crown to seek to claim some catholic advantage from these irreversible events, if only to mitigate the awful danger from Alva, the principal beneficiary of the massacre. In the estimation of William of Orange, he would otherwise have been swiftly overthrown: 'selon toutes apparences humaines,' he wrote, 'nous estions désjà pour cest heure maîtres du Duc d'Alve, et eussions capitulé à nostre plaisir. Maintenant au contraire . . .'[2] William arrived before Mons on 8 September and

---

[1] Printed in *Harleian Miscellany*, vii, 360, 'De Furoribus gallicis'.

[2] G. van Prinsterer, *Archives ou correspondance, série* i, vol. iii, 505, 21 September 1572, William of Orange to count Jean; vol. iv, app. 23-5, 15 November 1572, Saint-Gouard to Charles IX; Gachard, *Correspondance de Guillaume le Taciturne*, i, pp. xv-xviii.

immediately realised the hopelessness of the situation. Early in October he disbanded the forces he had gathered with such laborious pains, and withdrew into Holland.

Charles' frantic concern at the approach of Alva is clear from the rest of the letter to Mondoucet. If neither diverted nor propitiated, Alva might either invade France, or else release the prisoners of Valenciennes and Mons to avenge their confederates, while he himself concentrated upon the suppression of rebels in Flanders. Mondoucet was therefore ordered to maintain very secret contact with Orange, 'affin de ne luy donner occasion d'habandonner les entreprises quil a par delà pour en venir faire d'autres en mon royaume au secours de ceulx de ladite nouvelle religion'.¹ Meanwhile Alva must be mollified, and congratulated upon his felicitous and timely siege of Mons, containing, as it did, Charles' most factious subjects. But although, paradoxically, the massacre precipitated this immediate danger of the invasion of France by the Spanish governor of the Netherlands, Philip II himself sent the marquis d'Ayamonte to congratulate Charles, Catherine and Anjou, to encourage them to continue 'dans ce système,' and to offer help, as he had repeatedly done before, for the pursuit of violent measures.² The pope, for his part, struck a special medallion to commemorate the holy event.

If the massacre had cheated Orange of anticipated victory in the Netherlands, it may also, on the face of it, have deprived France of the long-pursued English marriage, since everyone in England was then favourable and Elizabeth had informed La Mothe on 17 August of her intention to marry Alençon upon the terms agreed for Anjou, provided a meeting were arranged, to which Catherine had already consented.³ This, at any rate, was the

¹ Fears that Orange would invade France were fairly generally expressed. Desjardins, *Negs. Tosc.*, iii, 806, 23 August 1572; Theiner, *Annales Ecclesiastici*, i, 330, 27 August 1572, Salviati to cardinal di Como; Albèri, *Relazioni*, 1st series, iv, 285, November 1572.
² Gachard, 'Particularités inédites sur la Saint-Barthélemy', *Bulletins de l'Académie royale de Belgique*, série i, vol. xvi (1849), 249.
³ La Mothe, v, 91–111, 28 August 1572, La Mothe to Charles IX and Catherine.

conclusion of La Mole's mission. But now everything had changed over night, and Charles' letter to Mondoucet reveals his terrible preoccupations. He had to prevent any provincial or general rising in France and to avert an invasion by William of Orange in support of his protestant confederates whose brief, inglorious liaison with the crown had proved even more disastrous than Coligny had always feared. He had also to prevent an invasion by Alva, and possibly a general war with Spain not merely without the declared alliance of England, but in which neither the huguenots nor the catholics could be expected to assist him. Thus Charles had finally reached a point at which paradox and confusion could hardly have been worse confounded. All the civil war elements – the weakness and indigence of the crown, the struggle for control of the council, the variegated, internecine rivalry of the nobility, subsequently engulfed into an international, ideological conflict, itself confused by a profoundly cynical struggle for power – all these elements were present in the collapse of France in the massacre of St Bartholomew in August 1572. The realistic validity of Catherine's reiterated fears and warnings could not have been more starkly apparent. Charles was isolated in ignominious impotence, and the duke of Alva could have marched upon Paris.

Whether or not it can be explained in this way, or indeed explained at all, it is certain that after Charles' declaration in the *parlement* of 26 August, the distinction between the assault, the subsequent death of Coligny and his lieutenants, and the general massacre became blurred. Later evidence must be treated with particular care because the royal assumption of responsibility both permitted the catholics retrospective wisdom, and played into the hands of the outraged protestants. Thereafter they no longer blamed the Guises, Lorraine or his adherents in France, but the crown. This confusion of thought, together with the plentiful purveyance of the pamphleteers, largely accounts for the traditional assumption that the massacre – as a complex of events – was Catherine's calculated crime, in spite of some eight major efforts – several of which still lay in the future – to establish the protestants within the law. While catholic extremists, whether

French or foreign – could easily have been accused, the royal declaration which enabled the protestants to blame the crown, shortly became their defensible pretext for a developing, political and military organisation, through which the civil conflict assumed a new and revolutionary turn.

The death of Coligny had extinguished the old vendetta, and Lorraine was the sole survivor of the original antagonists. He was also the only one known to have died a natural death – some two years later on 26 December 1574. He had, however, enjoyed a brief return to power with the accession of Anjou as Henry III who arrived back from Poland in August that year. Bereft of the cardinal's ability, Henry himself was about to reap, as king, the awful harvest of retribution he had previously sown as heir presumptive, simultaneously suffering the armed opposition of the organised protestants, and the sophisticated treachery of the catholic extremists.

Appendix

The 'treaty' of the Triumvirate

[1561] *Sommaire des choses premièrement accordées entre les ducs de Montmorency connestable, et de Guyse grand maistre, pairs de France, et le mareschal Sainct André, pour la conspiration du triumvirat, et depuis mises en délibération à l'entrée du sacré et sainct concile de Trente, et arrestée entre les parties, en leur privé conseil faict contre les hérétiques, et contre le roy de Navarre, en tant qu'il gouverne et conduit mal les affaires de Charles neufiesme roy de France, mineur; lequel est autheur de continuel accroissement de la nouvelle secte qui pullule en France.*

Premièrement, afin que la chose soit conduite par plus grande authorité, on est d'avis de bailler la superintendance de tout l'affaire, au roy Philippe Catholique; et à ceste fin, d'un commun consentement le tout chef et conducteur de toute l'entreprise. Ont estimé bon de procéder en ceste façon, que le roy Philippe aborde le roy de Navarre par plaintes et quérelles, à raison que contre l'institution de ses prédécesseurs, et au grand danger du Roy pupille, duquel il a la charge, nourrit et entretient une nouvelle religion; et si en cela se monstre difficile, le Roy Catholique par belles promesses, aissera de le retirer de sa meschanceté et malheureuse délibération, luy descouvrant quelque espoir de récouvrer son royaume de Navarre, ou bien de quelque autre grand profit et émolument, en récompence dudit royaume: l'adoucira et ployra, s'il est possible, pour le retenir de costé, et conspirer avecques luy contre les autres autheurs de ceste secte pernicieuse; ce que succedant à souhait, seront lors faciles et abregez les moyens de la guerre future: mais poursuivant et demeurant iceluy tousjours obstiné, néantmoins le roy Philippe, à qui, tant par l'authorité à luy donnée par le sainct concile, que par le voisinage et proximité, la chose touche de plus près, par lettres gracieuses et douces l'admonestera de son devoir, entremeslant en ses promesses et blandices, quelques menaces: cependant, tant secrètement et occultement que faire se pourra, se fera sur l'hyver quelque levée et amas de gens deslite au royaume d'Espaigne: puis ayant ses forces prestes, déclairera en public ce qu'il brasse; et ainsi le roy de Navarre sans armes et pris à l'impourveu, facilement sera opprimé; encores que d'aventure avecques troupe tumultuaire et ramassée, s'efforçast aller à l'encontre, ou voulust empescher son ennemi d'entrer en païs.

Or s'il cède, sera aisément chassé hors son royaume, et avecques luy sa femme et ses enfans; mais s'il luy fait teste, et plusieurs volontaires gendarmes et sans soulde, le deffendent (car plusieurs des conjurez d'icelle secte se pourroyent avancer pour retarder la victoire), alors le duc de Guyse se déclarera chef de la confession catholique, et fera amas de gens d'armes, vaillants, et de tous ceux de sa suitte. Aussi d'un autre part, pressera le Navarrois; en sorte qu'estant poursuyvi d'un costé et d'autre, tombera en proye: car certainement un tel roy ne peut faire teste à deux chefs, ni à deux exercites si puissants.

L'Empereur, et les autres princes allemans qui sont encores catholiques, mettront peine de boucher les passages qui vont en France, pendant que la guerre s'y fera; de peur que les princes protestans ne facent passer quelque force, et envoyent secours audit roy de Navarre: de peur aussi que les cantons de Souysse ne luy prestent ayde, faut que les cantons qui suivent encor l'authorité de l'Église romaine, dénoncent la guerre aux autres; et que le Pape aide de tant de forces qu'il pourra, lesdicts cantons de sa religion, et baille soubs mains argent et autres choses nécessaires au soustenement des frais de la guerre.

Durant ce, le Roy Catholique baillera part de son exercite au duc de Savoye, qui de son costé fera levée de gens si grande que commodément faire se pourra en ses terres. Le Pape et les autres princes d'Italie déclareront chef de leur armée le duc de Ferrare qui se viendra joindre au duc de Savoye; et pour augmenter leurs forces, l'empereur Ferdinand donnera ordre d'envoyer quelques compagnies de gens de pied et de cheval allemans.

Le duc de Savoye, pendant que la guerre troublera ainsi la France et les Souysses, avec toutes ses forces, se ruëra à l'imporveu

sur la ville de Genève, sur le lac de Lozane, la forcera, et plustost
ne se départira ses gens, qu'il ne soit maistre et joüissant de ladicte
ville; mettant au fil de l'épée, ou jettant dedans le lac tous les
vivans qui y seront trouvez, sans aucune discrétion de sexe ou
aage, pour donner à congnoistre à tous, qu'enfin la divine puissance a compensé le retardement de la peine, par la griefve
grandeur de tel supplice; et qu'ainsi souvent faict résentir les
enfans et porter la peine, par exemple mémorable à tout jamais,
de la meschanceté de leurs pères, et mesmes de celle qu'ils ont
commise contre la religion; en quoy faisant, ne faut doubter que
les voisins touchez de ceste cruauté et tremeur, ne puissent estre
ramenez à santé; et principalement ceux qui, à raison de l'aage ou
de l'ignorance, sont plus rudes ou grossiers, et par conséquent plus
aisez à mener; ausquels il faut pardonner.

Mais en France, pour bonnes et justes raisons, il fait bon suivre
autre chemin, et ne pardonner en façon quelconque à la vie
d'aucun qui autrefois ait fait profession de ceste secte; et sera
baillée ceste commission d'extirper tous ceux de la nouvelle
religion, au duc de Guyse, qui aura en charge d'effacer entièrement le nom de la famille et race des Bourbons; de peur qu'enfin
ne sorte d'eux quelqu'un qui poursuive la vengeance de ces
choses, ou remette sus ceste nouvelle religion.

Ainsi les choses ordonnées par la France, et le royaume remis
en son entier, ancien et pristin estat, ayant amassé gens de tous
costez, il est bésoing envahir l'Allemagne, et avec l'aide de
l'Empereur et des évesques, la rendre et restituer au Sainct-Siège
apostolique: et où ceste guerre seroit plus forte et plus longue que
l'on ne pense et désire, afin que, par faute d'argent ne soit conduite plus laschement ou plus incommodément, le duc de Guyse,
pour obvier à cest inconvénient, prestera à l'Empereur et aux
autres princes d'Allemagne et seigneurs ecclésiastiques, tout
l'argent qu'ils auront amassé de la confiscation et despouille de
tant de nobles bourgois et riches, qui auront esté tuez en France, à
cause de la nouvelle religion; qui se monte à grande somme;
prenant par ledit seigneur de Guyse suffisante caution et respon-
dant, par le moyen desquelles, après la confection de la guerre, sera
remboursé de tous les deniers employez à cest effect, sur les

despouilles des Luthériens et autres, qui pour le faict de la religion seront tuez en Allemaigne. De la part des Saincts Pères, pour ne défaillir, et n'estre veus négligens à porter aide à tant saincte affaire de guerre, ou vouloir espargner leur revenu et propres deniers, ont adjousté que les cardinaux se devoyent contenter pour revenu annuel, de cinq ou six mille escus; les évesques plus riches, de deux ou trois mille au plus; et le reste dudit revenu, le donner de franche volonté, à l'entretenement de la guerre qui se conduit pour extirper la secte des Luthériens et Calvinistes, et restablir l'Église romaine, jusqu'à ce que la chose soit conduite à heureuse fin.

Que si quelque ecclésiastique ou clerc a vouloir de suivre les armes en guerre si saincte, les Pères ont d'un commun consentement conclu et arresté qu'il se peut faire et s'enrouller en ceste guerre seulement, et ce sans aucun scrupule de conscience.

Par ces moyens, France et Allemaigne ainsi chastiées, rabaissées et conduites à l'obéissance de la saincte Église romaine, les Pères ne font doubte que le temps ne pourvoye de conseil et commodités propres à faire que les aultres royaumes prochains soyent ramenez au troupeau et sous un gouverneur et pasteur apostolique, mais qu'il plaise à Dieu ayder et favoriser leurs présents desseings saincts et pleins de piété.

Bibliography

The abbreviations and short titles which follow in square brackets are
those used in the footnotes.

I MANUSCRIPT SOURCES

PARIS
Bibliothèque nationale
Fonds français [Mss. fr.]
Nouvelles acquisitions françaises [Mss. n.a.f.]
Cinq Cents Colbert
Fonds Clairambault
Fonds Dupuy
Fonds Italien [Mss. Italien]
Institut de France
Fonds Godefroy, by courteous permission

CHANTILLY
Musée Condé
Archives de Chantilly
Papiers Condé

GENEVA
Archives d'État de Genève
Pièces historiques [P.H.]
Régistres du Conseil

LONDON
British Museum
Mss. Cotton, Vespasian
Public Record Office
State Papers (PRO/SP)

HATFIELD
Hatfield House
Cecil Papers, by courtesy of the late marquess
of Salisbury.

II PRINTED WORKS CITED IN THE TEXT

Albèri, Eugenio, *Relazioni degli ambasciatori veneti,* 15 vols (Florence, 1839–63)

Amirault, Moyse, *La Vie de François seigneur de la Noue* (Leiden, 1661)

Archives historiques de la Gironde, i (Bordeaux, 1859)

Archivo documental Español, Negociaciones con Francia, 1559–1566, 9 vols (Madrid, Real Academia de la Historia, 1950–54)

Atkinson, E. G., *The Cardinal of Châtillon in England, 1568–1571* (London, 1890)

Aubigné, A. d'. *See* Ruble, Alphonse de

Aumale, *Histoire des princes de Condé,* 8 vols (Paris, 1863–96)

Baguenault de Puchesse, Gustave, *Jean de Morvillier évêque d'Orléans, garde des sceaux de France* (Paris, 1870)

Bastard d'Estang, L. de, *Vie de Jean de Ferrières vidame de Chartres, seigneur de Maligny* (Auxerre, 1858)

Bonardot, François, *Régistres des délibérations du bureau de la ville de Paris,* vii (Paris, 1893)

Bonnet, Jules, *Mémoires de la vie de Jean de Parthenay-Larchevêque sieur de Soubise* (Paris, 1879)

Boulé, Alphonse, *Catherine de Médicis et Coligny* (Paris, 1913)

Bourquelot, F., *Mémoires de Claude Haton,* 2 vols (Paris, 1857)

Brantôme, Pierre de. *See* Lalanne

Bulletin de la société de l'histoire du protestantisme français [*BSHPF.*]

Butterfield, Herbert, *Man on his Past* (Cambridge, 1955)

Cabié, Edmond, *Ambassade en Espagne de Jean Ébrard de Saint-Sulpice, 1562–1565* (Albi, 1903)

—— *Guerres de religion dans le sud-ouest de la France* (1906)

Calendars of State Papers
  Domestic [*CSPDom.*]
  Foreign [*CSPF.*]
  Rome [*CSP Rome*]
  Spanish [*CSPSp.*]
  Venetian [*CSPVen.*]

Capilupi, Camillo, *Le Stratagème de Charles IX . . . contre les huguenots rebelles,* 1572, translated from Italian in Cimber et Danjou, *Archives curieuses, série* i, vol. vii

Castelnau, Michel de. *See* Michaud et Poujoulat

Catena, Girolamo, *Vita del Gloriosissimo Papa Pio Quinto* (Mantua, 1587)

Catherine de Médicis. *See* La Ferrière, H. de

Champion, Pierre, *Charles IX, la France et le contrôle de l'Espagne*, 2 vols (Paris, 1939)

—— *La Jeunesse de Henri III*, 2 vols (ed. Paris, 1942)

Charrière, E., *Négociations de la France dans le Levant*, 4 vols (Paris, 1848–60)

Combes, M. F., *L'Entrevue de Bayonne de 1565 et la question de la Saint-Barthélemy* (Paris, 1882)

Condé, Louis Ier, prince de, *Mémoires*, 6 vols (ed. London, 1743)

Courteault, P., *Blaise de Monluc historien* (Paris, 1908)

Delaborde, Jules, *Gaspard de Coligny amiral de France*, 3 vols (Paris, 1879–82) [Delaborde, *Coligny*]

De Potter, Joseph, *Lettres de Saint Pie V* (Brussels, 1827)

Desjardins, Abel, *Charles IX, deux années de règne, 1570–1572* (Douai, 1873)

—— *Négociations diplomatiques de la France avec la Toscane*, 6 vols (Paris, 1859–86) [Desjardins, *Negs. Tosc.*]

Desormeaux, Joseph-L.R., *Histoire de la maison de Bourbon*, 5 vols (Paris, 1772–88)

Digges, Dudley, *The Compleat Ambassador* (ed. London, 1655) [Digges]

Discours du Roy Henri III à un personnage d'honneur. Petitot, *Collection des mémoires relatifs à l'histoire de France*, série i, vol. xliv

Douais, C., *Lettres de Charles IX à M. de Fourquevaulx ambassadeur en Espagne, 1565–1572* (Paris, 1897)

Du Bouchet, *Preuves de l'histoire de l'illustre maison de Coligny* (Paris, 1662)

Dufey, P. J. S., *Massacres de la Saint-Barthélemy*, in *Paris révolutionnaire*, iii (Paris, 1838)

—— *Michel de l'Hospital, Œuvres complètes*, 3 vols (ed. Paris, 1824–5)

Duplessis-Mornay, Philippe, *Mémoires et correspondance*, 12 vols (Paris, 1824–5)

Dupuy, P., *Traité de la majorité de nos rois* (Paris, 1655)

Edwards, Francis, *The Marvellous Chance. Thomas Howard, fourth duke of Norfolk and the Ridolphi Plot, 1570–1572* (London, 1968)

Ellis, Henry, *Original letters illustrative of English History*, 11 vols (ed. London, 1969)

Erlanger, Philippe, *St Bartholomew's Night* (trans. Patrick O'Brian, London, 1962)

Este, Hyppolite d', *Négociations ou lettres d'affaires ecclésiastiques et politiques écrites au pape Pie IV* (ed. Paris, 1658) [Este, *Négociations*]

Fontanon, A., *Les Édits et ordonnances des rois de France*, 4 vols (Paris 1611)

Forbes, Dr *A Full View of the Public Transactions in the Reign of Queen Elizabeth*, 2 vols (London, 1740–1)

Gachard, L. P., *Correspondance de Guillaume le Taciturne*, 6 vols (Brussels, 1850–7)

—— *Correspondance de Philippe II sur les affaires des Pays-Bas*, 5 vols (Brussels, 1848–79)

—— *La Bibliothèque nationale à Paris. Notices et extraits des manuscrits qui concernent l'histoire de Belgique*, 2 vols (Brussels, 1875, 1877) [Gachard, *Notices et extraits*]

—— 'Particularités inédites sur la Saint-Barthélemy', *Bulletins de l'Académie royale de Belgique*, xvi (1849)

Geyl, Pieter, *The Revolt of the Netherlands, 1555–1609* (ed. London, 1958)

Gigon, S.-G., *La Troisième guerre de religion* (Paris, 1911)

González, Tomás, 'Apuntamientos para la historia de Rey Don Felipe segundo . . .', *Memorias de la Real Academia de la Historia*, vii (1832)

Goulart, Simon, *Mémoires de l'Estat de France sous Charles IX*, 3 vols (ed. Middelburg, 1578)

Granvelle, Antoine Perrenot de. See Piot, Charles and Weiss, Charles

Guise, François duc de. See Michaud et Poujoulat

Haynes, Samuel, *A Collection of State Papers . . . 1542–1570* (London, 1740)

Henry et Loriquet (Eds.), *Correspondance de Philibert Babou de la Bourdaisière, évêque d'Angoulême* (Travaux de l'Académie de Reims, xxvii, 1859)

Hirschauer, Charles, *La Politique de St Pie V en France, 1566–1572* (Paris, 1922)

Historical Manuscripts Commission, Calendar of the Manuscripts of the marquis of Salisbury, at Hatfield House (1883–1940) [HMC Hatfield]

Huizinga, J. H., *Dutch Civilisation in the Seventeenth Century and other Essays* (London, 1968)

Isambert, François André, *Recueil général des anciennes lois françaises*
29 vols (Paris, 1829–33) [Isambert, *Édits et ordonnances*]

Kervyn de Lettenhove, *Documents inédits relatifs à l'histoire du XVIe siècle* (Brussels, 1883)
—— *Les Huguenots et les gueux, 1560–1585*, 6 vols (Bruges, 1883–5)
—— *Relations politiques des Pays-Bas et de l'Angleterre sous le règne de Philippe II*, 11 vols (Brussels, 1882–1900) [Kervyn de Lettenhove, *Relations*]

La Ferrière, H. de, Catherine de Médicis, *Lettres*, vols i–iv (Paris, 1880–1895) [La Ferrière, *Lettres*]
—— 'La Troisième Guerre civile et la paix de Saint-Germain, 1568–1570', *Revue des questions historiques*, xli (1887)
—— 'L'Entrevue de Bayonne', *Revue des questions historiques*, xxxiv (1883)
La Huguerye. *See* Ruble, Alphonse de
Lalanne, Ludovic (Ed.), Brantôme, *Œuvres complètes*, 11 vols (Paris, 1864–82)
Lalourcé et Duval, *Recueil de pièces originales et authentiques, concernant la tenue des États Généraux*, 9 vols (1789)
La Mothe-Fénelon, Bertrand de Salignac de, *Correspondance diplomatique*, 7 vols (Paris, 1838, 1840) [La Mothe]
La Noue, François de. *See* Sutcliffe, F. E.
Léonard, Frédéric, *Recueil des traitez de paix* . . . 6 vols (Paris, 1693)
L'Hospital, Michel de. *See* Dufey

Marlet, Léon, *Correspondance d'Odet de Coligny cardinal de Châtillon* (Société historique et archéologique du Gâtinais, documents, i, Paris, 1885)
—— *Le comte de Montgommery* (Paris, 1890)
Martin, C. T., 'Journal of Sir Francis Walsingham, December 1570 to December 1583', *Camden Society Miscellany*, vi (1870)
Mergey, Jean de. *See* Michaud et Poujoulat
Michaud et Poujoulat, *Nouvelle collection des mémoires pour servir à l'histoire de France*, série i:
    vol. vi, *Mémoires-journaux de François duc de Guise*
    vol. viii, *Mémoires de Gaspard de Saulx-Tavannes*
    vol. ix, *Mémoires de Michel de Castelnau*
    Mémoires de Jean de Mergey
    vol. x, *Mémoires de Marguerite de Valois*

Monod, Henri, 'La Saint-Barthélemy. Version du duc d'Anjou', *Bulletin de la société de l'histoire du protestantisme français*, lviii (1909)

Navarrete, M. F., *Colección de documentos inéditos para la historia de España*, vols i–iv (Madrid, 1842 . . .)

Noailles, Henri de, *Henri de Valois et la Pologne en 1572*, 3 vols (Paris, 1867)

Olaegui. *See* Gachard, L. P., 'Particularités inédites sur la Saint-Barthélemy', *Bulletins de l'Académie royale de Belgique*, xvi (1849)

Pasquier, Estienne. *See* Thickett, D.

Piot, Charles, *Correspondance du cardinal de Granvelle 1565–1586*, 12 vols (Paris, 1877–96) [Granvelle, *Correspondance*]

Pommerol, M. J., *Albert de Gondi maréchal de Retz* (Geneva, 1953)

Prinsterer, Groen van, *Archives ou correspondance inédites de la maison d'Orange-Nassau*, série i, 8 vols (Leiden, 1835–96)

Ranke, Leopold von, *Civil Wars and Monarchy in France in the Sixteenth and Seventeenth Centuries*, 2 vols (trans. M. A. Garvey, London, 1852)

Regnier de La Planche, *Histoire de l'Estat de France sous le règne de François II* (ed. Paris, 1836)

Roelker, Nancy Lyman, *Queen of Navarre, Jeanne d'Albret, 1528–1572* (Cambridge, Mass., 1968)

Romier, Lucien, 'La Mort de Henri II', *Revue du XVIᵉ siècle*, i (1913)

—— 'La Saint-Barthélemy, les événements de Rome et la préméditation du massacre', *Revue du XVIᵉ siècle*, i (1913)

Roth, Cecil, 'Roberto Ridolfi et la sua congiura', *Rivista Storica degli Archivi Toscani*, ii (1930)

Ruble, Alphonse de (Ed.), A. d'Aubigné, *Histoire universelle*, 9 vols (Paris, 1886–97)

—— *Antoine de Bourbon et Jeanne d'Albret*, 4 vols (Paris, 1881–6)

—— (Ed.), *Commentaires et lettres de Blaise de Monluc maréchal de France*, 5 vols (Paris, 1864–72)

—— *L'Assassinat de François de Lorraine duc de Guise, 18 février 1563* (Paris, 1897)

—— *Le Traité de Cateau-Cambrésis* (Paris, 1889)

—— *Mémoires et poésies de Jeanne d'Albret* (Paris, 1893)

—— *Mémoires inédites de Michel de la Huguerye*, 3 vols (Paris, 1877–80)

Sainte-Croix, Prosper de, *Lettres adressées au cardinal Borromée*, in Cimber et Danjou, *Archives curieuses, série* i, vol. vi (1885)

Serrano, Luciano, *Correspondencia diplomatica entre España y la Santa Sede durante el pontificado de S. Pio V*, 4 vols (Madrid, 1914)

—— *La Liga de Lepanto entre España, Venecia y la Santa Sede, 1570–1573*, 2 vols (Madrid, 1918–19)

Šusta, Josef, *Die Römische Curie und das Concil von Trient unter Pius IV*, 4 vols (Vienna, 1904–14)

Sutcliffe, F. E. (Ed.), *La Noue, Discours politiques et militaires* (Geneva, 1967)

Sutherland, N. M., 'The Edict of Nantes and the Protestant State', *Annali della Fondazione italiana per la storia amministrativa*, i (2) (Milan, 1965)

—— *The French Secretaries of State in the Age of Catherine de Medici* (London, 1962)

Tauzin, J.-J.-C., 'Le Mariage de Marguerite de Valois', *Revue des questions historiques*, lxxx (1906)

Tavannes, Gaspard de Saulx-. See Michaud et Poujoulat

Theiner, A., *Annales Ecclesiastici*, 3 vols (Rome, 1856)

Thickett, D. (Ed.), Estienne Pasquier, *Bref discours de tout ce qui a este negotié pour la querelle entre les maisons de Guyse et de Chatillon* (1564)

—— Estienne Pasquier, *Lettres historiques* (Geneva, 1966)

Le Tocsain contre les autheurs du massacre de France (Reims, 1578), printed in Cimber et Danjou, *Archives curieuses, série* i, vol. vii (Paris, 1835)

Vaissière, P. de, *De Quelques assassins* (Paris, 1912)

Valois, Marguerite de. See Michaud et Poujoulat

Varamundus, Ernest, 'De Furoribus gallicis', *Harleian Miscellany*, vii (1811)

Vera et Brevis Descriptio Tumultus Postremi Gallici Lutetiani (Cracow, 1573). See Monod, Henri

Vogler, Bernard, 'Le Rôle des électeurs palatins dans les guerres de religion en France, 1559–1592', *Cahiers d'histoire*, x (1965)

Wedgwood, C. V., *William the Silent* (London, 1944)

Weiss, Charles, *Papiers d'État du cardinal de Granvelle*, 9 vols (Paris, 1841–52) [Granvelle, *Papiers d'État*]

Whitehead, A. W., *Gaspard de Coligny Admiral of France* (London, 1904)

Wright, Thomas, *Queen Elizabeth and her Times*, 2 vols (London, 1838)

Index

Albe, Dominique d', 102, 103

Albornoz, Bartolomé, secretary to the duke of Alva, 292

Alençon, François duc d', 49, 100, 105, 155, 186, 190, 216, 217, 228, 248, 266, 273, 274, 275, 281, 282, 283, 291, 298, 299, 300, 302, 339, 344

Alessandrino, cardinal, papal legate, 215, 218, 219, 220, 221, 222, 225, 316, 331

Alluye, Florimond Robertet, seigneur d', secretary of state, 62, 98

Alava, don Francés de, Spanish ambassador in France, 44, 98, 99, 100, 101, 102, 103, 104, 107, 155, 157, 167, 168, 176, 199, 224; instructions, 30 & n. 4, 37; fled to the Netherlands, 207; his recall, Aug. 1571, 208

Alva, Fernando Alvarez de Toledo y Pimentel, third duke of, 5, 25, 30, 31, 33, 34, 42, 45, 48, 49, 57, 66, 70, 74, 80, 84, 99, 104, 125, 146, 148, 176, 194, 195, 235, 236, 241, 242, 247, 280, 285, 286, 289, 290, 296, 302, 311, 343; and France, 5, 6, 30, 31, 34–5, 36–7, 39, 40, 41, 42, 43, 44, 61, 74, 91, 96, 108, 109, 118, 132, 155, 156, 197–8, 230, 231, 237, 240, 242, 243, 244, 294, 295, 307, 308, 336, 342, 344, 345; and England, 5, 6, 71, 82, 83, 84, 85, 91, 93, 106, 108, 114, 140, 141, 158, 195, 196, 197, 268, 269, 270, 310; governor of the Netherlands, 47, 49; instructions, 47 & n. 1, 81; and the Netherlands, 58, 74, 75, 93, 101, 108, 129, 130, 224, 225, 229,

231, 241, 245, 250, 260, 277, 279, 290, 291, 293, 301

Amboise, conspiracy of, Mar. 1560, 24, 59, 60

Amboise, edict of, Mar. 1560, 10

Amboise, peace and edict of, 19 Mar. 1563, 19, 20, 21, 22, 27–8, 36, 37, 44, 54, 118, 123; rumours of revocation, 34, 35, 36, 37, 57–8, 59; confirmed at Marseilles, Nov. 1564, 35

Andelot, François de', 8, 42, 53, 71, 76, 77, 88, 96, 97, 99, 107; death at Saintes, 100, 101, 102

Anjou, Henri, duc d', 18, 33, 90, 91, 95, 97, 98, 99, 107, 109, 112, 121, 122, 135, 137, 156, 158, 160, 164, 165, 186, 193, 194, 204, 210, 212, 213, 216, 218, 259, 344, 346; influenced by Lorraine, 49, 66, 67, 69, 106, 159, 215; enmity for Charles IX, 49, 67, 127, 128, 172–3, 190, 212–13, 322, 333; lieutenant-general, Nov. 1567, 54, 56, 67, 76, 128, 194, 202, 216, 249, 261, 319, 320; *chef du conseil*, 1567, 54, 55; ensnared by the pope, 1567, 55–6, 108; catholic figurehead, 56, 127, 128, 172–3, 179, 193, 207, 211–12; proposed marriage to queen Elizabeth, 56, 57, 72, 73, 102, 108, 128, 132, 134, 137, 139, 140, 141, 142, 153, 154, 155, 157–9, 161–2, 171–2, 190, 193, 204, 216–17, 344; suitor to Mary queen of Scots, 69, 72, 127, 158; and the death of Condé, 97; and the death of d'Andelot, 100; and assaults upon Coligny, 102, 103, 313, 316; described by Wal-